R. STEPHEN HUMPHREYS

BETWEEN MEMORY AND DESIRE

The Middle East in a Troubled Age

University of California Press

Berkeley   Los Angeles   London

University of California Press
Berkeley and Los Angeles, California

University of California Press, Ltd.
London, England

First paperback printing 2001

© 1999 by
The Regents of the University of California

Library of Congress Cataloging-in-Publication Data

Humphreys, R. Stephen.
    Between memory and desire : the Middle East in
a troubled age / R. Stephen Humphreys.
        p.   cm.
    Includes bibliographic references (p.   ) and
index.
    ISBN 0-520-22918-5 (pbk. : alk. paper)
    1. Middle East—Politics and government—1945–
2. Islam and politics—Middle East.   I. Title.
    DS63.1.H856 1999
    956—dc21   98-30576
                                              CIP

Printed in the United States of America

08 07 06 05 04 03 02 01
9 8 7 6 5 4 3 2

For Gail
in whom shines
"l'amor che move il sole e l'altre stelle"

CONTENTS

Contemporary North Africa and the Middle East. Gaza and the West
Bank are occupied territories, and there are disputed boundaries in both
Morocco and Cyprus.

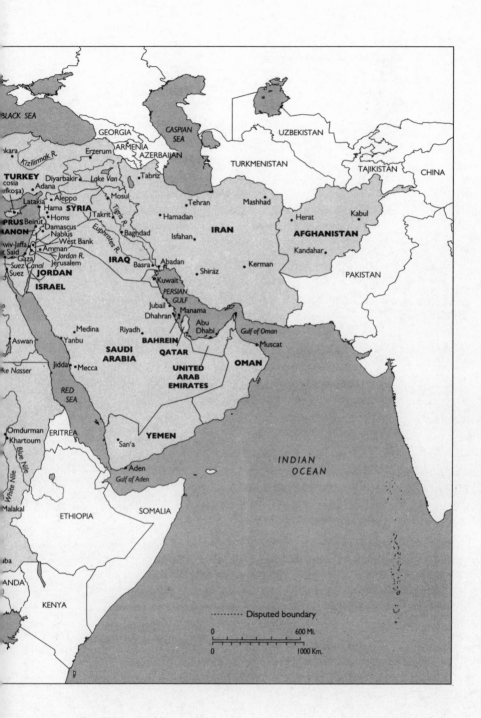

BLACK SEA

GEORGIA

ARMENIA

AZERBAIJAN

CASPIAN SEA

UZBEKISTAN

nkara

Kızılırmak R.

Erzerum

Tabriz

TURKMENISTAN

TAJIKISTAN

CHINA

TURKEY

Diyarbakir

Lake Van

cosia
(efkoşa)

Adana

Aleppo

Mosul

Tehran

Mashhad

Latakia

Hama

SYRIA

Tigris R.

Takrit

Hamadan

Herat

Kabul

Homs

PRUS

Beirut

Damascus

Euphrates R.

Baghdad

Isfahan

IRAN

AFGHANISTAN

ANON

Nablus

West Bank

Kandahar

viv-Jaffa

Amman

Jordan R.

Said

Gaza

Jerusalem

IRAQ

Basra

Abadan

Kerman

PAKISTAN

Suez Canal

Suez

JORDAN

ISRAEL

Kuwait

Shiraz

PERSIAN
GULF

Jubail

Dhahran

Manama

Medina

Riyadh

Abu
Dhabi

Gulf of Oman

Aswan

Yanbu

BAHREIN

QATAR

Muscat

ke Nasser

Jidda

Mecca

SAUDI
ARABIA

UNITED
ARAB
EMIRATES

OMAN

RED
SEA

Omdurman

ERITREA

YEMEN

Khartoum

San'a

Blue Nile

INDIAN
OCEAN

White Nile

Aden

Gulf of Aden

Malakal

ETHIOPIA

SOMALIA

ıba

ANDA

KENYA

- - - - - Disputed boundary

0   600 Mi.

0   1000 Km.

PREFACE

This book examines the unending and deeply frustrating struggle among contemporary Middle Easterners to infuse meaning, value, and moral purpose into the politics of their region. In so doing, it inevitably focuses on the uneasy coexistence between secular and religious politics in the modern Middle East. It also tries to show how Islam might play a far more positive and constructive role in the region's bitter political debates than it now does. In these ways, I hope it may be of value not only to American readers who know little about Islam and the Middle East but also to Muslims who are deeply and justifiably concerned about the direction things are taking in the ancient heartland of their faith. The book begins with a set of five essays on secular politics, because we cannot really deal with deeper issues of value and meaning until we have confronted the hard-edged, intractable problems of power and the distribution of resources that Middle Eastern politicians must grapple with every day. Chapter 6 then broaches the problem of a dual politics; it asks what we mean when we use the words "secular" and "religious" (or "profane" and "sacred") in the realm of politics and how these two registers of thought and action have manifested themselves in the history of Muslim peoples. In the last four essays, I explore several dimensions of sacred politics, the politics of godliness and salvation. I ask about the impact of Islam on public life—what specific ideas and values it puts into play, what challenges it poses to "ordinary" politics, what resources and possibilities it brings to the struggle for democracy and social justice. As we investigate these issues, it is well to keep in mind that politics in this register is a familiar part of American life—to name but one example, the Religious Right's "family values." No one acquainted with contemporary American politics should find anything inherently strange or odd about the issues discussed in this book, although of course they will have a distinctively Islamic and Middle Eastern twist.

I make no claim to explain the mysterious and exotic Middle

East. To begin with, the Middle East is no more mysterious, and is considerably less exotic, than Santa Barbara, California, or even Madison, Wisconsin. But more to the point, the time is long past when foreign experts can set themselves up as persons uniquely authorized to speak for the peoples and cultures they study, as if they alone hold the key to some objective truth that their subjects either do not grasp or cannot articulate. In the following pages I hope to do something simpler and more straightforward, to give an account of my interactions with Middle Easterners over a period of some thirty years and to explain what I believe I have learned about them and my relationship with them in the course of these interactions. My account is not the whole truth or the only possible truth, but I hope that my Middle Eastern friends will recognize themselves in it and will think that my words have not done them an injustice.

The audience I chiefly have in mind is that elusive creature, "the interested nonspecialist"—in this case, the reader with curiosity and a wide experience of the world, but possessing no particular expertise in things Middle Eastern and Islamic, apart from what he or she has gleaned from occasional travel in those parts or from the better class of print and broadcast journalism. On one level, this book will provide a context for this journalism, a way of making sense of the bits and pieces of information that such readers bring with them. These readers will naturally be Americans for the most part. Americans bring to the Middle East a particular body of background information along with a rather odd set of values and unspoken assumptions about how things are and ought to be. Because I have spent most of my life in the United States, I share these values and assumptions to a considerable degree, and I allude to them repeatedly in these pages. They are a crucial element in how I respond to the events and personalities and ways of life of the Middle East. But I am also aware that they are often exactly the wrong sort of baggage to bring along, and I try to point out places where I think that Americans' accustomed ways of thinking about things are getting in the way. As to my professional colleagues in the Middle East studies guild, I am certain that they will find much to criticize and that they would have gone about the task quite differently. But I hope that they will find my presentation both honest and productive of useful discussion.

The "interactions" mentioned above are sometimes direct, personal ones; I will be telling a lot of stories about my encounters with all sorts of people in Cairo, Fez, Tunis, Kayseri, or Riyadh because these encounters are one of the ways I have learned what I claim to know about the region. But I have spent a great deal more time in the United States than in the Middle East over the last three decades, and much of my interaction with the region has taken place through my reading—of medieval manuscripts, contemporary short stories, statistical abstracts, news reports, and scholarly writings of one kind or another. Some of this material was produced by Middle Easterners for other Middle Easterners, and the evidence it yields is just as direct and reliable as any face-to-face encounter in Cairo or a Lebanese village. But inevitably much of this writing represents a scholarly literature produced by and for people like me, professors of Middle Eastern studies. In that sense it is writing that claims (like the present book) to explain the region to foreigners, albeit foreigners of a peculiar kind. Obviously I have learned an immense amount from my colleagues, and I could not have undertaken this book at all without the work they have done. At the same time, I have used their contributions selectively and eclectically. The present book thus does not fit easily into the usual academic categories; it is neither a work of systematic original research nor a synthesis of the scholarly literature. It simply represents my own effort to make sense of a vast, complex region.

I have conceived of this book as a series of interlocking essays. Each essay is meant to stand on its own, but each also tries to build on the essay preceding it and to set the stage for the one following. The reason for this approach is in large part that I am an inveterate dabbler; I tend to start reading in the middle of things and assume that other people do so as well. Such an approach inevitably involves a certain amount of repetition from one essay to another, but since the material presented here will be unfamiliar to many of my readers, a degree of repetition may not be a bad thing. Moreover, I hope that the changing contexts in which the material appears as readers move from one essay to the next will provide contrasting and revealing perspectives on it.

Every book raises problems of language, of what to call things. That is particularly the case with the subjects I discuss here. Many issues of names and labels can be deferred until they come up in the course of the book, but two must be discussed at the outset, at least in a provisional manner. First, what is the entity that I am discussing? Sometimes I refer to "the Middle East," at others to "Muslim peoples," "the Islamic world," and so on. Why this maddening inconsistency? Second, much of this book deals with Islam in the contemporary political arena—what is typically labeled "Islamic fundamentalism" by the American media. I use this term, but very sparingly. Am I just being an arrogant academic who wishes to make life difficult for his readers by refusing to use ordinary words that everyone understands?

First, the terms "Middle East" and "Islamic world." These overlap in many respects, but they are not at all the same thing. The Middle East refers to a geographic region, one defined partly by natural features, partly by strategic and political interests and interactions, and partly by assumptions about shared social and cultural elements. In this book, "the Middle East" is a convenient shorthand for an immense tract of land covering some five million square miles: Africa north of the Sahara Desert (including Egypt and northern Sudan), the Arabian Peninsula, Turkey, the Arabic-speaking lands of the Fertile Crescent stretching from the eastern Mediterranean coast to the Tigris River, Iran, and Afghanistan. Sometimes (but in no terribly consistent way) I also include two contiguous regions: Pakistan and the Muslim countries of Central Asia (formerly republics in the Soviet Union) bordering on Iran and Afghanistan—Turkmenistan, Tajikistan, and Uzbekistan. Pakistan and the Central Asian republics sometimes seem to extend the problems and concerns of the Middle East farther north and east; and sometimes they seem connected to the very different realms of India and Russia.[1]

However its limits are defined, the Middle East includes an enormous variety of landscapes, ecologies, peoples, languages, cultures, and religions. What binds it together is history, for Islam first emerged in this region, and the peoples of this region are those who defined Islam's core doctrines, values, and concerns over a period of some six centuries. As the religion of Islam has spread into other parts of the world, however remote and however different, it has never quite lost its Middle Eastern imprint. More precisely, the interpretations of Islam shaped in the medieval Middle East have always retained a special prestige in the eyes of Muslims living in other lands and later periods. For a great many Muslims throughout the world, it is Middle Eastern Islam, as articulated between 610 and ca. 1250, that often seems truest and most authentic, even if they themselves have developed their faith along quite different lines.

Now, the Middle East is by no means synonymous with the Muslim world. A huge majority of Middle Easterners are in fact Muslims, but roughly 10 percent belong to other confessions (chiefly Christianity). More important, the largest Muslim countries lie outside the Middle East, in Indonesia and Bangladesh. Even India, where Muslims constitute only one-tenth of the population, has more Muslims than any Middle Eastern country. The region where Islam is being adopted most rapidly is Africa south of the Sahara. And by now there are very large "diasporas" in Europe and North America. Something like 10 percent of the population of France is Muslim, and the United States has a Muslim population of well over three million. There are places in this book where it seems more useful to speak about Muslim societies and cultures irrespective of where they are located—where what I want to focus on is people's Muslim identity, not where they happen to live. So, when I move in an apparently careless way from "Middle Easterners" to "Muslims" and back again, that represents a very deliberate choice of words. With the one phrase, I want to call attention to a particular region, with its own distinctive problems and characteristics. With the other, I am pointing to a religiocultural identity that may be shared by peoples at the opposite ends of the earth.

Explanation begets explanation. In this discussion I have used the phrase "Muslim countries," and in the following chapters that term, plus others like "Muslim governments," will often recur. What do these terms really mean? By a Muslim country, I mean simply a country most of whose citizens are Muslims; likewise, a Muslim government is one in which most of the high offices and functions are held by persons who identify themselves as Muslims. Obviously traditions, norms, and values derived from Islamic religious thought and practice will color the policies and legislation of such countries and governments, very much as "Christian values" (a vague term if ever there was one) permeate public life in the United States. But the mere fact that most of a country's people are Muslims, or that it is governed by Muslims, does not mean that this country systematically tries to shape every action or institution according to Islamic religious criteria. There are such countries and governments, to be sure—revolutionary Iran, Afghanistan under the Taliban, the Sudan, Pakistan from time to time. But these are rather the exception, and their efforts are often decried as profoundly un-Islamic by their neighbors. In the hope of creating a distinction with a difference, I will normally reserve the adjective "Islamic" for those policies, institutions, governments, or countries that are articulated within a framework of explicitly Islamic concepts and values.

Let us now turn to the second issue, namely, what we are to call those ardent Muslims who have seized the center of the political stage in the name of Islam. The usual term in the American media is "Islamic fundamentalists." This phrase is assailed by many academic critics as misleading and even demeaning, but in fact it can be a useful one. First, the people in question do stress the Islamic character and purpose of their actions. Second, if we do not insist on equating "fundamentalism" with American biblical literalism, but instead give this word a broader definition, it readily suggests that those so labeled are trying to go back to the foundations of their faith—in the case of Muslims, to the Qur'an and the teaching of the Prophet Muhammad. And in fact most "Islamic fundamentalists" do cite the Qur'an and the teachings of the Prophet to the exclusion of almost everything else; these are in their minds the sole valid foundation for the new order they hope to establish. The usefulness of the term can be seen from the fact that in recent years the Arab press has picked it up; they translate "fundamentalists" as *usuliyyun*—literally, "those seeking roots." Though coined as a translation of an English word, *usuliyyun* has a distinctive resonance in Arabic. The word *usul* was widely used in Classical Arabic for the "roots" or "underlying principles" of law and theology, while the modern word *asala* means "authenticity," a favorite mantra of Third World thinkers.

The problem with the term "Islamic fundamentalism" is not that it is wrong but that as normally used by the Western media it lumps together very disparate phenomena. Moreover, it distracts us from what its adherents really see themselves as doing. To take the latter point first, "Islamic fundamentalists" are far less interested in the literal truth of the Qur'an and Hadith (a point they simply take for granted) than in applying the statements of scripture to the moral and social problems of the present. They seek to build an Islamic Order (Ar., *nizam islami*), and their problem is to show how scripture provides the blueprint for that Order. As to the first point, "Islamic fundamentalism" is typically cited in the U.S. media to explain violence, some grotesque act of terror against apparent innocents. And indeed some "fundamentalists" are given to direct and even violent action, believing that nothing less is needed to purge the corruption of their societies. But many more find the right path in education, exhortations to moral reform, and charitable works. That fact suggests that we need to find more precise and less loaded language to characterize these people.

In the Middle East, the favored terms are still "the Islamic movement" and "the Islamic tendency." The latter term is especially helpful, in that it emphasizes that we are dealing with a direction of thought, a search for Islamic values and solutions, rather than some sort of centrally controlled organization. But a word like "tendency" does not capture the intensity and dynamism of what is happening. Other common words are "Islamism" and "Islamist," both coinages of French origin. In English, however, they come across a bit oddly. Since no perfect term exists, I will use now one, now another, depending on context and the point I wish to underline. However, two phrases recur more often than any others in the following pages: "Islamic activists," by which I refer to the broad spectrum of those working to define and institute an Islamic order; and "Islamic militants," which I use for that usually small but highly visible subset among the activists who are ready and even eager to use violence to achieve their ends.

One may well ask whether such a lengthy discussion was necessary simply to justify the use of a few words: Middle East and Muslim world, Islamic activist and Islamic militant. But I hope that it did suggest some of the difficulties we face in trying to discuss these societies and cultures. The problem is not that these societies are any more complex or exotic or elusive than our own. The problem is rather to find a genuinely transparent way of speaking, one that seems clear and self-explanatory to Western readers but does not achieve clarity at the cost of distorting the basic features of the societies we are trying to understand.

In light of these thoughts, it may be useful to discuss the title I have chosen for this book. *Between Memory and Desire* of course alludes to the opening lines of T. S. Eliot's "The Wasteland":

April is the cruellest month, breeding
Lilacs out of the dead land, mixing
Memory and desire, stirring
Dull roots with spring rain.[2]

A colleague was perfectly puzzled by the allusion: what has Eliot to do with the Middle East, a region about which he knew and cared nothing? The connection I intend is not one of subject but of sentiment, of a frame of mind. Eliot twisted Chaucer's cheerful opening to the *Canterbury Tales*,

Whan that Aprille with his shoures söte
The droghte of Marche has perced to the roote,
And bathed every veyne in swich licour
Of which vertu engendred is the flour,[3]

into a message of despair, the despair of ineffectual longing mixed with useless memories.

Middle Easterners likewise feel themselves trapped between deeply felt and ardently sought aspirations for freedom, prosperity, dignity, and cultural authenticity, on the one side, and the twice-bitter memories that suffocate these aspirations, on the other. These memories are bitter in part because they are memories of the twentieth century, with its hopes forever deferred, promises repeatedly betrayed, ideals twisted beyond recognition. They are also bitter, even more so, because they are memories of a past (now remote) of political grandeur, economic vitality, and cultural creativity. That these memories are only partly true makes them no less tantalizing. For Middle Easterners, memories of what once was and what has recently been mock hopes for the future. From this perspective, the struggle of modern Middle Easterners is a struggle for liberation from the past—from the allure of an unrecoverable Golden Age and from the frustration of the twentieth century. It is likewise a struggle driven by desire, the intensely felt need to seize what ought to be theirs.

The parallels between Eliot's fashionable despair and the many-layered frustrations of the contemporary Middle East go only so far, of course. Eliot, at least in his poetic persona, was content simply to talk about his problems; Middle Easterners visibly are not. Their frustrated desires boil over in intense debates, noisy street demonstrations, and occasional riots and political violence. These things are disturbing to outsiders, who prize stability and calm in other people's societies, but they are a sign of vitality. The hopes of Middle Easterners may be frustrated and blocked, but they are not extinguished. The struggle (however defined, and whatever its goals) seems endless but not pointless. In the pages that follow, in fact, we will see many solid achievements and a fair number of remarkable victories against high odds. These things are too often forgotten, by Middle Eastern as well as Western commentators, and they need to be remembered as an integral part of the story. Memory, after all, can propel hope as well as frustrate it.

ACKNOWLEDGMENTS

I began serious work on this book in the spring of 1993, so it has occupied me for much of the past five years. On another level, it represents simply what I know about the Middle East and Islam, and in that way it is the harvest of thirty-five years of trying to find my way into this vast subject and learning to communicate something about it. In all this, I have accumulated incalculable debts and owe thanks to more people than I can name. Some of this debt, but only a very small portion of it, will be visible in the notes accompanying each chapter; in fact, I have gleaned insights from hundreds of colleagues in many fields of study over three decades, and one of the difficulties in writing this book has been to distill all I have learned from them. It is of course no longer possible to attribute most of this in any specific way.

I do owe a special debt of gratitude to three Egyptian scholars who received me very generously during my visit to Cairo in 1993 and who shared with me a remarkable amount of time from their overbusy lives: Abd al-Azim Ramadan, Ali Hilal al-Din Dessouki, and Hasan Hanafi.

I was also generously welcomed in Indonesia in the spring of 1997 by several outstanding scholars: Nurcholish Madjid of Para Medina and the University of Jakarta, Abdul Aziz Saleh and Wahidar Khaidir of Andalas University in Padang, and Jimly Asshiddiqie at the Ministry of Education. The perspectives they provided on Indonesian Islam and its place in the broader Islamic world were of great value in my final revisions to this book. I also want to thank a friend of many years, Margaret Hanson, for arranging my meetings with these scholars and otherwise facilitating my visit to that country. James Hanson, at that time senior economist of the World Bank in Jakarta, likewise took time to collect materials and provide introductions.

I have been very fortunate in my colleagues at the University of

California at Santa Barbara. They are of course in no way responsible for this book, but they have contributed greatly to whatever knowledge and understanding I have of the matters discussed here. I would mention in particular Juan and Magda Campo, Robert O. Collins, Nancy E. Gallagher, Richard Hecht, Nuha Khoury, Scott Marcus, and Dwight Reynolds.

The readers of the manuscript for the University of California Press, Michael Cook and Leila Fawaz, supplied valuable criticisms and suggestions, and have thereby saved me from many embarrassments. Frederic Hunter brought the frankness of a friend and the sharp eye of an experienced foreign correspondent to an advanced draft of the manuscript. A second very attentive and constructive lay reader was my sister-in-law Barbara Valenta. All these readers were supportive of the project and very frank about what remained to be done. No one could hope for more patient or constructive editors than James Clark and Lynne Withey of the University of California Press. All these people have done their best for me; none of them is responsible for whatever errors and omissions still remain.

Various members of my family have read all or large parts of the manuscript at various stages. An honest exchange of views has always been encouraged in our household, and they did not disappoint me on this occasion. I want to make special mention here of my mother-in-law, Edna R. Simons, who passed away as this book was nearing completion; I benefited greatly from her love and caring support throughout my career. Finally, I thank my wife, Gail, for her energetic encouragement of this project, and even more for her love, friendship, and unwavering loyalty over thirty-five years. Most of what I owe her is a matter between husband and wife, but I could not have continued in my career, let alone prospered in it, without her.

CHAPTER I

HARD REALITIES

Population Growth and Economic Stagnation

First impressions can be desperately misleading, but revisited in the light of longer experience, they often point to basic truths. When my wife and I got off the plane and walked across the tarmac into the Cairo airport terminal for the first time on a hot spring night in April 1966, we were immediately engulfed in a crush of would-be porters, all clamoring for the privilege of carrying our bags to the taxi stand. We chose a likely prospect, who snatched up our stuff and carried it about fifty feet. There he passed it off to a second man and in the same motion stuck out his hand for the customary two-piaster tip. The second porter repeated the same act, and then a third and a fourth. I am happy to say that our first taxi driver took us all the way downtown without a break, but as soon as we stepped out of the cab a pack of boys materialized out of the shadows, all shouting and grabbing for our luggage. It was only about twenty feet to the door of our pension, so this time we fended them off with barking and a bit of pushing. By some miracle the elevator was working (just how rare a miracle it was in the Cairo of 1966 we would soon discover), and we were quickly and peaceably delivered to the door of Mme Seoudi's fifth-story hotel-pension.

Our initial experience was repeated hundreds of times over in the coming weeks. The simplest task required three or four or half a dozen people. What we were dealing with, plainly, was too many people chasing too few jobs.[1] The causes for this phenomenon were by no means obvious to the superficial observer, but a bit of reading and talking to the right people told us more or less what was going on. The countryside was jammed and could no longer provide any kind of living wage for agricultural workers, and so displaced peasants were flowing into the cities to find whatever work they could. In spite of a determined push toward industrialization

1

by the Nasser government, there were still few factory jobs. In any case, these rural immigrants were mostly illiterate and utterly without the skills needed even for assembly-line labor; all they could find was pick-up work at minuscule wages. As for the boys who swarmed around us wherever we went, they were supposed to be in school, but that was boring, irrelevant to any purpose they could see, and anyhow, their families desperately needed the pittances that they could scrounge from sympathetic or unwary tourists. Finally, however inadequate the high schools and universities may have been in view of the number of teenagers and young adults who needed an education, they were still producing far more graduates than the Egyptian economy could find room for. To soak up the excess, Nasser had decreed that the government would be the employer of last resort—hence the five sullen tellers and cashiers needed to stamp the sextuplicate forms that authorized us to exchange dollars for Egyptian pounds.[2]

To us the Cairo of thirty years ago seemed extraordinarily crowded. People were jammed into the buses, and it was common for a dozen or more boys to hitch a free ride by clinging to the outside of these careening contrivances. The buses were battered and had a perpetual list, and it is amazing they held together as well as they did. From a present-day perspective, however, the city was almost empty. It had a total population of only some 3 million, the medieval tomb cities to the south and east still housed mostly the dead, and the Pyramids stood alone in the bright, clear air, many miles from the small middle-class suburb of Giza on the west bank of the Nile. The streets were mostly narrow and ill designed for modern traffic, but there weren't a lot of cars and most of these were of astonishing antiquity. When I went back seven years later, in 1973, Cairo had 6 million people (many of them refugees from the Suez Canal cities, which were then inside a war zone), the buses were even more insanely packed, the tomb cities had been commandeered by squatters, and urban sprawl had infected the Nile's western bank and was moving up toward the Pyramids. But even this falls far short of the realities of 1997. There are something like 15 million people (though no one knows for sure) in Greater Cairo. The city sprawls across at least three separate governorates, high-rise apartment buildings reach almost to the base of the Pyramids (which are often masked in dense gray smog), and the traffic jams compete with any in the world. Over

the last decade Cairo has been outfitted with a good modern infrastructure, at least downtown; there is a complex throughway network and a good subway system, the water runs, the telephones
work, the electricity is reliable, faxes and copy shops are ubiquitous.
But the schools and universities continue to pour out graduates by
the hundreds of thousands, and after four decades of policies aimed
at making Egypt into a dynamic modern economy there are still not
remotely enough jobs to go around. The university class of 1985, for
example, was awarded its guaranteed government jobs only in 1993.

Egypt is now and has always been a peculiar place, even within
the Middle East. But its employment problems are quite typical of
most countries in the region—Morocco, Tunisia, Turkey, to name
only countries that have not been directly afflicted by war or political revolution in recent decades. Istanbul (which has grown from
about 1.5 to 10 million people over the past quarter century) and
Casablanca are just as overgrown and congested as Cairo. These
problems are no doubt partly the result of bad policy: wanting a
modern economy will not create one, especially if the goal is pursued through contradictory, constantly shifting, and ill-administered
policies. (Americans familiar with the anomalies of their own health
and welfare systems will surely understand how situations like this
can come about.) But Middle Eastern policy makers have been the
victims of paradox; some of their greatest successes—building comprehensive albeit desperately overcrowded systems of higher education or lowering the infant mortality rate by more than 50 percent
in a decade—have only intensified the economic problems they must
contend with. So we must ask, with genuine humility, how and why
they have fallen into their present quandary.

It is very common, and very misleading, to say that the modern
Middle East suffers from overpopulation. In fact the Middle East
and North Africa as a whole possess approximately the same size
population as the United States and a considerably larger land area—
300 million people in about 5 million square miles. The largest and
most populous countries in the region—Egypt, Iran, and Turkey—
each have some 60 million people. That is, they have populations
equal to those of France, Italy, and the United Kingdom, all of which
are much smaller in area. So we cannot talk about "overpopulation"
in an absolute sense, as if a given parcel of land could absorb some
fixed number of people and that barrier had now been breached.

The real problem is not the number of people in the Middle East but how rapidly and recently they have appeared on the scene.

The first thing one needs to know about the contemporary Middle East is that the average age of the population is about sixteen—half the average age in the United States. That one fact tells volumes about the intractable problems confronting the governments of the region, and why their record in solving these problems is such a spotty one. To begin with, it means that the majority of the population (taking both the very young and the aged) is a consumer of expensive services, especially education, housing, food, and medical care, while producing little wealth. It also means that the labor markets are flooded with young adults, increasingly well educated and equipped to participate in a modern economy, but also increasingly frustrated in their efforts to get even a low-paying entry-level job. That is why university graduates in law and engineering and philosophy, some with advanced degrees, serve as night clerks in luxury hotels or as tourist guides. I retain vivid memories of a wonderful précis of contemporary trends in philosophy in the Arab world, which I heard from a concierge in Fez in 1990; he held an M.A. from Muhammad V University in Rabat, and he delivered his disquisition impromptu in fluent and sonorous Classical Arabic (akin to speaking Latin off the cuff), but he could have told me the same things equally well in French or English. This represents, I believe, a standard that few American hotel clerks could match. (There are Ph.D. taxi drivers and waitresses in the United States, I know, but only as a temporary expedient; in the Middle East there is nothing temporary about it.) On a different level, young people everywhere are impatient with authority and in search of meaning for their lives—hence the magnetism of ideologies that explain and solve everything. When two-thirds of the population is less than twenty-five, the search for meaning and alienation from the stifling established order inevitably become a defining element of the whole society.

Each of the points in the preceding paragraph raises crucial questions. Why is the average age in these countries so low? Why have Middle Eastern economies failed to provide enough jobs for their people? Are there any positive prospects for the future, or must we expect worsening economic stagnation and involution? Finally, what are the ideologies that have most appealed to the restless (or desperate) young, and how can we account for their appeal?

We begin with the reasons for the very youthful median age. Sixteen is not in itself an astonishingly low figure—before the mid-nineteenth century it was in fact probably the norm in most of the world. At the time of the first U.S. census some two hundred years ago (ca. 1800), for example, the median age in this country was sixteen. However, that was due less to a high birthrate than to the very low life expectancies of that era—only some thirty-five to forty years. But in the contemporary Middle East the same figure reflects a very different phenomenon—namely, a massive population boom.

This is a relatively recent phenomenon in the Middle East, as it is in the rest of the world. In 1830 (a date I choose because it marks the first efforts at a modern-style census in the region, and also the earliest phase of the European colonial era) the population of the entire Middle East and North Africa from Morocco to Iran, including modern Turkey but not the Balkan possessions of the Ottoman Empire, did not exceed 34 million. (This number is admittedly only an educated guess.) By World War I the region's population had reached 68 million—which is to say that it had doubled in eighty-some years. (In this case the numbers are based on fairly good censuses, except in Iran and the Arabian Peninsula.) The current population of 300 million—again, after an interval of eighty years—is four and a half times the World War I figure and more than eight times the original number. This represents an average growth rate over the past one hundred sixty years of just about 2 percent per annum—a rate that allows a population to double in less than forty years, and a startling demonstration of the long-term impact of even moderate population growth.[3]

How can we explain the recent and very rapid population growth in the region? Birthrates, as far back as we can trace them, have always been high in the Middle East. No doubt this is partly due to a patriarchal culture that valued a large number of children both as a proof of virility and as a supply of manpower to defend the clan or tribe. But far more important was the crucial need, universally experienced in the ancient and medieval world, to compensate for cruelly high death rates among children and adolescents. To take just one example, it has been argued that in the relatively prosperous, well-fed, secure Roman Empire of the first and second centuries A.D., a woman needed to bear five children in order for two of them to reach adulthood and the age of reproduction.[4] In modern demographic parlance, a fertility rate of 5 was needed to ensure a stable population. (In modern times, a fertility rate of about 2.1 will do the trick.) A failure to produce children was no mere personal misfortune; small families were an unaffordable luxury. Precisely the same considerations held true for the Middle East at least down to the end of the nineteenth century.

In the first half of the twentieth century the region's birthrates remained high and possibly even rose slightly, but death rates were beginning to fall. The divergence between the two curves was at first fairly small, but after World War II things began to change quite rapidly, and in the last two decades overall death rates have fallen precipitously. In a few countries of the region they are now comparable to those found in Europe, Japan, and North America. Birthrates, in contrast, have been much stickier; in many countries within the region they have hardly budged at all, while in others they have begun to slip only in the last decade. As a result, the rate of population growth has remained quite high, on the order of 2.5 percent to 3 percent, throughout the region since the end of World War II. As a point of reference, with a growth rate of 3 percent a given population will double in twenty-five years. At the rate of growth experienced during the 1980s, therefore, the Middle East would reach a population of 500 million by the year 2015—a figure comparable to all Europe minus the former Soviet Union.

Broad generalizations of this kind of course mask great complexity and nuance, and they do nothing to explain the phenomena that they describe. We need to ask whether all Middle Eastern countries are following the same demographic track. Likewise, we need to understand the dynamics underlying the crude birth- and death rates— that is, what the region is experiencing in terms of the number of babies born and surviving, life expectancies, age pyramids, and so on. Some of the relevant numbers are given in tables 1 and 2, so that the discussion can continue without cluttering the text with numbers.

In terms of broad trends, the countries of the Middle East clearly have much in common. All have succeeded in raising their average life expectancy markedly over the past two decades—overall, from about age fifty-five to sixty-four, and in some cases more than ten years. For this there are many reasons, but the most important by far is the precipitous decline in infant mortality since the early 1970s. Drops of more than 50 percent are the norm for this twenty-year

Table 1   Demography and Fertility in the Middle East
and North Africa, 1965–1992

	Crude Birthrate (per 1,000 pop.)		Crude Death Rate (per 1,000 pop.)		Fertility (per woman)			
	1965	1990	1965	1990	1965	1975	1985	1992
United States	19	17	9	9	2.9	1.8	1.8	2.1
Middle East and North Africa	47	40	20	10	7.1	—	5.7	4.9
Big Three								
Egypt	43	31	19	10	6.8	5.5	5.1	3.8
Turkey	41	28	15	7	5.7	4.7	4.1	3.5
Iran	46	45	18	9	7.1	6.5	6.2	5.5
North Africa								
Morocco	49	35	18	9	7.1	6.9	5.4	3.8
Tunisia	44	28	16	7	7.0	6.2	4.9	3.8
Fertile Crescent and Arabian Peninsula								
Syria	48	44	16	7	7.7	7.7	7.4	6.2
Iraq	49	42	18	8	7.2	7.1	6.4	5.7
Saudi Arabia	48	43	20	7	7.3	7.3	7.3	6.4
Yemen	49	53	27	18	7.0	7.8	7.7	7.6

The data are taken from the relevant country tables in World Bank, *Social Indicators of Development, 1994* (Baltimore: Johns Hopkins Press for the World Bank 1994); World Bank, *World Tables, 1994* (Baltimore: Johns Hopkins University Press for the World Bank, 1994); and World Bank, *World Development Report 1992* (Oxford: Oxford University Press, 1992).

period. Egypt and Turkey have managed a decline of almost two-thirds, and Saudi Arabia a full 75 percent. This is by any standard a remarkable achievement, especially in view of the extremely high rates that existed at the beginning of the period. In percentage terms, European, Japanese, and North American rates have fallen as fast, but of course the initial mortality rate was much lower, about one-sixth the Middle Eastern rate. In the developed countries, changes in infant mortality are a question of significant but marginal improvements; in the Middle East, the same percentages represent a transformation of family life and structure—and of course a demographic revolution.

The causes for such a dramatic shift can be traced through national statistics for nutrition, clean water, the number of doctors and

Table 2   Mortality, Life Expectancy, and Population Growth
in the Middle East and North Africa, 1965–1992

	Infant Mortality (per 1,000 live births)				Life Expectancy			Population Growth		
	1965	1975	1985	1992	1975	1985	1992	1965–1980	1980–1990	1992
United States	25	16	11	9	73	75	77	1.0	0.9	1.1
Middle East and North Africa	151	—	—	58	—	—	64	2.8	3.1	2.9
Big Three										
Egypt	145	150	112	57	52	57	62	2.1	2.4	2.1
Turkey	169	140	83	54	58	63	67	2.4	2.4	2.1
Iran	152	122	103	65	56	60	65	3.1	3.6	3.2
North Africa										
Morocco	145	122	92	57	53	58	63	2.3	2.7	2.1
Tunisia	145	110	62	48	56	63	68	2.1	2.4	2.2
Fertile Crescent and Arabian Peninsula										
Syria	114	88	49	36	57	63	67	3.4	3.6	3.4
Iraq	119	96	75	58	57	62	64	3.4	3.6	3.1
Saudi Arabia	148	105	58	28	54	63	69	4.6	4.7	3.2
Yemen	194	168	135	106	43	48	53	2.3	3.1	3.6

The data are taken from the relevant country tables in World Bank, *Social Indicators of Development, 1994; World Tables, 1994;* and *World Development Report 1992.*

nurses, immunization rates, and so on. But improvements in these areas are not hidden in columns of numbers; they are immediately visible to anyone who has been traveling in the region since the mid-1960s. When I first went to Egypt in 1966, I was astounded by the number of people, including a great many children, who were blind or afflicted with serious eye infections. This was true not only in slum quarters but downtown as well. Less astounding, but still striking, was the appearance of the people: Cairo seemed divided, far from equally, between the gaunt and the obese. In 1993 I found a different scene. Eye disease was conspicuous by its rarity, in Cairo and Alexandria at least, and people in general looked much better fed—as indeed they were, because a wide array of fresh fruits and vegetables were now available in abundance. People my age were aware of both things (young adults tended to be puzzled by my comments, since their memories did not extend back into the bad old times), and commented that both government and mosque-based clinics had been quite effective in getting poorer mothers to keep their children's faces and eyes washed, in spite of fears about the Evil Eye. As for fruits and vegetables, those came from new lands opened up in the Sinai and Western deserts. Wealthy countries like Saudi Arabia have built an extremely impressive health care network, including well-equipped specialist hospitals. The facilities of the King Faysal Hospital in Riyadh, for example, would certainly be the envy of many American cities.[5] Only for very advanced or innovative treatment do Saudi citizens need to go to Germany or the United States these days. But even poor countries like Egypt have built an impressive number of rural clinics and dispensaries, readily available to most of their people. What these places can do is quite limited—but in fact effective health care is often a matter of simple treatment and early intervention rather than costly high-end technology. (Greece, for example, enjoys one-third of America's per capita GDP and relies heavily on primary care clinics staffed by newly minted physicians, but its life span and infant mortality rates are equal to or better than U.S. numbers.) Finally, a less direct but no doubt extremely potent cause for the radical improvements in infant and early-childhood health is the spread of public education, especially among the younger generation of women, in which much attention is paid to issues of hygiene and public health.

As is so often the case, policies have unintended consequences— or rather, success in one arena inevitably creates new problems in others. Thus it is that the rapid fall in infant mortality, combined with general improvements in public health and longevity, has created a population crisis. To repeat a basic point, this crisis is not one of absolute numbers. Quite apart from overall populations, no Middle Eastern country is as densely packed as Germany or Japan. Even Egypt, where almost the entire population lives on about 5 percent of the country's territory, has an effective population density no higher than Belgium and the Netherlands. The problem lies elsewhere. First, there is the demographer's favorite cliché, "If present trends continue . . . " If present trends continue, the population of the Middle East will reach some 700 million by 2025 and will top out at over a billion sometime after midcentury. That *will* be a lot of people, by any standard.

Consequences on economy/
of youth pop.

The second problem, already sketched above, is more complex. High birthrates mean an influx of young people into the economy. For the first fourteen or fifteen years these children are marginal producers and high consumers; they may be able to get low-skill (and miserably paid) craft jobs in the cities, for example, but of course they cannot earn enough to pay for the costs of their schooling, health, or housing. They cost the economy far more than they can contribute in wages and services. In many countries child labor is a fact of life. If one pokes into the workshops of Fez, where the city's wonderful traditional crafts are produced, one finds that most of the simpler tasks are performed by preteens and adolescents—for a wage totaling about $5 to $7.50 per week.[6] When they reach young adulthood, of course, these young people should be highly productive workers, especially if (as is increasingly the case) they are able to complete their secondary or university education. But a huge flow of new workers challenges any country to find jobs for them; only a very dynamic, growth-oriented economy can hope to succeed in this task. The anecdotes with which I opened this chapter suggest that Middle Eastern economies have in fact been unable to provide productive employment for their young people, and now we need to ask why.

The first thing any American does in such a situation is to blame the politicians, and Middle Eastern politicians are certainly not without fault. Since achieving political independence after World War II, they have pursued policies that made eminently good sense in many respects but failed to lay the foundations for sustained long-term growth. Quite the contrary, in fact. Of course, it is easy to point to failure; it is much harder to explain it—to show why a given policy has failed and to define more effective alternatives. As we look at the debris of Middle Eastern economic policy, both realism and a bit of humility will be in order.

Let us begin with the obvious. Every government's first goal is to stay in power, and it will bend every effort to direct its revenues toward programs that will help it achieve that goal. As we have already seen, most Middle Eastern governments since World War II have been haunted by the specter of illegitimacy, by the fear (usually quite well founded) that in the eyes of their subjects and of neighboring states they have no right to rule. They are afflicted by a kind of rational paranoia, induced by the military and/or revolutionary roots of so many regimes, the Arab-Israeli conflict, internal ethnic tensions, the colonial origin of national borders within the region, and the social turmoil provoked by intensely felt and perpetually frustrated popular aspirations. To a large degree, therefore, the policy of governments throughout the region has been driven first and foremost by the quest for security. The economic and fiscal consequences are clear; the last four decades have witnessed an extraordinary rate of military expenditures by almost every Middle Eastern country. There is an irony in this, of course; by far the greatest danger to these regimes came not from the armies of hostile foreign powers but from coups, revolution, or subversion—things against which tanks and aircraft are almost useless, as the late Shah of Iran could attest.

But however misdirected their response to an admittedly dangerous environment may have been, by the end of the 1970s Middle Eastern governments were spending an average of 14 percent of their gross national product on the military; fourteen cents of every dollar produced by those economies went for soldiers and guns.[7] Even if these expenditures had been entirely internal—that is, devoted to soldiers' salaries and the purchase of domestically produced weapons and materiel—they would still have represented a very high opportunity cost. It is not just a question of guns versus butter—of "national security" versus civilian consumption—but more important a question of guns versus roads, telephones, schools, and factories. Not only civilian consumption but long-term investment suffered gravely. And in fact, military expenditures in the Middle East (in contrast to the United States) have not been internally directed. Until very recently, almost all the advanced weaponry possessed by every country had to be purchased abroad. In 1978, 39 percent of arms imports throughout the whole world were obtained by Middle Eastern governments—or to put this number in a more telling context, fully one-half of the total arms imported by developing countries went to the Middle East. (What these purchases actually cost is less clear; France and Great Britain demanded cash on the barrelhead, but the United States and the USSR supplied arms to poorer countries through grants, long-term credits, barter, and so on. But even here there were important quid pro quos.)

The 1970s may have been a golden age for the international arms merchant, but the 1980s hardly saw a collapse in the market—even by 1988, Middle Eastern countries were spending some 9 percent of their GNP on the military, half again as much as the United States at the very climax of the Reagan arms buildup. The number of men under arms as a proportion of population was twice as high as anywhere else in the world (18.3 per 1,000 in the Middle East versus 9.1 in the United States). There were certain constraints, to be sure, not least those stemming from the abrupt collapse of oil prices after 1984. This massive fall in revenues coincided with other limiting factors. First of all, the 1979 Camp David Accords and the 1982 peace treaty between Egypt and Israel held firm, in spite of very serious points of tension like Israel's 1982 invasion of Lebanon. However, the peace was to a large degree secured by the willingness of the United States to supply the arms needs of both countries on very generous terms. Iran, mired in the excruciatingly long and bloody Iran-Iraq War (eight years, with at least a half-million combat-related deaths between the two countries), obviously enjoyed no peace dividend. But ironically, though it had been one of the biggest spenders in the 1970s, during the war it was reduced to drawing on existing arms stocks, clandestinely obtained weapons, and the uncounted bodies of its youth. Iraq, in contrast, must have spent enough for both countries with its massive mobilization of manpower and foreign arms purchases. It is worth recalling that Iraq's crippling wartime debt to Kuwait was the immediate pretext for its occupation of that country in August 1990. Finally, there is the distinctive case of Saudi Arabia and Libya, two wealthy but thinly populated countries. The Saudis and Libyans continued to build enormous stockpiles of weapons and materiel, in spite of a serious revenue crunch caused by falling oil prices. Both maintained only a small number of men under arms, however, so their manpower costs did not rise a great deal.

It does seem possible that the decade of the 1990s has witnessed a substantial change in this long-entrenched pattern.[8] The Gulf War has ended Iraq's capacity to buy arms at least temporarily, the USSR is no longer around to tempt the United States into funding a regional arms race, and the emerging though very uneasy modus vivendi between Israel and its Arab neighbors may ultimately reduce the feverish quest for military "parity" on that front. But even if the regional arms race stays cooled down, a lot of damage has been done, a host of opportunities have been lost for good. Even countries that have received arms on concessionary terms from sympathetic suppliers, like Egypt under Sadat and Mubarak, are now burdened by genuinely mind-boggling levels of foreign debt. And even the Saudis have had to strip their once-boundless cash reserves to maintain a high level of arms purchases.

Many commentators have argued that military expenditure produces important indirect benefits, of course. They point to the technological spin-offs from the U.S. space program, or new industrial capacity that can ultimately be converted—however inefficiently—from military to civilian production. However, it is doubtful that most Middle Eastern states have reaped such benefits in any significant measure. Even the United States could not figure out, after the cold war wound down, how to convert its military aerospace industry to (for example) the production of high-speed trains. Economists count military expenditures as consumption, for the very good reason that such expenditures do not in any direct way provide new capital investment that can fuel future growth. In general, military goods are either stockpiled in warehouses or smashed to pieces, much like children's toys. We might suppose that the training received by soldiers in high-tech weaponry would create a technologically sophisticated stratum in society—that is certainly how the U.S. armed forces sell themselves to potential recruits. Likewise, one could argue that massive and costly arms imports will lead to efforts to manufacture them locally, and thereby lay the foundations for high-tech manufacturing. But neither has happened.

Except for Israel (and to a lesser degree Egypt and Turkey), no state in the region has really learned how to manufacture modern weapons; even everyday staples like small arms are imported. Iraq clearly tried to develop a strategic-weapons capacity on its own, but the choice of chemical-biological weapons and nuclear bombs was not a happy one, even if the Gulf War had not derailed these initiatives. These technologies have few uses and little spin-off in the civilian sector, with the not very convincing exception (for an oil-rich state) of nuclear power. Iran might ultimately have developed an arms-manufacturing capacity—certainly the Shah intended to do so—but the revolutionary government quite systematically marginalized the country's regular armed forces, even in the face of the eight-year war with Iraq. Military service may lead to some enhancement in the quality of the labor force, but in every country apart from

Israel the armies represent large conscript forces possessing only rudimentary levels of training and expertise.

Military expenditures have obviously been a very conspicuous
form of government consumption in the region, but they have not
been the only one. Since the mid-1950s, most Middle Eastern regimes
have also devoted a substantial proportion of their resources to social welfare expenditures (though not as much as several other regions in the Third World): food subsidies for urban populations, clinics and hospitals, schools, and various kinds of social insurance. In a
very real sense, these too are expenditures aimed at political security.

Now obviously welfare expenditures reflect first of all the publicly expressed (and no doubt sincerely held) ideals of these regimes.
After all, many of them originally seized power with the claim that
they represented the neglected and impoverished masses and that
their mission was to use the powers of the state to improve the lot of
the people. On a second, more political level, such expenditures validate these governments in the eyes of their supporters; since many
of them have only a narrow basis of support, they can ill afford to
alienate the few groups who are committed to their success. Finally,
social-welfare expenditures reflect the need of governments that have
seized power by main force to purchase a morsel of legitimacy in
society at large, to demonstrate even to the hostile or indifferent
that they have acted not for their own selfish benefit but for the
good of all.

Many social-welfare expenditures are now widely considered a
fundamental obligation of government. A state that does not attempt to provide "free" public education or basic medical care is
regarded with contempt throughout most of the world. (American
debates on these subjects are found almost nowhere else.) Other expenditures are a matter of political prudence if not sheer survival.
For decades the International Monetary Fund has been demanding an
end to food subsidies that allow urban populations, even the well-
off, to buy bread, rice, sugar, and oil at prices far below the costs of
production and distribution. But few Third World governments can
stand up to the massive riots that are unleashed every time such
subsidies are slashed. Economic rationality is never a match for the
solidly entrenched demands of the urban masses, and it is hard to
blame people as poor as most of those in Cairo or Casablanca or
Tehran for struggling violently to hold on to the few breaks they get.

On balance, Middle Eastern governments do what is expected of them, and perhaps what they have to do, in the arena of social welfare and entitlements. But such policies inevitably mortgage the future, in that they reduce the resources available for investment and long-term economic growth. They do so also because these policies often disrupt the weak market mechanisms that exist in these countries, replacing them with systems of central planning and distribution that make the old Soviet Gosplan seem a model of efficiency.

If it is true that Middle Eastern regimes have been strongly consumption-oriented, this does not mean that they have ignored the need for investment. Even though they have been severely constrained throughout the century in the domestic resources they could devote to this task, they began developing investment plans even in the 1920s and 1930s, and since the late 1950s they have pursued these assiduously. They have certainly not fallen behind in the production of five-year plans and the design of grand projects. Nor have their efforts been entirely without practical results. If Middle Eastern five-year plans often possess the same detachment from reality as construction cost projections in the United States, several of the great schemes have in fact come to fruition. Everyone "knows" about Egypt's massive and controversial Aswan Dam. Far less known are the even more daunting Jubail and Yanbu industrial cities in Saudi Arabia, far advanced but still very much in midstream. Each of these deserves a glance, to grasp both the opportunities and the pitfalls created by such massive efforts, designed to jerk stagnant national economies into self-sustaining growth in one pull.

The Aswan Dam was the first of the giant schemes to be seriously proposed in the postwar Middle East.[9] It was modeled in a broad sense on the vast network of dams, impoundments, and canals that had transformed the American West in the decades after World War I, and it was conceived in an era in which most people still thought of this transformation as unquestionably a Good Thing, the creation of a garden in the desert. By permitting year-round irrigation, the Aswan Dam would almost double the cropped land in Egypt. As such it would provide the food for Egypt's rapidly growing population (25 million when Nasser and his fellow officers seized power). It would also provide the basis to support their ambitious land reform policies. Finally, the hydroelectric power it would produce would allow the industrialization of a country that possessed few other sources of energy. The dam was finally completed in 1970, with substantial Soviet financial and technical aid. In some respects it has lived up to its promise: vast new areas in the desert west of the Delta have been brought into production, there is a lot of hydroelectric power, and so on. Unfortunately, however, there have also been major environmental effects. The Nile Valley used to be a self-fertilizing basin due to the annual floods and the layers of rich silt they laid down every autumn. Moreover, the natural rise and fall of the water table each year ensured that there would be no waterlogging of the soil and that excess mineral deposits would be flushed out. But now all these problems (and many others) exist in abundance. Even the foundations of the historic buildings in Cairo are threatened from salts leaching into the limestone. Egyptian farmers are slowly learning to adjust to the new realities, to install drainage mechanisms, to use water parsimoniously. But the adjustment is inevitably a slow one.

The Saudis have embarked on a project even more ambitious than Aswan.[10] This is a bold attempt to create—in effect out of thin air—a fully integrated industrial project, stretching from the extraction of natural gas and petroleum through the production of bulk plastics and petrochemicals to the fabrication of finished, high-level goods. The project is embodied in two full-scale industrial cities, one in Jubail on the Persian Gulf, the other in Yanbu on the Red Sea. (Both Jubail and Yanbu are long-established but historically very modest seaports.) The two cities are massive both in conception and on the ground, and to my knowledge the project has no parallel anywhere in the world; it makes the Pyramids look like a whimsical game of building blocks. Jubail's development site totals nearly 1,000 square kilometers (approximately 400 square miles), with 80 square kilometers devoted to industrial facilities. The population is slated to reach some 250,000 by 2010. Yanbu is a good deal smaller—less than half the size of Jubail—but it is still an immense undertaking in its own right. The project draws on two obvious Saudi assets—its vast oil and gas reserves and its great (though now somewhat depleted) capital resources. It is also an attempt to exploit and indeed reinforce a process under way for some two decades, the creation of a high-level Saudi professional and managerial class. In addition, this project reflects a growing awareness among the Saudi political elite of the need to develop a cadre of technicians and production-line managers. The Saudis have been working for more than two decades to develop high-level professionals (engineers, doctors, university professors) and senior managers among their own citizens rather than expatriates, but the Jubail-Yanbu project also incorporates a newly perceived need to ensure that the country can provide its own electricians, machine-tool operators, and so on. The project is well advanced, but we cannot yet predict if it will succeed in the long run. That is a question of economics as well as engineering.

So the need for investment has been recognized, but for a long time the strategies followed have been almost inevitably self-limiting. In the earlier phases, from the interwar period through the mid-1960s, industrial policy in the region emphasized autarky, the creation of self-contained industrial economies that could sustain themselves and grow without any need for foreign imports and capital. Atatürk's Turkey was the country that pursued this policy most single-mindedly, somewhat on the Soviet model devised by Stalin, albeit without the massive famines and violent political repression that the latter unleashed in the pursuit of his schemes. But we can see at least elements of this same policy in Reza Shah's Iran and (through a government-encouraged private sector) in Egypt under the Constitutional Monarchy (1923–1952). The quest for autarky normally has two dimensions: first, import substitution of consumer goods, so that finished textiles, processed foods, and other consumer goods are manufactured at home; second, an effort to build heavy industry—typically, iron and steel factories.

The point, of course, is to escape the classic trap for Third World countries of being compelled to sell cheap and buy dear—to export highly volatile raw commodities (grain, cotton, oil, phosphates) to industrial countries in order to buy back these same commodities in the form of costly (and far more stably priced) finished goods. In this realm the policy of Middle Eastern governments has probably been driven less by theory than by historical memory. Almost any educated Middle Easterner knows that his region was reduced to the role of a raw commodities exporter by the late nineteenth century, and retained that role for much of the twentieth.[11] For example, no Middle Eastern country could claim any role at all in refining and marketing petroleum products until the mid-1950s (and in practical terms until the end of the 1960s); they owned the oil in the ground, but all the facilities for pumping, refining, and exporting were owned and operated by foreign concerns. Some of these, like Aramco in Saudi Arabia, operated with a certain sense of tact, worked out fairly generous terms of payment, and provided considerable international political support for their host governments. In other cases, like the Anglo-Iranian Oil Company (AIOC), the company operated in a condescending, high-handed way and could only be induced to take the host country seriously in the face of political crisis. The oil nationalization crisis and the downfall of Prime Minister Mossadegh is seared into the memory of every Iranian, as permanent a part of national mythology as Sherman's march to the sea was in post–Civil War Georgia. Another case in point would be Egypt. By 1900 she was far and away the world's largest producer of high-quality cotton but had no modern textile factories until well after World War I. This was due in part to the investment preferences of the Egyptian land-owning class, but equally to the hostility of Lord Cromer, the near-absolute ruler of Egypt on behalf of the British government from 1883 to 1907, and not coincidentally a most effective lobbyist for the cotton mills of Manchester. Apart from historical memories of this kind—memories of national weakness and humiliation—Middle Eastern governments could look at the enormous success of two nineteenth-century heavy-industrializer, import-substituting economies: Germany and the United States. Japan—an Asian country—had pursued a similar game during the 1920s and 1930s, and in spite of various problems was still able to hold its own for years in an all-out war with the United States. All around, it must have been hard in the 1950s to think of a more effective policy or more persuasive models than these.

However understandable, an exclusive focus on import substitution and heavy industry is inevitably self-limiting. For this there are two reasons. The least important is that most Middle Eastern countries do not possess the raw or processed materials needed for heavy manufacturing: they have to import coke, pig iron, rolled steel, copper, aluminum, rubber, and so on. Far more important, the machine tools, furnaces, and other equipment needed to make manufactured goods must be brought in as well. For a generation or two, at best, we are not talking about manufacturing so much as final assembly—that is, the last step in a long process, most of which is still located abroad. The cost of all this is very steep, and it can only be recouped if there is a broad market for the final product. And that leads us straight to the second point: the small size of domestic markets in the Middle East. In poor countries like most of those in the Middle East, a policy based on import substitution was inevitably going to run up against a lack of demand in very short order. Poor people can buy only so many clothes and cans of vegetables. The only way to achieve real economies of scale and substantial profits is to develop broad markets; broad markets mean an emphasis on exports; and exports must be desirable (cheaper, better, or otherwise unobtainable) to these external markets. But the kinds of goods emphasized in import substitution policies are typically more costly and less good than those they have replaced. Under these circumstances, potential foreign customers, even in neighboring Arab states, have absolutely no reason to buy Egyptian rather than Taiwanese televisions. In the marketplace, money is thicker than blood.

In all fairness, it has to be admitted that there is now a substantial modern-industrial sector in many Middle Eastern countries and that the level and quality of production is far higher than it used to be. As for the level of production, one need only compare the blue skies of Cairo twenty years ago with the smog-ridden city of today. As to products, the Turkish-made Fiat (called the Murat) is a perfectly sound compact vehicle, though it will pose no threat to BMW, Honda, or Ford in world markets. Two decades ago you could not buy an Egyptian-made bicycle in Cairo (they were imported from India), and no one would have been foolish enough to do so even had they been available. Nowadays Egyptian televisions and home appliances—assembled under license from imported parts from German and Japanese manufacturers—are of modern design and quite reliable. Good inexpensive clothing, of local manufacture, is now available in Turkey, Syria, and Egypt.

Why carp in the face of such visible success? Because even today not one Middle Eastern state (with the partial exception of Turkey and of course Israel) has followed the only economic growth strategy that has worked since World War II—namely, the export-oriented production of high-value-added manufactures. This is of course the modern Japanese model, which has been mimicked by the Asian tigers (including South Korea, Taiwan, Singapore, and increasingly China), and more recently (aided by a huge influx of Japanese capital) by Malaysia, Indonesia, and Thailand as well. But to date there is not one Middle Eastern manufactured item that can be sold competitively on world markets. (In fact I have recently begun to see clothing in major U.S. retail outlets marked "made in" Egypt, Kuwait, or the United Arab Emirates. Egypt makes sense as a textile producer. It possesses a significant comparative advantage in this sector, since it can draw on both a domestically produced raw material—long-staple cotton—and cheap labor. But exactly how a low-cost, low-skill item like mass-market clothing has come to be manufactured in two rich oil economies—or in what sense it is manufactured there—I have yet to learn.)

In view of these realities, Middle Eastern states are still compelled to rely on the sale of commodities to finance imports, earn foreign exchange, and obtain independent capital for economic development. As has been the case throughout the last one hundred fifty years, the demand for these, hence their prices, is set by uncontrollable market forces in the developed economies, chiefly in Western Europe, North America, and Japan. Sometimes there are huge windfall profits, as in Egypt during the American Civil War, when Southern cotton was no longer available to English mills, or during the oil boom of the late 1970s and early 1980s. At other times there are abrupt price collapses—for example, Egyptian cotton in the late 1860s, as the South recovered from the war, or international oil prices in the mid-1980s (an unpredicted event that struck hard at Texas and Oklahoma as well, of course). Efforts by Middle Eastern governments to gain local control over production have been highly successful, especially for oil. But the efforts to control marketing through cartels have enjoyed only short-term successes, and these have been rather like drunken binges, which inevitably end in raging hangovers.

Commodities are not in themselves such bad things; someone must produce them, and they are the essential foundation of any industrialized economy. The problem comes when there is no domestic market for them—when demand (and hence price) is set by uncontrollable external forces—and when a country must depend on only one commodity for its income. This in fact has been the pervasive pattern in the Middle East ever since independence after World War II, as in so much of the Third World: oil in Arabia and Algeria, phosphates in Morocco, cotton in Egypt—products that find troubling parallels in Cuban sugar, West African cacao, Kenyan coffee, and Central American bananas. Monoculture of this kind, in effect the growing of a single (it is hoped high-value) crop for sale on world markets, is a distinctively nineteenth-century phenomenon. It of course often replaced or squeezed out the mixed agriculture of earlier times, which was usually aimed at subsistence or local markets. Monoculture was typically introduced under colonial rule, and thus reflects the economic outlook and interests of the now gone (but hardly forgotten) imperial economies of Britain and France. In some cases, however, it was instituted by independent regimes that were pursuing the main chance with a vengeance. This was particularly the case in mid-nineteenth-century Egypt, whose rulers viewed long-staple cotton as the ideal vehicle to finance the modernization of the Egyptian army and state. Ultimately their cotton export policy led to disaster. Egypt's last independent monarch, the Khedive Isma'il (1863–1879), channeled the country's export revenues into a whole array of visionary schemes but found balancing a checkbook unworthy of his concern.[12] The resultant fiscal crisis led to the British occupation of the country in 1882, which lasted until 1936, and on some levels until 1954. Since the end of the imperialist era after World War II, Middle Eastern governments have complained persistently about the damage done by monoculture and commodities markets to their economic development, but they have found it quite impossible to wean themselves from them. The reason is that they desperately need foreign exchange, and the wrenching adjustments involved in placing their economies on new foundations have seemed too daunting to face. The monoculture-commodities system is regarded as only transitional, as an umbrella to shelter the country while a new modern economy is under construction, but the umbrella has proved amazingly durable, the modern economy frustratingly slow to take form.

From all this, it looks as though the Middle Eastern economies have worked themselves into a fine impasse, and every effort to extricate themselves either comes to nothing or draws them further into the quagmire. Every proposed solution to any given problem seems to create a host of new and worse ones, or (at best) to promise only long-deferred resolutions. Is there any plausible and likely solution to this situation? Certain things do give at least some glimmerings of hope. First, for the moment (though who knows for how long) the specter of constant war seems to be fading, and governments can contemplate spending money on something else—no guarantee of the millennium, to be sure, since Latin America has long spent a very small proportion of its GDP on things military, but it has not been spared either extended military rule or severe economic development problems. Second, most Middle Eastern countries have by now acquired a functional infrastructure of roads, airports, telecommunications, schools and universities, and clinics and hospitals. A few of them, like Saudi Arabia and the smaller Gulf states, are at a quite advanced level of development in this sector. Infrastructure of course provides the framework for economic growth; it is what permits a country to participate effectively in the modern world economy. Whether these possibilities are exploited is another matter, to be sure, but they are there. Third, in key large countries like Turkey and Egypt there is far less official hostility to private investment and business than there was twenty years ago. In principle that should be a good thing, since market-oriented economies have certainly performed better than centrally planned ones in recent decades. But questions remain. Will the regimes really encourage private large-scale investment in potential growth or export sectors? Will private investment, as in the 1940s and early 1950s, be channeled largely toward consumer and luxury import goods, which are very lucrative places to put one's money but contribute little to long-term development?

There are no easy answers to such questions. Even where the proper economic policy seems transparently obvious, economic rationality may well contradict political survivability. And most of the time, of course, economists disagree on almost everything about which governments seek their advice—which facts are really relevant to the situation, the consequences of encouraging consumer demand or restraining inflation, the best mechanisms for building domestic investment. Under such circumstances a sensible government might well decide simply to live with things as they are, since everyone is used to that and since an attack on major structural problems is certain to be extremely disruptive. Only governments that enjoy the confidence of their citizens, and are willing to impose almost certain short-term hardships for the sake of long-term benefits that may never come to pass, can really take the steps needed to break the logjam. Life is full of surprises, and occasionally they are pleasant ones, but a betting man would wager that the Middle East will be living with the current legacy of rapid population growth and economic frustration for decades to come.

CHAPTER 2

FROM IMPERIALISM
TO THE NEW WORLD ORDER

The Middle East in Search of a Future

For the peoples of the Middle East, and indeed for Muslim countries throughout Asia and Africa, the twentieth century has been an age of frustration, of expectations repeatedly raised to dizzying heights and then dashed to pieces. Although the century opened at the high tide of European imperial expansion, Middle Easterners had already developed great ambitions for political independence, constitutional government if not full democracy, and material progress and prosperity. Most of all, they had intense and apparently well-founded hopes for a revitalization of culture and society, so that the peoples of the Middle East could again take their rightful place in the forefront of world civilization.

That there were formidable internal and external obstacles to all this no one denied for a moment. But those obstacles seemed clearly visible and vulnerable to a bold, direct attack. If the peoples of the Middle East could drive off the powerful empires—British, French, and Russian—that then dominated the region and replace the existing corrupt and autocratic regimes with governments that would truly represent them, then the path to economic, social, and intellectual progress would be open. Poverty, ignorance, disease, and a crippling sense of backwardness could, and inevitably would, be overcome step by step.

It has not worked out quite that way. The foreign empires dissolved soon enough—sooner perhaps than anyone had imagined possible. The czarist empire collapsed during World War I, and although by 1922 Lenin had reconstituted it in a new form as the Soviet Union, it displayed few ambitions for expansion until World War II, and then only in quite limited ways. The French and British empires were longer lived, but the British were clearly contemplating home rule or dominion status for many of their possessions by the mid-1920s. The whole process was sharply hastened by World War II, which dealt a death blow to both empires. France suffered an irreparable loss of prestige from her humiliating defeat by Germany in 1940, and the implications of this loss were driven home by eight years of bitter and ultimately futile struggle in Indochina. Britain retained her prewar prestige for many years; indeed, at the time of my first visit to the Middle East in 1966 she was still seen as the supreme puppet master by many locals. But Britain's governments, both Labour and Tory, knew they had been bankrupted by the war; even though they spent the decade after 1945 trying to act the part of a great power, they felt compelled to withdraw from one crucial position after another—India first, then Palestine, finally the Suez Canal.[1] By 1962 both empires had exited the stage. As a power vacuum (or so it was perceived) developed in the Middle East after 1945, the United States and the Soviet Union inevitably moved in to fill it, but both, in spite of their immense power and resources, found themselves quite unable to turn the region's emerging states into reliable and predictable allies. At many points, in fact, both found themselves held hostage to the purposes and maneuverings of their would-be clients.

But political independence within the Middle East (as in many other parts of Asia and Africa) did not create a framework for the achievement of other, and in the long term more important, national goals. To many people in the region, an especially bitter irony was the utter failure of political independence to usher in an era of real democratic government. Apart from Israel, democracy remains a rarity in the Middle East and North Africa, though some countries (Turkey, Egypt, Jordan, even Yemen) seem to pass through cycles of authoritarian and democratizing rule. As we saw in the previous chapter, even real victories in the socioeconomic arena have turned out to be two-edged swords. Sharp reductions in mortality rates, for example, have created a so far unmanageable population explosion. Secondary and higher education has expanded dramatically, but it has also created a huge class of highly trained but unemployable young adults—even in Saudi Arabia, which thirty years ago had no modern universities at all and only a few government schools at any level. In the last decade of the twentieth century, some forty years since the achievement of real independence from foreign political domination, we are left with weak and frustrated governments, uncertain of their place on the world stage and unable to achieve key domestic policy goals. They themselves are under siege by frustrated, angry populations. It is a certain recipe for turmoil, perhaps ultimately a cataclysm.

It may seem strange to call the governments of the Middle East weak, for a quick overview demonstrates that they have been astonishingly durable. To begin with the "traditional" monarchies, King Hussein of Jordan has been on the throne since 1953, and King Hassan II of Morocco succeeded his father in 1961 and represents a dynasty that rose to power some three hundred fifty years ago. The Kingdom of Saudi Arabia was established by Abd al-Aziz ibn Abd al-Rahman Al Saud in 1933, and since his death in 1953 four of his sons have succeeded him without serious challenge from any group outside the Saudi ruling family.[2] The many regimes created by military coup have shallower roots but comparable records of longevity. Hafiz al-Asad seized power in Syria in 1971, and Saddam Hussein of Iraq has been around more or less as long, in spite of two devastating wars between 1980 and 1991. In Egypt, the political system dates back to the coup against King Farouk in 1952; Anwar Sadat succeeded Gamal Abdel Nasser (1970) and Husni Mubarak followed Sadat (1981) with barely a bump. This occurred even though both Nasser and Sadat died suddenly and Egypt was embroiled in major economic, political, and diplomatic crises at both junctures. Finally, Libya has been run by Muammar Qaddafi since 1969; he may be "erratic" and "mercurial," but he indubitably has staying power. Apart from Libya and Morocco, the other North African states are ruled by governments that emerged during the struggle for independence in the mid-1950s. Algeria has been ruled by the FLN since independence in 1962, and Tunisia has seen only two leaders since 1956, Habib Bourguiba (1956–1987) and Zine al-Abidine Ben Ali (since 1987). On the surface Iran is the exception to this almost unblemished record, for it did have a tumultuous revolution in 1978–1979—but before that the Shah had endured for thirty-seven years, and his father for sixteen years before him. In any event, the new Iranian political system seems solidly established; there is presently no obvious internal challenge to the Islamic Republic. The governments of the modern Middle East have not had an easy time of it during the past three decades; they have survived foreign invasion, internal revolt, and innumerable economic crises. So in what sense can they possibly be thought of as weak?

In two senses, I would argue. First, most of the regimes in the region are highly personalized—that is, the political system of each country is built around the particular individual who has founded it and keeps it going; if these governments collapsed tomorrow, no one can guess who or what might follow them. To put it bluntly, almost every regime in the Middle East is vulnerable to a heart attack or an assassin's bullet. There are important exceptions, of course: Egypt, Turkey, and Iran have well-articulated political systems, and Algeria is controlled, more or less, by the army high command. Saudi Arabia is a broad-based family enterprise, and should endure so long as the House of Saud, literally several thousand strong, can fend off potential opponents and maintain a high degree of internal cohesion among its members. The political systems of all these countries can survive, and often have, even abrupt and unexpected transfers of power from one chief of state to another.

However, even the stablest and most institutionalized of Middle Eastern governments is threatened, or potentially so, by acute public discontent and in some cases by overt revolutionary movements. On the most fundamental level, only a few of them are in any position to lay the foundations of long-term economic growth and a wider prosperity.

How has this impasse come about? What has led to the failure to achieve the great hopes, often dashed but always cherished, that have driven Middle Eastern political life throughout the twentieth century? There is no simple way to answer this question, for each of the countries of the Middle East and North Africa has its own history. This is true even for countries like Syria, Lebanon, Jordan, and Israel-Palestine, which were for many centuries simply parts of a single broad if vaguely defined region ("Greater Syria" in modern parlance, *bilad al-Sham* in the traditional Arabic expression), and which indeed had no separate political existence until after World War I. Since God (or the devil) is in the details, we may learn most by using specific cases to throw light on the broader issues that concern us. Choosing these is no easy matter, since every country has a fascinating tale to tell. There is a strong case for Turkey, because it has pursued (since the mid-1920s) the most determined and single-minded policy of Westernization—a policy that may be on the verge of fulfillment today as Turkey strives to enter the European Economic Community (EEC), or that may be blocked as it rebuilds its cultural ties with a Muslim world from which it tried to divorce itself seventy years ago. Algeria presents an equally compelling line of inquiry. It was born in a long, bloody revolution (1954–1962) that became the very model for the anticolonialist struggle in the Third World. It mobilized its revolutionary heritage to pursue a politics of cultural identity more obsessively than any other state in the region. It has had the natural resources (in the form of oil and natural gas) to fund a long series of radical social and economic initiatives. And finally, it has been embroiled in an increasingly savage civil war since 1992, one that evokes awful echoes of the struggle with France four decades ago. Among smaller countries, the tragic fate of Lebanon, with its once-appealing, now-shattered image of tolerance and prosperity, suggests a host of sad and terrifying lessons. Iraq, Syria, Tunisia, and Morocco would each throw a bright light on many intriguing problems. But Morocco is really like nothing else in the Middle East (that is of course part of its charm), and Tunisia is too small to be an effective actor outside its immediate environs; in this cluster only Iraq and Syria have ever been able to claim a major role in the politics and intellectual life of the Middle East as a whole—and the regional ambitions of both have been consistently stifled. The oil-rich states of the vast but thinly populated Arabian Peninsula, along with Libya, are remarkable in many ways, not least for their meteoric transformation into modern economies even while retaining much of their old tribal social and political values and structures. But their unique oil wealth makes them economically and culturally highly idiosyncratic; they too really do not reflect the major dilemmas of the region as a whole.

In the end, I think, three places exemplify more of the dreams and frustrations of the modern Middle East than any others: Iran, Egypt, and Israel-Palestine. In their very different ways, they have been the stage for the grand dramas of the twentieth-century Middle East, and the region's political mythology is most fully embodied in their histories. Iran is a very large country, both in land and in population, and though it is absolutely sui generis in many ways, it has possessed extraordinary cultural continuity and a deep-rooted sense of national identity over many centuries. Moreover, Iran has been a central player within the region's geopolitics throughout this century. Omitting it would be akin to omitting California or New York (both of them genuinely odd places also) from an analysis of American society. Egypt has been since the mid-nineteenth century not only the largest Arabic-speaking country but also the focal point of Arabic literary life and intellectual debate; the Arab world without Cairo is like France without Paris—altogether inconceivable.

Alongside these two giants, the tiny region of Israel-Palestine seems something of an anomaly. But of course the Arab-Israeli conflict is almost synonymous with "the Middle East" in American political parlance, and has been so for at least half a century. It is the lens through which we examine and interpret every other issue in the region. Obviously the American perspective is full of geographical, cultural, and political distortions, but in one sense it is not so far off the mark. More than any other issue since World War II, the struggle for the parcel of land lying between the Jordan River and the Mediterranean has shaped the regional and international politics of the Arab world. In at least two cases (Lebanon and Jordan), a country's internal evolution has lain hostage to this struggle. Nor has any other issue in this century so fully embodied the intense aspirations and bitter disappointments of the peoples of the Middle East. And in spite of diplomatic and military developments since 1989, the Arab-Israeli conflict is not merely a matter of historical interest. We are far from knowing whether the Oslo Accords of 1993 can provide a strong enough framework for two peoples so divided by suspicion and bitterness to pursue their lives within the same land, partly separate and partly intermingled. In a very real way, the termination of the cold war and the retreat of most Arab states from direct confrontation has reduced the conflict to its core; Israelis and Palestinians can no longer avoid dealing with each other and with their own internal divisions.

Iran

Iran began the twentieth century as the most backward and isolated of the major states of the Middle East. A comparison with its neighbor and ancient rival, the Ottoman Empire, is instructive.[3] In spite of the severe territorial losses and unrelenting foreign interference suffered by the Ottomans during the nineteenth century, their empire still possessed many assets in 1900. To begin with, it was very large: although its hold over its remaining Balkan territories was fragile at best, its control of Anatolia (modern Turkey), greater Syria, Iraq, and the Red Sea coast of Arabia was still uncontested. Through many decades of tortuous and erratic administrative reorganization, the Ottoman Empire had built an effective centralized government that by 1900 could control and administer its provinces. Even more important, it could count on the loyalty of its Muslim subjects (about 80 percent of the total population), whether these were Turkish, Kurdish, Arab, or members of some other ethnic group. In spite of severe but erratic censorship and police repression, the capital of Istanbul and a few other urban centers enjoyed a dynamic, creative intellectual life, conducted in close touch with all the latest currents in Paris and London. The Ottoman Empire had a vital and growing commerce and was just beginning to develop a viable modern industrial sector. Communications throughout most of the empire were primitive, but Istanbul was connected with Central Europe via the famed Orient Express, and plans for an ambitious railway line from Istanbul to Baghdad (largely supported by German capital) were well advanced. In addition, the Ottoman government used its own funds, generated through public subscription, to construct the Hijaz railway between Damascus and Medina—an enterprise of enormous symbolic importance as well as considerable strategic and economic merit. The Ottoman army was sporadically effective at best, but it was unquestionably a modern army. Under good leadership, it could be a tough opponent, as the British learned at great cost during World War I in Gallipoli and Iraq. Finally—and far from a trivial point in the world as it was then constituted—the Ottoman Empire had begun to build close military and economic ties with Kaiser Wilhelm II's Germany, the only Great Power in Europe that had made no claims against her peoples or territories. The Ottoman Empire in the first decade of the twentieth century seems comparable on many levels to Russia during the same period, though it was of course smaller, weaker, and (by force of circumstance) far less ambitious.

Iran in 1900 was simply not on this level. It did possess an emerging modern intelligentsia, which included lower- and mid-level bureaucrats, some religious scholars (especially the younger men in the major cities), and—a new group—journalists. The north-western metropolis of Tabriz especially was in close contact both with Istanbul and with the Russian city of Baku on the Caspian—an oil-boom town with a mixed Russian and Turkish population and a strong (though obviously illegal) Marxist political movement. But the capital of Tehran likewise had rapidly proliferating intellectual societies and publications of its own.

But the Iranian political system was a farce. The country was nominally ruled by monarchs who stemmed from the Turkish-speaking Qajar tribe; they affected the ambitions and style of abso-lute autocrats, but in fact they could assert little control outside their capital of Tehran and its immediate environs. Most of Iran was domi-nated by vast tribal confederations, and the Qajar shahs could rule these regions only by horse-trading with the chiefs of the tribes. They had a bit more control over the cities, but here too they had to work through powerful intermediaries such as great landholders or senior religious leaders (who were often considerable landlords in their own right). Desultory efforts at administrative reform and centralization in the later nineteenth century had produced much expenditure and few results. Nor was there an effective Iranian national army. For the defense of their throne and territories, the Qajar monarchs had long depended on a small palace guard, combined with tribal levies sup-plied by the great chiefs, when they felt like providing them. In the late nineteenth century, the Qajars had added the Cossack Brigade, an elite cavalry corps made up of Iranian troops mostly recruited from the country's Turkish tribes but funded by the czar and com-manded by Russian officers. The existence of the Cossack Brigade in fact reveals a sad truth: that the modern heir of such legendary em-pire builders as Cyrus, Ardashir, and Abbas the Great was hardly more than a pawn in the czar's hand. By its menacing military pres-ence on Iran's northern borders and its extensive economic invest-ments there (railroads, telegraph lines, mines, fisheries, etc.), Russia by now utterly dominated the northern third of the country.

Southern Iran was subject to the subtler but hardly less intrusive meddlings of the British. For Iran in 1900, there was no German Em-pire on call. Iran's economy was very undeveloped; what modern sector existed was in the hands of European concessionaires. As it happens, an enormously valuable new resource, one that could utterly transform the revenues available to the central government and thus the balance of power within the country, was on the verge of being discovered in the lowlands along the Persian Gulf. The Iranian government was somewhat out of touch with these things, however, and in 1902 it sold the rights to explore for and develop petroleum for an exiguous price to a British subject, one William D'Arcy. The D'Arcy Concession was spectacularly successful, and by World War I it had become the Anglo-Persian Oil Company, half owned by the British government—next to the Suez Canal, Great Britain's most precious strategic asset in the Middle East. A crisis was inevitable: in the eyes of their subjects, the Qajar monarchs were not only despotic but stupid, and had demonstrated many times over that they were absolutely incompetent to defend the country's borders and resources from the ambitions of foreigners. If drastic steps were not taken, Iran was doomed to go the way of almost every other country in Asia and Africa.

The fuse was lit by a trivial act. The arbitrary and brutal punishment of a couple of Tehran's sugar merchants in December 1905 led to a massive general strike against the Shah's government. The aspirations of Iran's emerging modern intelligentsia, as well as many of the bazaar merchants of the great northern cities of Tehran and Tabriz, emerged to the forefront in the Constitutional Revolution of 1905–1909, and their demands were embodied in the Fundamental Laws promulgated in 1906–1907. Though formally issued by royal edict, these laws were drafted by the new class of urban secular intellectuals and certain elements of the clergy, who thereby made themselves the spokesmen for a fundamental reshaping of Iranian politics and society. Although observed far more often in the breach than in actuality, the Fundamental Laws of 1906–1907 remained on the books as the constitution of Iran until 1979.

The new constitutional regime was sharply challenged by both traditional monarchists and (in close alliance with them) the Russians, but it endured until 1911, when the Russians moved to quash it and establish a puppet government. Iranians ever since have looked back to those few years as a beacon, a brief shining moment when progressive national forces took charge of the country's destiny and instituted a modern constitutional government, asserted national independence against the domineering great powers of the day (Britain and Russia), and laid the foundations for a renewal of Iranian society and culture. Obviously there is much idealization in this picture—a kind of golden haze effect typical of all national myths, including our own. Even so, the years from 1905 to 1911 were undeniably a period that opened up new possibilities for Iranians, a vivid sense of the things that could be if only they were allowed to work out their national destiny. The Constitutional Revolution is for Iranians the single most crucial event in their modern history, something that looms as large in the Iranian political imagination as does the Civil War for Americans.[4]

In a very real sense, the history of the following seven decades is a history of the struggle to recover that shining moment, and of the painful realization that it was always just out of reach. At two points there seemed a chance to set things right again: (1) the Cossack commandant Reza Khan's rise to power after World War I, when he ejected the last Qajar monarch and took the throne as Reza Shah (1925–1941), and (2) the decade of parliamentary ascendancy between 1943 and 1953, culminating in the government led by Prime Minister Mohammed Mossadegh in 1951–1953. For quite different reasons both opportunities failed, but politically engaged Iranians saw both failures as caused by foreign interference—Great Britain alone in the former case, Britain together with the United States in the latter. This perception is not mere paranoia or xenophobia: foreign interference was certainly not the whole story in either case, but in both it was a critical element.

Reza Khan was strongly supported by the British Embassy during the early 1920s, because they saw in him the only real hope for political stability in Iran, and hence the best guarantor for British oil and the security of the western approaches to British India. Once in power he proved very prickly, since he was an ardent modernizing nationalist with an agenda of his own. Among other things, in 1933 he demanded and obtained a substantial revision of the royalties paid by the Anglo-Iranian Oil Company. (There was in this period no question of nationalizing a British corporation.) Nevertheless, Reza Shah served bottom-line British concerns well enough, since he was a ruthless and effective autocrat who for the first time in centuries managed to assert direct administrative control over all of Iran. He tamed though he did not quite break the power of the great tribes, and he was also perfectly willing to use brute force to intimidate Shi'ite religious leaders at the smallest sign of opposition to his secularizing policies. He had of course no patience whatever with democratic processes, or with opposition of any kind, and Iranian intellectuals who had hoped that he might revive the moribund 1906 Constitution were doomed to bitter disappointment.

The case of Mohammed Mossadegh was far sadder and, in the short term at least, far more disastrous for the hopes of Iranian nationalists.[5] Mossadegh belonged to the landed aristocracy, and his family had a long record of service to the monarchy. But he himself had participated in the Constitutional Revolution, and he was known throughout his long career as a dedicated patriot and democrat. Moreover, in a political system almost wholly based on the buying and selling of favors, he was known to be utterly incorruptible. When Mossadegh was named prime minister in 1951 by the young Muhammad Reza Shah (1941–1979), he was already more than seventy years old. Though he gained power so late in life, he did not regard it as a retirement sinecure or as the due reward for his eminence. Rather, he used his opportunity to pursue the most fervently and universally held goal of Iranian nationalism, regaining control of the country's oil. The only way to do that, he believed, was to nationalize forthwith the Anglo-Iranian Oil Company, which held monopoly rights to produce, refine, and market Iranian oil throughout the world. Such a confrontation had both material and symbolic value; it was a declaration of Iranian sovereignty and economic independence, and it aimed at actual control over the material resources that were essential to that sovereignty and independence. Mossadegh's challenge naturally provoked a strong resistance from the British government, who (with only slight exaggeration) regarded it as a grave threat to the vital interests of a still prestigious but rapidly declining empire. In addition, Mossadegh's tactics, combined with his enormous personal popularity, also threatened not only the political power but also the very throne of the Shah who had appointed him. As negotiations over the future of Iran's oil dragged on for more than two years with no progress, this combination of opponents proved deadly, especially after the new Eisenhower administration weighed in on the British and royalist side. In the summer of 1953, the United States and Britain jointly organized and funded a military coup aimed at overthrowing Mossadegh and re-storing the Shah's authority.

The coup was in the short term brilliantly successful. The Shah was restored to his throne and for the next quarter century imposed a personal dictatorship (with occasional constitutional trappings), reinforced by a close alliance with the United States against ene-mies both external and internal. Iran's oil was transferred pro forma to Iranian national ownership in 1954; the transition to full Iranian control and management now began to take place after all, but it occurred smoothly over a couple of decades and was only com-pleted twenty years later. From one point of view, both Western and Iranian national interests had been handsomely served. But in con-trast to most Americans, Iranians were never fooled by the covert nature of the coup against Mossadegh. It was in their eyes a gross betrayal, and they never forgave either the Shah or the United States for it. In the end, the coup against Mossadegh was the cancer that killed the monarchy.

Because of events like these, the persistent foreign presence in Iran came to be perceived as the root of all evils. It was so perceived first of all by secular-minded intellectuals and politicians, both Marx-ist and non-Marxist, who saw it as subverting national indepen-dence and/or aspirations for democratic government. But it was no less bitterly resented by the Shi'ite religious leadership, who saw it as a threat to the independence of a Muslim people, and even more gravely, as poisoning the values and way of life espoused by Islam. The concurrence between these two groups on this point is crucial. After the Constitutional Revolution of 1905–1911 (and in many cases during it) Iran's religious leaders and secular intelligentsia were of-ten at loggerheads, to put it mildly, on many fundamental issues: education, the status of women, the true nature of Iranian national identity. Their mutual opposition issued in violence on more than one occasion. But both agreed that the suffocating foreign presence they had experienced throughout their lives, whether it took the form of overt intervention or insidious influence, was an abomination. By the late 1970s, this shared disgust and rage would have a cata-clysmic impact.

The revolution of 1978–1979 is full of irony. It began with vio-lence between government troops and religious students in Febru-ary 1978, but by the summer and early fall of 1978 it looked as though the course of events might bring about a rebirth of constitutional government under a secular nationalist regime—the remnants of Mossadegh's old National Front, in fact. To the astonishment of most observers (both Iranian and foreign), however, a loose-knit but astute and very tough-minded group of religious leaders soon placed itself in the forefront of the burgeoning revolution. Without ever quite specifying just what they had in mind, they used rituals of piety, protest, and mourning to drape the revolution in religious symbolism. In so doing they were able to bring together many disparate groups, from uprooted and impoverished rural migrants in the cities to restless intellectuals in search of an authentic Iranian national culture. One of their most senior and prestigious members, the fiery and bitterly antiroyalist Ayatollah Ruhollah Khomeini, in political exile in France, emerged as the spokesman and symbol of the Iranian nation.

In this way these religious leaders came to be in a very strong position to set the political agenda during the chaotic weeks after the Shah fled Iran in January 1979. The Ayatollah Khomeini had mobilized very broad (although not universal) support for his claim that only a government of the clergy had the right to lead a Muslim people. In the new order envisioned by him and his associates, secular politicians would be at best subordinate members. Even the most ardently religious-minded politicians quickly learned that no one could govern without Khomeini's support, and that he would give this support only to his fellow clergy—and among these, only to those who adhered to his line.

Even so, the Islamic Republic that they created was and remains a constitutional government. First of all, and common American perceptions to the contrary, Khomeini was no dictator; he made no effort to control everyday government affairs or to define concrete policy initiatives. He saw his role as assuring the Islamic character of the new republic. Hence he would remain on the sidelines even when there were serious policy disputes between the elected politicians. He would only intervene in cases where he believed that Islam itself was at stake. It is true that his interventions were rather unpredictable and very public, and once he had come down decisively on an issue it was impossible to oppose his will. It is likewise true that he knew how to use his interventions for maximum political leverage, and he demonstrated great skill in subverting his rivals and supporting his allies. Hence, he did not order the U.S. Embassy takeover, but he sanctioned it once it had occurred; no Iranian government could negotiate an end to the crisis until he permitted it to do so. When he decided that Iran's first elected president, Abu'l-Hasan Bani'Sadr, was departing from the true path, Bani Sadr had no choice but to flee Iran even though he had been an ardent supporter of the 1979 revolution and of an Islamic order. It was Khomeini who insisted on pursuing the war against the satanic Saddam Hussein even after Iraqi forces had been driven from Iran and a favorable negotiated peace was within easy reach. Most notoriously, it was Khomeini who issued the *fatwa* authorizing the death of Salman Rushdie; even after Khomeini's passing, this document has been a godsend for militants wanting to block any normalization of relations with the West, and particularly with the United States.

The new constitution, drafted by a mixed assembly of religious leaders and laymen, was overwhelmingly approved by a broad popular mandate in the fall of 1979.[6] It was very much a hybrid document. It assigned oversight powers—in effect, the power to veto legislation and any executive actions—to the Council of Guardians (a panel of clergy) and ultimately to the Jurist (an office that the constitution explicitly offers to Khomeini during his lifetime). In that sense the political system created by the revolution was, and even now remains, a theocracy. But the power to initiate legislation rests with a legislature elected by universal suffrage, and the country's laws and the ordinary affairs of government are to be carried out by an elected president. On this level, then, it is a government grounded in a concept of popular sovereignty. More than that, the 1979 Constitution is imbued with the mixed flavors of piety and a social-democratic welfare state. Access to elected office is strictly controlled; only candidates approved by the Council of Guardians may run—hence the piety and orthodoxy of members of parliament are assured. And yet the elections themselves are reasonably honest; over time they have led to a steady decline in the number of clergy in the parliament (it is now down to about one-third), and they have even produced real surprises, like the broad-based triumph of the moderate cleric Muhammad Khatami in the presidential elections of 1997. The new system has proved strong enough to survive both eight years of all-out war against Iraq and numerous internal political crises, a fact that demonstrates that it possesses practical as well as purely legal legitimacy.

At the same time, the chief success of the Islamic regime may be its durability. The Islamic Republic has never been able to decide quite what role Iran should play in the world. Early in its career it adopted a stance of ardent support for Islamic revolution every-where, in the manner of Lenin's Russia in the 1920s and Castro's Cuba in the 1960s. This ardor was indeed one of the things that pro-voked the bloody war with Iraq in 1980 and left the country almost isolated in a struggle for its very survival. Since Khomeini's death, Iran has searched for a new foreign policy without ever quite find-ing one. It seems clear that Iran does permit terrorist training camps on its soil and that it provides some financial and political support for Islamic revolutionary causes. However, these things would go on with or without Iranian support; in a sense, they are a device for a tired postrevolutionary regime to maintain a degree of legiti-macy and even leadership in the Islamic movement. Iran is no longer the proud symbol of the rejection of everything Western and un-Islamic. On the contrary, it has sought to rebuild economic and dip-lomatic ties with the West on at least a limited level.

In the arena of domestic policy, the record is just as befuddling. The Islamic Republic began in part as a drive for an Islamic social and economic order, one that would in effect create a Swedish wel-fare state through the application of Islamic values. But it has not happened; successive parliaments have been quite unable to develop a viable economic policy in any arena, because neither the parlia-mentarians nor the Council of Guardians can agree what an Islamic social order should look like. For example, does Islam demand the defense of the paramount rights of private property (the preference of the Council of Guardians), or does it support a broad-based re-distribution of land and resources (a perspective that has found some support in the Majlis)? The answer of course depends on how one understands Islam, and how one believes it should be applied to real life. Without a consensus on these points—and clearly there is no such consensus—the meaning of Islamic government remains completely up in the air.

There is thus a bitter irony in the Iranian Revolution of 1978–1979. It was a genuinely popular movement, one that mobilized wider support and more enthusiastic engagement than any political event in the modern history of that country. And yet it has, after less than two decades, left Iranians just as disillusioned and cynical as they were in the days of the Shah. There is no sign that the Islamic regime's existence is threatened, but it seems to be devoted more to keeping itself in power than to building a future for the country. In Iran even Islam has not been the solution.

Egypt

Egypt's modern history presents a very different picture.[7] In Iran, political tensions throughout the twentieth century have focused primarily on problems of foreign domination and constitutional government. In Egypt, foreign domination and constitutionalism certainly held center stage in the first half of this century (i.e., until the rise of Gamal Abdel Nasser and the Suez Crisis of 1956), and the struggle for constitutional or democratic government continues to be a matter of intense debate even today. But at least since World War II the front-burner issue in Egypt has been the need for economic development and some mitigation of the country's extraordinary disparities of wealth.

Egypt, in contrast to Iran, produced a functioning if thoroughly corrupt constitutional system from 1923 to 1952, and it has had such a system again (albeit with many restrictions and shortcomings) since Husni Mubarak came to power in 1981. As to foreign domination, it was certainly a core issue—indeed almost the only issue—throughout the half-century of the British Occupation, which lasted from the arrival of British troops in 1882 down to the Anglo-Egyptian Treaty of 1936. (It is worth noting that Iran, for all its problems with foreign interference during this century, suffered only a brief direct foreign occupation, a joint enterprise by the British and the Soviets during World War II.) The 1936 treaty certainly fell short of ending British domination in Egypt, since it left control of the Suez Canal Zone in British hands and leashed Egypt to British strategic interests. Nevertheless, the treaty's terms went well beyond pro forma independence; moreover, the bitterly resented unequal provisions it contained were essentially eliminated in the new Anglo-Egyptian Treaty of 1954, and the last vestiges of these were scrubbed away in the Suez debacle of 1956. For the last forty years, Egyptian governments have been quite free to choose their own friends and make their own enemies—one of Nasser's most enduring legacies to his country.

Nasser, like most members of his generation, was obsessed throughout his life by the humiliating memory of British domination. The mere fact that the British presence was decisively eradicated in 1956 could not lay these demons to rest. Not without reason, he believed that the British role in the region had not really disappeared but had been taken up (albeit in a somewhat altered form) by the United States. For that reason he regarded all American initiatives with grave suspicion and refused to get involved in anything but limited tactical relationships with the Western powers. The American connection with Israel, the key "imperialist outpost in the Middle East," only intensified his ingrained suspicion and distaste. With the Soviet Union he did build an alliance on several levels (investment in infrastructure, arms purchases, access to Egyptian bases, cultural exchanges), but he was confident—quite correctly, as things turned out—that he could keep this relationship within bounds and use it as a tool to manipulate American policy. The Soviet presence would keep the Americans involved in the region and thereby prevent a monopoly of Soviet influence but would block any efforts by the United States to interfere in Egyptian policy.

Egypt's foreign relations, however, were never Nasser's sole preoccupation. When he and his fellow army officers seized power in 1952 (i.e., before the final disposal of British military bases and the Suez conflict), Egypt's emerging economic crisis was already at the head of their agenda. In spite of such distractions as Suez, the struggle for Arab unity, and the Arab-Israeli conflict, the new regime devoted the bulk of its political and financial resources to economic and welfare issues: a major land reform, building the Aswan Dam, a vast expansion of health care and education, and (after 1958) large-scale state investment in and control over industry and commerce. This package of initiatives ultimately came to be labeled "Arab Socialism." Arab Socialism, like most efforts at state-controlled development, had a mixed record at best and might be faulted on all sorts of economic policy grounds, but it certainly does not reflect indifference to the well-being of Egypt's people. Insofar as Nasser fell short of his goals—and he unquestionably did—it was not for lack of trying.

In fact Nasser's policies did achieve rapid economic growth, especially in the industrial sector, during the early years of Arab Socialism between 1958 and 1965. Thereafter the economy began to stagnate—in part due to the internal contradictions of his development policy, in part due to external hemorrhages like the war in Yemen and the catastrophic June War of 1967. When Anwar Sadat succeeded Nasser in 1970, he began, in his unique improvisational manner, to dismantle the apparatus of Arab Socialism. He sought to free up the economy by a radical policy shift, the so-called Infitah ("Opening-Up"); this consisted of a partial privatization of Egypt's massive public enterprises, permitting new private investment in many sectors of the economy, and reopening the country to foreign investment. Since Egypt was essentially bankrupt by the mid-seventies, the latter step was obviously its best hope for garnering the massive capital required for economic development. But it had dark connotations for many, recalling those decades in the late nineteenth and early twentieth century when almost the whole industrial and financial sector of Egypt's economy was in the hands of foreigners.

Since Sadat's assassination in 1981, his policy has been extended and applied more systematically by Mubarak. As under Nasser's Arab Socialism, the new regime can boast substantial achievements—most strikingly, an immense though still incomplete overhaul of Cairo's once-disintegrating infrastructure. (One takes infrastructure for granted once one has it, but it is no trivial matter. During my first stay in Cairo in 1966, the water ran two hours a day—but never the same two hours—there were few telephones and they seldom worked, and electricity was spotty. In such circumstances, an orderly everyday routine was almost impossible to achieve. Just getting around was a major chore.) There is also a significant manufacturing sector, though it is oriented toward internal rather than export markets. But overall, per capita economic growth has been disappointing at best, and disparities of wealth have again become immense, perhaps as glaring as they were under the Constitutional Monarchy on the eve of the 1952 Revolution.[8] Vast numbers of rural migrants have poured into Cairo (which has swollen from about 3 million people in 1966 to more than 15 million today) and other cities. Every report indicates that the level of economic frustration is very high indeed; by now no level of skill or education ensures even the hope of a decent job to any young person.

Clearly almost any economic strategy one can imagine has been given a try in twentieth-century Egypt—import substitution, Arab Socialism, state-led industrialization, foreign-driven investment—depending on the reigning political ideology of the moment, running the gamut from the laissez-faire of the Monarchy to near-autarky in Nasser's later years to Sadat's hybrid Infitah. In the end nothing has worked very well. What about Islam? Can it provide a way out of this impasse? Islamic activists over the past two decades have indeed promised all good things, and their platform has attracted many adherents and sympathizers. Islamic groups have in fact done very well in sponsoring and operating charitable enterprises (urban clinics, child-care centers, schools, etc.), and they have established a number of workshops and cooperative enterprises. When Cairo was struck by a massive earthquake in 1992, the Islamic groups were far quicker and more effective than the government in bringing relief to stricken areas. But Islamic activists have been shy about presenting a comprehensive economic policy with concrete proposals for taxation, investment, labor policy, and so on. Many of them indeed argue that there is no need for such things; if Muslims simply follow the mandates of the Sacred Law, prosperity and social justice will be the inevitable consequence. But both elections and attitude surveys suggest that Egyptians are wary of such arguments; they have after all heard a lot of promises by this time. Moreover, the violence committed by extremist elements within the Islamic movements has tended to shift the debate away from economic policy to political power. In the face of such tactics, the question becomes not who can best assure prosperity and a hopeful future but who will seize or retain control of the government, by whatever means.

The issue of power and government has in fact been a central one throughout this century in estimating the balance of frustration and hope in Egypt. One of the key goals among the nationalists who struggled for the restoration of Egyptian independence in the early 1900s was to establish constitutional, parliamentary government. They had had a brief, tantalizing taste of this in the late 1870s, and especially in the two years just preceding the British invasion in 1882. The 1923 Constitution (under which Egypt was governed for thirty years) devised a nicely balanced constitutional monarchy that in theory put legislation and budgetary authority largely in the hands of an elected parliament. However, the 1923 Constitution assigned rather broad powers to the monarch, and these were exploited very adroitly by King Fuad (1917–1935) and his son Farouk (1935–1952). Their task was made all the easier by the rampant factionalism and corruption of the parliamentary politicians. Whether the king or parliament was in the ascendant, the result was a study in frustration for the bulk of politically conscious Egyptians. Bourgeois liberalism thus left a thoroughly sour taste in the mouths of many, and the authoritarian populism of Nasser seemed a welcome change, at least for a time.

Nasser was in fact a classic embodiment of a leadership style much esteemed by sympathetic students of the emerging Third World down to the mid-1970s. His program of anti-imperialism, forced-draft economic development, and radical social reform clearly could not be instituted by a few well-intentioned men at the top; it required the full, active, enthusiastic participation of the Egyptian people as a whole. Remaking the nation demanded mass mobilization— a total break with passivity and fatalism, petty traditional loyalties, and selfishness and egoism; a great awakening of the nation's will and the pouring of its energies into the great tasks of the future. The leader's role was in part to articulate the necessary programs, but chiefly to inspire. In such a task "intermediate institutions" like political parties were an obstacle at best. Rather, the leader should make himself the personification of the nation, answerable directly to the people and to them alone. He would intuitively grasp their aspirations and know how to give voice to them. Though the comparison was sometimes made, Nasser was no Hitler; he claimed no mystical union with the spirit of the folk, he was an ardent nationalist but not a racist, and though intensely ambitious he had a sense of limits. (Admittedly he overstepped them rather badly in a couple of crucial cases.) In his world there was room for many nations and peoples, so long as they respected the dignity and independence of Egypt and the Arabs. He enjoyed jokes in which he was the target (and Nasser jokes were one of the great popular literary genres of modern Egypt); he could take advice but did not tolerate opposition once he had made a decision. Nasser was undeniably a charismatic leader, but he tried to institutionalize his revolution not only through a long series of plebiscites but also by creating a mass party reaching down to the neighborhood and village level. His efforts in this direction came to little, however; the succession of party structures he created were always a dead weight, simply an addition to the already massive burden of bureaucracy and factionalism that have plagued Egypt throughout the twentieth century.

In the final analysis, of course, Nasser's style of mass mobilization was inevitably authoritarian; stripped of the niceties of political theory, it was one-man rule. Precisely because he claimed to embody and speak for the nation, he could abide no real opposition. The Egyptian parliament (which continued to be elected, to meet, and to pass legislation) was a puppet, and Nasser readily adopted police-state tactics to silence opponents or compel them to accept the party line. In this context, Anwar Sadat provides important contrasts. Sadat was a surprise successor to Nasser. Though he was one of the original members of the Free Officers and the Revolutionary Command Council of 1952, he was widely regarded in Egypt as a nonentity, a clown, "Nasser's poodle." His political toughness and acumen astonished his rivals, as one after another was cut out of the centers of power. Even more astonishing were the policies followed by Sadat once he had a firm grip on things (essentially by 1972); we look at these simply because they reveal the nature of his rule.

Sadat was one of the classic "mercurial" and "unpredictable" national leaders of modern Middle Eastern political folklore. The most experienced commentators were constantly left with mouth agape by his abrupt shifts in direction and startling improvisations. It suffices to cite his almost single-handed transformation of Egypt's relations with Israel: the October War of 1973, the Sinai Disengagement Accords of 1975, the journey to Jerusalem in 1977, the Camp David Accords of 1979. But there was far more, of course, including the breaking of the Soviet alliance and the restoration of close relations with the United States, the abandonment of Pan-Arabism as a guideline for regional policy, the partial return to a market economy and foreign investment signaled by the Infitah, the fitful tolerance of a legal political opposition, and the restoration of an occasionally meaningful role to parliament. Fatefully, Sadat also restored the Muslim Brothers to legality, a step that provided the opening for the proliferation of other and far more radical Islamic political groups during the 1970s—and ultimately for his own assassination in 1981.

In retrospect, it seems clear that there was nothing mercurial or unpredictable about Sadat's policies per se; taken in a long view, they embodied a well-defined and consistently pursued set of goals. Sadat felt that Egypt had reached a dead end by 1970; any solution of its problems required breaking the logjam with Israel, restoring steady economic and diplomatic relations with the West, finding a new path for economic development, and allowing some breathing room for Egyptian political and intellectual life. But all these goals were intensely controversial, especially within the political elite that had formed around Nasser. To pursue them required the ability not only to seize but also to create opportunities—a quality that Sadat possessed in abundance. Sadat's apparent impulsiveness and his instinct for the *coup de théatre* was a device for catching others off guard and outflanking them before they could figure out how to block him. Such political tactics are often brilliant, but they come at a price. They do not allow the building of a consensus in favor of a difficult decision, and in fact subvert such efforts. They win admiration when they are successful but incite bitterness and anger when they fail.

Sadat failed on many levels, and even his successes aroused bitter opposition. He unquestionably brought the struggle with Israel to an end—the Israeli-Egyptian Peace Treaty of 1982 has endured in spite of incredible stresses and tensions—and likewise he repaired Egypt's relations with the West. But to many Egyptians this represented nothing better than a sellout to the forces of Imperialism and Zionism against which Nasser had struggled for so long. Internally the record is more mixed. The Infitah brought rapid economic growth but little long-term development. This was confirmed by the collapse of international oil prices in the mid-1980s, which wiped out much of the apparent rise in Egypt's GDP over the previous decade. (Indeed, the collapse of the mid-1980s has not been fully restored to this day.)

Politically, Sadat was no institution builder, and while he had democratic impulses, he had equally strong autocratic ones. In the end, his regime, like Nasser's, was a personal one. He possessed much of Nasser's boldness but not his ability to persuade. Moreover, Nasser's personal life was austere, and hence it was easy for most Egyptians to believe that he was one of them. Sadat acquired a great deal of wealth during his years in power and was not reluctant to show it off; he also had a taste for grandiosity. It is no accident that his opponents called him Pharaoh. The label is an especially harsh one in a Muslim country, for in the Qurʾan Pharaoh is not merely an arrogant autocrat but the supreme rebel against God, the very symbol of human disobedience to the divine will. In contemporary Cairo, an observer sees quickly that Sadat is the official national hero, commemorated in a thousand monuments, streets, and city names, while Nasser's name is mentioned only discreetly (e.g., one of Cairo's subway stations is named for him). But it is Nasser who still has the heart of the Egyptian masses, even among many who concede the grave shortcomings of his rule.

Of Husni Mubarak it is too early to speak, even after sixteen years. It is easy, perhaps too easy, to describe him with negatives. He certainly does not share the boldness or imagination of his two predecessors. He possesses neither Nasser's charisma nor Sadat's sense of theater. In personal style, he is a man in a well-cut business suit, who falls in a nondescript middle between Nasser's austerity and Sadat's grandeur. But he is durable and steady, and that approach has perhaps gained him a degree of credibility. At least everyone admits that he has had to face difficult challenges. The collapse in international oil prices in 1984–1985 undid most of Sadat's economic growth in a stroke. The region has been wracked by repeated war and revolution, and the relationship with Israel has been difficult at best. In spite of periodic pauses in its offensive, the violent fringe of the Islamic movement no longer restricts its wrath to government officials but attacks every manifestation of secularism and Western influence, occasionally including tourists in their list of targets. In the nature of things, none of these problems will yield to dramatic posturing.

Mubarak has tried to deal with these matters by opening up the political system, by restoring a degree of democratic challenge and conflict, and thereby finding his way to a broad consensus. At the same time, he plainly has only limited confidence in where real democracy might lead the country. He has not been able to resist the temptation to rig and manipulate elections in various ways, and as president he retains massive powers to govern by decree and to impose harsh security measures. Mubarak's style of governance might best be called bureaucratic authoritarianism. Politics in Egypt is still plainly a work in progress.

The Arab-Israeli Conflict

It is popular among Americans to view the Arab-Israeli conflict as the very model of an age-old struggle, rooted in ancient and irrational antipathies, and utterly beyond rational analysis or solution.[9] If asked to describe the roots of the conflict, many would no doubt cite good biblical authority: Moses and Pharaoh, Joshua and the Canaanites, David and Goliath, Nebuchadnezzar and the Babylonian Captivity. Contemporary Muslim militants also tend to place the roots of the conflict in the distant past. But even though they are quite aware of the biblical sagas, they seldom identify themselves with Pharaoh and Nebuchadnezzar (both of whom have a thoroughly bad press in Islamic lore). Rather, they cite the bitter confrontation between Muhammad and the Jews of Medina at the very beginnings of Islam—a confrontation that in their minds exemplifies the innate and undying hostility of the Jews to Islam and the Muslims. (Many modern Jews cite the same events but of course reverse the thrust of the hostility.)

With apologies to all parties, they know a lot of things that just aren't so. The Arab-Israeli conflict is hardly more than a century old; it is decisively a twentieth-century conflict, and biblical or Qurʾanic texts are relevant only insofar as they are used to sanctify ideas and standpoints whose roots lie in modern times. These roots lie in the ideological currents of late-nineteenth-century Europe and in the breakup of the Ottoman Empire in the years around World War I. The key events that mark the beginning of the conflict in fact all occurred in Europe, not the Middle East: the publication of *The Jewish State* by the Austrian journalist Theodor Herzl in 1896, the formation of the World Zionist Organization in Basle in 1898, and the issuance of the Balfour Declaration in 1917 by the British government in London.

Ironically these years were a period of considerable security and rising prosperity for most Jews residing in Muslim lands. They benefited both from traditional Ottoman tolerance (going back to the end of the fifteenth century, when the Jews expelled from Catholic Spain found a refuge in Thessalonica) as well as from the empire's political reforms after 1856, which had decreed civil equality among all Ottoman subjects. Jews enjoyed a considerable degree of colonial protection in French North Africa (a fine irony in light of the Dreyfus affair about 1900) and in British-occupied Egypt. In sharp contrast to Europe at the turn of the century, nowhere in the Muslim Middle East was the political status and role of Jews a significant public issue. Some European Jews were already migrating to Palestine and settling there, but the favored place of refuge for the overwhelming majority of those seeking economic opportunity or trying to escape the rising tide of European anti-Semitism was the United States, where the gates to immigration (from Europe, of course, not Asia) remained wide open until 1920.

It is a strange thing that a thoroughly modern conflict, whose origins owe far more to Europe than to the Middle East, should have proved so infernally difficult to bring to a satisfactory conclusion. But that is how things have turned out, and we need to ask why.

There are a thousand reasons, not least the self-interested maneuverings of the superpowers and various Middle Eastern states, but ultimately it all comes down to the two principal protagonists, Jewish Israelis and the Arabs of Palestine. These are after all the peoples between whom a direct confrontation arose and who have the most at stake in any resolution of it. As different as each may be from the other on many levels, they are uncannily alike in at least one respect: both Israelis and Palestinians perceive themselves both as innocent victims and as terribly vulnerable. Each group is driven by deep-rooted, bitter resentment over past injury, and by the fear that any possible settlement will leave it gravely weakened. Moreover, each possesses the absolute moral certainty that it is in the right. And in the final analysis neither is in a position to impose its will on the other, at least over the long term. In a perverse way, many Israelis and Palestinians are most comfortable with continued confrontation, because at least they know where they stand. The whole situation is a negotiator's worst nightmare.

This shared sense of victimization is politically and psychologically crucial, because that is what drives the conflict between Israelis and Palestinians. In a political discourse framed in terms of victimization, we gain rights by the fact of having been a victim. From this perspective, a right is primarily a claim against an alleged oppressor or violator. If a specific oppressor/violator cannot be named or is beyond our reach, then some surrogate class of wrongdoers must be identified and a claim lodged against them. This way of thinking is reinforced by the psychology of victimization: to be a victim is to feel violated, humiliated, and powerless. There is a profound need to be made whole again, to regain a sense of power and dignity. This need often impels demands for violent revenge, since nothing else so starkly demonstrates that we are not powerless and contemptible, that we can take charge of our own destiny. But in any case, complete vindication is essential—the opponent must be forced to confess the wrongs he has committed and to make full restitution.

Both these elements of victimization, political and psychological, are readily in evidence in the confrontation between Palestinians and Israelis. In many ways the two parties are remarkably comparable, for both feel (certainly not without cause) that they are innocent victims of the whole process of twentieth-century history, of vast forces beyond their control and even their comprehension. As noted above, this historical process is primarily rooted in the politics of Europe—of Germany first and foremost, but also (in quite different ways) of Great Britain, France, and Russia. The forces that surged up there have thrown Jews and Palestinians face to face within the confines of a small parcel of territory (some 10,000 square miles all told). There they have been left to work out their mutual destiny as best they can.

The recent historical memories of both Israelis and Palestinians infuse them with fear and a profound sense of weakness, because both remember what they suffered precisely when they felt most secure, or at least were confident about their ability to shape the future. For each community, the struggle is not merely about land and sovereignty, though it certainly involves these things. It is rather about its very survival as a people with a name of its own. For each, it is not a particular state (or would-be state) that is threatened but its whole ethnic and cultural identity. These are admittedly very broad generalizations, but they are readily illustrated by the actual historical experience of Israelis and Palestinians.

The Israeli sense of victimization is rooted in the experience of European anti-Semitism. Although anti-Semitism has a long history in Europe, it seemed a force in decline, even to be slowly and fitfully withering away, between the mid-eighteenth century and the 1870s, as traditional religious hostilities in Western Europe weakened and were replaced by a broad concept of universal and equal citizenship under the law. But beginning in the 1880s, there was a strong resurgence of anti-Semitism throughout the continent. The reasons for this are still much disputed, but it was no doubt partly connected with the rise among many Continental intellectuals of the notion that national identity was rooted in race and that only racial purity could provide a solid foundation for national life. In any case, the catastrophe of the 1930s and early 1940s demonstrated conclusively to all Jews the truth of a proposition that only a minority had accepted until then—namely, that there was no future for the Jews as a minority in Europe and that they could secure their future only in a country of their own.

By that time, fortunately, such a country lay close at hand—the Jewish National Home in Palestine. Modern Jewish settlement in Palestine under the auspices of the nascent Zionist movement had begun in the 1880s, but the concept of a Jewish National Home there was only formally promulgated in the Balfour Declaration (1917) and the League of Nations Mandate for Palestine (1922). The Jewish National Home had been a fairly small affair during the 1920s and was a bit of a disappointment to Zionist activists; it had attracted fairly substantial financial support from American and European Jews but only limited immigration and settlement. The Ottoman census of 1911 had yielded a total population in Palestine of about 700,000, of which some 10 percent were Jews. The British census of 1931 revealed some growth in both sectors: an overall population of slightly over one million, of whom 176,000 were Jews. This was almost double their percentage in 1911 and an interesting harbinger for the future, but the Jews of Palestine were still a small minority, certainly far from an adequate demographic base for a country that Zionists believed should be "as Jewish as England is English."

Within the Middle East, the Zionist project had to confront a problem that was both simple and insoluble: neither the indigenous Arab population of Palestine (still some 80 percent of Palestine's population) nor the new Arab states of the region were willing to see the Jewish National Home become a Jewish state. Things careened toward a collision in the late 1930s as the Jewish flight from Europe increased, and the Palestinian Arabs at first staged a general strike and then an open revolt against British rule. World War II forced a momentary hiatus in the burgeoning crisis, but after 1945 it was clear that an armed conflict between Arabs and Jewish settlers was almost inevitable. European Jews who made their way to Palestine had escaped from one danger only to face another. Driven by the devastating experience of the Holocaust and the fervent belief that their backs were now to the wall, the Jews were compelled to vindicate their right to a national existence—in effect, their claims against Europe—at the expense of another group (the Arabs of Palestine) who had played little part in the wrongs they had suffered.

The Palestinians obviously saw things quite differently. In their eyes, they were the victims of a massive Zionist influx that threatened to submerge them in their own country. As some of their spokesmen noted at the time, they too were the victims (albeit indirectly) of European anti-Semitism, since they were being made the scapegoat for Europe's crimes. But Palestinians also saw themselves as direct victims of Europe, in the form of French and British imperialism. It was after all the British Empire that had decided there should be a Jewish National Home in Palestine, and had endeavored to impose it in spite of the expressed wishes of the overwhelming Arab majority (both Muslim and Christian) living therein. Whatever the complaints of the Jews against British policy in Palestine, and there were many, it was transparently clear to any Palestinian observer that the Zionist project could have made no headway without British political, administrative, and military support.

To begin with, the Jewish National Home could be established only because the British and French had dismembered the defeated Ottoman Empire after World War I. Some Arabs (though by no means a majority) had certainly welcomed this step, since they had been promised British support for an independent Arab kingdom in the Arabian Peninsula and Fertile Crescent after the conclusion of the war. The Arab nationalists felt both betrayed and humiliated by what actually ensued: an agreement between Great Britain and France to leave the peninsula more or less to its own devices but to partition the Fertile Crescent into five different entities. The new states of Syria and Lebanon would be placed under French control, while the British would oversee the futures of Iraq, Palestine, and Transjordan. Apart from the brazen negation of Arab independence, this scheme broke up an emerging Arab state in Greater Syria—the very region of which Palestine had historically been an integral part. Within the framework of Ottoman rule going back four centuries, Arab political leaders in Palestine had never been much more than ward bosses, and now they were left to face alone the purposes and resources of the vast British Empire. They were hopelessly outmatched and they knew it; their failure to block or even limit the British-sponsored Jewish National Home was foreordained.

Most galling of all, precisely when Syria, Lebanon, Iraq, and Transjordan at last claimed effective independence after World War II, the Arabs of Palestine quickly fell under the control of the new Jewish state of Israel or found themselves ejected from their ancestral homeland. They endured in a vast series of UN-supervised refugee camps in the surrounding countries and were integrated into the societies of their host countries only slowly and very partially. As refugees, the Palestinians were politically useful pawns for a lot of people, but for themselves and all Arabs they were an indelible symbol of weakness and humiliation. Israel thus took its turn as the oppressor and violator of Palestinian rights. But even so, for politicians and intellectuals throughout the Arab world, Israel (or as they usually called it, "the Zionist entity") was only the reflection of larger and more sinister forces. In their minds, the whole Zionist enterprise was from the beginning no more than a facade for British imperialism and then (after Britain's retreat from the Middle East in the mid-fifties) its American successor. Palestinians have indeed consistently held the Israelis and the Americans jointly responsible for the wrongs they have suffered—the Americans more than the Israelis, really, since they could have made Israel change her policies and have willfully refused to do so.

Israelis and Palestinians shared a common territory and a common framework of foreign control under the British Mandate between 1920 and 1948, but they have each had radically different (though intimately intertwined) fates during the half-century since the Mandate ended. Throughout that period, Israel has faced the vitriol of Arab rhetoric, and more important the material threat of force from the Arab states and/or various Palestinian guerrilla organizations. In the event, both rhetoric and military threat have proved largely ineffective. There have been five separate wars between Israel and the neighboring Arab states since the winter of 1948, and in all of them Israel has emerged with a decisive military advantage.

However, Israel has been much less successful in reaping long-term political gains from its battlefield victories. This persistent frustration has inevitably intensified the country's profound sense of insecurity, its fear that a moment's weakness or lack of vigilance will open the door to a second Holocaust.

There were two unambiguous victories. First, the War of Independence in 1948, which established the state of Israel. Second, the June War of 1967, which shattered the prestige of Nasser's Egypt and the whole Arab Nationalist movement and left Israel in control of all of Palestine plus the Sinai Peninsula. But even these triumphs did not spare Israel from frustration. After the War of Independence it did not obtain diplomatic recognition from its foes but only a tension-ridden armistice. Nor was it able to leverage the stunning success of June 1967 into a permanent settlement on terms acceptable to it. The results of the Suez campaign in 1956 and the invasion of Lebanon in 1982 were even more evanescent. Israel's crushing military superiority was self-evident, but in both cases it was compelled to surrender most of its territorial and strategic gains and retreat to a situation little better than the status quo ante. Finally, the October War of 1973 dealt a real shock to Israeli self-confidence, for it represented the first time since 1948 that any Arab state had dared to take the offensive (initially with surprising success), though it is important to recall that both Egypt and Syria attacked territories lost in 1967, not Israel proper. Ironically, this war—which seemed a near thing for a couple of weeks and created a genuine political crisis in Israel—led to the first serious moves toward peace since the foundation of Israel.

Apart from the periodic wars with the Arab states sketched above, Israel was forced to endure an interminable struggle with a variety of Palestinian guerrilla and "terrorist" organizations.[10] The earliest phase of this confrontation took place in the early 1950s; but however annoying the Palestinian raids of these years may have been, they were small-scale, ill-coordinated, and constituted no threat whatever to the integrity of the state. Clearly Israel gave as good as it got in its reprisals against Jordan and the Egyptian-occupied Gaza Strip. A far more dangerous and better coordinated guerrilla and terrorist campaign arose after 1967 and lasted throughout the 1970s; although many organizations (not all of them on speaking terms with one another) were involved, this phase of the struggle is indelibly connected in most people's minds with the largest and most complex of them, the Palestine Liberation Organization (PLO) led by Yasser Arafat.

As violent and ugly as the struggle was during the seventies, it too never threatened the existence of Israel, for the bulk of the violence took place outside Israel and the Occupied Territories; every effort by the Palestinians to establish a presence within historic Palestine was quashed before it could get started. Unable to strike effectively against military and strategic targets, the Resistance launched attacks against vulnerable civilian targets—passenger buses, airport check-in counters, schoolhouses—inside and outside the country. In keeping with the temper of the times, there was a lot of romantic nonsense about wars of national liberation and about the transformative power of terrorism. (It is worth remembering that several developed countries—West Germany, Italy, Japan, even the United States—were afflicted by domestic terrorist groups during this decade. For a brief time, terrorism was glorified as an ideology in itself, not just as a means to an end.)

The real object of the Palestinian Resistance, however, was quite concrete—namely, to demonstrate that Israel could not secure the safety of her citizens and thus to compel her to negotiate with the Palestinians as equals. What was in fact achieved was quite the opposite: the Palestinians were branded as terrorists and criminals, with whom no discussions of any kind were possible. Apart from the political-diplomatic stalemate, which in this case suited the Israelis very nicely, Palestinian losses in lives and property from massive Israeli reprisals (aimed at very broadly defined targets) were many times larger than those suffered by Israel. Even so, the PLO campaign of the early and mid-1970s did re-create a pervasive atmosphere of tension and insecurity among Israelis, almost wiping out the euphoria of June 1967. That general insecurity, coupled with the demand in the PLO's founding document, the Palestine National Charter, that the "Zionist entity" be dismantled and replaced by "a secular democratic state" in all of Palestine, reinforced Israel's deepest fears. Clearly, Israelis believed, any significant concession to the Palestinians for the sake of a momentary truce would only open the door for the ultimate extinction of Israel.

By 1977, most Israelis and most outside observers felt that peace was almost inconceivable, that the long twilight struggle would continue forever and ever until the end of the world. And then the logjam began to break. It started with Egypt's decision to go its own way, even at the cost of its relations with the other Arab states; Sadat's astonishing trip to Jerusalem in November 1977 led to the Israeli-Egyptian peace treaty of 1982. That peace has been a chilly one and has been severely tested many times, but it has held. The PLO ceased to be a significant threat, even on the symbolic level, as it became embroiled in the Lebanese Civil War after 1975 and then was driven from Lebanon altogether by the Israeli invasion in the summer of 1982.[11] The PLO had always been more an uneasy coalition of factions than a unified and centralized organization, and its internal divisions were intensified by the trauma of the 1980s. Its capacity to play any significant role in the Arab-Israeli conflict was rapidly disappearing; to save anything from a quarter century of struggle Yasser Arafat had to act, and he finally issued a reluctant and very painful recognition of Israel's right to exist as a sovereign state in 1989. The PLO's position was further undermined by the Gulf War in 1991, which deprived it of whatever financial support it could still glean from the Arab states. In this context, the Oslo Accords of 1993 were slowly and very secretively worked out. Israel's rigid stubbornness over two long decades had apparently achieved a great deal, albeit at an immense price; from the PLO it obtained recognition as a state, pure and simple, while the PLO was compelled to settle for a status as a vaguely defined Palestinian Authority possessing indeterminate administrative control over areas yet to be defined. However uncertain and inconclusive, the Oslo Accords and the consequent White House Agreement were enough to commit the PLO to the "peace process," and that in turn allowed Jordan at long last to sign its own peace treaty with Israel. A war half a century old seemed all but over.

But in the Middle East nothing ever just ends. So twenty years after Sadat went to Jerusalem, and on the verge of victory in its struggle for recognition and security, Israel has run into new obstacles—some would say it has created them for itself—and these seem as fiercely irreconcilable as any it has faced in the past. One of these obstacles is a new manifestation of the Palestinian Resistance—a manifestation not only independent of the PLO but representing a sharp ideological shift as well. Although there was plenty of Islamic sentiment driving many Palestinian resistance fighters during the 1970s, the official ideology of the PLO (as well as of the more radical groups) was resolutely secularist. In public forums, at least, the PLO always claimed to share in the Third World's struggle against colonialism and oppression and to be dedicated to the creation of a secular democratic Palestine. But by the end of the 1980s a militant Islamic movement (under the names Hamas and Islamic Jihad) had grown up in Gaza and to a lesser degree the West Bank, one absolutely unreconciled to the notion of a settlement with a Jewish state that had displaced a predominantly Muslim people from Islamic territory and occupied the holy city of Jerusalem. The Islamic movement grew up outside the PLO, almost in defiance of it, and the formally constituted Palestinian Authority now in charge of the everyday affairs of the West Bank and Gaza has found that they can neither suppress it nor co-opt it. On the contrary, the Islamic movement is able to challenge Yasser Arafat's "government" on almost every issue, and even to subvert its very legitimacy. When the Islamic militants do cooperate with Arafat, they do so on their own terms.[12]

As with the PLO two decades ago, the Islamic resistance in Palestine can hardly hope to bring down or even weaken Israel. Rather, they aim to cause the peace process to collapse and to rekindle the confrontation of decades past. To this end they have mounted a series of selected and spectacular acts of terror, typically aimed at Tel Aviv cafés, Jerusalem vegetable markets, or metropolitan bus lines. It is absolutely essential to understand that such acts of terror do not flow from unfocused rage or blind fanaticism, though they certainly exploit such emotions. On the contrary, they represent a carefully calculated political tactic—a perfect illustration of Clausewitz's famous dictum that war is politics pursued by other means. Moreover, though the direct targets of terrorism by the Islamic militants are invariably Israeli, these acts are in fact directed as much against Arafat and his lieutenants as against Israel itself. The irony cannot be lost on men who themselves first gained the world's attention through their own spectacular, made-for-TV strikes thirty years ago.

No Israeli government can negotiate with terrorists or those who collude with them; so incidents of this kind force the Israelis to become more intransigent, to break off contacts with Arafat and his regime or to increase pressure on them to act in pro-Israeli ways. In turn, that Israeli pressure either delegitimizes the Palestinian Authority in the eyes of its own people or radicalizes it. And in this way the slow, suspicion-laden groping toward an accommodation, a modus vivendi, between Israelis and Palestinians will inevitably fall apart. It must be admitted that over the past two or three years the Islamic resistance in Gaza and the West Bank has been quite successful in this agenda. They have kept the struggle and the sacred cause alive, they have bought time, and they continue to dream that, after infinite sacrifice, the conflict may at long last turn to their advantage. Many commentators point out the roots of this movement in the poverty, despair, and political frustration of the population of the Occupied Territories, and that assessment is not wholly without merit. But Israelis remember other ideologically driven movements rooted in despair and frustration, and they remember that the mere return of prosperity and national pride was not enough to assuage them. Among Israelis militant Islamic movements inevitably strike very deep chords of anxiety and terror.

The rise of an Islamic resistance in Gaza and the West Bank has not occurred in a vacuum, for the Israelis have a powerful "religious right" of their own, and this movement has been actively, not to say enthusiastically, encouraged and fostered by Likud governments in Israel since the 1977 elections. As time has gone on, Israel's religious right has become progressively more influential, its demands harder and harder to deflect or ignore by any government. As with Islam, religious activism among Jews encompasses many groups and shades of opinion, and it enlists many camp followers who find some element of its platform appealing without signing on to the whole thing. (In particular, politicians who are primarily concerned about strategic and security questions find Israel's religious right a strong source of electoral support.) But in essence Jewish activism stresses that Israel holds its land not by international law but by biblical covenant. And this covenant was vouchsafed for the whole land of Israel, including the heartland of the biblical kingdom, Judaea and Samaria. Since Judaea and Samaria are unfortunately coextensive with the present-day West Bank, inhabited by well over a million Palestinian

Arabs, we have here the seeds of yet another irreconcilable political confrontation.

The most extreme elements in Israel's religious right (though by no means a majority) hold that the Arabs have no real right to be living in the land of Israel at all and should be actively encouraged to leave. In spite of occasional outbursts of violence against the Palestinians (as in the Hebron mosque massacre in February 1994, when twenty-nine Muslim worshipers were gunned down by an American immigrant, Baruch Goldstein), Israel's religious militants prefer to operate within the Israeli political system to pursue their aims. They are skillful at this; at the very least they enormously constrain the options available to Israeli negotiators charged with working something out with the Palestinians. More than that, they pile new demands onto the political system, and these must somehow be addressed by vote-sensitive leaders. Finally, by the very nature of their program, which has a real resonance even among Israelis who reject it, they erode the legitimacy of any Israeli government that would presume to trade land for peace.

A Palestinian perspective on events since 1967 draws on the same body of facts reviewed above but of course places them in a very different framework of meaning. For Palestinians, the thirty years since 1967 almost replicate the course of the twentieth century as a whole. The Palestinian Resistance began with a burning determination to transform Arab defeat and humiliation into triumph, with the sure and certain hope that it could replicate the stirring if bloody victory of the Algerian Revolt a decade earlier. But then things moved into year after year of stalemate, full of spectacular but petty victories and smashing defeats. For a majority of Palestinians, the struggle has at last sputtered out into a melancholy recognition that even settling for half a loaf is no longer a realistic goal. They will have to take the heel and see what they can make of it.

Even this much was gained in the end not by the PLO but by the spontaneous uprising at the end of 1987 (the so-called Intifada) among the Palestinians living under military occupation in the West Bank and Gaza.[13] Israeli security forces were able to contain the Intifada fairly quickly, admittedly by severe and sustained repression, but they could not quash it. To maintain even minimal order in the Occupied Territories required a massive and extremely costly mobilization of military resources over many years, with no end in sight.

The cost in self-doubt and morale was even higher. In the end, the Israeli government decided that it could no longer afford to maintain the status quo; a solution was imperative, and at the end of the day that meant dealing with the PLO, something that every Israeli government since 1967 had sworn it would never do.

For the dispiriting situation in which they now find themselves Palestinians can find many to blame: not only the unrelenting hostility of Israel and the United States but also the bumbling support of the old Soviet Union and the repeated perfidy of the Arab states. In the end, however, their worst enemy has been themselves—their unrelieved factionalism, their lack of realism about what they could really achieve when times were better, their inability to define concrete intermediate steps that could move them closer to their final goal. Taken together, these things made it impossible for the PLO leadership to devise any effective long-term strategy; rather, they rewarded and indeed necessitated evasiveness and theatrical virtuosity. Through his mastery of these qualities Yasser Arafat has held the PLO together for three decades, but they are not the qualities needed to head a Palestinian Authority that must both negotiate with a tough, suspicious Israeli government and administer the everyday affairs of an angry and economically stricken people. The complexity of this challenge, and the uncertainty of the outcome, is almost beyond calculation.

The achievements and frustrations of Iran, Egypt, and Israel-Palestine symbolize those of the whole region. It is clear, I hope, that the political achievements of each have been impressive. In all honesty, we could probably have expected no better when we remember how things stood at the beginning of this century. But it is perversely true that every achievement has provoked greater frustration, an intense awareness of chances missed and promises broken. In the following chapters we will step outside the framework of national history to explore three areas where frustration has seemed particularly acute: ideology, foreign policy, and political development.

First of all, there is the vital role of ideology in modern Middle Eastern politics—in particular, the sort of grand overarching ideology that can lay out a comprehensive agenda and inspire people to make the heroic efforts needed to achieve it. The modern Middle East has not lacked for ideologies of this sort, though a stable and widely based consensus as to which one really marks out the path to the future has been hard to come by. Especially at the present moment, when so many ideologies have lost their capacity to challenge and inspire, when so many Middle Easterners feel that they are lurching about without direction, it is vital to explore the impact that a strongly felt ideology can have on political life.

Second, foreign policy is—and has been for the last two centuries—a crucial element in the way Middle Easterners pursue their political and economic goals. Much of Middle Eastern politics is conducted in the international arena, even on issues that might seem primarily domestic in nature. Moreover, the foreign policies of Middle Eastern states are often pursued in a manner that seems theatrical or even absurd to outside observers. For both these reasons, it is important to try to understand how these states conduct their foreign policy—what concerns drive them and why they choose the tactics they do.

Third, we need to look at the underlying structures of government in the Middle East. It is a region where democracy seems a terribly frail plant, and where authoritarianism and dictatorship are unusually vigorous. The pull toward authoritarianism slackens from time to time, but it has undeniably persisted from generation to generation throughout the modern era. This authoritarian tendency requires serious discussion; it cannot just be dismissed—as American commentators are so prone to do—as part of an innate and unchanging "Middle Eastern character."

CHAPTER 3

THE STRANGE CAREER
OF PAN-ARABISM

In American politics ideology is almost a synonym for political extremism. Every election campaign is filled with denunciations of left- or right-wing ideologues. Intriguingly, we hear no attacks on (or compliments for) ideologues of the center; presumably moderates are not inspired by anything as dangerous as ideas. It is not surprising, then, that we are suspicious or even fearful when politicians abroad self-consciously and proudly proclaim their adherence to this or that ideology. In their eyes, this means that their policies are not merely ad hoc solutions to separate, disconnected problems but rather flow from a comprehensive and logically integrated body of principles. In our eyes, it means that they are pursuing some mad utopian scheme, usually one hostile to vital American interests and values. Since Middle Eastern politics has been carried out in an explicitly ideological atmosphere for at least the last half century, Americans inevitably view the politicians of that region with apprehension and distrust. Europeans have tended to be more relaxed about it all, at least since they gave up their colonial empires about 1960. There are many reasons for the European frame of mind, but surely one is simply that they are accustomed to a highly ideological style of politics. Indeed, ideology is one of Europe's most enduring colonial legacies.

Guided (or misguided) by our traditional attitudes, we can make no sense of ideology in Middle Eastern politics unless we take it seriously. That in turn requires us to decide just what we are to mean by this notoriously abstract word. A full-scale analysis is out of the question, obviously, but a few comments may get us started.

To begin with, ideology arises in a context of change—in particular, the kind of massive, sudden change that threatens to overturn an existing political and social system. In the face of such disruptive forces, those who speak for the existing order must explain why it is right for things to be arranged the way they are. On the other side, dissenters will denounce what is wrong (more or less everything, as a rule) and show how they intend to set things right. It is debates of this kind that generate ideology. In formal language, we can say that ideology is a broad, systematic critique of a given sociopolitical system that both describes that system and calls on its members to defend, alter, or overthrow it. Ideology is both analysis and a call to action.

Next, ideologies are utopian. Each ideology claims that its program will establish the best possible society, a society whose rightness will be self-evident to all. This utopian goal may be portrayed as the recovery of a lost Golden Age, or it may represent the achievement of aspirations barely dreamed of in the past. Ideologies are often (almost always, in fact) connected with some metaphysical scheme, some interpretation of the ultimate nature of reality. To name only two possibilities, this metaphysics may be strictly materialist (as in Marxism-Leninism) or it may presuppose the active presence of a deity (as in the various Islamist ideologies). In any case, the claims of ideology tend to be absolute, because they are rooted in absolute truth. It is thus not surprising that ideologies readily slide toward extremism.

One final point. Ideology is conveyed to its audience in ways that are simultaneously rational and highly emotive. Ideology aims to incite people to action. To do that it must express its ideas through the use of values and symbols that inspire an intense, immediate, almost instinctive response by everyone who encounters them. A sophisticated ideology is quite able to support its program through elaborate rational arguments, but in the political arena it is more likely to resort to flag-waving and the chanting of slogans. For much the same reason, once an ideology leaves the seminar room or the salon, it prefers to keep things simple. One should never assume that a crude stump speech reflects a lack of important and complex ideas.

Of all the ideologies that have played on the Middle Eastern stage in this century—bourgeois liberalism, Marxism, Islamism—none has had a greater impact both within the region and throughout the world, none excited more hope and anxiety, than Arab Nationalism.[1] Like its cousins, the nationalisms of Turkey and Iran, Arab Nationalism aimed at the political resurrection of a people. But the nationalists of Turkey and Iran were working within the boundaries of an internationally recognized country. Arab Nationalists, in contrast, had to struggle against the artificial political divisions imposed on their homeland by a succession of foreign empires—Ottoman, French, and (most malign of all) British. In a very literal sense, Arab Nationalism sought to heal the wounds of history.

The year 1958 was the annus mirabilis of Arab Nationalism. It was a new ideology, hardly half a century old, but it already seemed the irresistible wave of the future. The energy and power of Arab Nationalism were manifested in three spectacular events: first, the February melding together of Syria and Egypt in the United Arab Republic (UAR); second, the violent overthrow of the monarchy in Iraq in July (a wonderful omen, since that was the same month that the Free Officers had seized power in Egypt six years earlier); and third, the Lebanese crisis of the autumn, which nearly led to the collapse of the strongly pro-Western regime of Camille Chamoun.

Beyond these headline-grabbing crises, 1958 marked a structural shift in Arab politics, the emergence of the progressive/reactionary split that would bedevil inter-Arab relations for the next decade and beyond. This rivalry would take many forms and pass through many phases, but initially it placed the revolutionary military regimes in the new UAR and Iraq against the conservative monarchies of Jordan and Saudi Arabia. (These alliances were marriages of convenience, to be sure; the ruling houses of Jordan and Saudi Arabia had been rivals since the end of World War I, while revolutionary zeal quickly proved unable to overcome the burgeoning rivalry— both personal and national—between Nasser of Egypt and Col. Abd al-Karim Qassem of Iraq.) The "reactionary" monarchies represented everything the new wave of Pan-Arabists despised: a commitment to traditional (supposedly despotic) forms of government, an attachment to backward social and cultural values, stagnant religiosity, alliances with reactionary social elites like big landlords, and—worst of all—subservience to foreign imperialism. The progressive states, in contrast, were led by young, future-oriented military officers. These states stood for all sorts of desirable things: cultural dynamism, rapid economic growth combined with social justice, the rise of new classes to social and political leadership (for most of the revolutionary regimes were led by men of modest rural or small-town origin), rationality and modernity, intense commitment to the Arab cause, and complete independence from foreign influence or domination.

The way had already been shown by such legendary leaders as Jawaharlal Nehru of India and Sukarno of Indonesia, and the Arab generation of 1958 was determined to strike off down the same path.

By the winter of 1967, however, the glowing promise of Pan-Arabism was already a bit tarnished, and the movement had suffered some real setbacks. First of all, the UAR, the very symbol of Arab unification, had split apart (peacefully but very acrimoniously) in 1961. Nor were the wounds easily healed; increasingly radical regimes in Syria ragged Nasser for his lack of zeal for the Arab cause, and Egypt's relations with Iraq grew more and more strained. Relations among the "progressive" states quickly degenerated into what Malcolm Kerr felicitously named the Arab Cold War, an unceasing mutual barrage of vitriolic propaganda, accusations of betrayal and subversion, and stillborn reconciliations.[2] Nasser had gotten involved in a lingering civil war in the Yemen and sent the bulk of Egypt's combat-ready forces to support a beleaguered military-republican revolutionary government in that country. But in spite of all these disappointments and frustrations, Pan-Arabism was still effectively unchallenged on the ideological level, at least among the most articulate and politically mobilized groups—young professionals, university students, and army officers. Imperialism and Zionism would be harder to defeat, unity harder to achieve, than many had supposed, but victory was inevitable. If the will to struggle was there, it still waited just around the corner.

By September 1972, when I arrived in Lebanon to complete a book on the great Arab Nationalist hero Saladin (who was in fact a Kurd and grew up in the service of a Turkish-speaking dynasty), things had not improved. The Arab Nationalist program had suffered catastrophic setbacks during the previous five years, though among younger people it still remained the ideological currency of the realm. Or at least it had no viable competition, for the Islamic movement was just beginning to stir, and the old ideas of European-style liberalism were still derided as bourgeois decadence. The crushing humiliation of 1967 had left people disoriented; some were seeking to redeem the disaster through direct revolutionary action, while others had fallen into passivity. That 1967 was a terrible wound to Pan-Arabism was obvious to all; that it was in fact a death blow had yet to sink in.

But now, a quarter century later, where is Pan-Arabism, or Arab

Nationalism in any form? As an effective ideology, able to mobilize and direct political action, it has failed; both Israel's unanswered invasion of Lebanon in 1982 and the Gulf War of 1990–1991 demonstrated that decisively. Arab Nationalism is of course not necessarily gone forever. As we will see, it is an ideology that embodies deepseated values and aspirations, and in a favorable milieu it may spring to life once again. But for the time being we have to ask why something once so brilliantly promising faded from the scene, and what if anything has replaced it? Arab Nationalism was not merely the victim of bad fortune and hostile circumstances, though it certainly encountered its full share of these. In its very origins and in the way it developed over half a century it had certain persistent weaknesses, and these may well have prevented it from ever achieving its full program.

First, Arab Nationalism was even in its heyday a new plant in the Arab world, with very shallow roots in the political tradition of that region. An Arab Nationalist ideology was just beginning to be articulated in the decade before World War I, chiefly in Beirut and Damascus, and it had not proceeded much beyond a few journalists, intellectuals, and army officers when war broke out. It emerged as a tangible political force only during World War I, and it did so then largely due to the failure of Ottoman policy and Ottoman arms in the Hijaz and Fertile Crescent. Even at the height of the war it was the cause of a small elite (largely in Damascus and Beirut, and to a markedly lesser extent in Baghdad) rather than of the masses. A majority of Arab military officers in the Ottoman army remained loyal to the empire down to the end of the war. The armies of the Arab Revolt, led by the Sharif Hussein of Mecca, were largely funded by British gold, and operated in close liaison with Britain's Arab Bureau in Cairo.

In the newly created Arab states of the 1920s and 1930s, however, Arab Nationalism did begin to sink deeper roots, for it provided a compelling ideology of resistance to European occupation and control under the Mandate system. By World War II it had undeniably become a broad-based popular movement in Syria, Iraq, and Palestine. At this point, however, Arab Nationalism still stirred few sympathies west of Suez. Even as late as 1940, Egypt's politicians and intellectuals chose to play only a marginal role in the movement, and the countries of North Africa (which remained under direct French rule throughout for a full decade after World War II) were fully preoccupied with their own situation.

If the concept of Arabism was a very new thing as a framework for political action, it unquestionably did have a long history as a form of ethnic identity. Down to the end of the nineteenth century, most inhabitants of North Africa, the Nile Valley, and the lands between the Mediterranean and the Tigris knew they were Arabs in the sense that they spoke the Arabic language as their native tongue. They were proud of their language and the remarkable literature it had generated over more than a millennium. Likewise, they knew that their ancestors had been the original and "most authentic" bearers of Islam, and of course they took pride in the noble lineage that they acquired from this fact. But none of these things implied in their minds that they should strive to form an Arab state. If asked to describe themselves, they would say that they were Muslims (or occasionally, Christians), residents of Damascus or Kairouan or wherever, members of such and such a clan, and subjects of the Ottoman sultan. Arabic speech was a crucial element in their cultural identity, but it had no political significance.

In the struggle for hearts and minds during the early twentieth century, Arab Nationalism—still raw and poorly articulated—had to compete with a deep-rooted and almost instinctive commitment to Islam. The relationship of Islam to Arab Nationalism was a tricky one for the publicists of the new ideology. If a person owed primary political allegiance to the Arab nation, what did that mean for the heretofore unquestioned loyalty to the worldwide Community of Believers? Whatever the historical role of the Arabs in Islam, most Muslims were not Arabs—and many Arabs were not Muslims. The early Arab Nationalists tried to make Islam a part of Arab identity by stressing its central role in their culture and history. But to many Muslims that was no solution at all, since it clearly made Islam less important than Arabism. In fact, early Arab Nationalists never quite resolved the conundrum, and they have not worked it out to this day.

It is undeniably true that Islam, in its origins, was deeply imbued with Arab elements. The Qur'an was revealed "in a clear Arabic tongue," the early Muslim Community was made up almost entirely of Arabic-speakers dwelling in the Arabian Peninsula and the Fertile Crescent, and the first conquests were aimed at uniting the peoples of this vast area within a single religiopolitical framework.

But the "Arabism" of early Islam began to evaporate as the Muslim armies penetrated into non-Arab lands and as non-Arabs slowly began to accept Islam—initially to the consternation of their conquerors. By the mid-ninth century the Arabs were no longer the political-social elite of the Islamic world, except for the caliphs themselves—and the caliphs' claim to rule lay in their kinship with the Prophet, not in the distant Arabian origins of their family. Arabic still remained the language through which all educated Muslims (and increasing numbers of non-Muslims) communicated with one another, whatever ethnic group they belonged to, and it would retain that role for centuries to come. But in fact a mastery of Arabic was increasingly the province of non-Arabs, of those who had spoken something else in their childhood homes and perhaps continued to do so as adults. Ironically, very few of the leading writers of Arabic prose and poetry in the ninth and tenth centuries could trace their family trees back to the Arabian Peninsula. Moreover, in the tenth century Arabic began to be supplanted in Iran and Central Asia by a revival of written Persian, and eventually even by Turkish. By the year 1000, to be an Arab in any sense—descendant of the conquering tribal warriors of the seventh century, or native speaker of Arabic, or desert dweller—conferred little or no religious preeminence. On the contrary, in most places political power was firmly in the hands of other peoples, often proudly and self-consciously identifying themselves as Iranians, Turks, or Berbers. A Muslim was anyone who confessed that God was one and Muhammad was His apostle; Arab roots and Arab identity had very little to do with it.

The idea that political action should be driven by the fact that one was an Arab still seemed new and strange by the eve of World War I. And even as the emerging ideas of Arabism began to take hold among the political elites of the new states of the region (particularly in Iraq and Syria), a second element of weakness emerged. Arab Nationalist thinkers and publicists from the very beginning had looked at the crucial problem confronting them and their people as one of identity rather than as one of institutions. The question was, Who is an Arab? not How can the Arabs build a common political life and effective institutions of government? If Arabs believed they were Arabs and acted on that belief, it was argued, they would inevitably be able to create an Arab national state. Very few writers asked seriously how this state would be constituted, how the relationships among its many disparate regions were to be defined, and how different social groups would be represented within the political system. Such issues were vital, everyone admitted, but they were premature.

The United Arab Republic of 1958, a slapdash marriage of convenience, was the perfect embodiment of these unanswered (and almost unasked) questions. It was never wholly clear in Nasser's own thinking whether he should aim at an alliance of Arab states that he would dominate (presumably through the Arab League) or whether he should try for something more. The proposal for a United Arab Republic, launched by desperate Syrian politicians trapped between the machinations of the CIA and domestic Communists, had caught him entirely by surprise, and when the union failed he found himself trying to salvage his prestige rather than looking for alternative structures.

The historical experience of Great Britain, the United States, and France might have suggested to Pan-Arabist ideologues that political institutions and common citizenship could provide a framework within which a solid national identity could take shape. However, the Italian and German models, based on race, culture, will, and struggle against internal division and foreign rule, had far more appeal. Given the hostile attitudes toward Great Britain and France among Arab political activists during the mid-1930s—attitudes that should be readily intelligible—the victory of the Italo-German style of nationalism was perhaps inevitable.

To be fair, the problem of identity was not a trivial one for the Arabs. The earliest Arab Nationalists (perhaps they should be called protonationalists), writing in the decade before World War I, originally focused on a Greater Syria comprised of the modern countries of Syria, Lebanon, Jordan, and Palestine. During the war, they broadened their focus to include the Arabian Peninsula and Iraq. It took Arab Nationalist writers a long time to come around to the argument that all the lands between the Nile and the Tigris should be included in the Arab nation. Indeed, the first to present this argument systematically was Sati al-Husri in the mid-1930s.[3] He is in fact an oddly paradigmatic figure for interwar Arab Nationalism. Born in Aleppo to a Turkish-speaking family of Ottoman officials, Sati al-Husri was educated in Istanbul and spent the war years there. After World War I he took up residence in the new state of Iraq and ultimately became minister of education in that country. He emerged in the 1930s as the most sophisticated and effective spokesman for Pan-Arabism. Ironically, Turkish was his mother tongue, and though he was devoted to the Arabic language he never was fully at home in it.

Apart from uncertainties about what lands and peoples belonged to the Arab Nation, there were important and deep-rooted counter-identities at play—Egyptian, Syrian, Lebanese, Muslim, and so on. These identities had to be dealt with; except for Islam they were dismissed as "regionalism." Moreover, several Arab countries contained large non-Arab minorities, especially the Kurds in Iraq and the Berbers in Algeria—some 20 and 15 percent of the population, respectively. Morocco had an even larger Berber population than Algeria, but most Pan-Arabists were willing to recognize that it possessed a distinctive character of its own within the larger Arab world.

It followed from the fundamental propositions of Pan-Arabism that the creation of the Arab state would come about by a supreme act of will, by a revolt that would shatter the rigid but brittle cage of historical accident and misfortune that imprisoned the Arabs. It was an article of faith among the avant-garde intelligentsia that the Arabs had been kept apart solely by the selfishness of local elites and the machinations of Franco-British imperialism. But once these artificial barriers could be smashed, the Arab nation would inevitably flow together and meld into one indissoluble union. The will demanded by history was first of all the will of the whole Arab people, but it was also the heroic will of a single actor, who would embody in himself the aspirations and ideals of the whole nation.

Not entirely by his own volition and certainly not by circumstances of his own making, Gamal Abdel Nasser found himself in this role after the Suez Crisis of 1956. The problem he faced was this: whatever his stature with the Arab masses—which had become almost overwhelming even for a man of his considerable self-esteem—he had to deal with rival political elites in other Arab states. In spite of Nasser's fiery propaganda machine, these were not the entrenched elites of the "reactionary" states, the old colonial period bureaucrats and landowners, wealthy merchants and tribal chiefs, whose wealth, privilege, and toadyism the progressives loved to assail. Especially after 1958, Nasser's chief rivals were for the most part the raw, insecure radicals of Syria and Iraq who had their own vision of the

Arab future. These men had just seized power and were determined to keep it in the face of domestic enemies, the CIA, and Nasser himself. In their eyes, Nasser fell far short of the unclouded vision and the pure ruthlessness that were needed to bring about the new world they envisioned so vividly.

In a sense the Pan-Arabism of the 1950s and 1960s was a surrogate for other impulses—the struggle to end the last vestiges of colonial domination, to eradicate the constant, burning humiliation of Israel, to achieve prosperity and social justice, and to realize the glorious aspirations of so many for the cultural and intellectual renewal of the Arabs. Through Arab Nationalism, the Arabs could once again become a great people who would command the respect of the world. But when Arab Nationalism—or Arab Nationalist rhetoric—did not bring those things into being but instead dragged the Arabs into the abyss of June 1967, it was inevitable that they and their leaders would look elsewhere for hope and inspiration.

In retrospect, all these points seem a sure guarantee that Pan-Arabism would have only a brief turn upon the stage. But for a moment it did triumph, or almost so. Every expert commentator in the 1960s (not only the Pan-Arabist intelligentsia, who obviously had a vital stake in the debate, but also the best-informed Western observers) took it for granted that some form of Arab Nationalism represented the future. And this universal assumption among intelligent and well-informed contemporary observers should cause us to ask whether the "failure" (as it now seems) of Pan-Arabism was rooted, not in the movement's structural flaws, but simply in the accidents of history. Suppose the Arabs had held their own in the June War—not winning the smashing victory that their propagandists had predicted, but simply stalling the Israeli offensive for three weeks or a month, long enough to compel the United Nations (or rather the United States and the Soviet Union) to intervene and compel a standdown. In such a case might not Nasser's dominance have been restored or even heightened, in the manner of 1956? After all, a merely creditable performance in 1973 earned a tremendous surge of prestige for Sadat, and this war too might have ended very badly for Egypt had not the Americans and Soviets, fearful of a nuclear confrontation between themselves, pressured the Israelis into a cease-fire. It is in any case a possibility that deserves more serious reflection than it usually receives.

But let us grant that events might have gone differently than they did. Even so it is hard to think that the maximum Pan-Arabist program was ever attainable, if only because the existing boundaries between the Arab states—boundaries that were pure colonial fictions created out of thin air in 1920 by Britain and France for their own convenience—had become sacred and immutable by 1950. Those boundaries provided the arenas in which the struggles for independence were fought, in which established social elites and their challengers strove to control the future. It is implausible to think that the young radicals who seized power in Iraq and Syria in the mid-1960s could have been induced to surrender their own aspirations for the greater glory of Nasser—whom they despised as a waffler in any case. And of course that is all the more true today, when those young radicals, now thoroughly middle-aged or worse, have enjoyed more than two decades of almost absolute power.

If Pan-Arabism, or Arab Nationalism in any form, can no longer inspire real hope and effective political action, has anything arisen to replace it? Is it possible that the Pan-Arabist dream has been replaced by state patriotism, a devotion to Egypt or Jordan or Iraq as they exist within their present boundaries? Can we imagine that the existing Arab states have so risen in the affection and esteem of their citizens that they are now the highest goal of political action, the focus of political loyalty? It is easy enough to be dismissive. But in fact the political experience of the Arab countries has been extremely complex, and we cannot answer the question without taking account of that complexity. A satisfactory reading of the shifting balance between Arab Nationalism and state patriotism demands that we look at the Arab states one by one. Ideally, we would survey every country from Mauritania to Oman, but that is not really necessary. The main struggle for Arab Nationalism took place in the eastern Arab world, in Egypt, Syria, Iraq, and the countries adjacent to them. By focusing on these, we will have some basis for deciding whether state patriotism can fill the void left by Arab Nationalism.

The shift from Arab Nationalism to state patriotism may in fact have taken place to some degree in the Egypt of Sadat and Mubarak, but Egypt (along with Morocco) is the odd man out in the Arab world, for Egyptian intellectuals and political activists long ago developed a strong sense of their country's historical identity and cultural personality. Modern Egyptian nationalism dates back to the 1860s and 1870s, and was forever crystallized by the trauma of the

British Occupation in 1882. In this context the Nasserist era (which lasted sixteen years, from his personal seizure of power in 1954 to his death in 1970) was a striking but atypical interlude. But even if Egyptians have no desire to dissolve themselves in a vast, undifferentiated Arab nation, they do not like going it alone either. Arabism is a significant element in what it means to be an Egyptian, and at some point it may well become once again the most important element.

When we turn to the countries of the Fertile Crescent and the Arabian Peninsula, however, we find few parallels to Egypt's well-articulated sense of national identity. Syria is a particularly intriguing test case for state patriotism in the Arab world, for Syria is a country that never wanted to exist at all, at least within its present boundaries.[4] Syrians quite rightly believe that the present boundaries of their country have no natural or historic roots but are rather a wholly artificial creation devised by France and Britain for their own purposes at the end of World War I. The political leaders who emerged in Syria between 1918 and 1920 had no delusions of grandeur. They hoped only for a truly independent Syria within its traditional boundaries—a region that stretches from Sinai in the south to the Taurus Mountains in the north and from the Mediterranean on the west to the Syrian Desert in the east. This region, called bilad al-Sham in Arabic (literally, "the lands of the North"), or Greater Syria, had never existed as a separate political entity with legally defined borders, but everyone knew what it was. Syrian politicians discovered very quickly that Britain and France were going to carve their homeland into pieces rigorously separated from one another and subjected to close imperial tutelage. In the Anglo-French settlement after World War I, bilad al-Sham—Greater Syria—became the modern states of Syria, Lebanon, Palestine/Israel, and Jordan.

The new Syria created by the World War I settlement was only two-thirds as large as the traditional Greater Syria. Moreover, it was isolated by being stripped of its ancient seaports, which were now located in the new entities of Lebanon and Palestine. Palestine was to be set aside for a Jewish National Home under British protection. Finally, the lands east of the Jordan (mostly desert, admittedly) were assigned by Britain to the amir Abdallah, as compensation for a host of broken promises made by the British to his father, Hussein, who had instigated and led the Arab Revolt against the Ottomans during the war.

During the interwar years Syria's politicians were compelled to focus on ridding themselves of French domination, since nothing else could be achieved until that was done. Since the final evacuation of French forces in 1946, however, Syrian leaders, whatever their political complexion, have felt it their mission to speak for some higher cause than the truncated country they inherited from the French Mandate. Even those who forswear the vast claims of Pan-Arabism have dreamed of reuniting the "historical" Greater Syria. The Syrian governments in the twelve years between independence (1946) and formation of the United Arab Republic (1958) could make no progress on either goal. They came and went with dizzying speed, leaving hardly a trace behind. By the winter of 1958, Syria's leaders were equally fearful of a CIA plot and a communist coup—and as many have remarked, even paranoids have real enemies. In desperation they turned to the one man whom they thought could save them, Gamal Abdel Nasser, by now at the peak of his prestige in Egypt.

To Nasser they offered the crown of his career, the formation of a United Arab Republic that would join together Egypt and Syria within a single state. The UAR would be the catalyst for the emergence of a dynamic and progressive Arab state stretching from the Nile to the Tigris—in effect the realization of the Arab Nationalist vision born in World War I. Nasser had serious doubts about the feasibility of the project, but against his better judgment he allowed himself to be persuaded. And thus Syria disappeared from the map, to be replaced by the rather less resonant "United Arab Republic, Northern Region." Far more upsetting to the Syrian politicians who had engineered the union, they were edged out of power and out of sight. From the Syrian perspective, the marriage proved an unhappy one in every way.

In 1961 the UAR broke up as suddenly as it had appeared, when a carefully planned conspiracy seized power in Damascus. Nasser prudently decided not to oppose the secession, and Syria was reborn. But the effort to return to "normal" lasted only a couple of years. In 1963 a mixed military-civilian coup put a new government in power and thereby founded a political system that has endured for more than three decades. The core of the new regime was the Baath ("Resurrection") party, founded in Damascus in 1943 by a Christian schoolteacher and a Sunni pharmacist. The Baath was the most ardently Pan-Arabist movement of all; its program combined a secularist worldview, populism, a vaguely Marxist socioeconomic program, and a visionary dream of a single Arab nation stretching from Morocco to Iraq. The Baath had been a fringe element in Syrian politics until the mid-1950s, but throughout that time it was building a clandestine power base in the Syrian armed forces. That was in itself not unusual: the armed forces were often a center of political dissidence and revolutionary action throughout much of the Third World during these decades.

But Syria presented an interesting twist on this pattern, for its armed forces were dominated by a deeply despised religious minority, the Alawis (or to give them their correct name, the Nusayris), who dominated the northwest coastal region and constituted about one-eighth of the population. Under French rule and early independence, the army was in effect the only channel of upward mobility for the Alawis, and they took full advantage of it. For them, the secularism, populism, and socialism of the Baath had an obvious appeal. But all this meant that a Baathist government, especially one dominated by the military, would be by definition an Alawi government. And so it turned out. In a country where two-thirds of the people are Sunni Muslims, this fact severely alienated the regime from its subjects down through the mid-1980s.

In 1966 an even more radical Baathist faction seized power. This new regime was determined to make itself the leader of the Pan-Arabist movement. To that end it sponsored a string of guerrilla attacks against Israel and mercilessly taunted Nasser for his passivity. Its efforts to put itself in the vanguard of the Arab world made little headway, but it was all too successful in setting the stage for the June War of 1967. Unlike Nasser, the Baathist junta lacked the stature to survive such a debacle. One of its members, the air force chief of staff Hafiz al-Asad, threw out his erstwhile colleagues and took charge himself.

Since seizing full power in 1971, Hafiz al-Asad—nominally a Baathist, but in fact a pure Machiavellian—has narrowed Syria's ideological focus sharply, though for tactical reasons he still attaches himself to the Arab Nationalist cause on suitable occasions. In particular, he has made himself an advocate for the more radical, "rejectionist" elements of the Palestinian resistance to Israel. However, he has played this card with such transparent cynicism that no one any longer thinks that he really believes in the Palestinian cause.

Some have argued that he dreams of creating or restoring a Greater Syria. In fact he has contrived to make Lebanon a de facto Syrian protectorate for at least the last decade, and his periodic bullying of Jordan has sometimes compelled King Hussein to toe the Syrian line in regional affairs. But we could just as well see this as old-fashioned sphere-of-interest politics, intended chiefly to secure his own position in a dangerous environment. It need not imply any grand design.

Deprived of any credible higher cause and quite devoid of personal charisma, Asad has stayed in power for more than a quarter century through extraordinary political skill and when necessary through an equally extraordinary ruthlessness. He is not called the spider of Damascus for nothing. To take only the most dramatic example, his suppression of the Islamic uprising in Hama in February 1982 drowned Syria's burgeoning Islamic movement in blood.[5] In another vein, after decades of denouncing U.S. imperialism and support for Zionism in the Middle East, he joined the U.S.-led coalition against Iraq in 1990–1991. Most recently, he has entered into direct if intermittent talks with the once-despised "Zionist entity" over the future of the Golan Heights and a possible peace treaty. These talks have gone nowhere in particular, and they may well be only a tactical diversion, but it is remarkable that they have been held at all.

Under Asad as under his predecessors, then, Syria remains a country in search of its role within the Middle East—a role that lends prestige and significance to Syria but is actually within its grasp. It no longer seems likely that this role will be defined by ideology; Baathist Pan-Arabism is exhausted, and a regime like Hafiz al-Asad's can hardly inspire a spontaneous surge of state patriotism. Apart from any long-term role within the Arab world, Syrians must worry about their immediate political future, for the Asad regime is. entirely a personal enterprise. Even the Baath party, with its complex apparatus reaching into every village, is simply an extension of the president. What hope does such a system have of outliving its creator? After all, even the most solidly constructed and impersonal party machinery can vanish into smoke with astonishing rapidity, as we saw in Eastern Europe between 1989 and 1991. It is hard to think that the Syrian Baath can expect a better fate. Of all the mysteries of the Asad regime, the darkest and most opaque is surely what will happen at the hour of his death.

Whatever quandaries Syria has faced in finding its place in the

Arab Nationalist and post-Nationalist eras, they fade into nothingness in comparison with Lebanon's travails.[6] From World War I until 1975, Lebanon was like nothing else in the Middle East. The country was created in its modern form by the French after World War I as part of the same package deal that produced Syria, Jordan, and Palestine. Though the new Lebanon was a very small place (some 1.2 million people in 1936, and 4,000 square miles), it encompassed almost every religious sect in the Middle East, with a slight overall Christian majority. Constitutionally, Lebanon was a parliamentary democracy with a strong president. In fact it was a system of shared power, in which the bosses of the various religious sects divided up government offices (as well as the other rewards of power) among themselves and their followers. Lebanon was in a sense the elder Mayor Richard Daley's Chicago transplanted into the Middle East, though its leaders did not get the garbage collected as efficiently as he did.

No one was entirely happy with this arrangement. As Muslims gained a larger share of the population, they felt increasingly shortchanged by it. Moreover, many of them wanted to align Lebanon closely with the rising forces of Arab Nationalism. On the other side, the Christians were uneasy at best about the implications of Arab Nationalism. On balance they felt a much stronger cultural affinity for the West than for the turbulent and "backward" Arab milieu in which they were imbedded. Moreover, they had no desire to abandon the only political system in the Middle East where they had the upper hand, however tenuously. In spite of such tensions, the Lebanese system worked fairly well as long as there was a modicum of prosperity and security; it even ensured a high degree of tolerance, though not mutual esteem, among the multitude of religious groups who lived there. And by 1970 there clearly seemed to be an emerging sense of a real Lebanese patriotism that could bridge the old confessional lines.

Under the stress of the decade after 1967, however—and the stress was undeniably enormous—Lebanon turned out to be less an integrated nation-state than a coalition of jealous interest groups. A hideous civil war broke out in 1975 and took at least 150,000 lives over more than a decade of intermittent fighting. Having no ambitions of its own, Lebanon became the target of everyone else's—Syria's drive for regional paramountcy, Iran's vision of a Shi'ite revolution,

Libya's hopes of revitalizing the Pan-Arabist dream, and most of all the savage struggle between the PLO and Israel. The civil war finally sputtered out in 1989, as the country's internal and external rivals fought to utter exhaustion. In a way, things have gone back to the way they used to be. The state of Lebanon still exists within its old French-drawn borders. The Lebanese have gone back to wheeling and dealing, and there is a vast program of rebuilding amid the ruins. But Lebanon is hardly an independent country any longer; it is a quasi-protectorate of Syria. In such a climate, state patriotism can be only a frail plant. Lebanon's relationship to Arab Nationalism is full of irony. It was never really a part of that movement even at its peak, but it was dragged into the struggle over Arab Nationalism's collapse and was almost destroyed by it. In the disarray of the contemporary Arab world, it is hard to know what role the Lebanese imagine for themselves.

Jordan's place in the Arab world is also uncertain though infinitely less tragic.[7] Since World War II at least, Jordan's role has been, first, to survive and, second, to serve as a broker between conflicting agendas and ideologies within the Arab world, or between the Arab countries and the West. In a very real sense, that remains its role today. The reasons for this are grounded in the country's history, size, and demography. Jordan began its career in the early 1920s as part of the British zone of control in the partition of Greater Syria. The arid regions east of the Jordan had previously been a thinly populated frontier zone (300,000 people in 1930), attached variously to Damascus or to Palestine. The first ruler of the newly created entity, the amir Abdallah, had been a significant figure in the Arab Revolt during World War I, and he should have had solid credentials within the emerging Arab Nationalist movement. But these prospects were wrecked by the chaos in Arabia and Syria after 1918. Abdallah could only restart his career when the British created a new country for him—the Amirate of Transjordan—east of the Jordan River. He was a highly ambitious and very astute politician, but he could never escape British tutelage or the taint of being regarded as a British puppet. When he was assassinated in Jerusalem in 1951, no one thought that his little state (by then called the Hashimite Kingdom of Jordan) had any future.

The Middle East produces prophets beyond number, but they seldom hit the mark. As things have turned out, Abdallah's grandson

King Hussein, who took the throne in 1953, has endured and at moments even prospered against a fantastic array of crises and enemies. In the teeth of every prediction, he has built a viable state and a considerable sense of loyalty among his people, but that is very much a personal achievement. King Hussein's achievement reflects uncommon, indeed uncanny, political skill. Even when he has committed the mortal sin of backing a loser (e.g., Nasser in 1967, Saddam Hussein in 1990–1991), he has done so with an astute calculation of the gains and losses involved in his choices. He has variously played the ardent Arab Nationalist, the staunch ally of the West, the thoughtful moderate—whatever the situation at any given moment seemed to demand. Hussein's impressive acumen is not the whole story, of course; the kingdom's survival also reflects the realities of international politics—in this case, a widely perceived need both within the Middle East and among outside powers, especially the United States, to have a stable buffer state placed between Israel, Syria, Iraq, and Saudi Arabia. As to Jordan after King Hussein, it is perhaps best not to speculate about the commitment of its people to the idea of the Hashimite Kingdom.

Ideology in Jordan tends to follow the fault line of the country's sharply divided population. This fact illustrates very neatly the limits both of Pan-Arabism and state patriotism in the modern Arab world. Even after the loss of the West Bank in 1967, a majority (some 60 percent) of Jordan's citizens are Palestinian in origin, not natives of the lands east of the Jordan River. For the most part, the Palestinians of Jordan are refugees from the wars with Israel in 1948 and 1967, and in Jordan they have regarded themselves as strangers in a strange land. They have on the whole been deeply committed to the struggle to restore their Palestinian homeland. Since this struggle could only be won with the united support of all Arabs, Arab Nationalism obviously had great appeal for them. The continuing force of these feelings exploded into full view in the fall of 1990, when the Palestinians enthusiastically backed Saddam Hussein in the hope that he would at last be the longed-for champion who could face down Israel and the United States. King Hussein had no choice but to swim with this powerful current; in effect, it was Palestinian sentiment that dictated the policy he would follow. In a very vivid way, the Gulf War demonstrated state patriotism's limited role in Jordan's political life.

Iraq, like Egypt, possesses an unmistakable geographic and historical identity of its own.[8] With the fading of the Pan-Arabist dream, it should be fertile ground for a vigorous state patriotism. Saddam Hussein's appeals to the glory of ancient Assyria and Babylon undeniably have a comic aspect, but Iraqis are well aware of the great civilizations that arose in their land and take a deep pride in them. Throughout Islamic times, moreover, Iraq was always seen as a region with a character all its own; from 762 to 1258, its metropolis of Baghdad was at least the nominal capital of a vast empire stretching from the Nile deep into Central Asia. Nor is there anything vague about Iraq's "natural frontiers"; these are quite clearly marked by the Zagros Mountains on the east, the Syrian Desert on the west, and— most important—the vast alluvial plain created by the Tigris and Euphrates rivers as they exit the mountains of southeastern Turkey.

But in spite of its geographic cohesion and ancient history, Iraq is ridden with profound and apparently unassuageable tensions; these have obviously been sharply aggravated by the Gulf War and the subsequent sanctions, but they were hardly caused by these very recent events. Iraq is split by social, ethnic, religious, and socioeconomic fault lines: Sunni versus Shi'ite, Arab versus Kurd, tribal chief versus urban merchant, nomad versus peasant. Nor did Iraq have a real history of its own during the four centuries of Ottoman rule (1534–1918), when it was divided into three major provinces, centered on Mosul, Baghdad, and Basra, respectively. In the face of these challenges, it has proved almost impossible for the governments of independent Iraq since 1921 to build a stable political order founded on the consent of the governed. Stability has indeed been achieved from time to time, not least under the Baathist regime in power since 1968, but it is a stability purchased at the cost of massive repression. This repression has been directed not only against the Kurds or (especially since 1991) the Shi'ites of the deep south but against every possible dissident as well.

Iraq's ethnic and religious divisions, together with the brutal political repression it has suffered, have done much to subvert any foundations for state patriotism there. Perhaps even more important, Iraq has tried to play the leading role in defining Arab Nationalism and has pursued the constantly changing agendas of this ideology almost since the country was established in 1920. In such a milieu, a solidly grounded state patriotism has had little chance to take root. Iraq's role within the Arab world during the two decades between the world wars was mostly one of trying to assert ideological leadership, and this effort had few practical consequences. With the bloody coup d'état of 1958, however, Iraq entered the struggle for leadership alongside, then against, Gamal Abdel Nasser—a hopeless contest. The rise of the radical nationalist Baath party in the late 1960s might have given Iraq an edge during an era (the 1970s) when radicalism seemed a rising tide in the Third World. But Iraq's opportunity to reinvigorate and lead the Pan-Arabist cause was squandered by the brutal Stalinism of Saddam Hussein and a squalid quarrel with a sister-Baathist regime in Syria. In the end, Iraqi patriotism is potentially a significant force in the country. But to become genuinely effective this patriotism will have to be ethnically and religiously far more inclusive than the doctrinaire forms of Arab Nationalism that have blighted so much of Iraq's twentieth-century history.

Saudi Arabia might seem a good candidate for an effective state nationalism or local patriotism.[9] To begin with, the kingdom was never an enthusiastic participant in the Pan-Arabist dance, although it is the oldest fully independent Arab state. Its roots lie in the late eighteenth century, and it was established in its present form by the relentless campaigns and astute diplomacy of the amir (later king) Abd al-Aziz Al Saud between 1905 and 1926. As the largest state within the ancient homeland of the Arabs, it is one of the few Arab countries whose ethnic identity is not subject to debate or self-questioning. But the official ideology of Saudi Arabia has been from the beginning, and remains today, religious rather than nationalist; the mission of the kingdom and its ruling family is to promote not Arabism but an intensely traditionalist version of Islam. Thus while Saudi Arabia was a charter member of the Arab League and has supported many of the usual Arab causes (especially the Palestinian resistance to Israel), it has vigorously and effectively resisted schemes for a union of Arab states, especially the kind of unity proclaimed by secularist-progressive leaders. The Saudis have, however, consistently supported Islamic causes of all kinds, whether missionary activity in the Philippines, funding Islamic political and social movements in Egypt and the Sudan, or providing arms to the Afghan resistance during the 1980s. King Fahd's principal title is Khadim al-Haramayn, Servitor of the Two Holy Sanctuaries (i.e., Mecca and Medina), and that fact says all we need to know about the ideological foundations of his regime.

Saudi Arabia does not face the long-term economic crisis of Egypt or the bitter sectarian and ethnic cleavages of Iraq, but it has very distinctive and quite intractable political problems of its own. In particular, the government and indeed the whole country are in a real sense synonymous with the ruling house. From the moment of its birth, Saudi Arabia has been very much a family affair; not only the throne, but every critical ministry (e.g., Defense, Interior), every provincial governorship, and a host of other government offices, is held by a senior prince of the House of Saud. Many of the kingdom's largest economic ventures belong to one or another of the princes. The Saudi regime has made considerable, indeed remarkable, efforts to "spread the wealth," and it has created a social welfare network that compares favorably to those in the European social democracies, along with a system of subsidies to politically sensitive centers. Even so, the House of Saud's strict monopoly of political power and its refusal to permit serious public debate on major issues have created serious tensions within an increasingly educated and politically aware public. Anything that goes wrong in the country can be blamed on the House of Saud—who else is there, after all? The liberal technocrats chafe, since they are denied any independent voice in policy making and face severe restrictions on their personal freedom. On the other side of the ledger, there is now a growing body of Islamic activists (many of them professional men with advanced modern educations) who denounce the regime as not Islamic enough. In their eyes the House of Saud is ridden with corruption and is all too ready to bend Islamic precepts to fit the demands of Western governments or corporations.

In the end, it is hard to think that state patriotism is the wave of the future in the Arab world; only a few of the existing Arab countries seem the right and natural focus of ultimate political loyalty. But in spite of all the weaknesses of the existing states—and many others could be cited—they have been the sole arena of political action in the Arab world for the last two decades. Pan-Arabism has fleeting moments of life—for example, the sporadic efforts by Muammar Qaddafi of Libya to construct two- or three-state federations, presumably as a step toward the ultimate goal of a unified Arab nation-state. But these federations have proved far more ephemeral

than the United Arab Republic; only a few super-experts can recall that they ever existed even on paper. The only two exceptions—
and in different ways each of them proves the rule—have been the
wealthy but tiny United Arab Emirates in the Persian Gulf (dating
back to 1969) and the more recent union of North and South Yemen
(1990), which remains a tension-filled though apparently functional
marriage.[10]

The most likely successor to Pan-Arabism may be the Islamic
movement, which has managed to combine a universalist program
with local tactics in a very effective way. The burgeoning Islamic
groups espouse political and social values that are universal in principle. They have grown up within particular countries, however, and
for the most part they aim only to establish an Islamic order within
those countries. Very few look toward a dissolution and transformation of the present state system in the Arab world. Even the Ayatollah Khomeini envisioned a vast Islamic alliance, not a unified Islamic state. And in fact, as several commentators have shown, his
own version of revolutionary Islam was so marked by Shi'ite symbols and Iranian culture that it was almost unexportable to Sunni
countries.[11]

It is certainly true that in an era when Islam seems to possess
enormous power to move and inspire, we could envision a situation in which Islamic movements seize power in two or three major
countries—for example, Egypt and Algeria—and consequently become highly influential in the policy making of several others. This
fact would certainly transform the international environment of the
region, but there is no reason to think that it would reshape the existing state system in any significant way. Such an event might even
harden the existing borders, for each of the various Islamist movements seems to be strongly rooted in its own local soil, to whatever
degree it may be in contact with other movements or be (as with
Hizbollah in Lebanon) a recipient of external financial and political
support.

But all this is mere speculation, and perhaps we should close by
recognizing that in some very important ways Pan-Arabism is not
dead. On the contrary, it is a living and vital force. Educated Arabs
(along with many from the lower strata of society) travel, work, and
study widely throughout the Arab world. In so doing they have developed a spoken *koiné* that effectively bridges dialect differences,

they watch Egyptian situation comedies on television, and they are aware of events everywhere among the Arabs. They retain and relish their regional differences—much like Southerners and New Yorkers—but in many ways they have indeed become one people with an acute sense of their peculiar identity. This shows up in many forms, but perhaps most characteristically in the way Arabs refer to one another as members of a family: the various Arab states are "sisters," the Arab people(s) are "brothers" to one another. Like many families, they quarrel incessantly and even violently, but against the outside world they tend to band together. When the chips are down, they believe deeply that they should support and defend one another. Such kinship language sounds odd in American and European politics, but it is an everyday part of Arab political speech. Moreover, this political kinship is taken seriously: Arabs agonized over Iraq's rape of its sister Kuwait and over the betrayal of the "family" involved in siding with outsiders (namely, the United States, Britain, and France) against one of their own, however brutal and egregious his behavior, however much he had violated the honor and integrity of the family. This deep-seated sense of Arab identity is almost certain to have political consequences. We cannot yet discern what form these will take, or what circumstances will call them forth. It is hard to imagine that the visionary Pan-Arabism of Nasser or the early Baath will ever reemerge as a serious political option, but that is not the only form in which nationalism may manifest itself or become a real force in Middle Eastern affairs.

Still, a cultural Pan-Arabism of the sort that now exists (and even flourishes) does not provide a framework for political action that goes beyond the narrow confines of state nationalism and presents a vision of a "greater destiny" or "higher good." The search among Arab politicians and intellectuals for such a framework has so far drawn a blank. If this is so, the crazy quilt of states that came into being as part of the process of colonization and decolonization must continue to provide not only the framework but also the sustenance for political life in the Arab world. To discover meaning and purpose and intellectual energy in that framework is the challenge confronting those who hope to lead the Arab world.

CHAPTER 4

THE SHAPING OF FOREIGN POLICY

The Myth of the Middle East Madman

No creature in the American political bestiary is more enduring than the Middle East Madman. This creature takes varying forms— the ranting dictator in khaki uniform; the bearded terrorist, head wrapped in the ever-present checked kaffiyeh, bearing a thin smile and a ghostly light in his eyes; the dour yet fiery fundamentalist cleric, likewise bearded and eyes aglow, but wearing a turban and gown. But at bottom they are all alike: men (along with an occasional woman) filled with a consuming hatred for America and the American way of life and dedicated to its destruction. They fill the air with terrifying threats, grotesque fabrications, and grandiose dreams of revenge and glory. Most of all they are simply out of touch with reality. They are madmen, impervious to reason and logic, utterly beyond the understanding of rational Westerners.

The Middle East certainly has its full share of extravagant rhetoric and preposterous claims—though some might say the same thing about the United States—but the Middle East Madman is a mythological beast, or nearly so. When we look beyond the facade of theater and posturing, we will almost always discern a hard-headed politician who knows perfectly well how to set his goals and to craft strategies for achieving them—and also knows that in the Darwinian struggle of international politics, both goals and strategies must normally be camouflaged. The problem for us is not that the goals of Middle Eastern leaders are impenetrable; most of the time they are quite transparent. The problem is simply that these goals are not the ones that we want them to have. Since we refuse to recognize their goals even when they are right in front of our eyes, we are easily misled by the rhetorical smoke screens they lay down to mask them. It is certainly true that the policies of Middle Eastern leaders often go awry, sometimes with catastrophic results. But the same thing

83

holds for almost any American or European politician. Misplaced goals and miscalculated strategies are the everyday stuff of politics; they are not in themselves the signs of irrationality and delusion. We will get a lot further in trying to penetrate the thinking of Middle Eastern politicians if we go on the assumption that their words and actions are the product of rational calculation.

Having said this much, we will have to backtrack a bit and admit that *no* policy is or can be wholly rational. Policy aims at future goals, but it is constructed within a web of memory. It is our experience of life, and more important how we remember that experience, that dictates to us what our hopes for the future ought to be and suggests the best ways of realizing those hopes. In analyzing the policies of political leaders, we must begin by asking what they believe the past has taught them. Let me stress that the issue here is not what "really" happened in some impersonal, objective sense but what these leaders remember or think they remember. As it happens, the historical memories of Middle Easterners are very different from our own. This simple fact should be intuitively obvious, but most pundits overlook it. In view of the gulf between their memories and ours, it is natural that the policies that Middle Easterners deem desirable and achievable should diverge (often in startling ways) from the policies that we think they ought to choose—in effect, the policies that we would choose for them if we were in charge.

The gap in memories comes about in large part from the profoundly different historical events and processes through which they and we have lived, and by which their societies and ours have been formed. The Abbasid Revolution (747–750)—a genuinely cataclysmic event with enormous long-term consequences—is completely unknown to most Americans, just as the American Civil War means nothing to Middle Easterners.

But there are also crucial differences in perspective on events we and they share in common. Few Americans, for example, recall the oil nationalization crisis in Iran between 1950 and 1953, even though the U.S. government regarded that crisis as a threat to vital American interests and played a decisive role in bringing it to an end. On the other side, no Iranian has ever forgotten those events for a moment; in Iranian national memory they carry enormous symbolic and tragic weight—at once the noblest embodiment and most crushing betrayal of the nation's dreams. For a host of Iranians, including many opponents of the Ayatollah Khomeini, the seizure of the U.S. Embassy by Iranian students in 1979 was a long overdue payback for what the CIA had done to Iran a quarter century before.

This example underlines several useful points. First, it is not what happens to us but what we remember about it that is crucial in how the past shapes our thinking about the future and about what we are going to do next. Second, we all forget far more of the past than we remember, but we do not all forget the same things. Finally, all of us tend to remember, sometimes very vividly, things that never happened. However rationally conceived and pursued a policy may be, then, it is ultimately grounded in fallible but extremely powerful images of the past. Policy is in a sense the struggle of memory to control the future.

By way of trying to demonstrate some of these points—in particular, the uncertain and always shifting relationship between cold rationality and subjective memories of the past in the making of policy—we will look at three paradigmatic "Middle East Madmen," each at a defining moment of his career. It must be admitted that the direct evidence for how each of them approached policy questions is ambiguous and hard to interpret. So in reconstructing the way they thought about these crises, we have to fall back on surmise and inference. But the very fact that their policies can readily be interpreted as the result of rational calculation suggests that this is a far more useful way of understanding them than just assuming that they were mad.

One of these moments may seem remote from current issues and concerns, but more than any other crisis it defined for Western statesmen of that era who the new breed of Middle Eastern leaders were and how they must be dealt with. On the other side of the ledger, it opened up to Middle Eastern politicians a whole new world of bold possibilities. This was the decision by Gamal Abdel Nasser to nationalize the Suez Canal in the summer of 1956.[1] The second two cases, in contrast, are indelibly imprinted in the recent political memories of both Americans and Middle Easterners, and their immediate consequences are very much with us: the Ayatollah Khomeini's seizure of the American Embassy in Tehran in 1979–1980; and Saddam Hussein's decision to occupy Kuwait in August 1990.

All three of these men, different as they were in so many ways, appeared to American and European observers to embody the rashness, the utter unpredictability, the heated rhetorical extravagance, and the bitter anti-Westernism of the modern Middle East. All of them—at least as they were perceived in America and Europe—demonstrated the profound gulf separating the Arabs or (more globally) Islam from the West, a gulf that would forever make each incomprehensible to the other. But I will argue that all three men were pursuing policies that made eminently good sense in terms of the struggles in which they were engaged, and moreover, policies that seemed to have real prospects of success. Indeed, both Nasser and Khomeini succeeded brilliantly in at least the short term, though not necessarily in just the way they expected to. And even Saddam Hussein, though badly defeated on the battlefield, remains solidly in power and entirely unchastened.

Nasser's Decision to Nationalize the Suez Canal (July 1956)

Early in the afternoon of July 19, 1956, Egypt's ambassador to the United States entered a meeting with Secretary of State John Foster Dulles.[2] He brought with him a proposal aimed at overcoming differences between Egypt and the United States over a package of American aid to help build a vast dam and hydroelectric project at Aswan. But without warning and with few niceties, the ambassador was informed that the United States had decided that Egypt could not successfully complete this project. The United States was therefore withdrawing the offer of assistance it had made only six months earlier, in December 1955. Even while the meeting between Dulles and the ambassador was going on, the State Department had issued an official statement canceling funding for the dam. The ambassador was left with his mouth open, with no chance to respond or even seek a delay.

The proposed Aswan Dam was a critical element in the domestic policy of Egypt's revolutionary government, for both material and symbolic reasons. A high dam in the far south of the country, impounding vast quantities of water and permitting year-round irrigation of the Nile Valley, had been talked about for half a century. However, serious proposals were put forward only after the military government seized power in 1952. By 1955, Egypt's population had reached 23 million and was continuing to grow rapidly. Egypt's stagnant economy could not easily absorb such numbers. Most Egyptians were peasants, but the amount of arable land was severely limited by the natural flood patterns of the Nile, which permitted only one crop per year on a very narrow floodplain. Moreover, a key policy of the new government—indeed, the centerpiece of its whole policy of social justice—was a wide-scale land reform that would distribute farms to landless peasants, but this could not be done unless new farmland was made available. The high dam at Aswan would extend year-round irrigation all the way down the Nile Valley and vastly increase the amount of land that could be cultivated. The dam would have another material benefit as well: it would produce an immense quantity of hydroelectric power, enough to underwrite a massive industrialization program that would bring Egypt's economy into the twentieth century. It would become a significant industrial nation, not merely an exporter of agricultural commodities. And this point leads to the symbolic element of the project. To its own people, the revolutionary government would show that it could build monuments worthy of the Pharaohs—but monuments for the living rather than the dead. To the world, Egypt would demonstrate its determination and capacity to become an advanced nation. Probably no single project was more crucial to the new government's vision of its historic mission.

In spite of the dam's great value, everyone knew that Egypt had neither the technical skills nor the financial resources to build it. For that reason the Egyptian government started searching for partners in 1953. At first few were sure that such a vast project could be built at all; in any case, it was certain that extraordinary time and expense would be needed. Egypt's inquiries thus encountered doubt, hedging, and severe conditions on every side. But the World Bank found it a realistic if ambitious project. It estimated a construction time of one decade and a total cost of $1.3 billion. (To get a sense of these costs in current dollars, multiply these figures by five.) Most of this would be generated and spent within Egypt (on labor, housing, etc.), but about one-third—that is, $400 million—would be hard-currency expenditures for heavy industrial equipment, foreign engineers, and the like. Such a sum Egypt could not afford. The World Bank was willing to lend $200 million, but the rest would have to come in the form of cash grants. The British were eager to join the consortium, but they had severe financial problems of their own. In the end, the United States was the only game in town. In December 1955, Secretary of State Dulles was persuaded to commit $56 million in grant money; Britain would chip in $14 million. Further grants and loans would depend on satisfactory progress on the dam. It took the whole winter of 1956 to get Nasser to accept this three-part offer because foreign loans had very unpleasant connotations for Egypt. Moreover, some of the World Bank's conditions in effect allowed it to oversee Egypt's financial affairs. To any patriotic Egyptian, the whole thing stirred bitter memories of the crushing foreign debts of the 1870s; these had led to the collapse of Egypt's state finances in 1876 and ultimately to the British military occupation in 1882. Only in March was a satisfactory agreement with the World Bank reached, and there were still many loose ends as regarded U.S. and British participation. It was to iron those out, on the basis of a very accommodating proposal, that the unfortunate ambassador had entered Secretary Dulles's lair on July 19.

When Egypt's President Nasser was informed of the U.S. decision and the grave insult to his ambassador, he predictably hit the ceiling. But the question remained, what to do now? Should the high dam still be built, and if so, how? Could anything be done to redeem Egypt's public humiliation? And in the broadest terms, what kind of relationship should Egypt seek now with the great powers—with Britain (still the paramount power in the Middle East), the United States (overwhelmingly the richest and most powerful country in the world), and the Soviet Union (with the appeal of its socialist ideology, its stern anticolonialist line, its rapid industrialization, and its vast military apparatus)?

Perhaps the American decision should have come as no surprise, for relations between the revolutionary government of Egypt, the United States, and Britain had been deteriorating since early 1955, and of course the British and Egyptian governments were incurably suspicious of each other. But the British and American governments had initially taken a distinctively favorable attitude to the young military officers who had overthrown King Farouk in July 1952. Why had things gone sour?

In his dealings with Britain and the United States, Nasser faced a multidimensional situation shaped both by historical memories and by current problems and frustrations. It included the following elements, each of which was entangled with all the others:

1. Egypt's changing relationship with Great Britain since 1882;
2. the status of the Suez Canal, an autonomous entity on Egyptian soil;
3. Egypt's relations with other Arab states, directly and through the Arab League;
4. Egypt's role in the Arab-Israeli conflict brought about by the war between Israel, the Palestinians, and neighboring Arab states in 1948; and
5. cold war pressures, and the impact of these on the broad international role that Egypt was trying to define for itself.

For Nasser, as for any Egyptian government, the relationship with Britain seemed particularly central and delicate. Britain had sent an expeditionary force to Egypt in 1882 and occupied the country so as to restore order and secure the throne of the then-reigning viceroy. One thing had led to another, and the British not only maintained their military occupation but also closely supervised Egypt's domestic affairs down to the end of World War I. The rationale for staying was no doubt first and foremost to ensure the security of the Suez Canal, which had become a critical link in Britain's communications with India.

Even after Egypt was granted autonomy in its internal affairs in 1922, most Egyptians felt that their country continued to be a British puppet, since the High Commissioner felt free to intervene whenever things were not going to Britain's taste. Britain's main concern in the 1920s and 1930s was to negotiate a treaty of alliance with Egypt that would ensure the primacy of British security interests. To this end, the British government often instructed the king of Egypt as to which politicians were or were not acceptable negotiating partners. As a result, even when the British were neutral bystanders in Egypt's political quarrels, it was assumed by everyone that they were really running things behind the scenes.

A viable Anglo-Egyptian treaty was finally negotiated in 1936. The Occupation was terminated, the High Commissioner became an ambassador, but the British maintained massive bases on Egyptian soil, supposedly with a maximum of 10,000 men in peacetime. (In fact, the number after World War II reached 80,000.) With one startling exception in February 1942, when the British ambassador surrounded the Royal Palace with tanks and ordered King Farouk to name a pro-Allied government, there was no further interference in Egypt's internal affairs. But the British military presence in the Canal Zone, and the treaty terms that compelled Egypt to follow Britain's lead in foreign affairs, left Egyptian nationalists bitterly discontented. Under such circumstances they could not regard Egypt as a truly independent country.

After World War II, continuing discontent over the British presence, plus the Palestine crisis, led to an upsurge of guerrilla activity against Britain's Canal Zone bases. Egypt unilaterally renounced the 1936 treaty in 1951. Open warfare was avoided chiefly because of changes in both countries. In Britain, these were the country's near-bankruptcy after World War II and the decision by Labour and Conservative governments to reshape the empire into a close but voluntary association of free countries. In Egypt, the military coup of July 1952 changed the political chemistry, though Egyptian demands were still stiff. A new agreement was finally signed in October 1954, due largely to the determination of Foreign Secretary Anthony Eden and Gamal Abdel Nasser to break the deadlock. The new agreement called for the prompt evacuation of all British troops, although Britain could use the Suez Canal bases in the event of outside attack on an Arab country or Turkey. That was an opening that left some Egyptians unhappy, but on the whole it seemed to mark an end to the unequal relationship. Still, could they ever really trust the British to deal honestly with them?

Apart from the nagging headache of relations with the British, Nasser had urgent concerns about Egypt's role in the Arab world. This was partly a problem with the British, for even after the Anglo-Egyptian agreement of 1954, Britain still had a strong position in the Middle East. The Jordanian army (the so-called Arab Legion) had been commanded for decades by a British officer, Gen. Sir John Bagot Glubb (locally known as Glubb Pasha). Kuwait, Aden, and several Persian Gulf emirates were British protectorates. Most important, Britain had two major airfields in Iraq, along with the support of a thoroughly corrupt but generally pro-Western government headed by that perennial survivor Nuri al-Saʿid, whose political career had begun in the Arab Revolt in World War I forty years earlier.

Iraq's generally pro-British stance was crucial for many reasons— oil resources, location, and so on—but particularly because between the two world wars Iraq's leaders and intellectuals had portrayed themselves as the appointed spokesmen for the Arab Nationalist movement. During those two decades Egypt's writers and politicians had played no real role in that movement, and when Egypt emerged as the most important Arab state after World War II many Iraqis regarded her as usurping their role. Within the Arab world, then, there was an underlying tension between Iraq and Egypt in any case. This was exacerbated in the early 1950s as Nasser and Nuri each tried to assert his leadership within the Arab world. Their opposing views on this matter, and their search for external allies, would inevitably drag them into the international rivalries of the cold war.

Like many leaders of the newly independent states, Nasser did not want to get caught in the U.S.-Soviet rivalry, and thus by 1955 he was increasingly identifying himself with the neutralist bloc led by Nehru of India, Sukarno of Indonesia, and Tito of Yugoslavia. To Nasser, this approach seemed to offer the fewest entanglements in superpower tensions, along with the least likelihood of foreign domination. In his personal political experience, of course, the greatest threat of entanglement came from Britain and the United States. The Soviet Union, in contrast, was just beginning to play a significant part in the Middle East, and then only in the northern fringes—Turkey, Kurdistan, northern Iran. Nasser was willing, or at least he said he was willing, to develop positive relations with the Western powers, but he would abide no conditions; Egypt had to be treated as a sovereign country, not as a client. At the same time, Nasser bitterly opposed any attempt by other Arab states to line up with the West, since this would undercut his own position.

Nuri al-Saʿid, in contrast, took a darker view of Soviet intentions. For one thing, the Soviets periodically supported Kurdish independence movements in northeastern Iraq. He did not find British attentions suffocating. With British encouragement, Iraq and Turkey entered into negotiations for a regional mutual security pact. The new pact was ostensibly aimed at the Soviet Union, but its implications for Nasser were clear enough. Agreement was reached in

February 1955 and the Baghdad Pact was born. Britain signed on in April, Iran and Pakistan in the autumn. The Baghdad Pact created a solid Northern Tier of Middle Eastern and Islamic countries along the Soviet border. It thus implicated the Middle East in the U.S.-Soviet rivalry, wherever that might lead. Just as bad, it threatened to put Nasser's Egypt in dangerous isolation: Nuri was a rival for Arab leadership, Iraq and Iran were conservative monarchies, Turkey was a member of NATO, and British membership gave the whole thing a sinister cast.

The American role in all this was fairly cautious. Dulles and Dwight D. Eisenhower were of course deeply concerned about the threat of "International Communism," and Dulles in particular was perpetually trying to enlist the newly independent states of Asia in one anti-Soviet alliance or another. However, neither the president nor the secretary of state ever thought that the Baghdad Pact was a good idea, if only because it was sure to alienate Egypt. On balance, the United States preferred to cultivate direct relations with Egypt's revolutionary regime, in the hope of bringing Egypt into a mutual security system.

Although the United States was represented in Egypt by three capable and sympathetic ambassadors, the kind of relationship the United States wanted proved extremely difficult to build. One problem, of course, is that Egypt would abide no entangling alliances with the West. The second problem was Egypt's continuing state of war with Israel. The Eisenhower administration was convinced that there was no way to link Middle Eastern governments into a broader mutual security system until the Arab-Israeli conflict was resolved. It thus devoted enormous diplomatic efforts to this problem throughout 1955 and early 1956. Some of these efforts were public, but the critical negotiations were strictly secret. These were the so-called Project Alpha, a series of proposals submitted alternately to Egypt and then to Israel, designed to discover whether there was any basis for a comprehensive peace between the two countries. Nasser professed interest but would never make any definitive commitments, nor would he exercise any public leadership on the search for peace. He was afraid, he stated, of being blindsided by Israeli recalcitrance. On the other side, Israel did ultimately yield on a few points, but not enough to compel Nasser to negotiate seriously.

The ultimate failure of Project Alpha had critical consequences. Nasser wanted to build a more effective Egyptian army, and to do this he needed modern weapons—tanks, artillery, and planes as well as rifles and helmets. He was not asking for grants; he would pay hard cash. Britain and the United States were willing to sell such arms, but only if there was substantial progress on a peace with Israel and only if Egypt expressed interest in a mutual security arrangement. No one knows how long this dance might have gone on, but it was brought to an abrupt end on February 28, 1955, when Israeli forces staged a massive surprise raid on an Egyptian command post in Gaza. Thirty-eight Egyptian soldiers were killed, along with nine Israelis. The Gaza raid was certainly not unprovoked, but it was far out of proportion to the Palestinian commando raid on a water-pumping station that had triggered it. Over the previous year Nasser had made some efforts to clamp down on such raids, but the Gaza raid ended that policy. Faced with riots and demonstrations by the Gaza Strip refugees, Egyptian officers were soon equipping and training Palestinian commando forces. The incident also made Nasser's calls for U.S. and British arms far more urgent; he could not risk another such humiliation.

Britain and the United States dithered and stalled to buy time, but Nasser was no longer willing to wait. In the spring of 1955, he undertook highly secret negotiations with the Soviet Union. Inevitably hints of what was going on leaked out, but there was no clear confirmation until September 1955, when Nasser made a formal announcement of a major arms pact. The Soviet Union, using Czechoslovakia as the nominal supplier, would provide a generous package of heavy arms that would (in theory) make Egypt more than a match for Israel. The arms would be paid for in cotton, a commodity that Egypt then held in surplus, so they would be no burden on Egypt's scarce foreign exchange. Desperate but belated U.S. and British efforts to match the Soviet offer were of no avail.

Egyptian ideas about the significance of the Soviet arms package were quite different from those of Israel, the United States, or Britain. In British and American eyes, Nasser was on the verge of becoming a Soviet puppet. Some senior officials thought that in one way or another he would have to be replaced. The strategic implications of the deal were very troubling; Dulles commented privately, "We did not all work so hard to get a Suez base agreement in order to turn the base over to the Soviets." Harold Macmillan, then British foreign secretary, stated, "The world will not allow the USSR to become the guardian of the Suez Canal."[3] There were further rumors (with some substance) that the Soviet Union had offered to finance the Aswan Dam.

It was in the context of Nasser's "betrayal," ironically, that Prime Minister Eden contrived the idea that Britain and the United States should help build the Aswan Dam; he quickly persuaded Dulles to go along. The hope was that Nasser might be prevented from joining the Soviet camp outright—and if he could not be and had to be removed, at least some goodwill with the Egyptian people might be earned. A viable offer took time to assemble, but by December 1955 a package was ready to lay before Nasser.

Israel's response to the Soviet arms deal was more direct. For Israel, and especially Prime Minister David Ben-Gurion, it posed a deadly threat that had to be stifled as soon as possible. Few Israelis ever believed that Nasser was serious about peace, and the arms deal confirmed their suspicions. By the end of October 1955, the Israeli General Staff had been ordered to prepare a plan to occupy the Sinai Peninsula. International conditions did not permit Ben-Gurion to act immediately, but he was willing to bide his time until an appropriate opportunity came along.

In Egypt, the arms package looked like the dawning of a new day. For the first time the Western monopoly on arms sales to the Arab countries had been broken. That monopoly had always been exercised in such a way as to rub in Arab dependency and inferiority. Soviet arms, however, came with no strings attached. There was no requirement to join a Soviet-sponsored security pact, and no restriction on the deployment and use of the arms.

Altogether, then, the Middle East situation in mid-July 1956 was tightly strung. None of the principal players (Egypt, Iraq, Israel, Great Britain, the United States, and the USSR) could guess the real intentions of any other, nor was anyone inclined to think that these intentions were benign. Nasser found himself deeply enmeshed in U.S.-Soviet rivalries in spite of his often-stated intention to avoid that at any cost. Two years of intensive negotiations had left Egypt and Israel on the verge of war. The United States and Britain were frustrated with Nasser's constant backing and filling on issues of deep concern to them, and they were also acutely anxious about the new Soviet initiatives in the region, however modest they had been to this point. In this context Dulles made his decision to withdraw American support for the Aswan Dam. It was in the same context that Nasser had to decide what Egypt's policy was to be.

On hearing that Dulles had withdrawn American support for the high dam, Nasser exploded. Egypt, he said, would build the dam itself, even if it had to be done with shovels and fingernails. But then he had to consider his options in concrete terms. The problem was, as always, hard currency. Egypt's foreign-exchange income from cotton sales abroad was barely enough to offset the importation of essential goods; there was no surplus for the vast amounts required by the Aswan project. To get the money he needed, he had three obvious choices: (1) to try to rebuild a working relationship with the United States and Britain; (2) to pursue the Soviet connection, since they had already indicated some interest in assisting with the high dam; and (3) to identify some other *internal* source of hard currency.

Apart from cotton, the only big foreign-exchange earner in Egypt was the Suez Canal. The canal was owned by a private corporation that behaved like a sovereign entity; it was on Egyptian soil, but the Egyptian government derived little financial benefit from it. In 1955, the Suez Canal had earned gross revenues of $103 million, with a net income of $32 million. Indeed, the rapid growth of oil shipments through the canal promised far higher revenues. In 1955, oil shipments from the Persian Gulf producers totaled 67 million tons, two-thirds of the total traffic through the canal. By 1968, it was predicted, oil shipments would reach 250 million tons. But as things stood this growth would be of modest benefit to Egypt, since the great bulk of profits were repatriated to company shareholders in Europe. The British government, for example, received about $8 million per year on its shares during the early 1950s—shares it had purchased from the bankrupt Egyptian government in 1875.

For some time the notion that Egypt might nationalize the Suez Canal had been floating about in a vague way in politically engaged circles, but since the canal would revert to Egypt anyhow in twelve years (1968), most regarded such a step as mere bravado and needlessly provocative. But under the new circumstances, it might make sense to look at nationalization again. After all, the current and predicted earnings from the canal could liberate Egypt from the need for burdensome and dangerous foreign loans. And on the symbolic level, to nationalize the canal would complete the work begun by the Anglo-Egyptian Agreement of October 1954; Egypt would again enjoy real sovereignty over all her territory and all her resources. For Nasser, the benefits of nationalization were clear. What were the risks?

On the evening of July 20, we are told, Nasser sketched the possible consequences of nationalizing the canal.[4] In particular, he had to guess the likely reactions of four outside actors: Great Britain, the United States, Israel, and the Soviet Union.

As to Great Britain, Nasser expected a violent reaction from Prime Minister Eden, who would surely try to organize some military action to "recover" the canal. Britain after all depended very heavily on the canal for its oil supplies from the Persian Gulf; it could not permit an "unpredictable dictator" like him to have a stranglehold on this absolutely vital resource. Likewise, nationalization could compromise Britain's communications with its possessions and military bases east of Suez. The British government's 45 percent share of Suez Canal Company stock represented a major financial interest, although that could be offset by the projected dissolution of the concession in twelve years and Egyptian compensation to the shareholders. Most important, perhaps, would be the blow to British prestige—the idea that Great Britain would no longer be the guardian of the great highway between Europe and the Indian Ocean.

If Britain decided on military action, what resources did it have, and how long did it have to act? On the latter point, Nasser estimated that the likelihood of a British-led attack would decrease with time: it would be high at the beginning of August but wither away by the end of September. With time, inertia would set in, voices of caution would be heard, the irreversibility of a fait accompli would become clear to all. As to the short term, when an attack seemed most likely, it was clear that Britain did not have enough men and materiel in Malta and Cyprus to do the job. A buildup there would take months, by which time such action would be politically almost impossible.

If an attack did come, it would probably be directed against the Canal Zone; this was the place to concentrate Egypt's defense forces. Any campaign against Alexandria and Cairo would require far more money, men, and time than Britain could spare.

Britain would need allies. France was a likely possibility, since the French believed that Nasser was actively supporting the Algerian revolt. The United States would certainly object to the nationalization and work to reverse it. Militarily, however, they would not take an active role, though they would probably give financial and political support to Britain and France.

Israel was of course openly hostile to Nasser, and there had been many clashes between Egyptian and Israeli troops in Gaza and other places. Israel might seek to join forces with Britain and France to get rid of their mutual nemesis. However, it was certain that Eden would block this. Britain had valuable assets and a privileged position in Iraq, Kuwait, and the Gulf emirates. Any collusion with Israel would wreck all that, and Eden would never make such a blunder. Nasser therefore felt free to strip Egyptian defenses in Sinai to protect the canal against a possible Franco-British attack.

To see the nationalization through, Egypt would need diplomatic support. Nasser felt he could count on his mentors Nehru in India and Sukarno in Indonesia. The UN General Assembly would as a whole be favorable. But all this was just moral support.

The attitude of the Soviet Union would be critical, since it was the only power capable of checking the United States. As shown above, Egyptian-Soviet relations were progressing quite well, and the Soviets would certainly like to see a blow dealt to Britain's position in the Middle East. But the relationship was new and untested, and the Soviets were notoriously cautious about such grand theatrical gestures. Moreover, tensions in the Soviet client states of Eastern and Central Europe were very high, and the Soviet government would have to focus most of its attention on these. Best not to tell them, Nasser believed, and to hope they would fall into line later on. Of course, the very possibility of Soviet intervention might be enough to hold Britain and France back. Altogether, the Soviet role was a big IF.

Nasser could sum up his analysis as follows. He would certainly face shock and outrage, but these could be minimized by fair compensation to the Suez Canal Company and by announcing strict adherence to international treaty obligations regarding passage through the canal. As to diplomatic pressure, he could stand up to that. Finally, military action by Britain and France was a possibility, but it seemed extremely unlikely that they could really bring it off. With all this in mind, he decided to go ahead. He would announce his decision in Alexandria on July 26, in a speech commemorating the fourth anniversary of King Farouk's abdication.

If we are correctly informed about Nasser's calculations, they represented a cool, perceptive reading of the international arena. He acted quickly, but he did not shoot from the hip. Still, even the best poker players are wrong most of the time, and obviously things did not turn out as Nasser planned. After months of diplomatic comings and goings, marked by proposals by the United States that had had no prospect of being accepted by either party, Britain and France did enter into a secret alliance with Israel to occupy the Canal Zone and bring down Nasser. The joint military operations at the end of October were brilliantly successful, but they led to diplomatic disaster for Britain and (to a lesser degree) France. The United States had not been consulted about all this, and Eisenhower publicly demanded a cease-fire and the prompt withdrawal of foreign forces from the Canal Zone. In the end, a UN-supervised armistice between Egypt and Israel was patched together, though of course it only put off a full-scale military confrontation until another day. France and Britain withdrew, having lost the last vestiges of their influence in the eastern Arab world. And by February 1957 Nasser found himself in uncontested possession and control of the Suez Canal after all, albeit not in the way he had planned. He also found himself the hero of the entire Arab world, a man whose every word could stir the Arab masses and terrify their leaders. That fact created new challenges for Nasser; he exploited these brilliantly in the short run, though in the end he could not maintain momentum. But at least for the short term, his nationalization of the Suez Canal can only be considered a triumph of daring but utterly rational policy making—rational in the motives that propelled it, in the goals it was intended to achieve, and in its estimate of the obstacles to be overcome.

The Ayatollah and the President: The U.S. Embassy Hostage Crisis (November 1979–January 1981)

No Middle East event in this century has so deeply scarred America's political memory, or left such lasting emotions of humiliation and rage, as the hostage crisis that erupted in November 1979 and dragged on until the inauguration of President Ronald Reagan on January 20, 1981—444 days altogether.[5] Everything tumbled together: the shock of the initial takeover of the U.S. Embassy in Tehran by chanting students; the cat-and-mouse game played with American negotiators for months on end by cunning and unprincipled Iranian politicians; the embarrassing inability of the United States to cut the Gordian knot through direct action. During the crisis, Iranians and (more especially) Shi'ite Muslims were demonized as the inveterate enemies of American values and the American way of life, and so they remain; in American politics, "Shi'ite Muslim" is still a synonym for "fanatic." And in the American political imagination, the Ayatollah Khomeini has been linked to the twentieth century's darkest villains—Hitler, Stalin, Pol Pot. Even the name Saddam Hussein cannot boast the same resonance.

As it happens, Khomeini did not instigate the seizure of the embassy, nor did he have much direct involvement in the agonizing negotiations that eventually freed the fifty-six hostages. But once the crisis was upon him he exploited it masterfully to achieve ends that were very much his own. In a sense, his role was a triumph of skillful opportunism, not of long-term design.

Khomeini's goals seem clear enough, at least in retrospect. First and foremost, he wanted to secure the *Islamic* character of the revolution. In view of the chaos in Iran after the fall of the Shah and the number of would-be leaders of every stripe who were contending for preeminence, that was far from a sure thing. An Islamic revolution required an effective monopoly of political power for the Shi'ite clergy—or at least that segment of the clergy which was unquestionably loyal to him and his vision of a new Islamic order. It likewise required the eradication of all Western influence in the country, both to ensure the purity of an Islamic society and to block any possible influence by Western-oriented political elites.

In Khomeini's mind, a victory for the clergy and the elimination of Western influence could only be ensured if he made himself the focal point of the political process. There were many prominent men of religion, and some of them had shown themselves to be tough, skillful political operatives. But none had Khomeini's unique prestige as an implacable opponent of the old order, none could draw on the devotion that Iran's urban masses lavished on him. The problem was to convert this prestige and devotion into real political power.

He could not expect to control events by playing the role of a revered but distant symbol. At the same time, he could not take all the strings into his own hands and did not desire to do so. He was too old and had too little administrative experience to bring that off successfully. Even more important, he could not afford to tarnish his immaculate image by the inevitable compromises and failures of everyday politics. By the fall of 1979, nine months after his triumphant return to Tehran, it was not at all clear that he could do what needed to be done. In spite of Khomeini's immense prestige, he was not in any sense the dictator of Iran, for he controlled no machinery for enforcing his will on the country.

Nor at this point did Iran have a working political system that Khomeini could manipulate to achieve his goals. It was true that a new constitution had been drafted in the spring of 1979 and was now before the voters for their approval. This constitution ensured him a paramount role in charting the future course of the country in exactly the manner best suited to his talents and standing; it placed him above the sordid everyday political battles but empowered him to intervene at the times and places of his choosing, on just those issues that he regarded as crucial. Approval of the draft constitution was an absolute certainty, but in itself it would hardly restore political order in the country. As matters stood in the summer and autumn of 1979, the central government's control over policy making and even routine administration was almost nonexistent. The armed services and state bureaucracy, discredited by their close identification with "the criminal ex-Shah," were demoralized and leaderless. Neighborhoods and localities were largely run by self-created and uncoordinated revolutionary *komitehs*, each with its own agenda and its own list of enemies to be purged. The level of political violence was extraordinary and would remain so until 1982. Khomeini's power to intervene in or manipulate government policy required first of all an effective government.

Restoring political order was one thing; ensuring that it was the right order was quite another. The revolution had been brought about by a momentary coalition of religious militants, secular democrats, and leftists in the fall of 1978, and this coalition was rapidly coming unglued. In the current free-for-all, Khomeini sought the victory of a faction that would be loyal to his own very specific vision of an Islamic republic. During his long years of exile (1964–1979), Khomeini had elaborated a concept of government that he portrayed as a return to the original principles of Islam but that in fact represented a radical innovation in Islamic political thought. This was the famous *vilayat-e faqih*, "authority of the jurist." Essentially, Khomeini held that the powers of government should be invested solely in the scholars of religious law (the *faqihs*), because they alone understood the commandments laid down by God and his Prophet. Hence they alone were qualified to establish and implement these commandments in society. That religious scholars should advise rulers, and even hold certain offices (judgeships in particular, but other administrative posts as well), was a very old idea and practice in Islamic history. But in their traditional role as judges and officials, scholars worked for and under the rulers. As advisers, they were independent and could sometimes be brutally frank with near-impunity—but of course they were only giving advice, not governing. Khomeini argued that religious scholars should rule, pure and simple.

This vision was the official ideology undergirding the largest and best-organized party, the clergy-dominated Islamic Republican Party (IRP), which had been founded and led by the heretofore obscure Ayatollah Beheshti. Beheshti proved a brilliant political strategist, but the IRP had to face severe competition in the struggle for power. On the left there was the communist Tudeh Party and an armed guerrilla movement, the Mujahidin-e Khalq; the Marxist left had had a powerful appeal to university students and young professionals in the fifties and sixties, and the Shah had always regarded it as his deadliest enemy. In the center the secular-nationalist National Front maintained its devotion to democratic parliamentary government under the 1906 Constitution; it was a shadow of what it had been in Mossadegh's day, but it still possessed the magic of his name. Among religious militants on the right who regarded the IRP as dangerously lax, there were a host of factions. In the midst of the chaos the provisional government struggled to guide the country's political evolution in accordance with its own lights. It was led by a highly esteemed layman, Mahdi Bazargan, who was both a nationalist with close ties to Mohammed Mossadegh's movement and a longtime disciple of Khomeini. But in spite of his strong religious and nationalist credentials, Bazargan was very much a pragmatist. Hoping to devise an effective political consensus, he struggled to keep as much of the revolutionary coalition together as possible; he also believed that the new Iran could only achieve security and prosperity by keeping open its lines of communication with the outside world, even with the United States. Khomeini saw clearly that if Bazargan stayed in power, his own vision would surely have to make some room for competing visions of what an Islamic regime should be. And in Khomeini's eyes, some of these competing visions were not Islamic in any true sense of the word.

Finally, there was the delicate issue of Western influence. This went far beyond the fear that the United States, the sinister force that had masterminded the overthrow of Mossadegh in 1953 and had been the Shah's strongest supporter ever since, would revert to its old tricks. Rather, it was an intense resentment at the whole range of American and Western influence in the country. In the eyes of Khomeini and many others, the entire body of American culture was an assault on everything that was authentically Iranian and Islamic. More insidious than the CIA were the manners and values of the Western-educated social and economic elite spawned by the Shah— thousands of men (and many women) educated in Europe or the United States and now infecting the whole country with their licentious morals. It was absolutely clear that an authentic Islamic state and society could not be erected on a foundation of consumerism and sexual license. Mecca and Hollywood could not coexist. The only way to rid Iran of the plague of Westernism was to purge the political system of those who had been infected by it. In effect, the Western-educated laity, even those who seemed sincerely committed to an Islamic vision, would have to go. Or at least they would have to surrender all real power to the clergy and content themselves with the role of technical advisers and subaltern officials—an ironic reversal of the centuries-old relationship between regime and religion in Iran.

We cannot know just how Khomeini planned (if in fact he did plan) to address the political challenges that lay before him. But the unexpected seizure of the U.S. Embassy by students "following the line of Imam Khomeini" in November 1979 gave him an opening. At first he played for time to see how things would develop, neither sanctioning nor condemning the takeover. The government of Prime Minister Bazargan could not persuade the students to evacuate the embassy and release the hostages. When it received no support from Khomeini (Bazargan's old spiritual mentor), it was forced to resign in humiliation. Only at this point did Khomeini lend his public blessing to the enterprise. In so doing, he subjected Iran's politicians to a rigorous litmus test. Henceforth they could only work to resolve the crisis on lines that Khomeini approved, and that meant that they had to submit to his sometimes erratic supervision.

Khomeini never gave Iran's negotiators any clear guidelines as to what conditions they should demand, what compromises they could accept. He kept them guessing, and only after they had committed themselves to one plan or another did he intervene, almost always to subvert whatever initiatives they had taken. This approach left U.S. negotiators angry and frustrated, but of course they could do nothing without endangering the hostages. It made excellent sense within the Iranian political milieu, however, for Khomeini did not need a solution to the crisis. As far as he was concerned, the longer it went on the better, since the situation gave him maximum leverage to work Iran's political system to his own advantage. *ahh...*

In effect, the hostage crisis, and Khomeini's skill in using it, undercut the authority and legitimacy of Iran's senior officials (most of them still laymen at this point) by demonstrating their fecklessness and incompetence. In contrast, it allowed their opponents (mostly clergy) the luxury of an uncompromising hard-line stand. In the end, Khomeini brought down the last government headed by a layman (President Abu'l-Hasan Bani Sadr) and ensured that the clergy would control Iranian politics for the balance of the decade. In so doing, he ensured that his own vision of an Islamic state would remain the sole vision permitted to operate within Iran's political discourse. Likewise, he closed all channels for the infiltration of Westernist ideas and sympathies. Once the revolution was complete, of course, Khomeini could permit the hostage crisis to wind down. By the fall of 1980, the impossibility of ignoring or sidestepping his authority was manifest to every Iranian politician. Khomeini would face no further political challenge for the rest of his life.

Complete victory in the struggle for the soul of Iran was by this point not the only incentive to end the crisis, to be sure. The tensions between Iran and Iraq had now boiled over into open fighting. Though no one could have guessed how long the war would go on or how bloody it would be, it was clear that Iran had to refocus its energies on a new enemy, this one more than a symbolic threat to the future of the Islamic Republic. It is arguable that Khomeini's manipulation of the hostage crisis backfired in the international arena, for American hostility left Iran hopelessly isolated in its deadly struggle against Iraq. Indeed, America's support for Saddam Hussein in that war, however fitful and hesitant, almost certainly ensured the stalemate that brought it to an end. Khomeini might well have concurred with this judgment; he might also have said that it was well worth it to win the greater victory within Iran itself.

Saddam Hussein's Decision to Occupy Kuwait
(July–August 1990)

On January 15, 1991, Saddam Hussein found himself confronting a large and superbly equipped expeditionary force, made up of contingents from three Western powers (the United States, France, and Britain), and a combined force of several Arab states under Saudi command.[6] He was diplomatically hopelessly isolated, condemned by the United Nations, with his old ally the Soviet Union (now in the late stages of decay) standing helplessly on the sidelines. It is true that he had recently rediscovered the power of prayer, and perhaps he yet hoped for a miracle. But in this case God was on the side of the big battalions; Iraq's cities and military installations were exposed to a relentless and almost unopposed bombardment, and her ground forces dissolved within hours before a crushing ground offensive at the end of February. Only a decision by the allies to stop the carnage prevented their forces from occupying Basra and advancing to the gates of Baghdad. It must be admitted that Saddam Hussein has proved extraordinarily resourceful in the face of devastating military defeat, and over the past seven years he has wrested—at enormous cost to the Iraqi people—at least a diplomatic stalemate with his opponents. But that is another and very different story; here we are only concerned with the seven months leading up to and encompassing the Gulf War.

Why did Saddam Hussein want to seize Kuwait in the first place? And how did he suppose that he could prevail over the massed forces of the United States and its European and Arab allies? Could it be that he was just colossally stupid (and, it follows, that the allies were just lucky)? I would argue the contrary: Saddam Hussein had strong reasons to want Kuwait; he likewise had every reason to think that he held a pretty good hand in the Kuwait affair and that he was playing it cleverly.

His positive reasons for annexing Kuwait are straightforward and need not detain us long. First, he owed an enormous war debt to Kuwait, some $30 billion, incurred during the previous decade's struggle with Iran, and the Kuwaitis were insisting that it be repaid. For Iraq, almost bankrupt and suffering severe war damage, that was a near-impossibility. Apart from the fact that ridding oneself of debt by murdering an importunate creditor is an ancient and widely attested practice, Saddam Hussein could accuse the Kuwaitis of rank ingratitude. Only Iraq's heroic sacrifice had saved them from the imminent threat of Iranian domination.

Saddam Hussein's grievances against Kuwaiti greed were no doubt intensified by Kuwait's immense oil reserves, which were equal to those of Iraq. Taken together, Iraq and Kuwait sat on top of some 20 percent of the world's known oil—nearly equal to the staggering 25 percent held by Saudi Arabia. To occupy Kuwait would not only solve Saddam's war debt problem; it would give him the resources to rebuild his country's exhausted army and devastated economy. Indeed, Kuwaiti oil could underwrite his very bold ambitions for the Gulf region and the Middle East. Iraq would inevitably become the paramount power in the Persian Gulf, and indeed a superpower within the Middle East as a whole.

On a deeper and morally more compelling level, Saddam Hussein believed that Kuwait had no right to exist in the first place. He believed that Kuwait was historically an integral part of Iraq, and had only come into being through the machinations of British imperialism at the end of the nineteenth century. Saddam was not alone in this belief; it was an article of faith for every politically articulate Iraqi, and had been for at least half a century. Like many devoutly held national myths throughout the world, this belief was ill supported by the evidence. Nevertheless, it was a part of every Iraqi's ideological baggage. To occupy Kuwait was simply to rectify a long-standing historical wrong. Such a step would thus recoup the political as well as the economic and human losses of the war with Iran.

If we grant Saddam Hussein's case for seizing Kuwait, what about the obstacles this bold initiative would face? He had very good reasons to be confident about the outcome. First, there was his own experience of U.S. policy in the Middle East over the past fifteen years. Second, almost every serious Middle East expert, political commentator, and military critic in the United States supported his judgment. When Saddam's armies seized Kuwait on August 2, 1990, he could have had a reasonable expectation that there would be no effective opposition. It must be admitted that we possess almost no reliable firsthand information on Saddam Hussein's evaluation of the situation that he had created. However, I suspect that any well-informed politician would have thought along the following lines as he contemplated the risks and rewards of seizing Kuwait.

(1) The United States would surely not go beyond pro forma verbal protests and dispatching a couple of frigates to the Persian Gulf. To begin with, whatever Ambassador April Glaspie did or did not say in her interview with Saddam Hussein on July 25, it was perfectly clear that the United States had invested too much in building good relations with Iraq over the preceding decade to sacrifice them for Kuwait. Iraq, after all, was now a valuable trading partner, a bloodied but victorious opponent of Iran's revolutionary Shi'ism, and a potentially crucial element in the search for an Arab-Israeli settlement. Kuwait was just another oil patch. Such general considerations would have been fully supported by the record of U.S. action in the Middle East for the previous fifteen years—essentially, since the fall of Richard Nixon and the communist victory in Vietnam. The United States had done nothing to save its closest regional ally, the Shah of Iran, in 1978–1979, even though he was the linchpin of the whole Gulf and Northern Tier security system, which had been painfully constructed and meticulously maintained since the early 1950s. Likewise, the United States had placed a small Marine peacekeeping force in Beirut in 1983 to support the fragile Lebanese government created in the aftermath of the Israeli invasion of 1982; this force represented a minor commitment of material resources but a considerable investment of prestige, yet the Americans scuttled and ran after a single terrorist attack. Finally, there was the whole Irangate imbroglio, which demonstrated among other things that American policy could almost be paralyzed by the fate of a few hostages. Jimmy Carter had spoken softly, Reagan had talked tough, but from

1976 to 1990 American policy had stayed the same—tentative, hesitant, and irresolute. It could only have inspired total contempt in a man like Saddam Hussein.

(2) If, contrary to Saddam's expectations, the United States did try to put real pressure on him, it could not possibly hope to succeed. Economic sanctions were the likeliest course of action, but these would require the assembling of a vast international coalition, possessing unprecedented cohesion and unity of purpose. In view of the sharply disparate interests of the United States, Europe, Japan, and the Soviet Union, even an oil boycott (to take only the most obvious step) could not possibly hold.

If a military response was contemplated, a major network of bases and logistical support within the region would be required. But since the mid-1950s, the powerful surge of Arab Nationalism had made it abundantly clear that such bases and communications would not be available to the Western powers—and the Soviet Union had learned a similar lesson in the early 1970s when its access to Egypt was abruptly terminated. The Iranian debacle of 1978–1980 represented the final confirmation of this process. If the United States could not work through local surrogates (the sort of policeman's role that the Nixon Doctrine had contemplated for Iran), it could surely not act at all. Among U.S. allies in the region, only Israel, Turkey, and Egypt were militarily comparable to Iraq in any way, and none of these powers could possibly threaten Iraq's position in Kuwait or the Persian Gulf. In short, bitter Arab memories of Western imperialism, and a deeply ingrained suspicion of foreign intervention, would keep the United States out of the picture.

(3) Suppose that Saddam Hussein's calculations, as we have imagined them above, were all wrong—and that possibility is of course one that every strategist must always entertain. Suppose George Bush did nail together a strong, durable coalition, able to support tough economic sanctions and willing to take military action; suppose he did obtain effective diplomatic, military, and logistical support within the region. Could the United States really project adequate force into the Persian Gulf to eject Iraqi forces from Kuwait? Saddam must have known, from watching "Sixty Minutes" if nothing else, that the United States had a hollow army—untried volunteer forces, a demoralized officer corps still humiliated by Vietnam, and a mountain

of high-tech gadgets that cost tens of billions of dollars to manufacture and did not work. Under such circumstances Saddam Hussein would have been a fool *not* to invade Kuwait.

To explore this point in greater detail, let us move forward, from August 1990 to early December of the same year. By now the situation had altered greatly, and not to Saddam Hussein's advantage. President Bush had in fact shaped a coalition of NATO states plus a few major Arab members. Working through the United Nations to gain maximum international legitimacy for his position, he had imposed stringent economic sanctions, which were proving surprisingly effective, at least for the short term. Moreover, substantial and rapidly growing military forces had been placed in Saudi Arabia, though no one knew how much they could actually achieve. Now Saddam Hussein had to confront the real likelihood that war would break out. What would happen if the coalition armies proved capable and the high-tech gadgets actually worked?

Fortunately, Saddam still had an ace in the hole, perhaps several aces. He had a very large, battle-experienced army, which had amply demonstrated during the preceding decade that it could fight long and hard, at least on the defensive. Saddam thus had good hopes of being able to force the U.S.-led coalition into a long, bloody, indecisive war. And with the time that such a struggle would purchase for him, he could expect a dramatic turnaround in the political situation.

First, he knew that a massive peace movement would bloom overnight in the United States and Western Europe—indeed, it had already put forth vigorous shoots. (Surely everyone remembers the deathless slogan, "No Blood for Oil!") As soon as the Persian Gulf looked like another Vietnam, domestic opposition would snowball. Weak democratic governments, Saddam knew, simply could not absorb high casualties for any length of time.

Second, a war would instantly ignite Arab Nationalist rage, Islamic solidarity, and the bitter resentment of poor peoples against the rich—not only the Americans but Kuwaitis and Saudis as well. It should be remembered that the coalition against Iraq combined old imperialist powers like France and Britain (still the bête noire of Arab intellectuals), a United States tainted by its close ties to Zionism, and corrupt, selfish oil-rich states like Saudi Arabia. The whole thing was custom designed to scratch every raw nerve in the Middle East and North Africa.

Naturally enough, Saddam Hussein did everything in his power to bring these issues to the fore. He made himself the chief spokesman for the sacred if now somewhat shopworn Palestinian cause. His propaganda machine purveyed lurid tales of moral corruption on the holy soil of Arabia and its holy places—for example, that five thousand Egyptian prostitutes had been sent to look after U.S. troops in forward bases. Indeed, he issued a formal call for jihad against the infidels. He pointed to the greed, extravagance, and arrogance of the oil-rich countries—an appeal nicely calculated to send Moroccan and Egyptian youth, who had no jobs and no prospects, into the streets. He wrapped himself in the glorious mantle of Gamal Abdel Nasser, the great Arab hero who would stand up to Imperialism, Zionism, and Reaction, even in the face of overwhelming force. And finally, when the war started, he could use (and did) his notorious SCUD missiles to drag Israel into the fighting, thereby demonstrating the real nature of the coalition against Iraq—namely, that the whole affair was nothing more than a war on behalf of Zionism.

Let me repeat once again that in all these calculations Saddam was no fool. Almost to a man and woman, every Middle East expert in the United States (and I must include myself in this unfortunate company) foresaw the same possibilities. All the best people agreed with Saddam, in short. So, we now have to ask a rather different question: Why didn't all these things happen after all? How could so many smart, well-informed people be so wrong? (One is reminded of Harry Truman's famous dictum, "An expert is someone who doesn't want to learn anything new, because then he wouldn't be an expert.")

One paradoxical answer is that Bush and his people took the experts' advice. Fully aware of what might happen, they decided to confront these problems by making the war as short and decisive as possible. If they could bring the fighting to a quick conclusion, they would cut the legs out from under domestic opposition to the war, and likewise keep Arab Nationalist and Islamist opposition from having time to crystallize. Happily for them, and to the astonishment of many observers, General Schwarzkopf and his troops proved equal to the task.

At least as important were two crucial failures by Saddam Hussein himself. One was his complete ineptitude as a military leader.

To win by losing, as Nasser had done at Suez in 1956, he had to put up a real fight. Heroism in a lost cause is only effective when there is some real heroism. Second, he did not perceive his own political liabilities as an Arab Nationalist or Muslim spokesman. For the Arab intelligentsia or the Arab masses to accept him in these roles, they had to forget a lot of things—his brutal suppression of the Shi'ite clergy in Iraq, for example, or the unhappy fact that he had created the crisis by annexing a sovereign Arab state. He had no credentials as a spokesman for the Islamic cause—quite the contrary. As to Arab Nationalism, he had played no substantial role in old struggles for the cause to which he could appeal, as Nasser in 1967 was able to recall his struggles over the previous twenty years.

In spite of these slips, Saddam's estimates (as we have reconstructed them here) proved very close to the mark. The Palestinians did respond to his call, and with enthusiasm; indeed, he won over not only the isolated and desperate PLO leadership but also the mass of Palestinians in Jordan and the Occupied Territories in Israel. By so doing, he compelled King Hussein of Jordan—normally a key U.S. ally in the region—to lend diplomatic and economic support to Iraq. In spite of King Hussein's immense political skill, including his willingness to subject his country to enormous economic deprivations as a sign of his commitment to Iraq, the situation in Jordan throughout the crisis and fighting was explosive. Likewise, the terrible socioeconomic stresses in North Africa sent huge crowds into the streets in Tunis and Casablanca, bearing the banners of Saddam Hussein. No doubt there was a bit of opportunism in all this; the protest leaders were likely using Saddam as a bogeyman to frighten their own governments. But the demonstrations might well have mushroomed into mass popular movements capable of toppling the Tunisian and Moroccan regimes had things continued much longer. In Egypt, finally, the signs of stress were growing daily. Had the fighting gone on two more weeks, had there been any significant loss of Egyptian lives, would the universities have exploded into massive riots? It is a very real possibility.

In the final analysis, what can we say about Saddam Hussein and his hypothetical exercise in risk analysis? This much at least: he may have been brutal, thuggish, arrogant, and unprincipled, but he was not crazy. Seizing Kuwait made very good geopolitical and economic sense. Apart from solving Saddam's immediate financial problems, Kuwait would have given Iraq unchallenged access to the Persian Gulf and provided it with the resources to dominate the whole region, and perhaps far beyond. Many leaders have gone to war for much less. Moreover, he must have known that he was incurring significant risks in seizing his neighbor, but Saddam Hussein was used to big risks. And as our analysis has tried to show, the risks here hardly seemed excessive. If Saddam's analysis had been borne out on a single point, he might well have carried the day in 1990–1991. Nor should we forget that he is still in power, still unchallenged within Iraq itself, still sitting on an enormous pool of oil, still waiting for a favorable change in the wind that will restore all his fortunes.

If our analyses of the conduct of three Middle Eastern leaders during three major crises are reasonably sound, the myth of the Middle East Madman can be safely laid to rest. Even in cases in which these leaders stunned the world (our corner of the world at least) with sudden and outrageous demands, they had well-defined, concrete goals, which they pursued with carefully calculated strategies. In pursuing their goals they have chosen ways of acting and rhetorical styles that speak to the cultural expectations and the political crises of their world. There is nothing odd or irrational about this; one need only contrast the campaign styles of a Brooklyn politician with another in rural Georgia. It is likewise true that they did not and do not choose the goals Americans expect them to. But these are goals that in a sense have been chosen for them; they are the residue of the history and diplomacy of the twentieth-century Middle East.

In analyzing the three cases above, we stumbled across some of that residue—Egyptian memories of British military occupation and the multiple humiliations brought about by the Suez Canal concession of 1856; Iranian resentments over shabby treatment by the Anglo-Iranian Oil Company, periodic foreign intrusions and manipulation, and the swamping of a distinctive national identity by alien cultures; Iraqi aspirations to "reunite" their country and revive a moribund Arab Nationalist vision. In a very direct way, nationalizing the Suez Canal, seizing the American Embassy, and occupying Kuwait were all a vindication of vividly remembered wrongs and a restoration of the rightful order of things. The Suez Canal, the U.S. Embassy in Tehran, the very existence of Kuwait—all were powerful symbols that embodied bitter memories and frustrated hopes. In attacking these symbols, Nasser, Khomeini, and Saddam Hussein were able to fire the enthusiasm of their peoples and sympathizers in a very powerful way. Moreover, their reckless daring was of the essence; prudent, step-by-step policies could never have engaged Egyptians, Iranians, and Iraqis in the struggle to redeem the past and claim the future.

At the same time, these bold initiatives obviously served the immediate political interests of the men who took them. The Suez confrontation regained a major economic resource for Egypt at a critical moment and confirmed Nasser's place as the uncontested leader of the nation. The American Embassy crisis consolidated the Islamic Revolution in Iran and reinforced Khomeini's place at the head of that revolution. Finally, a successful occupation of Kuwait would have doubled Iraq's petroleum reserves and made it incontestably the paramount power in the Persian Gulf, perhaps of the Arab world as a whole. In short, we should never assume that a leader is driven by the power of symbolism and historical memory, let alone by "irrational emotion." On the contrary, history and symbolism may suggest any number of possible goals, but it is the politician's art that decides which ones will actually be pursued and with what intensity.

CHAPTER 5

MILITARY DICTATORSHIP AND POLITICAL TRADITION IN THE MIDDLE EAST

Between 1949 and 1969, the three most populous and advanced countries in the eastern Arab world fell into the hands of military juntas, and in these power soon devolved on a single strongman. Syria was the first to go—temporarily between 1949 and 1954, then definitively in 1966. In 1952, the so-called Free Officers took control in Egypt, and though at first they governed as a collective body, within three years all effective power lay with Gamal Abdel Nasser. In 1958, an Iraqi faction also calling itself the Free Officers overthrew the monarchy there in a bloody coup; here the concentration of power was faster—within six months Abd al-Karim Qassem emerged as the strongman, though his position was never as secure as Nasser's in Egypt, and he was bloodily overthrown in 1963. Libya, of course, produced Muammar Qaddafi in 1969. Syria, Iraq, and Libya are all ruled today by the very men who had become the dominant political figures there in 1970, almost three decades ago. The government of Egypt has changed hands twice since 1954, but Sadat and Mubarak are products of the political system that Nasser created. Military government may well not be good government, but by the standards of the twentieth-century Middle East it is—sometimes, anyhow—stable government.[1]

In other countries of the region—Iran, Turkey, Algeria—the military has had a major political role since World War II, and indeed since World War I in Iran and Turkey. But only sporadically, in particular and temporary circumstances, has the army taken direct, front-stage control of the political system. These countries provide very interesting cases of the military in politics, but since they complicate things I will omit them in this chapter.

Military rule is nothing new in the Middle East. It first emerged in Islamic times during the late ninth century, and the last of the precolonial warlord states were only extinguished, or transmuted into

something more respectable, in the mid-twentieth century. It is therefore natural to wonder whether the rash of coups in the 1950s and
1960s was somehow linked to this millennium-long tradition.

If we are looking for a direct, causal linkage, we will not find it.
To understand military rule in the contemporary Middle East we
need to keep two things in mind.

(1) The region's postwar dictatorships are the natural and almost
inevitable outcome of the social and political processes of the twentieth century. These processes are sufficient in themselves, with no
reference to earlier Islamic times, to explain the emergence of some
form of military rule in the Middle East.

(2) The social origins of the postwar dictators are radically different from those of the precolonial warlords who dominated the region for so many centuries. Almost without exception, the latter were
foreigners in the lands they ruled—or at least their immediate ancestors were. They had been born elsewhere, spoke a different language from their subjects, and had distinct customs. In medieval Iran,
Egypt, and the Fertile Crescent, people commonly expressed the distinction as Turk and Tajik, or Turk and Baladi. The Turks, it was understood, were the military class who dominated the state as well
as the army. (Many of these so-called Turks were in fact not ethnic
Turks; they might be Circassians or Armenians or even Slavs, but
they had learned to speak Turkish and adopted Turkish manners and
dress.) In contrast, Tajiks and Baladis were the indigenous Persian
or Arabic-speaking townsmen. Insofar as they became members of
the state apparatus, they served as clerks and tax collectors or judges
and notaries.

Twentieth-century dictators, however, have emerged precisely
from among the native populations of their countries. They have
typically represented the lower middle classes—classes that had
been powerless and socially contemptible for centuries and that had
only begun to achieve political significance since World War I. In a
very real sense, the postwar dictatorships were and remain populist governments—which is possibly a damning thing to say about
populism.

Let us then begin with two questions. First, what circumstances
brought the modern military dictators to power? Second, how do
these circumstances compare with those that produced the warlords
of medieval and early modern times?

The military states of the Islamic Middle Ages began proliferating in the late ninth century as the universal caliphate fell into collapse. By "collapse" I do not mean the end of a particular dynasty but rather the failure of a whole political system. For two and a half centuries, the whole body of Muslims from Central Asia to Gibraltar had been members of a single empire, under a single ruler, who claimed to govern them as the direct heir of the Prophet. This political system was not only a widely shared ideal; it was substantially a reality. Once it failed, however, it could not be reconstructed. One military regime spun off another, and for six hundred years these warlord states formed, dissolved, and recoalesced in literally hundreds of evanescent polities.

In about 1500 the turbulence abated. There was a political consolidation in three very large, relatively stable, and remarkably durable states: the Safavids in Iran; the Mughals in India; and, most impressive of all, the Ottomans, who had first appeared in northwest Anatolia about 1300, and by the 1550s were lords of two-thirds of the Mediterranean Basin, southeastern Europe, and the Fertile Crescent. In spite of a rough passage in the late eighteenth and nineteenth century, the Ottoman Empire remained a viable—and territorially very large—state down to the end of World War I.

Within the Ottoman imperial framework, a number of new military regimes emerged after 1650. The chiefs of these were in principle Ottoman provincial governors; with few exceptions they were loyal to the Ottoman ideal, though as a practical matter they thumbed their noses at imperial rescripts from Constantinople. As its power was diffused and decentralized, the Ottoman Empire might seem to have been mimicking the classical caliphate, but it had far greater powers of recovery. By 1840, the regional warlords had either been suppressed by a resurgent Ottoman central government, or (as in the case of Egypt) they had become formally recognized autonomous rulers under imperial suzerainty. There is clearly no direct connection at all between the precolonial and the modern dictatorships, and they are in fact separated by more than a century.

How then do we account for military dictatorship in the twentieth century? Here I think four issues are crucial:

1. The collapse of the Ottoman state in World War I, after which its former territories were carved into the modern Turkish Republic

as well as several Arab successor states created and controlled by Great Britain and France. That is, the war brought about the abrupt end of a centuries-old political system that had been almost universally accepted as the legitimate framework of political action by the Muslim peoples of the Balkans, Anatolia, and the eastern Arab lands. When the Ottoman Empire was forcibly dismantled after 1918, there was nothing to replace it—or at least nothing that seemed intuitively right. The new governments of the region had to start all over again in the business of winning hearts and minds.

2. The failure of the new regimes in Egypt and the Fertile Crescent to win real legitimacy for themselves between their formation around 1920 and the years following World War II. The governments of these Ottoman successor states were in an unenviable position, to be sure. On the one hand, they had been created by the colonial powers (France and Great Britain), and were very much under their thumb. They were thus in no position to pursue policies that contradicted the regional goals and interests of those powers. At the same time, the new governments sought to reflect the popular will of their citizens, who wanted nothing more than to drive out the French and the British and all their works. Caught in such contradictions, they were inevitably perceived—both by the European powers and by their own citizens—as weak, ineffectual, and even clownish.

   Because these new countries had adopted constitutional and parliamentary institutions, the very system of government that we regard as most legitimate was seriously tainted in the eyes of many Middle Easterners. Even radical factions in these countries adhered to the constitutional-parliamentary ideal at least until the 1950s, but the governments and politicians actually in power were regarded with such contempt that the ideal itself ultimately seemed corrupt.

3. The rising social and economic tensions that first clearly emerged in the 1930s and intensified during the following two decades. The crisis of the 1930s and early 1940s was in certain respects simply a reflection of the Great Depression and the war. But it was exacerbated by purely internal factors—by rapidly rising populations facing a shortage of viable agricultural lands; by a

sharply increased incidence of rural-to-urban migration, which created a *Lumpenproletariat* of uprooted rural migrants dwelling in shantytowns and living by badly paid day labor; by exploding disparities of wealth and opportunity between a new landlord and export-merchant class that profited enormously from wartime and postwar shortages and the bulk of the population, consisting mostly of peasants but also of key urban groups such as industrial workers, retailers, clerks, and low-level bureaucrats.

The interwar and postwar governments were part of the problem, not the solution. In Egypt and Syria, they were dominated by civilian politicians who themselves either belonged to the landlord class and upper bourgeoisie or were at least securely in their pockets. Iraq was a somewhat different matter, but in the end it came to the same thing. As Middle Eastern populations became politically more mobilized in the face of these crises, existing systems of government lost all credibility. This was the case in spite of progress on the traditional nationalist agendas, for by 1945 the old regimes were obtaining not only formal independence from the colonial powers but also some real freedom of action in both the domestic and the foreign arenas.

4. The final blow was the catastrophic military and political performance of the newly independent Arab regimes in the first Arab-Israeli War in 1948. The bravado of May soon enough became the bitter humiliation of July. With these events, the end of the existing liberal-parliamentary—or pseudo-liberal-parliamentary—governments was a foregone conclusion.

Who then replaced them? The soldiers, of course—but who are they, and where do they come from? First of all, we need to recognize that they represent markedly disparate groups and interests in each country; Egypt is not Syria, Syria is not Iraq. This is the case even though every military regime seized power on the basis of the same pretext—that is, the corruption and weakness of the old civilian governments—and proclaimed the same program—that is, some form of nationalism, rapid economic development with social justice, and neutrality in the U.S.-Soviet confrontation. With this as a preface, we can look in turn at the social origins of the revolutionary military governments in Egypt, Iraq, and Syria.

In Egypt, the revolutionary officers emerged out of a complex class structure, which was partly (but not wholly) correlated with ethnicity. Down to 1950, the higher aristocracy in Egypt was not constituted of native, Arabic-speaking Egyptians. As had been the case for many centuries, the elite was made up of Turkish-speaking outsiders. In the nineteenth and twentieth centuries, these were the so-called Turco-Circassians—men who stemmed from the Ottoman military and bureaucratic class and continued to speak Turkish as their principal language. They had begun their careers in the Turkish-speaking lands of the Ottoman Empire (Anatolia and the Balkans) and then migrated to Egypt to seek their fortunes. The ruling dynasty in Egypt welcomed their presence, since it had been founded in 1805 by an Ottoman soldier of Albanian origins.

Down to the 1860s, the officer corps of the Egyptian army was drawn entirely from the Turco-Circassian aristocracy. At that point, officer rank was opened up to native Egyptians of some wealth and family, but they had only risen to middle rank by the time of the British Occupation in 1882. Since these Arab-Egyptian officers had been at the center of the nationalist agitation that had brought about the Occupation, the British excluded such a subversive element from the officer corps. Only in 1936, when the British Occupation was formally terminated, were Arab-Egyptians again admitted to the Military Academy.

In the first class were two men of note in later Egyptian politics: Gamal Abdel Nasser and Anwar Sadat. Their background reflects quite accurately the kind of men who were now seeking military careers: Nasser was the son of an Upper Egyptian postal clerk; Sadat came from a prosperous independent peasant family in the Delta. Both men were of respectable family, with strong rural or small-town roots. Like the other field-grade officers (majors and colonels) who emerged by 1950, they represented a second stratum, to borrow a phrase of Leonard Binder's. They were not the sociopolitical elite but the group whose hopes and ambitions were most directly frustrated by the existing system—by Turco-Circassian social and economic domination, a useless monarchy of foreign origin, and parliamentary politicians propelled only by greed and personal advantage.[2] This second stratum in Egyptian society constituted a rather broad middle class, made up of the better-off peasants (those with 20 to 50 acres of land), urban artisans and retailers, lower-grade professionals and bureaucrats. It was this group that had been the heart and soul of Egyptian nationalism since the turn of the century, and it had the most to gain from an assault on the established order.

Hence, when the so-called Free Officers seized power in July 1952, they were asserting not only political leadership but also the centrality of the political concerns of a social class—or better, a coalition of social groups—that had long been active and mobilized. Although Egyptian economic policy took a radical turn in the early 1960s, and then an equally marked conservative turn after Nasser's death in 1970, the social foundations of the regime have remained solid throughout. Doubtless that explains its remarkable stability, for Mubarak's political lineage goes back in a straight line to the Revolutionary Command Council (RCC) of 1952. The regime's social roots also help to explain its evolution over the past forty years. Nasser was undeniably a dictator, at least from late 1956 on. The current regime, in contrast, continues to be highly authoritarian, but state power rests in the hands of a fairly broadly based political elite, not of one man or even a party apparatus. In modern Egypt, military dictatorship in the strict sense seems to have been a relatively brief phase in its political life.

It is true, obviously, that nothing lasts forever. Since the mid-1970s, new groups have emerged with grievances and frustrations of their own. Moreover, many elements in the "republican-military coalition" have felt betrayed, not only materially but also in the arena of national values, by the very men who originally represented their perspective. No doubt this accounts for the country's powerful Islamic movement, at least to some degree. But whatever the discontents in contemporary Egypt, a clear alternative to the current regime, with a sufficiently broad base of social support to displace it, has yet to appear.

Iraq presents significant parallels to Egypt, in that the military-republican governments since 1958 have been rooted in the middle and lower middle class. But there are important differences as well. First, Iraq has a much stronger professional military tradition than does Egypt, reaching right back to the country's formation in 1921. In Iraq, the military was always hip-deep in politics throughout the constitutional monarchy, whereas the army in Egypt did not become strongly politicized until the Arab-Israeli War of 1948. Like-wise, though police repression is no stranger to Egypt, its military-republican governments have commanded a fairly wide base of pub-lic support. But such a broad-based political consensus has eluded Iraq. Since 1958 (except for a five-year respite in the mid-1960s) vio-lence and terror have been the essence of government in that country.

Finally, Iraq faces profound ethnic and religious cleavages; while these exist in Egypt, they are far less threatening to the political sys-tem. About 25 percent of Iraq's population are Kurds, who dominate the northeastern quadrant of the country. As everyone has now learned, they are not Arabs and do not wish to be. They are at best reluctant citizens of Iraq, and from 1921 to the present they have assiduously sought a maximum of political and cultural autonomy. This has repeatedly been promised and ignored—Saddam Hussein in this respect simply continues the unbroken policy of independent Iraq. He continues traditional policy in another domain as well. Al-though more than half of Iraqis belong to the Shi'ite branch of Is-lam, the Shi'ites have always been drastically underrepresented in Iraq's governments. Under the monarchy, under the military dicta-tors of the 1960s, and under the Baath, political power in Iraq has rested overwhelmingly with the 20 percent of its citizens who are both Sunni Muslims and Arabs.

The men who clustered around King Faysal in 1921 when he took up his new crown were for the most part former Ottoman military officers—men of Iraqi birth and ancestry who had trained at the Imperial Military Academy in Istanbul and served in the Ottoman army between 1890 and 1914. Several of them had remained loyal to the sultan even after the Arab Revolt broke out in 1916 and had only rallied to the Arab Nationalist cause after the war. By way of example (and there *are* many others), one of the most prominent Iraqi politicians of the interwar period was Hikmat Sulayman (prime minister, 1936–1937); he was a half-brother of Mahmut Şevket Paşa, the man who led the Young Turk seizure of power in Istanbul in 1909. This group of former Ottoman officers, all of them born in the 1880s and early 1890s, dominated Iraqi political life throughout the interwar period, and the most prominent of them, Nuri al-Sa'id, re-tained his extraordinary influence until his death in 1958.

As a group, these former Ottoman officers had come from fami-lies belonging to the lower and middle ranks of the old Ottoman bureaucracy in Iraq, though there were a few sons of landowners and men of religion as well. In general, the class origins of the new officers who entered the Iraqi army down through the 1940s and early 1950s were not drastically different—in a sense they are the mirror image of the older generation. It is true that more of the newcomers came from small landowning and retail-merchant families, fewer from middle-grade military and bureaucratic families.

It was in the 1960s that a new group pushed to the fore. Their instrument was the Baath party, which had emerged from utter obscurity in the struggles following the 1958 coup, momentarily seized power in 1963, and then was driven underground until 1968. (There are obvious parallels with the history of the Syrian Baath in this period, though the differences are no less important. It is important to note that although the Syrian and Iraqi branches of the Baath have common ideological and organizational roots, the two parties have never gotten on well at all. On the contrary, the hostility between the Syrian and Iraqi political elites has been intense and unvarying for the last quarter century.) During the 1960s, the Iraqi Baath was assiduously reorganized by a radical group from the small mid-Euphrates town of Tikrit, led by Ahmad Hasan al-Bakr and his much younger cousin, Saddam Hussein. The social backgrounds of the Baathist leaders marked a distinct departure for Iraqi politics:

1. They were much poorer—a full quarter of Baathist leaders were from peasant and working-class families.

2. They were markedly civilian rather than military by occupation, as one might surmise from Saddam Hussein's generalship in the Gulf War. Only one-third of the Revolutionary Command Council during the first decade of Baathist rule had been military officers. Saddam Hussein's inexorable rise to sole power during the 1970s marked the definitive victory of the party apparatchiks over its military wing. Saddam Hussein reminds one of Stalin in more than one way.

3. They tended to come from the countryside rather than the city. Only four members of the RCC were Baghdadis by origin, while six were from Tikrit. Hence the usual epithet of the Syrian media for the Iraqi regime: "fascist Tikriti bandits." The balance were from small towns and rural districts along the middle Euphrates and Tigris.

The Baathist regime in Iraq has demonstrated astonishing stay-ing power. It does not have the broad social roots of the Egyptian regime, though its nationalism and social welfare policies certainly reflect the long-standing values and aspirations of politically articu-late Iraqis. It is a highly personal regime, reflecting the goals, ambi-tions, and ego of one man. That man has been brilliant in gathering all the threads of power into his own hands, but he has built noth-ing that he can transmit to a successor. When he passes from the scene, his political system will dissolve—whether into chaos or some new order, who can say?

Finally, we turn to Syria. Although Syria mirrors Iraq in that it too is ruled by an intensely personalized and repressive regime dat-ing back two decades, the social and political milieu differs sharply from that in Iraq or Egypt. First, like Iraq but unlike Egypt, Syria did not exist as a political entity until 1919. Like Iraq, Syria is a creation of the Anglo-French partition of the Ottoman Empire be-tween 1918 and 1920. Syria does have ethnic minorities—some 15 percent of the population are non-Arabs—but politically the salient cleavage in Syria is religious. Moreover, the religious differences that count are those between Muslims: about two-thirds of its people are Sunni Muslims, while another 20 to 25 percent belong to various radical Shi'ite sects. The sense of religious difference is sharpened by the fact that each of the Shi'ite minorities inhabits a distinct area within the country, and in that area it constitutes a solid majority. Fi-nally, the Shi'ite sects are predominantly rural—traditionally among the poorest and most isolated peasants of Syria. Religious, regional, and class loyalties all reinforce one another. As to the Sunni majority, it is found everywhere in the country, but it dominates the four larg-est cities: Damascus, Aleppo, Hama, and Homs. Since cities are the age-old base of political power in the Middle East, it is not surpris-ing that the Sunnis had things pretty much their own way during the interwar and early postwar periods. The leading urban families were, as they had been under the Ottomans, the political elite in this era. Precisely these families were the natural targets of any seri-ous political challenge to the existing system.

Where would such a challenge come from? In sharp contrast to Iraq and even Egypt, there really was no Syrian army when inde-pendence came in 1946. The French kept Syria on a tight leash. A small native gendarmerie, the Troupes Spéciales du Levant, was re-

cruited in the usual French manner, from among the religious minorities, since these (or so the French hoped) would not be tempted
to align themselves with the urban Sunni nationalists. The Troupes
Spéciales were an exiguous force—some 7,500 at their height—and
they were of course demobilized when the French left. Not much
was done about building a new army until the Arab-Israeli War
loomed in 1948; the existing one's performance in that conflict did
little to enhance its prestige. When three colonels in succession seized
power in 1948–1949, the army was too weak to constitute a solid
long-term base of support, and it had few roots in society at large.
The three coups represented simple opportunism rather than a new
social movement. That is no doubt why Syria's first experiment in
military government was terminated quite painlessly in 1954. There
would be no new efforts from that direction for more than a decade.

In 1951, an air force academy was founded. In the first class was
one Hafiz al-Asad, then twenty years old and a recent high school
graduate from Lattakia. Like Nasser and Sadat in Egypt fifteen years
before, Asad accurately reflected crucial characteristics of the emerging Syrian army. He belonged to the Alawis, the largest, poorest, and
most isolated of Syria's radical Shi'ite sects, who lived in the coastal
mountains of the northwest. For Asad, the first member of his impoverished peasant family to gain a formal education, a military career presented great opportunities—a free education, vastly enhanced
social status, and of course a chance to be at the forefront of the nationalist struggle. Such a career appealed to many young men from
Syria's dispossessed groups—not only the despised Shi'ites, but the
Sunni peasants of the Euphrates valley as well. It had little to offer the sons of the urban Sunni elite, however; their political careers
seemed assured without the rigors of military life. It would not be
correct to say that the Shi'ite sects dominated the Syrian officer corps
in the 1950s and 1960s, but they were certainly overrepresented.
Moreover, their regional solidarity, class resentments, and sense of
religious apartness made them an exceedingly cohesive group within
the army.

Not surprisingly, men who shared Asad's background were
strongly attracted to the radical ideologies that proliferated in Syria
in the 1940s and 1950s. He himself, like many Alawis, had been an
activist in the Baath party since the late forties.

The Baath actually seized control of Syria in March 1963. Although the coup was carried out by a coalition of several groups, made up of both military and civilian members, a very secretive, tight-knit military bloc within the Baath party was decisive in its success. By 1966, this military bloc had uncontested control of the government. The new regime was heavily Alawi—for a few years almost half the members of the party executive, the cabinet, and the high command were Alawis—and was thus easily identified as a sectarian government by its opponents. In his three decades of personal power since 1970, Asad has made substantial concessions to the urban Sunnis, but the Alawis have retained a disproportionate position throughout. Because the new regime was surrounded and permeated by enemies, and no doubt because it was the creation of a conspiracy, Syria under the Baath almost at once became a single-party police state. Under Asad, moreover, in spite of an extremely complex party and governmental apparatus that reaches into every nook and cranny of the country, power has become as personalized, as focused on the kinsmen and clients of one man, as Saddam Hussein's regime in Iraq.

Syria represents the militarization of a once thoroughly civilian-dominated polity. It also represents a real and very sudden social revolution—the victory of the countryside, the peasantry, and the Shi'ite minorities over the city, the great merchants and landowners, and the Sunni Muslim majority.

In all this, there is really nothing that connects the modern military dictatorships of the Middle East to those of medieval times. However, I hinted at the outset that there might be links to the thousand-year-old traditions of political thought and action in the Islamic world. Two of these seem particularly tantalizing. Both, I should say, have rather a negative character.

First, especially among governments that rest on coercion and terror rather than the consent of society—or at least the consent of society's politically relevant groups—there is a perpetual but never fulfilled quest for legitimacy. Legitimacy is a big word that deserves extended discussion, but here I will settle for a few bald assertions. On a pragmatic level, legitimacy is simply a government's right to make mistakes and still remain in power. In a more abstract sense, legitimacy rests on a society's agreement that a small group of persons is rightfully empowered to make decisions, even decisions of life and death, on behalf of everyone else. Assent to such power is not easily given, and normally it flows from two beliefs: (1) that a regime has come to power in an orderly, legally sanctioned manner; (2) that the regime is dedicated to some higher end than sheer self-preservation, that it aims to serve both the material interests and the fundamental values of the society it governs.

Military dictatorships typically possess weak legitimacy, because everyone knows that their rule rests on nothing more solid than force. Force in and of itself is undeniably effective, but only when you have more of it than any possible rival. The bitterness of force can be sweetened through material and psychic rewards for those who join your side, but this happens only when you are in a position to give such rewards. It is precisely when times are bad—when your treasury is empty and your armies are in disarray—that you really need your subjects' loyalty and support, and then you cannot get it. In their pure form, then, military dictatorships are highly vulnerable; they are no more than a dense but frail web of fear and vested interest.

Where then is a military regime to find legitimacy? Medieval Islamic warlords sought this precious commodity in several areas. They claimed to be delegates of the caliph (the successor of the Prophet as the sole head of the universal Muslim community) and to be invested with their offices by his authority. They portrayed themselves as monarchs elected by God Himself; as such they were charged to uphold the divinely ordained social order on earth just as God sustained the cosmos as a whole. They asserted that they were the faithful servants of God's law, the Shariʿa, which had been revealed by God to His creatures through the Qurʾan and the authoritative teaching of His Prophet. As the upholders and defenders of God's law, they had an unquestionable right to the loyalty of their Muslim subjects, who were bound by that law.

All these ideologies seemed credible in themselves, and in fact all were widely accepted among both rulers and their subjects. But they all had a fatal flaw. They legitimized political power as such, in the abstract, but they did not say who should wield it. They did not distinguish between the claims of those who currently held power and the claims of those bent on getting it. The implicit logic of these ideologies is that a man had the right to rule only if he actually did rule—they conferred a retrospective legitimacy, so to speak.

Much the same problem has confronted the recent dictatorships of the Arab world. As in medieval times, contenders for power have stressed their unique capacity to realize the aspirations and fundamental values of their subjects. For example, they point to the need to unify the Arab nation, to achieve prosperity and social justice, or—especially since 1979—to build a true Islamic society. It is a politics of hope and frustration, and on the deepest level, a politics of cultural authenticity. But as in medieval times, anyone can lay claim to those hopes and frustrations. There is no way to choose between one contender and another save intuition or faith. Moreover, if a government comes to power on the basis of such lofty values and then fails to achieve them, it is in trouble. A government whose right to rule rests on its ability to achieve fundamental values and aspirations can seldom stand the test of reality. It will either fall to its rivals or be driven to preserve itself through coercion and terror. In short, for Middle Eastern dictatorships both medieval and modern, legitimacy has lain in the ultimate values that they claim to pursue, not in the processes by which they have attained and exercised power.

Legitimacy conferred by institutional processes—popular election, for example—would seem much more solid, simply because such processes spell out the rules by which power is to be won and identify those who may play the game. But neither traditional Islamic nor modern Middle Eastern political thought has been able to produce generally accepted ways of achieving legitimacy along these lines. Insofar as such criteria have been adopted, they have been borrowed from Western Europe. For almost a century, between about 1870 and 1960, European criteria of legitimacy were in fact widely appealed to if only sporadically adopted, to the point that they became the common coin of political discourse. But again for reasons already discussed, process- and institution-oriented legitimacy came to be regarded by the early 1960s as an ugly remnant of political and cultural domination by outsiders. The old rhetoric did not die out altogether; there were and are plenty of verbose constitutions, full of assertions of the sovereignty of the people and complex decision-making processes. But few take them seriously. From the early 1950s down to very recent years, political discourse in the Middle East has not been about constitutional government.

The problem of legitimacy leads us to a second and perhaps deeper level of similarity between new and old dictatorships—the dichotomy between society and the state. As political scientists like to put it, states in the Middle East have a high degree of autonomy. That is, they can do what they want, when they want, and their citizens can do very little to stop them. Middle Eastern societies since the ninth century have been unable to generate institutions of self-government on any but the most local and informal level. Nor have they been able to intervene in and control state policy through formal procedures. On the whole, they have had to rely either on the personal influence of respected individuals or on sporadic riot and rebellion.

I want to stress that this situation is not intrinsic to Islamic societies as such. There is nothing in Islamic religious doctrine that requires or even implies such a gulf between state and society. Nor did one always exist in Islamic times. Down to the third Islamic century (ca. A.D. 800), Muslims had a strong sense that their government, the caliphate, belonged to them. They assigned wide powers to their rulers, but if these failed to govern in accordance with God's commandments as Muslims in general understood those commandments, they had the right and indeed the duty to overthrow the existing regime and install a new one. According to the majority point of view, at least, God had called the Community of Believers into being and assigned to this Community the obligation to obey His commandments. To fulfill that obligation, the Community vested its political powers in one man, the caliph, who was literally and symbolically the successor and deputy (*khalifa*) of the Prophet. In this way, the caliph acted not as God's vicegerent but on behalf of the Community.

However, this sense of the ultimate sovereignty of the Community of Believers under God eroded during the 800s, and by the mid-tenth century it was a mere legal fiction. Having lost access to effective political power, the Community strove, with considerable success, to reserve certain crucial realms of life for itself. From these realms it was able to exclude or at least sharply limit state power, largely because the warlord states of the tenth to fifteenth centuries were really very weak. They possessed neither the resources nor the desire to control the everyday lives of their subjects. They had gone into politics for the money; as long as subjects paid their taxes and kept the peace they would be left alone.

In this way, the Community kept control of religious doctrine and practice, the law of contract and personal status, and the basic institutions of family life. All this was done in highly localized, informal ways, without parliaments or councils or chartered corporations. Even those great international institutions, the Sufi confraternities and ritual-legal associations, which linked together Muslims throughout the world in a community of faith and practice, were no more than networks of men who knew and respected one another, and who claimed allegiance to the teaching of common spiritual ancestors. The whole apparatus of community life was amorphous, but it also proved adaptable and incredibly durable. It survived drought and famine and invasion, the Mongols and the Black Death.

It survived everything, except the power of the modern state to penetrate into the most intimate crevices of life. Some inkling of this heightened state power could be glimpsed in the heyday of the Ottoman Empire, which between 1453 and 1600 was able to dominate and shape religious life within its dominions as no Muslim state ever had. But it was the colonial state of the nineteenth and early twentieth century that really marked a new age. The British tried to respect the religious and family institutions of their Muslim subjects, though of course in their deference and respect they utterly transformed them. The French approach was more direct, more arrogant, and equally transformative. Against the power of the colonial police and the efficiency of the colonial bureaucrat, the informal mechanisms of traditional Islamic society—consensus, mutual reputation, personal influence—were helpless. The colonial powers needed a chain of command by which to impose their control, and they created it. It is likewise true that the colonial powers provided a model for political action by society itself, in the form of political parties, labor unions, voluntary associations, and the like. But where they allowed these things to exist at all in the lands under their control, they controlled them so tightly that there was little opportunity for Middle Eastern societies to rebuild institutions of self-government along modern lines. This same control was exercised by the independent (or semi-independent) governments of the interwar and early postwar era. The traditional mechanisms by which these societies had regulated their affairs continued to wither away, even as newly created institutions were stifled and unable to function effectively.

All of this gave the dictators of the last four decades wide scope for action. On the one hand, they inherited and did much to reinforce the enhanced power of the state to intervene in its subjects' affairs. On the other hand, they were dealing with societies whose capacity for political action on the state level had been very limited for a thousand years, whose traditional institutions of political influence were atrophied, and in which new institutions capable of replacing them were still in embryo. The dictators have thus been in an enviable position to restructure society in their own image. Even so, they have not been able to heal the breach between state and society. Their efforts at social mobilization—single parties, credit cooperatives, women's clubs, universal public education—have been very much a top-down affair. These efforts have elicited much cynical opportunism but little popular enthusiasm or spontaneous participation. The modern dictators have indeed arisen from among the people they rule, and they espouse populist programs. And every now and then, as with Nasser between 1956 and 1961, there is a moment of glowing enthusiasm. But on the whole, Arab societies seem to regard their governments as an alien entity; they endure them, and they wait for them to go away.

At least this has been the pattern of things until the last decade. We are witnessing a struggle to bring about a fundamental shift in the relations between state and society in the Middle East. There has been much discussion of the concept of a secular "civil society" among Middle Eastern intellectuals.[3] However, the shift in state-society relations is in large part embodied in the Islamic movement, which represents a powerful and often well-organized challenge from below to the powers that be. Ironically, it is the Islamic Republic of Iran that most clearly expresses this shift. Ironically, because the Iranian government possesses in spades two key characteristics of the modern military dictatorship. First, it bases its legitimacy on its claim that it can make a reality of the loftiest possible political values, in this case no less than the government of God on earth. Second, it asserts the right and duty to watch over every aspect of social life. Even so, Iran has the most effective constitutional regime in the region apart from Turkey. However restrictive the 1979 Constitution may be, and (even as amended in 1989) however great the power this constitution assigns to the clergy, the Iranian government operates within the rules laid down by it. The presidential elections of 1997, with their restricted franchise and their preapproved slate of candidates, still produced a real surprise in the election of a moderate cleric, Muhammad Khatami. And that surprise, however unwelcome, has been accepted by the powers that be in Iran.

All this suggests a real effort to reintegrate state and society. If the effort has been partially successful at best, it still merits notice. Within the Arab world also, we are seeing persistent demands for popular participation and control, for restrictions on the power of elites, whether they call themselves revolutionary or traditionalist. The most effective demands are coming from the Islamic movements, and since (as we will see in greater detail later) these are not always democratic in form or ideology, we can only guess what will come of these demands. Even so, the present ferment does hint that the constitutional experiments of 1920 to 1950 may not have been utterly in vain. The age of dictators in the Middle East has been a long one, but perhaps it is not forever enshrined in the order of things.

CHAPTER 6

PROFANE AND SACRED POLITICS

The Ends of Power in the Middle East

"In Islam there is no distinction between religion and politics." No cliché is more deeply imbedded in Western thought about Islam, none is more fervently proclaimed by contemporary Islamic activists. Certainly no observer can help noticing how deeply religious language and action have permeated Middle Eastern politics (and the politics of every Muslim country) in recent years. Since the late 1970s all the most visible protest and revolutionary movements have marched under the banner of Islam. Nationalist movements, formerly stridently secular in their program and rhetoric, have now draped themselves in Islamic attire, and Marxism has all but disappeared from the public arena. Among Muslim thinkers and spokesmen, fundamental theological issues hardly seem to be discussed these days; all debate focuses on Islam in the realm of politics.[1]

In light of events in the contemporary Islamic world, can we realistically imagine a politics among Muslims divorced from religion? Is every political statement, every gesture, every act of policy in the world of Islam freighted with sacred meaning? Is every major issue a matter of salvation or perdition? The earlier chapters in this book certainly appear to contradict that view. For the most part, we have been looking at a politics of this world—that is, at conflicts over wealth and power, and hence at conflicts that at least in principle allow for accommodation, negotiation, and compromise. We have seen politicians struggling to win independence for their countries, to stay in power or wrest it from their opponents, to gain control of critical national resources, to increase the wealth of their societies and to distribute it among their citizens in some minimally satisfactory way. Only rarely have we seen them claiming that in doing all this, they are about God's work.

So we have a puzzle. On the one hand, most Muslim politicians are only politicians; on the other, Islam has become almost an obsession in political debate for the past two decades. We can only resolve these contradictions, real or apparent, by taking Islam seriously. In the balance of this book, therefore, I will put Islam at center stage. I will look at some of the political and social issues that have seemed most important to people who are operating within a consciously Islamic framework, and I will ask how they have dealt with these issues. When such issues are examined from a specifically Islamic perspective, how does that change the way we think about them?

However widely accepted it may be, the idea that Islam does not distinguish between religion and politics is a troubling one, for it presupposes that Islam is a monolith, a single, universal, unchanging system of belief and practice. This presupposition is demonstrably false, however deeply many Muslims might wish it otherwise. Any reasonably objective and attentive observer quickly sees that Islam provides enormously varied ways of understanding and grappling with the world. Muslims do not march in single file; they follow many paths (some leading in quite opposite directions) in applying the rich traditions of their faith to their lives. This is of course exactly what we ought to expect of any social and cultural system that goes back fourteen hundred years and has at least a billion adherents living in almost every part of the globe.

The complexity of human behavior obscures any clear-cut distinction between profane and sacred politics within Islamic countries. But that such a distinction exists Muslim thinkers have never doubted. Though some writers (both medieval and contemporary) have bitterly denounced ordinary politics as mere greed and ambition, and hence as rebellion against God's law, many others have recognized not only the reality but also the legitimacy of a politics aimed mostly at winning the goods of this world. The issue is not whether Muslims are in touch with reality—namely, that politics obviously does operate according to rules of its own, and that these rules do not always fit with the dictates of religion—but rather what degree of legitimacy Muslims assign to purely profane politics.

Traditional conceptions of the relationship between religion and politics were hammered out over many centuries of sophisticated and sometimes vitriolic debate, beginning with the Qur'an itself. The key conclusions of this debate were summed up in a three-part scheme devised by the fourteenth-century Tunisian scholar Ibn Khaldun

(1332–1406).[2] He argued that government fell into three broad categories: natural kingship, rational kingship, and caliphate (i.e., Islamic rule). Each type of government was ultimately defined by the
moral and psychological impulse from which it stemmed. Ibn Khaldun's argument on the nature of government began with the prem-
ise that the innate selfishness and aggressiveness of human nature
makes some sort of government essential. Better sixty years of tyranny than a single night of anarchy, as an often-repeated saying had
it. Even so, he condemns natural kingship, rule that aims only at
power and domination, for such kingship grows out of the basest
human instincts. However, when political power is restrained by
reason and exercised by a ruler for the benefit of his subjects as well
as himself, it merits the assent and obedience of these subjects. Indeed, when a ruler must operate without the benefit of a divinely
revealed law—the common lot of most nations before the coming
of Islam—such rational kingship was the best that could be hoped
for. Ideally, of course, political authority would be exercised within
the framework of the commandments and norms provided by the
Qur'an and the example of the Prophet. In this case, a ruler would
be acting as a caliph—as the successor and deputy of the Prophet—
and his political authority would be exercised with the aim of bringing prosperity in this life and salvation in the next. In Ibn Khaldun's
scheme, then, legitimate secular government is clearly possible, but
only in the absence of true religion. To put it another way, now that
Islam has come and has spread throughout the world, no ruler—
and certainly no Muslim ruler—has any excuse for trying to govern outside the framework provided by Islam.

   In the second half of the nineteenth century, however, this long-
established view of things was increasingly subject to doubt and
challenge, though it was never completely abandoned. During this
period, regimes in North Africa and the Middle East were beginning to deal with Islam's institutions and representatives more and
more in the manner of a state church on the European model. That
is, religion was compartmentalized; it was largely removed from the
political process, and its representatives were excluded from deciding or executing the major issues of public policy. Rather, religion became a matter of social utility; it would be the framework through
which personal morality and socially responsible conduct could be
inculcated, and it might also serve as a useful (though not the most

important) symbol of national identity and culture. To this end, Muslim rulers strove to bring all pious endowments, mosques, and religious schools and colleges—heretofore decentralized and autonomous—under the control of government ministries. Theological and legal curricula were made subject to the oversight of ministries of education. Scholars had to be officially licensed to hold positions in schools and mosques, and official religious hierarchies were created.

This process went furthest in the Ottoman Empire (including Egypt) and in French colonial possessions in North Africa. The Ottoman Empire presents a particularly striking example of it. Between 1870 and 1917, the Ottoman government undertook a systematic simplification and codification of the Shariʿa.[3] That meant that Muslim scholars were stripped of their centuries-old authority to interpret this immense corpus of discussion and debate, and to decide how it should apply to specific cases. Henceforth, bureaucrats would decide what the law was, and the scholars would be reduced to applying their formulas. There was admittedly barely a trace of all this in Iran, where the central government in Tehran was extremely weak, and the Shiʿite clergy were easily able to fend off the few feeble efforts by the inept Qajar shahs in this direction. For different reasons, India too followed its own trajectory, for the British were very chary of fiddling with "native" religious practices and institutions. However, while the Raj scrupulously upheld what it understood to be Islamic law and practice among its Muslim subjects, men of religion were awarded no role whatever in policy making or government administration.

The convulsions of World War I produced a whole series of new or reconstructed states, and these took decisive steps toward stronger state control of religion, even in Iran and British India. Most premodern regimes in Muslim countries had claimed that their role was protecting Islam and ensuring that Islamic norms and values were actually carried out. They had legitimized themselves as representatives of and advocates for Islam. The new states, in contrast, supported Islam financially and institutionally, and they drew on its teachings for legislation and policy. But upholding Islam was only one of their goals, and not the most important of them. On the contrary, the crucial thing as they saw it was to inculcate a sense of nationhood (Turkish, Arab, Egyptian, Lebanese, or Iranian as the case might be) and to ensure the material progress and prosperity of their citizens. Now the interests of Islam would not only be subordinated to needs of state, but would in fact be defined and closely supervised by the state. This policy certainly went furthest in the new Turkish Republic under Atatürk, who felt a deep personal alienation from Islamic belief and tradition. However, Reza Shah of Iran (1925–1941) made energetic, not to say violent, efforts to control the Shi'ite clergy of his country, and at least temporarily he cowed them into silence and passivity. Even in India, the ever-discreet British established the Shariat Act of 1937, which made the formal Shari'a the sole and uniform basis for legal action in the Anglo-Muhammadan courts of that country, to the exclusion of local custom or established practice, which had previously entered into many decisions.

By the 1950s and 1960s, Islam seemed thoroughly excluded from the central policy-making and legislative processes in almost every country from Indonesia to Algeria; scholars were state licensed and approved, mosques had to be officially registered to operate (at least openly), and the only parts of the Shari'a that were still widely applied in the courts concerned family law. Politicians certainly displayed due deference to religious values and sentiments among their peoples, and when it seemed advantageous to do so they would try to whip them up. (Muslim politicians are not the only ones to play this game, needless to say.) Nevertheless, for half a century, between 1920 and 1970, politics in the Middle East and throughout the bulk of the Muslim world was conducted largely within a secular frame of reference. Moreover, this approach appeared to be quite acceptable to the great majority of Muslims. There were a few regimes, such as Saudi Arabia, that continued to found their authority on traditional concepts of religion and power, but such exceptions were thought only to prove the rule.

The temper of the time is neatly conveyed by a story told by the British anthropologist Michael Gilsenan. In a fit of youthful idealism, he had gone to South Yemen as a volunteer teacher for an organization called Voluntary Service Overseas.

> A friend and I were in Seyyun, one of the ancient towns of the great eastern wadi of the Hadhramaut . . . dominated by a highly influential clan of sherifs, descendants of the Prophet Muhammad.
>
> Two young men of that family met us in the street, walking in the heat of the morning. The green band around their turbans, their flowing cream-colored outer garments, and their trim beards all signified the holiness and precedence of their position. Their wealth,

from large local landholdings and overseas business in Indonesia, showed in the quality of the fine material of their clothes and in the size and equal elegance of the luxurious house to which we were being guided.

It was all an enchantment, a desert, an oasis, a holy town, an age-old tradition. The fullness of sanctity and a ritualized sense of gracious order and harmony were added to when a student of mine encountered in the street stooped respectfully to kiss the young sherifs' hands as we passed. . . . The world was a perfectly formed magic garden. And I was entranced. All my images of Islam and Arab society were brought unquestioningly together.

The front door slammed behind us. The spell was broken. Our companions quickly closed the window shutters so that no one could see us, lights were switched on, a Grundig tape recorder played Western pop music, and the strictly forbidden whiskey came out of the cupboard. Turbans were quickly doffed, and there was no talk of religion but only of stifling boredom, the ignorance of local people, the cost of alcohol, and how wonderful life had been in Indonesia. . . .

A day later I met the student, a boy in his late teens like myself. He delivered the second blow. "We kiss their hands now," he said, "but just wait till tomorrow." He was a Nasserist. . . . A member of the first generation of peasants to be educated, he belonged to a cultural club in which most of the young men were sympathizers with the cause of the Egyptian president, then at the height of his power. That cause was identified as that of all Arabs against imperialism and the control of conservative and reactionary forces. He would talk to me, but I, too, was part of the apparatus of colonial administration, a fact that he realized much more clearly than I did.[4]

By the early 1970s, every reputable political scientist and sociologist in the West, including many who had been born and educated in the Middle East, had concluded that religion was a rapidly declining force in the politics of the Muslim world. Islam would soon cease to play a serious role outside the family and local community. (Religion had "low saliency," in the jargon of the time.) Islam was still the professed faith of the overwhelming majority of people, and even many members of the political elite were sincere and observant believers. But these people did not frame their political goals or even their political rhetoric in Islamic terms; the currency of the realm was liberal modernization theory or (far more often) some sort of Marxism.

Things did not turn out quite as we all expected, and religion

has surged back into the political arena with a force that has astonished even its proponents. But that did not happen merely in Islamic
countries. On the contrary, as Mark Juergensmeyer has demonstrated,
politicized religion is a worldwide phenomenon that has made itself felt even in such self-consciously "modern" societies as Israel and
the United States.[5] However, it is crucial to stress that we have not
reverted to the conceptual world of Ibn Khaldun, which allowed only
a limited and conditional acceptance of profane politics. Rather, what
we have now is a heated debate in almost every Muslim country
about the proper boundaries between religion and politics—a debate that implicitly recognizes that these are distinct and perhaps
incommensurate things, that they inhabit overlapping but separate
realms. It is true that the more ardent Islamists ("intégristes," as
the French call them) hope to obliterate the boundaries, but their
opponents are equally determined to maintain them, whatever tactical concessions they may be willing to make. In other words, the
nineteenth-century transformation of political thought in the Islamic
world is still in place.

Even when we put ourselves within a specifically religious frame
of reference—that is, one that declares that the chief end of politics is to lead people to salvation—we find that Muslims view the
relationship between religion and politics in very complex ways.
Within this complex and always shifting relationship, however, there
are a few consistent and enduring patterns that seem to recur in almost every period and region. In my judgment, these patterns can
easily be grouped into three distinct models of political thought and
action that seem to hold good over the fourteen centuries of Islam's
history. These three models of action—we might call them paradigms—do not represent different periods of history, nor are they
successive phases in a broad scheme of historical evolution. Rather,
each of the three is always and everywhere in evidence—certainly
within the vast boundaries of the Muslim world as a whole, but
also (and more to the point) within the confines of any given country or sociopolitical system.

These paradigms of political action have grown out of two contrasting and probably irreconcilable attitudes that Muslims have
about their religion. One attitude holds that Islam is simply what
Muslims actually do and believe. This is a frame of mind that sees
the established order in Muslim societies as inherently Islamic, and

hence as essentially right and proper. Viewed from this perspective, Islam is a body of values, beliefs, and practices that undergirds and legitimizes the way things are. This attitude is very widely held, but it is seldom consciously recognized or openly stated. The reason, no doubt, is that it is a hard position for a thoughtful Muslim to defend in a principled, logically compelling way. The statement, "We've just always done things this way," sounds fine to an anthropologist or comparative religionist; it is not persuasive to a Muslim who needs to be sure that he or she is living in accordance with the true teachings of Islam. The second attitude that Muslims hold about their religion could hardly differ more sharply. In this case, Islam is seen as a profound challenge to the corruption and evils of society as it now exists. Islam represents God's demand that every Muslim enter the struggle to create a social and political order in accordance with His revealed commandments. If this struggle leads to a violent confrontation with things as they are, so be it. This is of course an attitude of the discontented and disaffected, but those are the very people who are most likely to demand explanations and make pronouncements.

Among our three paradigms of political action, the first and by far the most common one throughout the course of Islamic history clearly grows out of the more relaxed attitude. It is a style of mutual indifference between the realm of politics and the realm of religious belief and practice. This does not mean that religion and state are seen as wholly separate. On the contrary, even within this paradigm, the government and organized religious life are interdependent in a host of ways, though each tends to take the other for granted so long as it knows its place and stays there. The key point is this: within this paradigm of mutual indifference, political action per se aims at winning and retaining power. How that struggle is waged, and by whom it is won, is religiously irrelevant. For the ordinary believer, the one crucial thing is that the winner of the struggle be committed to upholding those institutions through which Muslims can observe God's law. In particular, the winner of the struggle must maintain mosques, where communal worship is held, and courts of law, which apply the commandments of the Shariʿa to the affairs of everyday life—commercial contracts, family disputes, criminal punishments, and so on.

If the government provides this irreducible minimum of support, ordinary Muslims are free to pursue their religious commitments as far and deep as they wish, so long as they do not disrupt the lives of other Muslims. Within this latitudinarian approach to religion and politics, questions about the nature of Islam—what Islam truly is and ought to be—may be (and often are) spiritually and morally urgent, but they are politically irrelevant. These issues are worked out *outside* the contest for worldly power.

It is worth repeating that this pattern is the norm for most Muslims in most times and places. It is a "go along, get along" style of religious politics. As such it does not aim for the highest and best, but by that very fact it does not sow dissension, intolerance, and violence among the believers. It is a paradigm that, in the current state of things, looks pretty good—not only to confused Westerners, but to a great many weary or frightened Muslims as well. However, this paradigm does not operate merely because it is a good thing; it requires a certain set of conditions. In fact, the sort of relaxed tolerance embodied in this paradigm tends to work in those times and places where Islam is well established among the bulk of the population, where there is a broad consensus as to what constitutes sound belief and good morals, and where there are no major perceived threats to the existing order.

However stable this first style of political action appears to be at any given moment, it is readily disrupted by the rise of intense revivalist or puritan movements from within the Community of Believers, because such movements attack the established consensus of belief and practice as formalistic, hypocritical, and corrupt. They make it impossible for people to be relaxed about the way things are; everyone must be mobilized, however reluctantly, to attack or defend the status quo. The live-and-let-live style is no less vulnerable to threats mounted against "Islam" (i.e., the existing way of life) by non-Muslim outsiders, whether these threats are seen as political or cultural or both. In modern times, "the West" provokes anger and anxiety because it represents foreign, non-Muslim rule ("imperialism"), and equally because it represents moral corruption, subversion by secularist ideologies, uncontrolled female sexuality, and "The Bold and the Beautiful."[6]

The inherent fragility of the first paradigm of political action leads us to the second and third, which grow out of the idea that Islam is essentially revolutionary, a challenge to build a new society founded on God's law. These two paradigms are mirror images of each other, for each involves a determined struggle by one party to control the territory of the other. Within both paradigms, politics remains a struggle for power over worldly affairs, but it also becomes a struggle for salvation. Control of the political arena takes on a profound, literally apocalyptic significance. The two paradigms differ, not in their view of the nature of politics and religion and the proper relationship between them, but in where they locate the center of religious authority.

In the second paradigm, it is the rulers who claim the full and exclusive right to control religious life and expression. The regime defines what Islam is and how it should be lived, and the regime asserts the right and obligation to enforce that definition on its Muslim subjects. These are extremely bold claims, and to bring them off a government must possess very specific characteristics. It must have high prestige and legitimacy, an extraordinary capacity for coercion, and a strong ideological identity that intimately binds the nature of the regime to its vision of religion. Many governments, of course, aspire to possess these characteristics, but in the nature of things such regimes are very rare. Hence they constantly struggle to impose their view of their mission on subjects who may not believe a word of it. More complex is the situation in which a regime does indeed have the support of some elements of society while arousing the indifference or active hostility of others.

Among Muslim regimes today there are a few that fall more or less within this second paradigm. Pride of place, at least in the political awareness of Westerners, surely belongs to the Islamic Republic of Iran—though it must be said that the intensity and fervor of the first decade (1979–1989, from the revolution to the death of the Ayatollah Khomeini) have now faded considerably. By far the oldest regime of this sort, however, is Saudi Arabia, which has its roots in the late eighteenth century, although the present kingdom was established only seven decades ago by its founder Abd al-Aziz Al Saud (d. 1953). The fiercely puritan public morality of the two regimes has something in common, but the Saudi government speaks for a drastically different theological and legal interpretation of Islam than does Iran, and it certainly affects a very different tone in international affairs. The list of Islamist states would also include Sudan, whose military rulers claim to be guided by the vision of Hasan al-

Turabi and the Muslim Brothers, and (in a completely idiosyncratic fashion that is also completely typical of that country) Morocco, where the authoritative interpretation of Islam is the exclusive province of King Hasan II.[7]

It is fair to ask whether these self-proclaimed Islamic states are in fact fundamentally different from their less ideological neighbors. In all times and places, after all, Muslim governments have claimed to represent Islam and to be motivated solely by service to the faith. This is as true of the twentieth century as of any previous era. All governments in Muslim countries have tried to supervise the key institutions that shape the public practice of Islam—for example, the major mosques and colleges of religious studies, the Shariʿa courts, and the great public religious observances (Ramadan, the Prophet's birthday, the Feast of Sacrifice at the end of the pilgrimage season). Ironically, the most determinedly secularizing governments (such as Atatürk's Turkey, Nasser's Egypt, Bourguiba's Tunisia, or Baathist Syria and Iraq) are the ones that have in fact asserted the strongest control over Islamic life and institutions, although these secularist regimes do not so much support Islam as build a fence around it, with the aim of confining it to its "proper role" of instilling moral values, supporting the family, and calling for obedience to the duly constituted authorities. Moreover, few modern governments, even those with a clear pro-Islamic stance, officially adhere to any particular interpretation of Islam; on the contrary, they have quite consciously followed a latitudinarian or "broad and hazy" approach of permitting whatever does not give serious offense. If I may attempt a fine distinction, the mission of most governments in Muslim countries has been to shelter and supervise ordinary religious belief and practice, not to establish the Kingdom of God on earth. And of course all regimes, whether secularist or pro-Islamic, have shared the solid pragmatic (if unspoken) aim of not permitting Islam to fall into the hands of anyone who might use it against them.

In short, these governments co-opt Islam—precisely what governments commonly do when they are confronted by a potentially independent force that might be turned against them. They seek to neutralize opponents by giving them a vested interest in the existing political order. It is also an implicit demand that Islam's recognized spokesmen lend support to the regime. However, co-optation is not a claim that the regime possesses the exclusive right to define

Islam and membership in it. It rather fits with the "go along, get along" style of my first paradigm. The mere fact that a regime oversees Islamic affairs and claims to be an ardent supporter of Islam does not make that regime an embodiment of a state-led struggle to build an Islamic society. It is admittedly sometimes difficult to decide whether the acts of a given government at a given moment should be interpreted in terms of the first paradigm or the second, but the distinction between the two conceptions is real and enduring.

The third style of Islamic politics, in contrast, can hardly be mistaken for anything else. Here Islamic consciousness and practice are mobilized by discontented elements in society at large and aimed against the existing political system. Under this paradigm, Islam becomes a language of reform and protest, even of revolutionary action. (It seems ironic but is inevitable that the third paradigm is often transmuted into the second: the Iranian and Saudi regimes, for example, began as revolutionary movements.) As such, Islam provides a devastating critique of the existing order, a critique that may empty that order of every shred of legitimacy. At the same time, Islam becomes the template for a radically new way of life, one that will bring about prosperity and justice through the struggle to do God's will here on earth.

In the mind of its advocates, this striving to do God's will, to build a godly society, is no vague aspiration or pious hope but a very concrete imperative. Such a perfect society once did exist here on earth, we know all about it, and all we need to do is reclaim it from the debris of history. This perfect society is of course the community established and led by the Prophet Muhammad in Medina in the decade 622–632 C.E. The memory of this society is accurately and fully preserved for us in a multitude of stories, first told by the Prophet's own Companions and faithfully transmitted from generation to generation thereafter. And of course this society is reflected in God's own speech, the Qur'an. It is right there in front of our noses for the taking, if only we have the will and faith to act.

To most non-Muslims, and certainly to those of a secular frame of mind, this sounds like a headlong retreat into the golden haze of a distant imaginary past. And so it is important to recognize that Islamic activists are not (for the most part, at least) foolish, naive persons. They know perfectly well that we do not live in seventh-century Arabia and cannot pretend that we do. They have no intention whatever of giving up modern medicine, electronics, transport, and the like; they see these things as perfectly harmonious (*if* they are properly used) with an ideal Muslim society. The activists are not trying to re-create Muhammad's Medina in the material sense—an isolated date palm oasis of a few thousand souls. Rather, they are trying to recapture the social solidarity, the intense moral commitment, the religious urgency that they believe characterized the first Muslim community. They are trying to infuse these qualities into a modern world afflicted by moral anomie, congestion, vast economic disparities, and mass culture.

Having said this, I must confess that at least to me, the activists have always seemed rather vague about the concrete programs through which they would bring about the titanic moral, cultural, and social transformations that they call for. As one political spokesman said when he was asked how an Islamic regime would attack the looming agricultural crisis in his country, "We don't need a program; the Qurʾan is our program." Rather in the same vein, the Islamic coalitions in Egypt rest their case on a simple slogan, visible everywhere in graffiti and wall posters: *al-Islam huwa al-hall*: "Islam is the solution." It is as simple and cryptic as the things my calculus teacher used to tell me, and it is irrefutable.

In all fairness, the Islamists do have fairly clear-cut programs in a few areas: those touching on public morality and those that have taken on great symbolic significance because they mark the distinction between Islamic morality and justice and Western corruption. The sale of alcoholic beverages would be banned; women would be compelled to adopt "modest" dress in public (at least a broad shawl covering the head, if not a face-covering veil), and in general the sexes would be highly segregated outside the home; financial institutions would not charge interest, though they would generate income from their activities in Islamically acceptable ways (e.g., profit-sharing). Moral derelictions (drinking, adultery, etc.) would be severely and publicly punished, though not all Islamists are quite willing to resort to the Qurʾanic penalties of flogging and the like. But all this, however visible and powerful as symbolic action, falls far short of a comprehensive public policy.

We might determine the likely course of Islamic policies by examining the programs instituted by Islamic regimes once they have come to power. But here the record is not altogether enlightening.

Iran, the largest and boldest of Islamist experiments, is rather hard to assess at this point, as we have already seen in chapter 2. The Islamic Republic has clearly put much effort and money into public welfare (clinics, schools, etc.), especially in rural areas, and it has devoted considerable attention to rural development as well. But all these policies were launched under the monarchy, and in fact had proceeded quite far in aggregate terms, however unevenly their benefits were distributed. Some of revolutionary Iran's shortcomings, especially in industrialization and modern services, can surely be excused by the enormous costs of the Iran-Iraq War, one of the bloodiest regional struggles of this hideously bloody century. But even so, things that could have been done have just not happened; after years of meandering debate there is still no clear-cut legislation on land tenure, import-export policy, or financial institutions. This is so because the Islamic experts who have dominated the country since 1979 cannot agree on what Islam calls for in these areas. The Ayatollah Khomeini always said he wasn't interested in traffic lights, and that may yet prove the epitaph of the revolution he led.

Saudi Arabia presents a very different picture. Since King Faysal assumed the throne in 1964, the Saudi authorities have been fairly clear-headed about what they wanted to achieve and how they meant to get there. Since 1970 they have built an astonishing physical infrastructure of highways, airports, and telecommunications; a perhaps wasteful but indubitably productive agriculture (Saudi Arabia is now a substantial net exporter of wheat); and a considerable higher education network, in which approximately one-third of the students are female. However, Saudi Arabia sits on 25 percent of the world's proven oil reserves; even with the abrupt collapse of oil prices in the mid-1980s, the country continues to have financial resources unmatched by any other large Muslim country. It is hard to claim that there is anything specifically Islamic about Saudi Arabia's development programs, though so far as I know there is nothing in them that contradicts traditional Islamic teachings.

In the arena of culture and public morality, of course, Saudi Arabia has notoriously adhered since its founding to a severely puritanical interpretation of Islam. This is part and parcel of the country's legacy. The House of Saud first arose in the mid-eighteenth century as the political and military arm of the fiery teaching of Muhammad ibn Abd al-Wahhab (1703–1792).[8] Since the dynasty's legitimacy is grounded in its claim to represent and enforce Wahhabi moral and religious teaching, the country's rulers cannot very well relax these policies even if they might wish to do so.

If we turn from Iran and Saudi Arabia to other countries, we find even less enlightenment as to the practical meaning of an "Islamic state." Sudan is a basket case, to put it plainly, and has no public programs worth discussing.[9] Pakistan under General Zia (1977–1988) was pursuing an effort to Islamize its legislation and legal system, but the results of this policy were at best ambiguous. (The same might well be said of General Zia's intentions.) In any case, this policy has not been pursued in any systematic way, though it has likewise not been reversed, under succeeding governments.[10]

So much, then, for our three paradigms. To repeat a point already made, all three styles of political action are at work simultaneously— any one of them may seem particularly visible and important in a given place at a given moment, then suddenly fade into the background as another emerges into prominence. Before the late nineteenth century, these paradigms operated in a relatively localized manner. The fact that one region was locked in revolutionary ferment did not mean that other regions were similarly affected. To be sure, political and intellectual elites knew quite well what was going on beyond their own borders, but direct contacts between regions were sporadic and narrowly channeled.

Since World War II, however, the rapid rise of instantaneous communications and mass audiences means that no one can remain insulated from what is going on anywhere else. This is doubly so when social and political conditions are tense, not to say explosive, throughout the Islamic lands. In spite of the astonishing wealth of a few oil-rich countries (Libya, Saudi Arabia, the Gulf states, Brunei), massive poverty is endemic in most high-population countries. Even more ominously, the economic stagnation of these countries has created a dead end not only for young people entering their working years but also for much of the professional middle class of all ages. For this and a host of other reasons, there is a general disillusionment with alternative ideals like socialism or liberal nationalism. Under conditions of this kind, Islamic protest anywhere (whether reformist or revolutionary) echoes everywhere. Islamic activists in any one country thus have the sense—and they are not deceived—that they are part of a worldwide movement.

The universality of this ferment is the genuinely new element in contemporary Islam. What makes 1998 quite different from 1898, and radically different from 1798, is the sense among Muslims that people in Malaysia are directly, immediately, and powerfully affected by what is happening in Sudan or Algeria or Pakistan. This universality—not only of ideas and values but of emotions and aspirations and frustrations as well—is no doubt the key (or at least an important key) to comprehending the future of the societies of the Muslim world. Note that I do *not* say predicting the future, but comprehending it—that is, understanding the forces that drive the events going on before our eyes.

At this point, two notes of caution. First, a stress on the universality of religiopolitical currents throughout the contemporary Muslim world must not blind us to the enormous differences within that world. Recall again that it encompasses a billion people living in the most diverse geographic conditions over many millions of square miles. A very similar set of concepts, symbols, and values may be invoked by Muslim activists everywhere, but there are enormous differences in the social, political, and cultural milieus within which these ideas are played out. The political systems—not only the formal institutions of government but the way politics is performed—of Malaysia, Pakistan, Iran, Egypt, and Morocco are not the same. Economic and demographic problems may be similar on a global level, but on closer inspection each country has its own distinctive profile. And finally, a very elusive and admittedly slippery point, but a crucial one: different countries possess their own cultural styles, and hence have their own ways of absorbing and acting on the ideas and stimuli pouring into them.

The second caveat I have already alluded to: part of the appeal of political Islamism lies in the lack of credible ideological alternatives, although as we have seen elsewhere, these seemed plentiful and appealing in the first two-thirds of this century. Even when liberalism, secular nationalism, or socialism was the favored cause of the intelligentsia, to be sure, Islam was always a powerful and readily mobilized political force, but it did not have the field to itself. One of the questions we must ask, therefore, is whether the future will again generate serious alternatives to contemporary expressions of political Islam—if not alternatives to the impulse to formulate and apply Islamic policies, at least alternatives that will connect with Islamic ideologies and reinforce the constructive tendencies within them. At the moment the answer to this question is uncertain at best. It is almost impossible to imagine that there will be no such alternatives, but it is equally impossible to surmise what they may be. For some years to come, we will do well to accept flux, confusion, and ambiguity as the normal state of things.

CHAPTER 7

ISLAM AS A POLITICAL SYSTEM

Is there an Islamic system of politics? Are there political institutions and forms of government that are laid down in the basic scriptures of Islam, or that can at least be traced back to the actions and practices of the Prophet and his closest associates? We have identified distinctive styles of political action that are characteristic of Muslim societies. But forms of political action very much like these can easily be found almost anywhere else in the world. All we need to do is tweak a few key terms and adjust certain emphases to find ourselves in twentieth-century Europe with its mad array of politicians, from the blandest time-servers to the most extreme ideological fanatics. But we are still left with a crucial question: can we identify a set of basic political concepts and institutions of government within the historical experience of Muslim societies, growing from the same roots as their religious faith and practice?

In exploring this problem, we need to begin literally at the beginning. All the forms of Islam throughout the world, disparate and varied as they are, spring logically and historically from a common source—the word of God as given in the Qur'an and the life and teaching of His chosen prophet Muhammad. These are the foundation and core of every version or interpretation of Islam. Even though (like the sacred texts and events of every religion) the Qur'an and Muhammad's life are apprehended and interpreted in strikingly diverse ways, they are absolutely binding and normative for every serious Muslim. From the perspective of an individual believer, Islam can be defined simply as the effort to shape his or her life in the light of God's commandments and Muhammad's teaching and example. From another perspective, that of the whole historical edifice, Islam can be imagined as an immensely complex debate, sustained over fourteen hundred years, on the human meaning of a book (the Qur'an) and of the life (Muhammad's) in and through which that book was revealed to mankind.

Clearly, then, an examination of Islam and politics has to start with the Qur'an and the life of the Prophet. In principle we might want to keep these distinct, but as a practical matter that is simply not possible. Almost all Muslims regard the Qur'an as literally the word of God, existing with Him without change from all eternity; strictly speaking, Muhammad was simply the instrument that God used to proclaim His word to the world. But even so, it is still true that Muhammad not only received the word but also preached it, acted on it, and gave it practical effect within a new moral, social, and political order. Most Muslims, I think, would agree with the proposition that Muhammad's life is in itself the clearest and most complete exposition of the meaning and significance of the Qur'an.

Contemporary Muslim activists fill their speeches and election posters with a few favorite slogans—for example, "The Qur'an is our constitution," "Islam is the solution!"—and these slogans naturally lead the unwary to suppose that the Qur'an is mostly a book about politics.[1] The reality is quite otherwise. The Qur'an contains a little bit of law—that is, injunctions to perform or avoid specific acts—a number of verses urging unity among the believers and obedience to God and His prophet, and almost nothing that gives explicit instructions on how to build and run a government. Overwhelmingly, the Qur'an focuses on moral exhortation, on God's power and absolute oneness, on the need to fear and worship Him alone and obey His commandments. It is a book, in short, that spells out the nature of God and the fundamental relationship between Him and His creation. It is crucially important to understand that the Qur'an is concerned not only with the relationship between God and the individual believer—though that relationship is very important—but also with the bonds between God and a community of people who have been called to obey him, and who must choose whether or not to heed that call. God saves or condemns individuals only at the Day of Resurrection, but he saves or condemns communities here and now.

The verses that modern non-Muslims would regard as "legal" in content number less than 100 out of a total of some 6,200. They are scattered in several places, and deal with very disparate topics: marriage, divorce, inheritance, a few criminal acts (these include murder—which is treated as a tort rather than a crime—robbery, adultery, slander, and the drinking of intoxicating beverages), and the division of battlefield spoils.

In contrast, verses with political import are quite numerous but highly general and repetitive. They outline a very simple order of things. God is the sole possessor of sovereignty over the Community of Believers, and his sovereignty is instituted through the agency of His chosen prophet. As God's spokesman and vicegerent, the Prophet conveys His teachings and commandments. He also works to build his followers—that is, those who have accepted the divinely sent message he has brought—into a community that conducts its affairs in accordance with God's commandments. In so doing, the Prophet demands complete obedience to his own judgments and decisions, though he is admonished to consult with his followers in making them. In what might seem an astonishing and crucial omission, the Qur'an does not tell us what happens to the Community of Believers when the Prophet is no longer there to teach and govern. The Qur'an simply does not envision a believing community without a prophet at its head. In light of this gap, we might infer that the community is now free to consult its own needs and interests in accordance with the divine commandments left in its care. However, the unhappy example of the Jews and Christians shows how readily people will go astray from the true path when they no longer have a divinely appointed messenger to guide and control them.

As to the social structure of the Community of Believers, the Qur'an says almost nothing. It presupposes the extended family or clan as the basic building block of society, for the family is made responsible for the well-being and protection of its members, demands vengeance from those who have injured or murdered one of its members, and distributes the estates of its deceased members in accordance with precisely spelled out rules. Such clans had for centuries been the constitutive elements of traditional Arabian society. The Qur'an takes the patriarchal family as the norm; it stipulates the authority of men over women, specifically of husbands over wives. Whether this simply continued a long-established patriarchal order or represented something of an innovation we do not really know; there are arguments on both sides of this question, none of which are terribly convincing. The Qur'an clearly recognizes and sanctions the right of the individual to own and dispose of property, though believers are constantly admonished to obtain and use it in a fair and just manner. In particular, they are enjoined to care for the poor and weak in their midst, particularly orphans and widows. As head of the community, the Prophet sees to its common interests and needs, but the taxes and booty he receives for this purpose are his to dispose of in accordance with his discretion; they are not really common property. In general, the prosperity of the community and the salvation of its members demand unity and mutual support before all else. "Hold fast to the rope of God, and do not break into factions. Remember the favor God has bestowed upon you. He reconciled your hearts, and by his grace you became brothers after you had been enemies of one another" (Qur'an 3:102).

It is in the context of these general observations that we can understand what Muhammad's life means to Muslims, how it is the living embodiment of the Qur'an.[2] According to Islamic historical tradition, Muhammad's life falls into three segments—one of some forty years and two of roughly a decade each. The first two-thirds of his life (ca. A.D. 570–610) he passed unremarkably as a citizen of his native Mecca in western Arabia. During the next ten years, he was (as he understood his experience) called by God to reform the belief, worship, and morality of his fellow townsmen. Frustrated by Meccan indifference and hostility, he sought refuge with his small band of followers in the neighboring oasis of Medina (A.D. 622), and there, in exile, he shaped his teaching into the kernel of a world religion and made himself the paramount power in Arabia.

Mecca was a regional trading town and shrine center, and as such it surely had a rather mixed population, but politically and economically it was dominated by a single tribe, the Quraysh. Muhammad was a member of this tribe and had been born into one of its most prestigious clans, but though his clan enjoyed high status it seems to have been neither wealthy nor powerful during his lifetime. Islamic tradition represents the young Muhammad as a man respected for his probity and moral seriousness, but had his life not taken a shocking turn in his early forties, there would have been no particular reason for later generations to remember him.

Sometime around 610, after a long period of spiritual uncertainty and searching that led him to turn away from the traditional gods and cult practices of Mecca, he began to see visions and hear voices. This was initially a terrifying experience, as one can well imagine, but bit by bit he became convinced that he was not a victim of demonic forces; on the contrary, he came to realize that he was being called by the one God to summon his fellow tribesmen of Quraysh to repentance, obedience, and true worship. This God was no local deity of Mecca; he was the same God who had sent the ancient prophets—Noah, Abraham, Moses, Jesus, and many others—to warn and teach their peoples. Initially, the message was simple and stark: God would soon bring the present world to a cataclysmic end, the graves of the dead would be opened, every man and woman who had ever lived would be confronted with his or her deeds and then led into the gardens of Paradise or thrown headlong into the everlasting fires of Hell. Every human action counted on the Day of Judgment, but one was critical: to have confessed that God is one, unique, and eternal, and to have worshiped Him alone.

The message brought by Muhammad at first seemed addressed to individuals, but underneath it had a communal significance as well. First, the human actions subject to divine judgment (apart from the confession of God's oneness) were largely social in character— honesty in one's business dealings, charity to those in need, and so on. That is, one would be judged on how he had conducted himself within his community. Second, the new teachings were profoundly subversive of the established order in Mecca, even if unintentionally so, for the leaders of the Quraysh derived much of their wealth and status from their control of the city's pagan cult practices. If Muhammad's message were accepted by the people of Mecca, he would ipso facto supplant them as the town's leading figure.

In addition, Muhammad's proclamations soon incorporated a broader message. This message is conveyed through a long series of exhortations and parables, but perhaps most vividly in the story of Noah's people, which is repeated many times throughout the Qur'an. Noah tries to warn his neighbors of God's imminent wrath, of the need to turn back to Him at once, but he is scorned. Then "they were drowned and led into the Fire" (Qur'an 71:25; see also 11:25–49; 26:105–121). God's commandments are sent down not merely to individuals but to whole communities. Individuals can sometimes reject God and get away with it during their lifetimes, though they will be judged sternly at the end of time. But communities are subject to mercy or wrath here and now in this present life. To reject God and His messengers is to invite destruction at any moment. The Qur'an contains scores of warnings on this point, all summed up in the terse words, "Nay, your Lord has not destroyed towns unjustly, while their people knew not their sins" (Qur'an 6:131).

In spite of the dire fate that surely awaited them, the Meccans ul-

why maybe some muslims believe renewed fate will salvage community in the present...

timately found their kinsman unendurable and compelled him to leave. After two years of fruitless searching for a place of refuge, he found a place for himself and his followers in the oasis of Medina, some two hundred miles to the north. In inviting Muhammad to settle among them, Medina's leaders clearly solved his most urgent problem, but he likewise solved one of theirs. Medina was inhabited by two tribes that had in recent years been locked in a bloody, unresolvable feud. The chiefs of the two factions apparently discerned in Muhammad the qualities of a good traditional arbitrator: a reputation for justice and fair dealing, firmness and resolution in the face of hostility, the appearance of one who had contact with supernatural forces, and—not least—an outsider with no ties to either warring faction and with no local basis of support. In ancient Arabia an arbitrator's capacity to settle disputes was ironically rooted in his very political weakness and marginality.

Thus Muhammad came to his new home in two somewhat contradictory capacities—as the man the Medinans had chosen to arbitrate their bloody conflicts and as a refugee dependent on them for protection of his family and himself against his Meccan kinsmen. Through a path that we cannot trace here, Muhammad skillfully transformed these frail beginnings into a position of uncontested leadership within the oasis. More than that, he made this prosperous but previously obscure agricultural settlement into the political center of gravity of all Arabia. Medina became in less than a decade the heart of a dynamic and rapidly expanding tribal confederation that pulled into its orbit most of the nomadic tribes and oasis settlements of western and central Arabia. Some of these were subdued by conquest, but the majority entered the confederation voluntarily. In this way they became allies within a loose tributary relationship that required them to confess that God was one and unique, that Muhammad was God's apostle, and to pay a modest annual tax to support the common needs of the confederation. In the end, even the obdurate Meccans, left hopelessly isolated politically, militarily, and economically, were compelled to acknowledge the revelation Muhammad had brought and therefore to accept his political supremacy.

The basic principles of Muhammad's polity were drawn from long-established Arabian tradition in many ways, but he gave these traditions a unique twist and wound up creating something very new indeed. To begin with, most Arabian tribal confederations were

in Medina

fly-by-night affairs that depended for their power on a momentary balance of power and the charismatic leadership of the man who had assembled them. As power shifted from one tribe to another, or when the founder passed from the scene, the confederation dissolved. Muhammad's confederation, in contrast, had remarkable staying power. Even in its most transitory dimension—a coalition of nomadic and sedentary tribes capable of imposing their rule on their neighbors— it lasted more than a century. In its permanent form—a vast body of men and women scattered throughout a host of separate countries but bound together by a common confession—it flourishes down to the present day. Apart from its sheer longevity, Muhammad equipped his new confederation with a set of institutions that, however rudimentary at first, had the potential to evolve over time into the machinery of a centralized, bureaucratic state. This transformation from tribal coalition to state was slow and sometimes violent, but the new political structure was clearly in place sixty years after Muhammad's death, and it was strengthened and elaborated for some centuries thereafter.

It was in Muhammad's time very common for a tribal movement to coalesce around a sacred shrine or a holy man—that is, a person infused by supernatural knowledge and powers. But Muhammad alone brought a coherent set of values and doctrines capable of reshaping (without entirely supplanting) the Arabian Peninsula's old way of thinking. More than that, his new outlook was capable of adapting to and being effective within enormously different social and economic milieus. The real glue of Muhammad's confederation, especially its core elements in Medina and Mecca, was the demand that its members accept the revelation he had brought. In so doing, family and tribal loyalties were subordinated to Islam—first of all, one must obey and serve God and His prophet. Through this confession, a loose, temporary confederation of independent tribes was transformed into a community of believers; the ancient word *umma* indeed soon ceased to mean a confederation or people and came to refer specifically to a community defined and bound together by a common religious belief. The message had such power that it was able to survive the passing of the man who had brought it.

What the leaders of the early Muslim community distilled from their experience of the Qur'an and Muhammad was that their new religion, Islam, was not merely a system of personal belief and morality. Rather, Islam was a call to build a new community based on obedience to God's commandments and dedicated to spreading His religion to all humankind. To this task, all Muslims, men and women, should contribute to the best of their abilities, in the sure and certain knowledge that they would have to answer for it before God. Islam, in brief, had a political mission, and political action was an essential element in personal salvation.

On this point most Muslims have agreed. The question is how Muslims over the last fourteen centuries have tried to go about fulfilling this urgent mission. On the largest scale, that of the Community of Believers as a whole, Muhammad of course had already laid the foundations; the task at hand was to maintain the political structure that he had erected. As his immediate followers interpreted his example, there must continue to be a single commonwealth of those who accepted Islam, unified and governed under the broad authority of one man, Muhammad's successor. This "successor" to Muhammad quickly acquired a variety of titles. According to Islamic historical tradition, he was first called *khalifat rasul Allah*, "the deputy or vicegerent of God's apostle"—that is, the one who acted in Muhammad's place now that he was no longer here, anglicized as "caliph." But he soon adopted the additional title *amir al-mu'minin*, "commander of the believers"—literally, the one invested with authority over the believers—and this was the way he was usually addressed. Finally, he came to be called *imam*, a word that initially referred to the person (always an adult male) who stood in front of the assembled body of worshipers and led the ritual prayer. Soon enough, however, the title *imam* acquired in addition the sense of a revered and authoritative religious teacher. That is, Muhammad's successor was the community's mentor and guide as well as its ruler.[3]

The nature and scope of the powers wielded by the caliph were disputed from the outset, and remain so even today. Most Muslim and non-Muslim scholars agree, however, that the caliph was no prophet—that is, he was no longer a recipient and transmitter of divine revelation; with the death of Muhammad, God had forever ceased to speak to humankind. However, he was certainly the chief guardian of the revelation vouchsafed to Muhammad. As such, he was responsible for maintaining the integrity and purity of this revelation, for preventing any contamination or corruption of the words that had been sent down to the Prophet. But just as important, he

was responsible for ensuring that revelation was upheld throughout the lands of Islam as the standard of belief and conduct, that it
was the foundation for law and administration. In this perspective,
his authority was unambiguously religious; his job was to ensure
God's continuing protection and blessings toward the Muslims, and
hence their felicity in this world and the next.

His authority was also very much of this world, of course. The
caliph was a monarch, albeit of a peculiar kind; in his person were
invested all the political powers of the Community of Believers. If
the Muslims were to live their lives in accordance with God's word,
the community's territories had to be expanded or at least defended
from its enemies, there had to be law and order, disputes had to be
settled peaceably, malefactors punished, commerce and agriculture
encouraged, and so forth. All this required armies, police, courts, bureaucrats, and, inevitably, taxes. Everything ordinary monarchs did,
the caliph had to do as well. That is, his office required piety and religious learning, but it also imperatively demanded political skills
of a high order, skills that were then as now in desperately short
supply.

So far we have asked what the caliph did, but who was he? That
is, who could hold this lofty office, and how was he chosen? On this
issue, from the very beginning down to the present day, Muslims
have disagreed, often very violently. One faction called the Kharijites—never a very large one—held that since the caliph acted on
behalf of the community, he had to be elected by it (i.e., by its most
prestigious senior males). If the caliph fell into sin—and almost any
policy error might be regarded as a sin—he should be deposed at
once, so as to prevent the community as a whole from being tainted
by his fault and thereby risking God's wrath. At the opposite pole,
another and much larger group believed that the caliph was chosen
not by men but by God and that every caliph had been so chosen
from all eternity. God did not choose at random, of course, but from
the blessed family of his chosen prophet. Who belonged to this family was long disputed, but eventually membership was narrowed to
the progeny of Muhammad's only surviving child, his daughter Fatima, and her husband, Ali (who was also Muhammad's first cousin).
The group holding this opinion were called Shi'ites, from *shi'at 'Ali*,
"the partisans of Ali." From time to time they succeeded in putting
one of their candidates on the throne in some corner of the Islamic

world, but they have almost always been a minority of Muslims—
currently, some 10 to 15 percent of the total in the world.

Finally, the great majority of Muslims (the so-called Sunnis) took
a mixed—their opponents would say opportunistic—position, one
that tried to base itself on the complex historical realities of the office. The caliph ruled on behalf of the community, but once in office
he could be deposed only for manifest disbelief. Mere tyranny and
injustice did not suffice, since "sixty years of tyranny is better than
one night of anarchy," as a famous adage had it. In principle he was
elected by the community's leading men, though in fact he was almost always nominated by his predecessor, who was typically his
father or older brother; that is, the office was effectively transmitted
by hereditary succession, unless it was seized by violence and conspiracy. The fundamental goal, for both the caliph and his subjects,
was to maintain the unity of the community. Schism must be averted
at almost any cost.

Described in this way, the Sunni view of the caliphate may seem
hardly better than a counsel of despair, and in fact it does sometimes come across as a tissue of unprincipled compromises. But it is
the view that ultimately commanded the broadest and most persistent support among medieval Muslims. It did so for two reasons.
First, it assured Muslims that they had never fallen from God's saving grace; whatever traumas and disasters the believers had suffered,
they were linked to the golden age of the Prophet through an unbroken chain of his lawful successors. Second, it recognized the all-
too-human fallibility of rulers and made their role instrumental and
symbolic. Caliphs might help the Community of Believers live in accordance with the divine commandments, and they symbolized its
ideal unity, but in the final analysis the community was responsible
for its own salvation, for knowing and maintaining the truth that
God had revealed to it.

As the above remarks no doubt intimate, the actual history of the
caliphate was extremely checkered; at many points it seems, as Edward Gibbon said in a different context, "little more than the register of the crimes, follies, and misfortunes of mankind."[4] When Muhammad died, it was by no means certain that he would have a
single successor, or that his infant community would hang together
at all. When that crisis was surmounted, the Muslims soon fell into
another extended period of political crisis; Muhammad's second,

third, and fourth successors were all assassinated, the latter two by Muslim dissidents, and the glittering century of expansion between 632 and 750 was disfigured by three major civil wars. There was then another half century of internal peace before the caliphate became the object of another civil war. The ninth century witnessed an accelerating decline of real caliphal power, until at the end a caliph could hardly visit the privy in his own palace without permission from the military despots who now controlled the government.

By 950, the caliph was a puppet ruler; his very title was challenged by anticaliphs in Spain and North Africa, and almost all the territories nominally under his authority—territories that extended from Spain to Central Asia and parts of Pakistan—were in reality run by local warlords. The warlords were happy to put the caliph's name on their coins and ask God's blessing on him at the Friday prayers, but otherwise they paid him little heed. Under such circumstances one might suppose that the caliphate would slowly fade from the scene altogether, but that was not the case. Whenever opportunity offered, in the messy transitions between one warlord dynasty and the next, the caliphs tried to reassert the prestige and power of their ancient, sacred office. By the 1150s, they were in fact able to reestablish themselves as the actual rulers of a petty state in central and southern Iraq, and for the next century they exploited their status as the head of the community of Muslims to play a more than symbolic role in the complex diplomacy of the Muslim world. The historic Sunni caliphate was only brought to an end by the cataclysm of the Mongol conquest of Baghdad in 1258, after a history of 625 years.

Even after the death of the last caliph—he is said to have been wrapped in a carpet and clubbed to death lest the blood of a monarch be spilled on the ground—the idea of the caliphate did not disappear among Sunnis. It did in fact manifest itself in many new ways. To recall a point made in the last chapter, the historian and philosopher Ibn Khaldun argued that any ruler who governed in accordance with the Shariʿa—that is, who strove to carry out God's commandments and adhere to the model set by His blessed prophet—was a caliph. There could in principle be several caliphs at any given moment, or none at all. In any case, the central meaning of the office in earlier times—that the caliph should be the symbol and guarantor of the unity of the community—was abandoned.

Rather, the caliph was the symbol of government in accordance with God's law. Other theories of the caliphate were not so ready to abandon the tradition of universalism; these theories asserted that the caliphate could only be claimed by a powerful Muslim empire, that one state which was preeminent among the rest in size, power, and prestige, and which was best able to expand the boundaries of Islamic rule. In the sixteenth and seventeenth centuries, this theory was adopted by two mighty empires, the Ottomans and the Mughals of India. Happily these powerful claimants to universal sovereignty in Islam were separated by Iran and the Indian Ocean, and hence had neither need nor opportunity to resolve the merits of their respective claims.

In the eighteenth and nineteenth centuries, the idea of the caliphate took yet another turn. The Mughal Empire dissolved into chaos and was ultimately absorbed by the British East India Company, a peculiar hybrid enterprise of commerce and politics. The Ottoman Empire endured but did not prosper. To claim some standing among the Great Powers of Europe, to maintain a certain credibility as the peer of Britain, France, Austria, and Russia, the Ottoman sultans reasserted their title as caliph in the late 1700s. The claim had a certain resonance among the world's Muslims, since the Ottoman Empire was soon the only major independent Muslim state still in existence. For European consumption, however, the Ottomans made a somewhat different claim; as caliph, the sultan was the "spiritual head" of the world's Muslims, much as the pope was the spiritual head of the Catholic church. This claim in effect renounced political leadership, but exactly what it meant in a positive sense was never clear. The pope after all claimed to define faith and morals for Catholics, and he was indubitably the chief of a great international institution, the Church of Rome. But the Ottoman sultans made no claim (as the earliest caliphs may well have done) to be authoritative teachers of Islamic doctrine, and their political and administrative authority certainly did not extend beyond the boundaries of the empire—nor even within a great part of it.

Whatever the real meaning of the late Ottoman caliphate, it was apparently terminated for all time in 1924, when the new Turkish Republic under Atatürk abolished the office and banished its last holder. There was widespread shock and concern among Muslims, especially in India, but efforts to restore the office in the 1920s and 1930s came to nothing. Initiatives by Muslim governments were often perceived, quite rightly, as masks for dynastic ambitions, and by World War II the caliphate seemed as dead as the divine right of kings.

But it is not quite so, even now. Although the contemporary Islamic movement is in fact a thousand local movements, each rooted in local conditions and aspirations, there is a renewed sense among Muslims of the ideal unity of Islam and its myriad peoples, and of the acute need for them to combine their struggles against the enemies of poverty, corruption, tyranny, and imperialism. There have been some efforts (largely under Saudi aegis) to create an Islamic Conference as a bloc roughly comparable to NATO. A revival of the caliphate has been mentioned, though so far not seriously pursued, and it may be that an institution created to resolve a religiopolitical crisis in seventh-century Arabia cannot be made to fit a very different one on the eve of the twenty-first century. But the caliphate has always been a protean idea, changing in whatever way necessary to meet the realities imposed by the world. It survived a great deal— assassins and the Mongols, the French and British empires, modern secular nationalism—and throughout it has never ceased to be a fundamental element in Muslim political thinking. When a daring young professor at al-Azhar, Ali Abd al-Raziq, published a treatise in 1924 arguing that Islam per se—Islam as revelation—had nothing to say about the political institutions by which Muslims should govern themselves, and that the caliphate was a purely human creation, he was savagely denounced by his colleagues and quickly stripped of his post by an embarrassed Egyptian government. Among modern Muslim activists the caliphate is recalled as the political framework for the vividly remembered Golden Age that they struggle to reclaim. It is far too early to consign it to the dustbin of history.

The above comments obviously oversimplify things in many ways; most gravely, they sketch the historical evolution only of the Sunni caliphate. The Shi'ites—those loyal to the memory and lineage of Ali—naturally had a different experience and interpreted it differently.[5] For them, the idea of the caliphate soon faded in importance; their loyalties and intellectual concerns focused on the concept of imamate—that is, on the ethical and theological rather than the political dimension of authority over the Muslims. For Shi'ites, the imam did not require earthly power; he was a divinely appointed and infallible guide to salvation for those who recognized him, and he retained his supreme religious authority whether or not he actually ruled. Since Shi'ism had begun as a matter of personal loyalty to Ali and his sons, it was natural that later Shi'ites would believe that this unique religious authority could belong only to the direct lineage of Ali. The office of imam was thus transmitted from generation to generation within this divinely elected family, with each imam using his infallible knowledge to designate his own successor.

Just as Sunnis soon had to face the embarrassment of a powerless caliph, Shi'ites (most of them, at least) had to deal at more or less the same time with the problem of an imam who had disappeared from human view ca. 875. But they could not imagine that God would leave them with no teacher and guide. Hence they developed the idea of an absent imam, one who was still living and present on earth but hidden from the eyes of his followers, until that day when God would choose to bring him forth to reclaim his rightful power over the affairs of mankind. During the imam's absence, when no human being could have direct access to him, religious scholars steeped in the written and oral record of his teachings would provide provisional guidance to the faithful, and of course to any rulers who cared to heed them. How long the era of occultation would last no one knew, but the mere knowledge that the imam was really (if invisibly) present in the world allowed life to go on.

The above discussion gives us an answer to the question with which I opened this chapter. There is indeed a distinctively Islamic system of politics, a set of institutions and patterns of government that has had sacred meaning for Muslims since the earliest decades of Islam. It is true that this system of politics was not laid down directly by scripture but was rather created out of concrete historical experience. However, Muslims made sense of this experience through appeal to the theological and ethical teachings of the Qur'an and the Prophet. Among Sunnis, the caliphate was seen as a living link with the life and work of Muhammad, and as the instrument through which Muslims could carry out the collective obligations that God had laid upon them. Even as the caliphate gradually ceased to be an effective organ of government, and metamorphosed first into a symbol and then into a memory, it remained a powerful ideal. Among the Shi'ites, the historic caliphate represented a bald theft of the rights of Ali's lineage, but the idea of the imamate provided a very productive framework for political and theological discussion.

In spite of the central role of the universal caliphate in Islamic political consciousness, for most of the last fourteen centuries the actual government of Muslim territories took place within far smaller arenas than the whole Community of Believers and under rulers whose claims to religious leadership were exiguous at best. Indeed, for more than a thousand years the lands of Islam were divided up among a constantly shifting cast of quarreling warlords, tribal confederations, and hereditary dynasties. Was there any sense at all in which these regimes could claim to embody Islamic political values and purposes?

To answer this question, it is worth knowing how this unhappy situation came about. From the outset, the caliphs probably never exercised any real administrative control over the extremities of their enormous empire—Spain and Morocco in the west, the lower Indus River valley and steppe lands beyond the Oxus River in the east— but by the early 800s, even places far closer to home were slipping away from them. At first it was simply a matter of recognizing hereditary governorships in Tunisia and eastern Iran, turbulent regions far from the caliphal residence in Baghdad which required stable, long-term rule to be governed at all. Since these governorships were founded by men who had been loyal and effective servants of the caliphal regime, they posed no real threat to the legitimacy and primacy of the caliphate. But by the late 800s, for reasons that are still poorly understood, even the caliphate's central provinces were falling into the hands of a host of rival warlords. These warlords were constantly at war with one another, and few of their states survived as long as a century; many indeed came and went in months. They regarded the caliphs with ill-disguised contempt, but they rarely thought of supplanting them. On the contrary, when possible they tried to control the caliphs, to make them puppets and figureheads for their own jerry-rigged regimes.

The warlord states dominated the politics of the Islamic world for nearly four hundred years (ca. A.D. 850–1250) before they, like the caliphate, were submerged in the tidal wave of the Mongol invasions. Though these states were such a persistent feature of the political terrain, every one of them, taken individually, was internally unstable and vulnerable to attack by its rivals. The crucial political problem faced by every warlord was that of legitimacy—that is, of discovering some convincing reason (beyond brute force) why his subjects should obey him and his rivals should respect his right to exist. In this quest they certainly did not lack for ingenuity. They tried out every idea in the rich treasury of medieval Islamic thought, which drew not only on the Qur'an and the teaching of Muhammad but equally on the political traditions of ancient Greece, Christian Rome, Iran, and even India.

Ultimately the warlords and their apologists came up with a package of claims that seemed intellectually fairly satisfying, even if they were seldom effective in fending off the ambitions of their rivals.[6] First of all, most warlords claimed to be, not independent monarchs, but simply authorized deputies of the caliph; that is, they had the right to rule their territories because the caliph had formally appointed them as his governors. These caliphal appointments were highly prized; to get them, a warlord would pay handsome sums as "tribute" or, if a caliph seemed reluctant to go along, make highly credible threats of force. On one level, the caliphal delegation of powers may well seem an empty sham, but it did preserve the idea of a unified community of believers conducting its affairs under the authority of a single head. Moreover, the caliph's "governors" maintained the apparatus of Islamic life: they enforced the great public observances (the Friday worship, the Ramadan fast, the annual pilgrimage to Mecca) that were the symbol and foundation of Islamic identity; they built mosques and appointed preachers; they named judges who implemented the Shari'a's imperatives in all phases of civil and criminal law. Not least, the caliph's name was mentioned in the public sermon on Friday and engraved on the coinage. For ordinary Muslims, all this was enough to guarantee the Islamic character of the regime under which they lived; they had little reason to know or care how any given governor had actually come to power, or what his real relations with the caliph might be.

By the year 1000, few warlords were still content to be merely the caliph's deputy within the lands they ruled, though they jealously guarded that title as long as they could. After the destruction of the historic caliphate by the Mongols in 1258, they could of course no longer make much use of this convenient fiction. But by that time they had already elaborated another, quite separate source of legitimacy: namely, the ideals of kingship that had emerged in ancient Iran and were still preserved through the writings and attitudes of the Persian landholding elite that supplied most of the bureaucrats in Iran and Iraq.[7] The ideology of ancient Iranian kingship was not of course Islamic in inspiration; such religious content as it had was more Zoroastrian than anything else. But the advocates of this ideology did not find it difficult to mask that awkward fact and to develop a workable synthesis of Islamic and Iranian values. In the simplest terms, they argued that just as God governed the cosmos, so He chose kings as His deputies to govern and maintain the social order that He had created. The king was literally elected by God and was kept in power by divine favor. As God's vicegerent, the king was answerable only to Him; he was, in short, an absolute monarch, an autocrat. The king's duty as ruler was to uphold justice—and justice in this case referred less to individual rights than to the balance and stability of society as a whole, so that every group would fulfill its obligations and none could oppress any other.

So far there was nothing at all Islamic about this theory; it was simply a claim that kings had the right to govern because God had given them that right. What linked kingship to Islam was the mechanism through which the king maintained justice; this he achieved by implementing the Shariʿa as the law of his state. Shariʿa, God's law, was the substance of royal justice. By this deceptively simple equation, ancient Iranian kingship was made Islamic kingship. In this theory, it should be noted, the caliph had no real role. The king (i.e., the local warlord who actually ran things) upheld Islam and enforced the Shariʿa directly on God's behalf; the caliph was a dispensable intermediary. In part for lack of any better alternative, no doubt, Shariʿa-oriented political theorists in the later Middle Ages ultimately accepted this formulation as religiously sound: a regime was Islamic, and was hence owed all due submission by Muslims, insofar as it strove to uphold Islamic law and values and insofar as a ruler ensured he was on the right track by consulting actively with qualified religious scholars. But whatever their subjects might think about this approach, the warlords and hereditary dynasts found it altogether satisfactory, and Perso-Islamic kingship remained a keystone of political thought in the Islamic world down to the mid-nineteenth century. The Ottoman sultans, to take one very important example, relied far more heavily on this concept than on their somewhat tenuous claim to the caliphate to legitimize their authority.

Muslim thinkers in the late nineteenth and twentieth centuries have generally rejected Perso-Islamic kingship; they have not been impressed by its Islamic trappings, and they regard it as an embarrassing relic of an age of despotism, oppression, and stagnation. But since Sunnis have not devised any practical and intellectually convincing way to revive the caliphate and Shi'ites must put something in place while they wait for the hidden imam to come forth, modern thinkers have had to confront something of a theory vacuum. In view of the overwhelming military power, economic dynamism, and cultural effervescence of Europe during this period, it is not surprising that they were attracted to the possibility of adapting the latter's characteristic political institutions—in particular, constitutionalism and elected parliamentary government—to the needs of Islamic societies.[8]

Obviously, these notions flew in the face of centuries-old tradition, wherein rulers obtained their thrones either by hereditary descent or open conflict and their autocratic power was restrained only by the demand that they adhere to the Shari'a. That was of course a substantial part of their appeal: constitutionalism and parliamentary government were self-evidently "modern" and in that sense highly desirable. But were they authentically Islamic? There was after all no clear (or even murky) precedent for them in some thirteen centuries of Islamic history. The first to argue that Islam and constitutional government were compatible—that Islam, correctly understood, indeed demanded constitutional government—was a group of Istanbul writers and activists in the 1860s and 1870s who were called the Young Ottomans. Their argument was based on two points: first, the widely accepted advice that rulers should consult with their subjects—a point that they grounded in a terse Qur'anic command to the Prophet to "take counsel with them [his followers] in the matter" (Qur'an 3:158); and second, the historical fact that the first caliph Abu Bakr had been chosen by the acclamation of the Muslims (adult males, of course) assembled together after the Prophet's death. In fact, the classical Sunni theory of the caliphate had always maintained the fiction that the caliph was elected by the leading men of the community, although the manner of election and the number of electors were ambiguous in the extreme. To the Young Ottomans, these two points were sufficient to demonstrate that Islam was essentially democratic and that all the intervening centuries of autocratic rule had been a tragic diversion from the true path.

For reasons we cannot examine here, the Young Ottomans acquired considerable political influence for a few years, enough to have the sultan promulgate a constitution for the Ottoman Empire in 1876 and to have a parliament elected under this constitution in

1877. The parliament was summarily dismissed by the same sultan in 1878 and did not reconvene until 1908, when there was a return (not always untroubled) to parliamentary government, which lasted until the end of World War I. But the Ottoman Constitution of 1876 stayed on the books and remained a focus for the aspirations of many democratic and reform-minded groups throughout three decades of frustration. It was in most ways a thoroughly secular document (e.g., in its grant of equal citizenship to the large non-Muslim communities within the empire), but the point in the present context is that it had been conceived and legitimized through an argument appealing to specifically Islamic concerns and concepts.

The drama of the Ottoman Constitution was repeated on a different stage, with different actors, in Iran in 1905–1907.[9] Again there had been years of argument and debate (sometimes clandestine, sometimes public) among intellectuals and activists disillusioned with the country's inept monarchy. In Iran, however, this ferment ended not in an alliance (however momentary) between the intellectuals and the throne but in a massive popular uprising. The reigning shah was forced to allow the election of a constituent assembly in 1906, and this assembly drafted a constitution under the form of a series of Fundamental Laws, with some amendments in 1907. We have already examined (in chapter 2) the turbulent history of Iran's 1906 Constitution, but a few points need underlining here. First, several of the intellectuals involved in agitating for and drafting the constitution were either members of the Shiʿite clergy themselves or the sons and grandsons of clergy, and some of these were concerned to preserve a special role for the men of religion in the new order. Hence the 1907 amendments provided for a panel of clergy outside the parliament to assess the conformity of parliamentary legislation with the demands of the Shariʿa. In fact, the panel never met and never acted, but even as an empty formula it was a symbol of the Islamic nature of Iran's constitutional regime. Perhaps even more telling was the clause that specified that the new constitution would operate only "in expectation of the longed-for return of His Highness the Lord of the Age"—that is, the hidden imam. In short, the 1906 Constitution established a provisional government, albeit a very long term provisional government.

In spite of the possibilities for Islamic constitutionalism adumbrated by the Ottoman Constitution of 1876 and the Iranian Constitution of 1906, however, the first (and so far only) full-scale attempt to mold a constitution entirely in accordance with Islamic criteria is the Iranian Constitution of 1979.[10] It is a remarkable, not to say astonishing, document—a blend in almost equal parts of democratic liberalism, Swedish welfare-statism, Third World revolution, and Islamic political thought as interpreted by the Ayatollah Ruhollah Khomeini. The new constitution created an extremely complex balance of powers between a popularly elected president with wide executive powers and a parliament headed by a powerful speaker. The fact that each institution could effectively block the other seems odd to European commentators but is of course familiar and perhaps even reassuring to Americans. But the powers assigned to the president and the parliament were further checked, in fact almost vitiated, by organs superior to both. First of all, there was a supreme court with the power of constitutional review. But apart from this, a council of experts—essentially a panel of Shi'ite clergy—had to approve each piece of legislation for Islamic criteria. This is reminiscent of a similar institution in the 1906–1907 Constitution, but this time the council of experts was actually put in place, and it has successfully (or unsuccessfully, depending on one's perspective) made it almost impossible for parliament to pass any major piece of legislation in several areas, simply because the experts cannot agree on what the relevant Islamic criteria are. Finally, as a court of last resort and a source of continual guidance, there is the Faqih—the supreme Jurist who provides definitive interpretations of Islamic doctrine as needed, who can overrule any other organ of government, and who can take over the president's prerogatives or, if need be, even depose him from office.

This latter arrangement made the whole apparatus unworkable, and soon after Khomeini's death in 1989 the constitution was amended to reinforce the president's powers and enable him to act with some prospect of success. But it is necessary to know what the 1979 Constitution was attempting to do to understand why the office of the Faqih was created in the first place. First and foremost, the framers of the constitution wanted to build an authentically Islamic government, not just a Western parliamentary knock-off with a few Islamic trappings for local color. The constitution aimed at ensuring that legislation and policy would be developed in an Islamic spirit, with close attention to the doctrines and rulings of traditional

Shari'a jurisprudence. Of course, there were many ways to pursue that goal, but the framers instituted the office of the Faqih because of the unique role of Khomeini in the revolution.

Khomeini had rallied the people during the long autumn of 1978, when everything was in doubt, through his sermons from exile and his unyielding stance that the Shah must go.[11] He had thereby become the symbol of the revolution. But his role went well beyond that; among all the opponents of the Shah, he was the one who had insisted throughout on the creation of a specifically Islamic regime, and whose writings and teachings had demonstrated just what such a regime should be. In his extraordinarily influential 1970 treatise, *Vilayat-e Faqih veya Hukumat-e Islami* (The Authority of the Jurist, or Islamic Government), he had argued that the only people qualified to govern a Muslim people were the scholars of religion, because only they understood the commandments of Islam and how these should be instituted in public life.[12] Then taking an extremely bold step (which he masked in highly traditionalist rhetoric), he went on to argue that the scholars were not only uniquely qualified to rule but indeed were mandated to do so by the Qur'an, the teaching of the Prophet, and the doctrine of the imams. The only legitimate government in a Muslim country was government by the clergy, in strict accordance with the precepts of Islam. Khomeini had little to say about the formal institutions of an Islamic regime; the one crucial thing was that the right people should be in charge.

When it came time to draft the new constitution during the summer of 1979, it was intuitively obvious to all that a special place had to be set aside for Khomeini, not as head of state but rather as Iran's mentor and spiritual guide. It was equally obvious that this place would be defined in terms of his concept of vilayat-e faqih. Hence he became the Faqih, the Jurist, who was ultimately responsible for the country's government and whose presence guaranteed the legitimacy of the whole complex edifice. In the eyes of its founders, revolutionary Iran unquestionably embodied an Islamic system of politics, one that gave equal recognition both to the final authority of scripture and its recognized interpreters, on the one hand, and to the contemporary need for democratic institutions, on the other.

The Islamic Republic of Iran has no real counterpart in the Sunni world—that is, there is no state that has moved from a highly secularized political system to one claiming to be systematically Islamic in character. There are at least two Sunni regimes that have solid Islamic credentials, Morocco and Saudi Arabia. However, both of these represent very old political formations that can no longer be replicated in the contemporary world. Hence neither seems a terribly useful model for aspiring Islamic political theorists. The Moroccan monarchy dates back to the mid-seventeenth century (in some ways even a century before that). It is based on the unique religious charisma of the ruling family, originally a Sufi lineage that arose in one of the major Saharan oases and claims direct descent from the Prophet. The king of Morocco rules in part through an elected parliament, which he manipulates with consummate skill, but he also makes highly effective use of his religious authority and of the rich religious symbolism that surrounds his office.

As for Saudi Arabia, it began in the mid-eighteenth century, in a manner that has numerous parallels in Islamic history, as a close alliance between an ardent, intensely puritanical religious reformer (Muhammad ibn Abd al-Wahhab) and a powerful oasis chieftain in central Arabia, Muhammad ibn Saud. In effect, Ibn Saud built a polity (not so much a unified state as a complex tribal coalition) under whose umbrella Ibn Abd al-Wahhab could pursue his religious reform. After an explosive growth in the late eighteenth and early nineteenth century, the Saudi confederation was violently crushed by the Ottomans, but it sprang to new life in 1902 under a gifted new leader, Abd al-Aziz ibn Abd al-Rahman Al Saud, the founder of the modern Saudi kingdom. The Kingdom of Saudi Arabia (formally proclaimed under that name in 1932) has become in many ways a modern state over the last three decades, but it still struggles to retain its original mission as the political protector and supporter of the highly puritanical Wahhabi interpretation of Islam. It is no accident that King Fahd's chief title is Servitor of the Two Holy Sanctuaries (i.e., Mecca and Medina). Saudi Arabia very self-consciously clings to a late medieval political and legal structure: the king is an autocrat, who seeks advice widely but is not required to take it, and for cases that arise within the kingdom the Shari'a is interpreted and applied through highly traditional mechanisms. And apart from its formal institutions of government, Saudi Arabia is very much a family enterprise; all key executive and military posts are in the hands of one or another member of a very large royal family. For all these reasons, very few contemporary Islamic activists would think of imitating the Saudi system of government. However they imagine the future of Islamic politics, it is not this.

At this point, it needs to be emphasized that many Islamic movements have a far more modest goal than that of establishing an Islamic state, in the sense of creating a system of government whose institutions are systematically imagined and elaborated in terms of Islamic criteria. For them, the critical issue on the floor is *tatbiq al-shariʿa*—the application of Shariʿa. It seems a simple phrase, its meaning self-evident. But that is not altogether how things are.

What precisely is this Shariʿa that is to be applied? It can hardly be something as vast and amorphous as the whole body of debate and discussion on the obligations of a Muslim to God and his fellow creatures, although this is precisely what the word ought to mean. And if we restrict consideration to those parts of the Shariʿa that have produced concrete and legally enforceable rules for conduct (e.g., conditions of marriage and divorce, commercial contracts, crimes) we will hardly be better off. The reason, first of all, is that there are several different schools of interpretation, all regarded as equally orthodox, and these schools disagree on hundreds of very basic points. Worse, within each school we find a multiplicity of opinions on almost every issue. Not all opinions are equal, to be sure. Some carry great authority because they are shared by all leading scholars and are contested only by a few oddball dissidents. But in other cases the most revered and learned scholars simply do not agree with one another as to what a given rule of conduct ought to be. In view of this, should we force the Shariʿa, with all its loose ends and unsettled issues, into the straitjacket of a statutory code, in which there is one and only one authorized solution for each issue? If we do that, how shall we decide whose opinions to accept, whose to reject and silence? Finally, what about those parts of the Shariʿa that now seem socially unacceptable, such as the sections relating to slavery and concubinage? If we decide to exclude these, are we not ignoring God's law and the considered judgment of generations of Muslim scholars in favor of the whims and fancies of the present age?

If the very nature of the Shariʿa creates difficulties, these are only intensified when we turn to the first half of the phrase, *tatbiq*, "application." First of all, who is to apply it? Until the late nineteenth century, this was done by judges in the Shariʿa law courts. Each judge acted independently of all others; he applied the law as he understood it to the facts before him in each case. He was not bound in any way by precedent, by earlier decisions made by himself or by other judges in his jurisdiction. Nor, apart from taxes and a few other matters that were really not his concern, was there any body of statutes issued by the sultan or any other legislative agency. But since no contemporary state (apart from Saudi Arabia, at least) can function without statutory codes or case law, most of those advocating tatbiq al-shariʿa clearly expect to work within the modern framework of legislatures and appeals court hierarchies. Legislatures in particular are a problem. Should they have independent authority to enact legislation applying the Shariʿa, or do they need to be guided by councils of experts—and if the latter, who chooses the experts? What about the makeup of legislatures: can they include women or non-Muslims—people who in traditional Islamic settings had been barred from interpreting and applying the Shariʿa?

We need not pursue this line of questioning any further; it is already clear how problematic the concept of tatbiq al-shariʿa really is. But the debate does reveal an important point. For many, a political system is not Islamic because it has a particular structure or incorporates a specified set of institutions. Rather, it is made Islamic by the content of its laws, the substance of its policies. The mechanisms through which these laws and policies are generated are a matter properly left to human discretion and judgment. The moderate Islamist movements, sure of the appeal of their message to the Muslim masses, are usually quite democratic, at least in principle. (Once in power, of course, they might well face the ordinary human temptation to ensure that they stay there.) For this reason, they are willing to work within a parliamentary system more or less on the European model. In their experience, authoritarian or dictatorial governments are the ones that have most strenuously tried to exclude Islam from the political arena and to restrict its influence to the narrow realm of personal life.

With this we have come back to our starting point. Is there a distinction between religion and politics in Islam? The answer falls into two parts. On the level of broad values, the response would be no. Most serious Muslims do agree that Islam aims to build a society based on God's commandments, living in fidelity to those commandments, and this is preeminently a political goal. On the level of concrete goals and actions, however, the answer must be ambiguous; it depends very much on which group of Muslims we are talking about. We have seen that over the centuries Muslim peoples have developed an enormous array of political institutions (or had these institutions imposed on them), and they have found many ways of harnessing these institutions to their own purposes. Many Muslims, though certainly not all, would say that political institutions are religiously neutral in themselves; any given system of government may be more or less appropriate according to circumstances. What they do ask is that this government devote itself to building and defending an Islamic way of life.

That demand, bland and innocuous on the surface, of course raises a host of problems. To enter the debate on the "Islamic way of life" is often like plunging your fist into a hornets' nest. In the next three chapters I will explore a few dimensions of what Muslims believe their religion demands from them as they bring it into the public arena.

One of the most important of these dimensions is the defense—or perhaps I should say the vindication—of Islam against those who would attack or corrupt it. Any community, any system of belief, must be able to protect itself; obviously, it is essential to understand how Muslims have thought about this issue. Almost everyone knows the keyword—*jihad.* Very few have any sense of how complex and plastic a word it is.

A second dimension is even more crucial, that of the place of women within Islam. This is not a matter of ritual or theology but of the role that women ought to have, and historically have had, in building an authentic Islamic community. It is intuitively obvious to anyone that no such community is possible without their participation; it seems equally apparent to most observers that women have not been regarded as equal partners in this enterprise. But in any case, what Muslims mean by an "Islamic way of life" will remain completely opaque until we discover the place (or rather the many, constantly shifting places) that women occupy within the Islamic social imagination.

The issues raised by jihad and women, disparate as they are, suggest a third dimension of Islamic social and political thought. If jihad is resistance to the enemies of Islam, how should we define who these enemies are, and what limits or restraints must we observe in opposing them? Likewise, if women are full members of the community of Islam, and have the same hope of salvation as men do, how can we justify the host of restrictions on the roles they can properly play within the community's life? Both jihad and the "problem" of women thus lead us toward the issue of human rights. Does Islamic thought have any real contribution of its own to make to this issue, or is human rights talk in the Islamic world simply a foreign importation? The idea of human rights sets the claims of individuals against the claims of the community. For that reason, it brings together many of the issues confronted in this book and allows us to revisit them in a new context.

Simply because the debate among Muslims on these subjects is never-ending—it has been going on for some fourteen hundred years—I will not attempt to come to any categorical conclusions about them. What I will try to do is spell out a range of important perspectives, those that are always taken seriously because they have had a large number of advocates and supporters over many decades and centuries.

CHAPTER 8

JIHAD AND THE
POLITICS OF SALVATION

The image of American hostages, blindfolded and bound, being herded from the U.S. Embassy in Tehran into a shameful, helpless captivity, surrounded by exultant bearded or veiled youth, has become to many the image of Islam itself—a religion of fanaticism and hatred of everything not itself. As everyone knows, this fanaticism does not express itself simply as inchoate, unfocused rage; on the contrary, it is crystallized in the quintessentially Islamic doctrine of jihad, of unending and unlimited Holy War against the infidel.

People know a lot of things that aren't so, of course, and these statements about Islam fall squarely into that category. It is certainly the case that Muslims are capable of hatred and violence in the name of Islam. But so are we all, in the name of the beliefs and ideas that move us. One need only recall the roles of National Socialism and Marxism—thoroughly secular ideologies both—in the struggles of twentieth-century Europe, an era whose bloody savagery is almost without parallel in the history of the world. It is likewise true that jihad is a central doctrine in Islam—the sixth pillar of the faith, according to some authorities, though not all. Moreover, we have seen that Islam is a religion of social and political action, because it is rooted in the imperative to create a godly community. Human nature being what it is, that imperative sometimes requires a resort to jihad. But on closer inspection jihad turns out to be no simple thing; on the contrary, it contains a remarkably complex and wide-ranging cluster of ideas. To explore this cluster will tell us a great deal about the moral impulses that drive Muslims when they are trying to act as Muslims. It will also tell us how Muslims have translated these impulses into action in the real world.[1]

"Fight them until there is no more rebellion [against God] and religion is God's" (Qur'an 2:192; also 8:39). "The reward of those who go to war against God and His Apostle and spread corruption in the land is but to be killed, or crucified, or to have their hands and feet struck off alternately, or to be driven from the land" (Qur'an 5:33). The Qur'an has many such calls for armed struggle against the enemies of God. These commands to fight are far more nuanced and moderate when they are read in context, but they are undeniably there. Likewise, our oldest historical texts (a group of treaties dating from the Prophet's years in Medina) refer to the members of the new community as "those who struggle with their bodies and their goods alongside the Prophet." The crucial importance of warfare against the enemies of God and His prophet in Islam's early years is beyond dispute. The new religion might not have survived, and it almost certainly would not have flourished, without it. Yet this armed jihad was part of a larger struggle, one aimed at the creation of a new community on new foundations, and this struggle had to be waged on a very broad front. It is within this broader context that we must seek the meaning and importance of jihad.

The struggle to build a godly community takes two forms—or better, falls into two categories of moral action—jihad and (a long but weighty phrase) *al-amr bi'l-ma'ruf wa'l-nahy 'an al-munkar*. As we will see, each of these two categories of moral action unquestionably possesses its own tone and emphasis; a Muslim who appeals to one or the other is calling for quite different forms of action. Both, however, grow out of one and the same moral impulse.

To begin with, the term "jihad" does not mean "Holy War," as it is commonly and misleadingly translated. It means, literally, "to strive with all one's might" and is related to one of the fundamental concepts in Islamic legal thought, *ijtihad*, which is to strive through reason and knowledge to discover the truth—hence, to exercise independent judgment to resolve a disputed question of law. *Jihad* seldom occurs by itself in the Qur'an; the full phrase is normally *jihad fi sabil Allah*, which can be precisely translated as "striving in the path laid down by God"—that is, struggling to assure that God's purposes for mankind are achieved even in the face of obdurate opposition. In its broadest sense, jihad is struggle against all the forces that attempt to subvert God's purposes for mankind.

It is important to underline that jihad has a strongly positive purpose. It is not carried out merely to defeat the enemies of Islam, but is first and foremost a struggle to create a just and righteous social order. This struggle may be, and wherever possible should be, peaceable. Force is a last resort, as the Qur'an states many times; it is what you do when reason and persuasion get nowhere, when your efforts to use these methods are met not merely with indifference but with hostility and persecution.[2] Nor is jihad necessarily or even primarily directed against foreign nonbelievers. On the contrary, Muslims have from very early times regarded corruption, tyranny, and irreligion within the Community of Believers as even more critical targets of jihad. The internal health and integrity of the Community take precedence over the expansion of the faith. All this having been said, it remains true that the word *jihad* implies direct, vigorous action in the world; it proceeds from the perception of some overt evil, some malicious impediment to the fulfillment of God's will among mankind, which must be combated by all appropriate means. Jihad expresses the dynamism and activism of Islam.

The associated notion of *al-amr bi'l-ma'ruf wa'l-nahy 'an al-munkar* is on one level simply a form of jihad. The phrase means literally "commanding what is known to be good, and denouncing or forbidding things of ill-repute." (To save space and frustration, I will henceforth simply say "commanding the good.") It is the form taken by the struggle to build a godly community when talking is still possible, when preaching and remonstration are a plausible means of attaining this goal. It is an obligation incumbent on every Muslim, but only within the capacities of each. It might be something as ordinary as encouraging one's neighbor to come to prayer, or as bold as a fiery public denunciation of moral turpitude at the sultan's court. "Commanding the good" does not demand or even imply direct action, however. It is really a doctrine that reflects the moral awareness of the individual believer; if one calls attention to a wrong, one has done one's duty.

Now, what happens when one, as a concerned Muslim, is allowed to go on talking but nobody is listening—when, for example, the ruler goes on merrily with his drinking parties, his bribes, and his illegal taxes? Here Muslims part ways. Some ardent souls argue that such willful indifference to God's law is tantamount to unbelief and apostasy, and therefore calls for true Muslims to undertake the jihad. But the majority of religious authorities, adhering to the frame of mind inculcated by "commanding the good," have always taken a

more accommodating tack. They say that one just has to go on trying. It is up to God, not the individual believer, to bring down punishment on an errant community or corrupt leaders. Indeed, a rash
call for outright rebellion might burden one with the grave sin of
tearing the Community into warring factions (see Qur'an 3:102–105).

This last point leads us to a third doctrine, which has its origins
in the Qur'anic verse, "Obey God and His Prophet and those invested with authority among you" (4:59). This doctrine holds that
so long as one lives in a society where one can live an authentic
Muslim life—that is, where the prayers are performed, where judges
make their decisions on the basis of the Shari'a, and where the rulers
profess Islam, however hypocritically—Muslims should focus less
on overthrowing evil or correcting wrongdoing and more on upholding the central values and institutions of the community's religious life. Normally, we come closer to the goal of constructing a society built on God's commandments by performing the daily prayers,
observing the annual Ramadan fast, and giving alms to the poor
than by confrontation or violence. It is the believer's personal contribution to daily life, multiplied thousands and millions of times
over, that actually builds a moral and God-fearing community. This
sort of pious quietism in fact represents the mainstream teaching of
medieval Islam, the doctrine espoused and inculcated by the great
majority of religious scholars over many centuries, even down to the
present day. It is also the unspoken doctrine that has guided the public action of the great majority of Muslims throughout most of their
history. It may seem an oddly minimalist interpretation of a faith
born and spread through intense dynamism, but it reflects the inevitable political outlook of a group (i.e., the religious scholars) whose
very raison d'être was building a society governed by divine law
but who perceived all around them the threat of uncontrollable social and political violence.

At one time or another, any one of these doctrines—jihad, commanding the good, or pious quietism—may well appear to embody
the true "essence" of Islam, but the truth is that all three exist and
are at work simultaneously in every era. It is really a matter of circumstances which one comes to the fore and puts its mark on a
given period. All this having been said, however, it must be admitted that jihad is the doctrine that is most highly privileged in the way

Muslims remember and recount their own history. That is, when Muslims recall their past and appeal to it for guidance in the present, they most often see it as a story of overt struggle against the faith's enduring enemies—infidelity, tyranny, and moral corruption.

I have already cautioned against seeing jihad as a Holy War against the infidel, fought for the grandeur and aggrandizement of Islam. In fact, a deliberate policy of expansion through the conquest of non-Muslim territories, though it seems altogether typical to many non-Muslims (and not a few Muslims), is actually not terribly common throughout the fourteen centuries of Islamic history. Conquest under the banner of jihad was undeniably decisive—just as Manifest Destiny was for Americans during the mid-nineteenth century—in building the broad territorial framework in which Islamic life and culture evolved during its early history. However, most wars of jihad either have been directed against other Muslims, whether sincerely or cynically, or else have been clearly defensive in character.

Still, it is true that Islam's beginnings were deeply marked by wars of expansion, and these wars were important not only for the vast territories they brought under Muslim rule but also as a living epic that still possesses a profound mythic power in the Muslim imagination. To some degree this epic is embodied in works of systematic jurisprudence (which I will discuss briefly below) and serious history. But the consciousness of most Muslims over the centuries has been molded less by formal scholarship than by a huge body of folklore that began to take shape in the eighth and early ninth centuries—that is, one hundred to two hundred years after the conquests. (Much the same is true of Americans, obviously; most of us "know" our Western history only through Hollywood.) The folklore took many forms. There were hundreds of cryptic prophecies ascribed to Muhammad which linked the events and persons of the early conquests to cataclysms still to come. Anonymous poets composed immensely long verse epics, cherished among both urban and rural audiences and sung and elaborated for many centuries before they were captured in writing. Other writers concocted prose romances both short and long, preserved orally and in writing, whose contents often slipped into works of serious scholarship. It is hardly surprising that Arabic prose romances on the conquest of Syria were especially popular in that country and Egypt during the age of the Crusades, an era of heightened awareness among Muslims of the en-

during conflict between the forces of Islam and infidelity. The art of
the village epic poet and street-corner storyteller is now all but ex-
tinct, but their work has been taken over by cinema and television.
In addition, a suitably sanitized version of history is part of the curricula of the government schools, which now capture the great majority of children for at least a few years. We cannot say that most
Muslims have a critical or scientific knowledge of the early conquests.
But over the centuries popular culture has ensured that these events
are deeply embedded in their sense of who they are and where they
came from.

At this point it is clearly essential to look more closely at the
expansion of Islam during its first century, to see what it can teach
us about the place of jihad in Muslim thought.[3] The nature of the
warfare that marked Muhammad's career in Medina (622–632) is
sharply contested among both Muslim and non-Muslim historians.
The Qur'an and the most ancient historical texts explicitly call this
struggle jihad, and the willingness of Muhammad's adherents to participate in it and commit all their worldly possessions to it was the
real test of their commitment to his message. Even so, I think that
Muhammad's wars are best understood not as wars of conquest in
any simple sense. Rather, they were one element (a highly visible
element, admittedly) of a long and often desperate struggle to vindicate the new revelation against enemies who had explicitly proclaimed their intention to destroy it, or at least to isolate it and leave
it to wither on the vine. Moreover, Muhammad was a skilled diplo-
mat, and many of the tribes and regions that fell under his aegis during this decade did so as allies and tributaries rather than defeated
adversaries. But however he did it—and war and diplomacy are
hardly mutually exclusive—Muhammad was by his death in direct
or indirect control of much of the Arabian Peninsula (essentially, modern Saudi Arabia, Yemen, and Oman). The confederation he built,
with its core among his inner circle of followers in Medina, provided
both a political framework that could sustain and protect the new
religion he had brought and a powerful strategic springboard for
further expansion.

In the last three years of his life, Muhammad had in fact sent a
few columns northward into Syria to probe the Roman frontier districts east of the Dead Sea. These expeditions clearly suggest that his
views of his community's future encompassed something more than

Arabia alone. Still, we cannot be sure precisely what he himself had in mind. His immediate successors, however, launched a series of massive offensives that in two years subdued all Arabia, and within a decade after that gained dominion over Iraq, Syria-Palestine, and Egypt. Thereafter the pace of expansion slowed, but it did not cease; by 715, Arab-Muslim troops had penetrated beyond the Oxus River in Central Asia and stood at the foot of the Pyrenees in Spain. The great Sassanian Empire of Iran, four hundred years old, with its roots in the kingdom created by Cyrus and Darius a millennium before, was utterly destroyed, though it left a wondrous and evocative memory. The Roman Empire, shorn of its Near Eastern and African provinces, now had only a tenuous hold on what is now Greece and Turkey, though it would survive (at moments almost miraculously) and sometimes flourish for another seven centuries.

The causes of the Arabs' astonishing conquests in the decades after 632 have been endlessly debated, but to no avail. We can explain why the Romans and Iranians lost, but not why the Arabs won. Even more obscure are the motives that drove Muhammad's successors to such an incredibly bold policy. We might surmise—but it is no more than a surmise—that the initial goal of the Muslim armies was simply the conquest of Palestine, in particular the holy city of Jerusalem, already regarded by Muslims as sacred. But since Palestine was Roman territory and even more sacred to Christians than to Muslims, such a policy inevitably implied a wider war, for Palestine could not be held unless the Arabs also controlled all Syria, and ultimately Egypt as well. The attack on Iraq, which occurred more or less at the same time (the mid-630s) involved a different dynamic. Iraq was the political and economic center of the Sassanian Empire of Iran, but the conquests there seem to have been something of an accident, or perhaps inspired opportunism. They began as an alliance with local Arab tribes who were contesting Iran's rulers for control of the lower Euphrates valley and then turned into something more as early victories opened up new and grander possibilities.

But though the original nature of these events is a crucial issue, it is almost irrelevant to our concerns in this chapter. For when later generations of Muslims, writing in the late eighth and early ninth centuries, shaped their own historical interpretation of the conquests, they inevitably saw them from the perspective of what these titanic struggles had wrought. By that time no one could doubt that they represented the mighty hand of Providence, the fulfillment of God's eternal purpose in human history. Muhammad's successors, so later generations of Muslims believed, were simply following God's command to conduct jihad—the struggle to make His commandments prevail in this world—against the age-old but arrogant empires that had rejected the new revelation. The great conquests were all part of God's plan for spreading Islam to the ends of the earth. Through them the Muslims would build a vast political edifice within which His truth could grow and prosper and eventually win over the masses of people now placed under Muslim rule. Apart from this providential purpose, of course, the conquests were also the glittering reward that God had bestowed on the community that had embraced His word and messenger. (Obviously, the objects of these campaigns saw the matter in a rather different light, but that is a question for another day.)

The conquests of Islam's first century provided an extremely durable legal paradigm for appropriate relations between Muslim and non-Muslim governments and their subjects, a paradigm that would guide Islamic thought on the subject for many centuries. The whole edifice of Islamic legal doctrine dealing with jihad is distilled from debates during the eighth and ninth centuries on the events of the early Arab-Muslim conquests. The conquest era paradigm stayed on the books, so to speak, until the end of World War I, though it had become progressively harder to apply in any meaningful way to the realities confronting Muslim states throughout the nineteenth century. The traditional legal doctrine of jihad has retained a vestigial role in interstate relations in the twentieth century (particularly in the various wars with Israel), but almost all Muslim regimes have preferred to carry out their dealings with foreigners and with other countries on the basis of standard international law.

What then is the doctrine of classical Islamic law as regards jihad?[4] In simple terms, the medieval jurists divided the world into two parts: the Realm of Islam (Dar al-Islam) and the Realm of War (Dar al-Harb). The former was made up of all those territories that had a Muslim government; non-Muslims living under these governments suffered a number of legal and civil disabilities, but they were to be secure in their persons and property and were granted a substantial if limited freedom of religion. As non-Muslim subjects of a Muslim government, they lived under a formally defined pact of protection (Ar., *dhimma*) and were normally called *ahl al-dhimma* or *dhimmi*s.

The Realm of War was a different matter; this encompassed all the lands whose rulers and peoples had refused to accept Islam or rule by a Muslim government. These lands were therefore assumed to be in a permanent state of war with the Muslims, and a Muslim government could authorize warfare against them at any time. The object of such warfare was not conquest per se but either to defend the Muslims against attack or to bring nonbelievers into the Islamic fold. Only war conducted with those two intentions, and formally authorized by a lawful Muslim government, could be qualified as jihad, because only such a war was a struggle carried out in the service of God and His religion.

The appropriateness of defense is self-evident, but the idea of offensive warfare aimed at spreading Islam requires further explanation. The expansion of Islam through warfare could be achieved essentially in three ways. First, the peoples of the lands under attack could agree to accept Islam as their own religion; with that, fighting was to cease forthwith, and the only question concerned the political relationship between the existing regime and the Muslim government that had launched the struggle. Second, the nonbelievers could agree to accept Islamic rule while retaining their old religions. That is, they would surrender on terms. In this case, they would have more or less the same protected status as nonbelievers who had always lived under a Muslim government. Third, if they refused both alternatives, they were subject to forcible conquest, with all that this implied in the ancient and medieval world.

Islam's medieval jurists were usually realistic men, and they provided for several mitigations of this permanent state of war. First, if a Muslim government was too weak to attack a non-Muslim territory with success, it should by no means do so, since that would endanger the lives and well-being of its own subjects. Second, doctrine allowed for limited-term truces with non-Muslim rulers; in principle these were only to last a short time, but in fact they were almost indefinitely renewable. Third, a Muslim ruler had broad discretion to make military alliances with non-Muslim regimes for the benefit of the Muslims, and these alliances sometimes lasted for generations. For example, the Ottoman Empire was perpetually at war with the Holy Roman Empire and Habsburg Spain but maintained treaty relations with France and Great Britain from the late sixteenth century on. A glance at the map will reveal the sound geopolitical thinking behind Ottoman diplomacy. Fourth, trade was a good and lawful thing in itself, and apart from military truces with non-Muslim governments, treaties of commerce could be signed which would grant their subjects the privilege (always revocable) of living and working within Islamic territories.

Law and reality are not always the same thing, of course. By the early 800s, the jihad impulse in its optimistic, expansionist form was beginning to wane, and in most Islamic lands it faded away during the following two centuries. The famous Harun al-Rashid (who reigned over most of the Muslim world from 786 to 809) was the last caliph to make the jihad of expansion the heart of his foreign policy, though in fact his unrelenting attacks against the Byzantines achieved very little. As a formal concept, the idea of jihad as a war of expansion against the foreign infidel was never abandoned (at least until the mid-nineteenth century, and then only partially), but it was invoked only occasionally and very soon ceased to be a practical framework for state policy. On the contrary, by the mid-800s (i.e., some two centuries after the initial burst of conquests) we see a clear tendency among the major Muslim states toward permanent accommodation and coexistence with their Christian and other neighbors. Increasingly, the more powerful monarchs treated these non-Muslim states as elements in a secular balance of power, even as allies whom they could enlist against Muslim opponents if need be. The jihad, when and where it occurred, fell to pirates and frontier barons, who fought with their Christian or pagan counterparts on a basis of near-equality.

A remarkable index of this transformation is the place of Constantinople in Muslim thought. Three times between 677 and 715 the caliphs launched a massive expedition to conquer this city, not only the largest and wealthiest in Europe and Western Asia but also the capital of the Roman Empire and the heart of Christianity. Its fall to the caliphal armies would seal the end of the old order and manifest the final triumph of Islam. But Constantinople was a superb fortress, superbly defended, and all three sieges were beaten off. Muslim losses in the last siege (715–717) were so catastrophic that the caliphs never tried to mount another. After 717, Constantinople quickly ceased to be a concrete military objective and instead became the stuff of myth. The city would at last submit to Muslim arms, people believed, but only at the end of time, in the titanic convulsions preceding the Last Judgment. Constantinople symbolized broader changes in Muslim thinking: ideally, at the end of time, all the world would fall under Islam's shadow, but for the here and now . . .

There were, to be sure, other moments of enthusiasm after the glory of the first conquests had faded: the conquest of Byzantine Anatolia (modern Turkey) by the Seljukid Turks in the late eleventh century, the thrust into Hindu India by Mahmud of Ghazna around 1000 (although contemporaries understood perfectly well that his wars were as much about booty and empire as about Islam), and finally, during the sixteenth century, the nearly simultaneous conquests in India by the Mughals and in eastern Europe by the Ottomans. But all of these dynasties spent as much or more time warring against their fellow Muslim dynasts, and normally they tried to legitimize these wars too as jihads, though their subjects did not always believe them. In the latter case, they were fighting a jihad against heretics and schismatics within the Community of Believers rather than infidels outside it. Moreover, these rulers understood perfectly well how to pursue long-term balance-of-power politics with their non-Muslim neighbors. Where we find jihads against non-Muslim states after 850 or so, the great majority of them were defensive in character, struggles to defend the lands and peoples of Islam against invasion by powerful foreigners. For American readers, the best-known case in point would no doubt be the Crusades (ca. 1096–1291), but there are many others—the Spanish Reconquest (ca. 1080–1492) and the terrifying Mongol invasions of the Middle East between 1220 and 1300, to name but two.

By the time we come to the modern era—roughly 1700—Islam's wars of expansion already belonged to a glorious but remote past. When jihad against the infidel was invoked in the eighteenth and nineteenth centuries, as it often was, it was done to mobilize the Muslims against the growing threat from Europe, a region that had heretofore been treated with condescension and disdain but whose relentless economic dynamism and military power now threatened to subvert not only Muslim political independence but also the very foundations of Muslim society. By the 1820s, Muslim armies were suffering one disastrous defeat after another. Even the most powerful rulers were being compelled to sign humiliating treaties with Britain, France, and Russia.[5] These treaties varied greatly. Some led to major losses of territory. Others created "protectorates" under whose terms Muslim rulers formally retained sovereignty over their lands but surrendered all real powers of government to European advisors. Still others simply created extraordinary privileges and immunities for Europeans living in Muslim countries. In the end, these latter, which took the innocuous form of commercial treaties, were perhaps the most dangerous of all. They led to the destruction of many parts of the traditional economies of Muslim countries (most notably in textile manufacturing, for handlooms could not compete with the notorious steam-powered mills of Manchester) and ultimately placed all the most dynamic economic sectors—for example, banking and finance, import and export marketing, even transportation—in European hands.

Under such circumstances, it would surely be no surprise if we witnessed a surge of violent resistance among peoples who were on the verge of losing all control over their futures. And in fact we do see some evidence of this—the long Chechen resistance to Russian expansion in the Caucasus from the 1820s to the 1840s, the Algerian opposition to the French occupation led with such futile skill and tenacity by Abd al-Qadir at about the same time, the Indian Mutiny of 1857, the turmoil that surrounded Col. Ahmad Urabi's rise to power in Egypt between 1879 and 1882, anti-Dutch rebellions in northern Sumatra at the end of the nineteenth century, the long struggle by the French and Spanish to "pacify" the Moroccan highlands in the 1920s, and the Turkish resistance to Allied and Greek occupation led by Mustafa Kemal (later Atatürk) between 1919 and 1922.

These struggles can hardly be seen as evidence of "Mohammedan fanaticism," though European journalists and politicians of the era almost invariably did so. People have fought bloodier wars with far less provocation, after all. The leaders of these anticolonial struggles often called them jihads, and jihad was for the mass of Muslims the most obvious and immediate way of understanding what was going on. "Freedom," "self-determination," and "national destiny" were meaningful and effective concepts among Europeans and Americans but not among Sudanese cattle herders and Moroccan peasants. "Islam" in contrast was a very powerful idea indeed, one that required no explanation or justification. As late as World War II some anti-imperialist struggles were portrayed as jihads.[6]

However, these struggles were almost uniformly conducted by traditional-style leaders, or at least by leaders who donned a traditional cloak for the occasion and who claimed to be defending Islam and preserving the God-given values and institutions of their societies. Modern-style politicians and intellectuals were increasingly uneasy with a concept that seemed so redolent of a tradition-bound past and religious fanaticism, and few among the Muslim masses would have regarded them as authentic spokesmen for Islam in any case. These leaders preferred to use a more modern idiom, defining their struggles as secular nationalist revolutions grounded in a people's aspirations to shape its political destiny free of foreign control. In this category of secular resistance to imperialism would fall the Egyptian nationalist struggle, including the great uprising of 1919, and the Arab revolt against the Ottomans during World War I. (Ironically, the Ottomans formally proclaimed that their war against France, Britain, and Russia was a jihad.) Such struggles often had religious overtones, but they were defined in this-worldly terms, not as struggles to achieve or restore a divinely mandated order of things.

Indeed, far more remarkable than the occasional anti-imperialist jihad during the nineteenth and early twentieth centuries would be how many traditional social and cultural leaders opted to suffer in silence, or how many statesmen and intellectuals sought to grasp and instill in their own societies the technologies, institutions, and frames of mind that had made the Europeans so powerful. Jihad was thus only one response, and seldom the most salient one, to the European military, economic, and cultural onslaught. Indeed, several of the nineteenth-century jihads primarily targeted corrupt or tyrannical Muslim regimes. When the Sudanese Mahdi launched his massive revolt in the Sudan in the 1880s, his wrath was aimed at Egyptian domination in the region. In cases of this kind, any European presence on the scene was either accidental or secondary.

More widespread was the effort to reform society from within—that is, the ancient tradition of "commanding the good," now deployed in a new context. Many European commentators in the early twentieth century in fact dwelled on the resignation and passivity of

Muslim societies, the dispirited effort simply to maintain the institutions and values essential to an Islamic way of life, which they perceived among Muslim peoples. Absurd as it now seems, for many
decades the most influential foreign "experts" asserted that Islam
was inherently a religion of fatalism and lethargy, though of course
it might be punctuated with unpredictable, brief, and irrational outbursts of violence.

The European response to these trends in the Islamic lands was
rational and pragmatic if not always ennobling. Jihads in regions
under European control, or abutting those regions, were crushed by
overwhelming military force and meticulous administrative control.
In what seems a paradoxical and self-contradictory demand, Muslim governments were constantly hectored to mount major political,
legal, and social reforms but were usually halted in their tracks whenever they seriously attempted such a policy. Had reform worked,
after all, both the pretext and the opportunity for imperial control
would have been seriously compromised. In contrast, the efforts of
conservatives and traditionalists to maintain what could be saved
of the old ways, especially religious practices and family structures,
were often encouraged, albeit in varying degree. The British particularly prided themselves on defending freedom of religious practice, native customs, and the like, and the Austrian administration
within a largely Muslim Bosnia after 1878 was remarkably tactful
and even-handed. (Remember that Archduke Ferdinand's assassin
in 1914 was *not* a Muslim.) Russian and French policy was much more
interventionist, but on the whole they were willing to leave the natives to their own devices as long as they accepted foreign control. The
reason for such tolerance was partly ideological, though it is hard to
think of Czarist Russia as a wholehearted defender of liberal values,
but even more Machiavellian. After all, peoples who restricted themselves to the passive defense of tradition within a rapidly narrowing
social and cultural arena were easy to marginalize, to exclude from the
centers of political power and potential economic growth, to exploit
as food growers and servants. They were charming, picturesque, and
to all appearances quite harmless.

World War I shook the imperial edifice but left it standing. World
War II, in contrast, brought incalculable change to Asia and Africa,
and in the Islamic lands the war ushered in some very complex
shifts in the nature of resistance to imperialism. On one level, the

public discourse of resistance—that is, the vocabulary and symbols through which the spokesmen for a struggle presented it to the outside world—now became almost wholly secularized. All the classic conflicts from the late 1940s to the mid-1960s—the Arab-Israeli conflict, the British and Egyptian confrontation over Suez, the oil nationalization crisis in Mossadegh's Iran—were primarily articulated in the language of secular nationalism by Middle Eastern politicians and intellectuals. In the dominant ideological framework of that era, the peoples of the Middle East—Egyptian or Arab or Iranian as the case might be—were simply demanding the same rights of self-determination that European nations had long since demanded for themselves. Where religious (Islamic) symbols were allowed to creep in, they did so only as part of the larger cultural patrimony of these peoples. The nation was primary and religion was harnessed to its service.

But even as nationalism was becoming the primary ideology of resistance and renewal in the Middle East, or at least the one most loudly proclaimed in front of international audiences, Islam emerged from the war in a new form, with enormously enhanced power and vitality. This new energy inevitably meant that the doctrine of jihad would be revitalized as well; it had been (and remained) rather an embarrassment to Muslim modernists and secular-minded intellectuals, something to be minimized or explained away. But when struggles against imperialism, domestic oppression, or cultural crisis were articulated within an explicitly and consciously Islamic framework, jihad was bound to become a crucial concept within the rhetoric of resistance. Had the nationalist regimes not bent every effort to controlling the resurgence of Islam, including recourse to severe repression, it might well have swept the boards even by the mid-1950s, two decades before it at last burst on the consciousness of the outside world.

As many commentators have pointed out, it can be quite misleading to talk about an "Islamic revival." Islam always remained not only the religion of the great majority of Middle Easterners but also the heart and soul of their identity; it was the thing that made them who they were. But even conceding this point, Islam did have a new energy, a revitalized capacity to mobilize political action after World War II. To this new capacity there were two dimensions. First, Islam was now linked to the new forces of nationalism, though of course its adherents made the nation the handmaid of religion—a nice inversion of the nationalist formula. Second, the new Islam was no longer the traditional religion, a complex and highly variable blend of folk belief and practice, classical Shariʿa, and Sufi-influenced theology. On the contrary, it was an Islam that claimed to rest directly on the Qurʾan and the teaching of the Prophet, stripped of the deadening accretions of medieval and Ottoman times.

In spite of all claims to the contrary by Muslim activists and many Western commentators, this version of Islam was a radically new interpretation of the faith, with few real precedents from earlier centuries, and it was aimed not at recovering the past but at controlling the future. This purified Islam was sharply confrontational in its rhetoric and manner, for it had been constructed precisely to challenge the religious status quo, to rid the faith of superstition and corruption, to compel Muslims to reject the enticements of the West and live in accordance with God's revelation. As the reformers saw it, Islam was a religion of action, and to that end it had to be stripped down to its essentials.

The reform of Islam had important roots in the militant Wahhabi movement of eighteenth-century Arabia (to which the modern Kingdom of Saudi Arabia traces its origins). However, it emerged in its modern form in Cairo and Damascus in the last decades of the nineteenth century.[7] The key tenets were articulated by the Egyptian scholar Muhammad Abduh (1849–1905), an earnest and gentle man who sought to restate Islamic doctrine in a way that would make it meaningful and persuasive to Muslims exposed to, and in a sense mesmerized by, the dynamism of Western knowledge and institutions. What he argued was that Islam was a religion peculiarly suited to the demands of the modern world. The Qurʾan commanded man to use his reason, and the life of the Prophet and his Companions demonstrated that Muslims must not be bound by time-encrusted tradition. The modern world had brought new circumstances, new challenges, new values and forms of thought. Muslims could not deal with these effectively by adhering slavishly to the teachings of medieval lawyers and theologians, however revered these might be. On the contrary, Islam's true teachings demanded bold, original solutions to the problems of one's time—solutions securely anchored in the Qurʾan and the practice of the Prophet but unfettered by the dense, tangled legal doctrines of later ages.

By the time Abduh died, he had succeeded only in developing a sketch of his new interpretation of Islam, but that was enough to break open new paths for his successors. Some of these led in unexpected directions; Abduh's disciple Qasim Amin was the first to demand, at first cautiously and then very boldly, expanded rights and social roles for women. Others were more conservative in temperament, but even while readier to adhere to existing social norms and values, they were still bent on reinvigorating the faith. Among these the most influential was Abduh's closest collaborator during his last years, the Syrian Rashid Rida (1865–1935). Rida called for the use of independent judgment (*ijtihad*) in the rethinking of Islamic law, for example, but his own interpretations were conservative in tone and usually stayed rather close to traditional ways of looking at things. Rida was politically quite active in a number of Islamic and Arab Nationalist issues, but he was no militant. He accepted, at least de facto, the legitimacy of existing Islamic governments. Even so, his interpretation of Muhammad Abduh's intellectual legacy sketched the outlines of the activist Islamic ideology that burst on the scene after World War II.

This ideology was actually articulated and brought into the political arena, however, by a publicist and organizer of genius named Hasan al-Banna' (1900–1949), the real father of contemporary political Islam in the Sunni world (in effect, the Arab countries and Pakistan).[8] In the movement he founded we see both a model for effective political action and a stunning revival of the traditional concepts that had guided such action in previous centuries: "commanding the good" and jihad. Banna' was born and grew up in a small town, a village really, in Middle Egypt, where his father was a watchmaker. From him he received a thorough but narrow Qur'anic education. He then attended the national teachers' college in Cairo, and on graduating he was posted to a school in Isma'iliyya, the key city within the British-controlled Suez Canal Zone. His dismay at the degree of foreign domination in Egypt, and what he saw as the flagrant immorality of European life, drove him in 1928 to found an association aimed at supporting and revitalizing Islamic values and ways of life among Egyptian Muslims. When he was transferred to Cairo, he founded a new branch there and soon thereafter in several cities and towns throughout the country. He called his movement the Muslim Brothers (al-Ikhwan al-Muslimun, "the Ikhwan" for short).

Banna' was not a trained theologian or lawyer; the Islam he knew
was the Islam of the Qur'an, pure and simple. For him, the reformist
Islam of Rashid Rida, with its emphasis on going back to the very
sources of the faith and on the need to apply these sources directly
to the solution of contemporary problems, was made to order. He
of course lacked Rida's profound knowledge of and respect for the
medieval legal-theological tradition, but he made up for it with a
remarkable personal dynamism and intensity. For Banna', the key to
every problem lay ready to hand in the Qur'an; moreover, any intelligent, pious, and sincere Muslim could find and utilize that key.
Hasan al-Banna''s Islam was a layman's faith, which had little need
for the subtleties and erudition of scholars.

Hasan al-Banna' is a genuinely crucial figure; he was not simply
the originator of modern Sunni Islamic activism but the very embodiment of it. He represents precisely the kind of person who has
found the Islamic movement most appealing throughout the second half of this century, and who has provided much of its leadership. He was a layman but possessed an intense sense of Muslim
identity. He came from a small provincial town; it is in fact these
places, not the polyglot, foreign-influenced capitals or the villages,
that have been the real stronghold of conservative Islam in this century. He had a quasi-modern education, though not on an advanced
level, and within the Egyptian socioeconomic system he could only
aspire to a very modest status and standard of living. Finally, he lived
in an era when Islam as he understood it seemed threatened on every side; the Muslim peoples lived under the thumb of arrogant imperialists, good Islamic moral values were sneered at by Egypt's
intellectual elites and received only lip service from politicians. Under the circumstances, one had to choose; he could go with the flow,
or suffer in silence, or act.

Throughout the 1930s, the Muslim Brothers grew steadily, but
during that decade it was really an educational and charitable association, aimed at revitalizing Muslim consciousness and local or
neighborhood-scale action. Only in 1939, with a famous open letter
to King Farouk, then still a slender youth at the height of his short-
lived popularity, did Banna' make a decisive move into the political
arena.[9] The letter calls in essence for an Islamic state and asserts that
Islam contains all that is necessary for a dynamic modern society.
It describes this state and society in terms of a few key actions: a

ban on alcohol, abolishing interest, rigorous segregation of the sexes. These actions hardly constitute a social and economic policy, but they are in fact the visible symbols that would distinguish an upright Islamic way of life from the moral corruption and religious infidelity sown by the foreigners.

The outbreak of World War II, and the assertion of de facto British control over Egypt, blocked any further political action by the Muslim Brothers for several years. After 1945, however, the country suffered a near-collapse of any semblance of orderly parliamentary life, an intensifying economic crisis, and general hysteria induced by the first Arab-Israeli War. Under these circumstances the Muslim Brothers quickly seized center stage as the most dynamic, and by far the best-organized, political force in the country. Hasan al-Banna²'s version of Islam had an enormous appeal to many groups in Egypt, but especially to people much like him, what we might label the urban lower middle class—low- and middle-echelon bureaucrats, shopkeepers and artisans, schoolteachers, and some doctors and lawyers—people who combined strong Islamic roots with at least elements of a modern education. (At this point it is absolutely crucial to avoid any simplistic assumption that "lower middle class" equals "political Islam." The thoroughly secularist Baath party of Syria was founded at about the same time by and among the same sort of people—schoolteachers, pharmacists, low-ranking army officers.)

Like Hasan al-Banna², these groups were disgusted by the corruption of parliamentary politics, infuriated by the domination of foreigners over the country's politics and economy, and profoundly distressed by the fear that Egypt's Islamic character was being submerged in the moral chaos of a foreign-rooted modernity. For such people, Islam was indeed the solution. To some degree, no doubt, they were also frustrated by their own social and economic marginalization, but this point can be overdrawn; many Brothers were decently successful, though it is true that the movement had little appeal at that time for Egypt's elites.

Banna² was an unusually gifted and systematic organizer; he clearly intended for his movement to have staying power. An elaborate centralized hierarchy led up to him, the Supreme Guide. The Muslim Brothers became an international (though never centrally controlled) movement, with autonomous branches in Lebanon, Syria, and Jordan. Although the Brothers never made themselves into a political party per se and even denounced partisan politics as a matter of principle, they had enormous influence in the electoral process. Egyptian politics during those years was not merely turbulent but violent, and the Brothers could not avoid the maelstrom.

Some of their actions were perfectly acceptable in the context of the times, as when they joined the guerrilla war against British troops and installations in the Canal Zone or sent volunteers to Palestine in 1948. But for reasons unknown, Banna' took a fatal step in 1948, when he established a secret unit that engaged in focused acts of terrorism against political opponents. One of his agents assassinated the prime minister, and shortly afterward he himself fell victim to a government-sponsored reprisal killing. The Muslim Brothers did not disappear from the scene with Hasan al-Banna''s violent death; the new Supreme Guide, a Shari'a court judge named Hasan al-Hudaybi, had little of his predecessor's charisma, but he kept the Brothers a major political force until the army coup d'état of 1952 which ultimately brought Nasser to power. Hudaybi did away with the "special units," but that did not prevent a disgruntled Brother from trying to assassinate Nasser on his own in October 1954, on the grounds that the treaty that Nasser had just signed with the British to evacuate the Suez Canal Zone was a sellout to imperialism. Nasser did not take such challenges lightly. Egypt's jails were soon filled with Muslim Brothers; some leaders were executed, others were given long jail terms, and the movement was forcibly dismantled, or at least driven deep underground. There was a second attempt to assassinate Nasser in 1965, again savagely repressed. Thereafter the Muslim Brothers would not again be a force in Egyptian politics until the early 1970s, when Anwar Sadat briefly gave them free rein as part of his own campaign to quash the Nasserist left.

The actions of the Muslim Brothers after World War II combine quite neatly two of the dimensions of moral action in Islam. Down to 1949, at least, the Brothers would have claimed that their action within the Egyptian political system fell under the rubric "commanding the good": sincere advice, admonition, and remonstrance. They were trying to heal a sick society, not destroy it. But the struggle against the British in Suez and the Zionists in Palestine was a

jihad even by the strictest definition, an overt armed struggle to defend the Muslims from their enemies. After 1948, however, and especially after the violent Nasserist repression of 1954, there was a
real shift in attitude. According to Sayyid Qutb (1903–1966), who
emerged as the most important ideologue in the movement after
Hasan al-Banna''s death, Egypt—and indeed most of the Muslim
world—was a *jahiliyya* society, a society that called itself Muslim
but was in fact built on the brutish paganism of Arabia in the era
before Muhammad's mission. Such a society could not be reformed;
it had to be destroyed and rebuilt from the ground up. Against it jihad was not merely lawful but imperative. A true Muslim had no
choice but to struggle to overthrow it by whatever means necessary.

Qutb's ideas were obviously unwelcome to the regime, and in
1966 he paid for them with his life, in the aftermath of a second attempt against Nasser.[10] But his wholesale condemnation of the secularist regimes and his demands for a thorough purge and renewal of
Islamic society have had a tremendous impact on Muslim activists
everywhere. His *Milestones* at once became and has remained (to
use an odd but useful image) the Bible of Islamic activism. His call
for jihad against the forces of tyranny and moral corruption within
the Islamic world—in effect, for an Islamic revolution—bore fruit
in Egypt itself by the mid-1970s. The country was periodically con-
vulsed by acts of "terrorism" directed against the state and its officials, culminating of course in the spectacular assassination of Sadat in October 1981. It should be noted that these acts were not
perpetrated by the mainstream "Muslim Brothers" but by an array
of clandestine splinter groups. During this period, likewise, the Egyptian government was the enemy, not civilians or foreign tourists.[11]

After Sadat's death, the new government was temporarily able
to quiet the militancy of Egypt's Islamic movements through a deft
combination of leniency and selective repression, but the Islamic
movement continued to sink deeper roots in Egyptian society. Ultimately, it came to dominate the country's universities, even that
once unassailable stronghold of secular liberalism, the University of
Cairo. The impact of this change is immediately visible to any visi-
tor to the University of Cairo campus today, where a huge majority of women students and many female faculty have more or less
voluntarily donned some sort of Islamic dress. It is audible in the

streets and shops as well; twenty years ago the radios blared political speeches, soccer matches, and popular music. Today even the immortal Umm Kulthum is almost drowned out by a cacophony of Qur'anic chanting and religious harangues. The bookstalls are stuffed with Islamic tracts, while left-wing and Arab Nationalist books are hardly to be found anywhere.

Ultimately, there was a resurgence of terror, at first in militant strongholds like Asyut and Minya, but soon enough in Cairo. Initially aimed at the police and state officials, violence and threats of violence soon struck a broader class of enemies: secularist intellectuals like Farag Foda (assassinated in June 1992) and occasionally even foreign tourists. The latter, classic "innocents," have become useful targets on both ideological and pragmatic grounds. From a pragmatic perspective, such attacks rob the government of crucial tourist dollars, as well as demonstrate its inability to maintain security. From an ideological perspective, tourists are seen as a key source of the infection of foreign ways, of the notorious Western immorality, sexual license, drunkenness, and so on; to drive them out is in a sense to cleanse the country of this disease.

By the end of the 1970s, Sayyid Qutb's call had found an echo in Syria, where Muslim militants conducted a guerrilla war against the regime of Hafiz al-Asad, which they regarded as an apostate tyranny. Here, however, they made the unfortunate mistake of challenging an icy-blooded realist determined to stay in power whatever the price. The Islamic movement in Syria was almost literally drowned in blood when Asad's troops obliterated the old city of Hama in 1982, and has hardly been heard from since.

Hama Rules

In spite of the acute tensions in Egypt and occasional outbursts of violence there, the heart of Islamic militancy at this writing (June 1998) is probably found in the Armed Islamic Movement in Algeria and Hamas in the Occupied Territories (especially Gaza). That Islamic movements have come to dominate the stage in these two regions is profoundly ironic, for Algeria and Palestine are the home of the two prototypical "national liberation movements" of the twentieth-century Middle East, the FLN and the PLO. Both these movements drew on classic secularist Third World national liberation ideologies—and Algeria was in many ways the original model for this ideology. Both the FLN and the PLO were founded on armed struggle against colonial occupiers, France and Israel respectively, and both, in admittedly very different ways, achieved a real measure of success against their adversaries. The FLN did so by compelling the French to recognize Algerian independence, although it required a bloody struggle of eight years' duration (1954–1962) to achieve that end. The PLO prevailed (on a far more modest level) simply by enduring an incredible array of vicissitudes over thirty years and by at last inducing the Israelis to accept it as a negotiating partner, the legitimate representative of the Palestinian people.

The two movements have had rather different relations with Islamic activism. On its side, the PLO has always formally eschewed an Islamic identity, and the Palestine National Charter indeed calls for the establishment of a "secular democratic state." Such a state, it is important to stress, would have been a multicultural and multinational one, composed of Muslims, Druze, Christians, and some elements of the Jewish community. Some observers have doubted the sincerity of this call, and certainly it was made in part to legitimize the PLO in the international arena—as well as to delegitimize the explicitly Jewish state of Israel. Nevertheless, the fact that international approbation was sought is telling.

This much having been said, it is certainly the case that many Palestinians, perhaps especially those still residing in the refugee camps, have always looked at the conflict with Israel in a religious light, as at bottom a struggle of the Muslims against infidels who have dared to occupy an Islamic land and dispossess a Muslim people. That was the case during the Arab Revolt against Britain in 1936–1939, and again during the first Arab-Israeli War in 1948. In both of those struggles, a significant element of the Palestinians' political and military leadership was provided by men claiming religious authority and making an explicitly Islamic appeal to their followers. The secularist leadership clearly had the upper hand during the 1960s and 1970s, but throughout this period many observers noted the strong persistence of Islamic feelings and loyalties among the "Palestinian masses." In any case, it is certain that the strong if far from universal appeal of Hamas did not spring up in a vacuum. The conflict between Palestinians as to the kind of society and state they would like to build, assuming they are given the chance, will surely go on for a very long time.

As things have turned out, the PLO has become the bitter rival of Hamas—and one must suppose an increasingly hostile rival, as the PLO struggles to shape some sort of Palestinian future through a tense collaboration with Israel and takes the security measures necessary to maintain the peace with the Zionist enemy. (The further irony is that Israel allowed Hamas to flourish in its early years as a useful counterweight against the PLO, a decision that it now deeply regrets.) Moreover, insofar as the PLO is able to make itself the established regime, it will become the inevitable target of social-economic frustration and anger and of scathing critiques by Hamas for its un-Islamic or even anti-Islamic policies. Indeed, that is already the case. Whether Hamas will deal with its rival within the framework of "commanding the good" or jihad still remains to be seen; the militants within Hamas have certainly demonstrated that they are willing to use terror against Israeli targets in order to embarrass the PLO.[12]

The effectiveness of Hamas within the Palestinian community in Gaza and the West Bank deserves some attention. Most commentators stress its appeal as a movement of social and political protest, which rallies the impoverished and jobless, especially the youth, along with all those who have felt suffocated for a quarter century by the harsh, omnipresent control of the Israeli army. Certainly Hamas's fiery and uncompromising rhetoric speaks to this anger, just as its clinics and schools provide some response to the poverty and economic frustration of the Occupied Territories. But it is dangerously reductionist to argue that Islam is only a rhetorical mask for rage rooted in socioeconomic conditions. There are after all many secular ideologies that attack the same problems as the militant Islam of Hamas—for example, Marxism or Arab Nationalism. Why do the people of Gaza not embrace these with the same fervor? Or, to put the matter in a different perspective, would a call to jihad have the same impact in Chiapas or Guatemala? The answer is that Gazans and West Bankers are no doubt Palestinians and Arabs, but most of all they are Muslims; an appeal to act as Muslims is bound to have an immediacy and power that no foreign ideology can possibly match. In normal circumstances, Islam's commandments call for piety, prayer, and moral uprightness. But in the circumstances of the Israeli occupation (which in the eyes of Hamas and its adherents still continues, even if it wears a PLO disguise), a Muslim must combat corruption, infidelity, and tyranny with every resource he has. It is a struggle that gains both intensity and dignity from the fact that it is waged in God's name and for His purposes.

The FLN never identified itself as an Islamic movement per se, but it did, following the once fashionable theories of Franz Fanon, seek to fashion an Algeria that would be simultaneously revolutionary and culturally "authentic."[13] In the Algerian context, cultural authenticity meant a country that would again sink its roots in Islamic social and cultural values, and would express its ideas and aspirations in the Arabic language. The FLN's success in this enterprise has been mixed at best. The current Algerian leadership, for example, is still more at home in French than in Arabic, in spite of three decades of official "Arabization." Algerian property and contract law is rather a mélange, but it is probably more socialist in inspiration than anything else. However, the Algerian code of family law represents a very conservative, restrictive interpretation of Islamic legal norms, and this was the case long before the Islamist pressures of recent years.

In Algeria, the FLN of course is the regime, and as such it is also the Pharaonic tyranny that oppresses the Muslims, blights their aspirations, and blocks the establishment of a truly Islamic order.[14] In the eyes of many Algerians (not just Islamic activists), the FLN has long since frittered away the extraordinary fund of legitimacy it won as the liberator of the nation from French colonialism. The Islamic movement, having been cheated in 1992 of almost certain victory through democratic processes, has turned to violence in a particularly terrifying form, with attacks on professional women, foreign teachers and technicians, and many others. Since the beginning of 1997 there have been repeated massacres of unarmed villagers by ill-identified night marauders. The struggle on both sides has been ugly, brutish, and bloody—current estimates give more than 60,000 dead—and there is no clear end in sight. In this kind of confrontation, the more moderate or politically minded Islamists—the very people who began the movement for an Islamic order in Algeria—have no voice at all. They are silenced by government repression on one side, blazing militancy on the other.

The kind of violence espoused by extremist elements in Palestine, Egypt, and Algeria raises important issues for the theory of jihad. In any of the standard classical or modern doctrines, attacks against innocent civilians or visiting foreigners are wholly illegitimate. A remarkable commentary on this point comes from an imam in a West Bank town near Nablus, Shaykh Nayef Rajoub. When asked to comment on the recent suicide bombings in Israel, he responded, "The Israeli occupation has deprived the Palestinians of the right to act according to the principles of Islam. We are existing in circumstances outside the usual strictures of Islamic law."[15] He is in effect appealing to the venerable albeit easily abused principle of necessity—the principle in Shariʿa jurisprudence that allows the explicit commands of the law to be violated when the consequences of obedience are unacceptable. For example, a starving man may eat pork or carrion, a tyrant may be accepted as a lawful ruler if there would otherwise be anarchy. It is intriguing that Shaykh Nayef does not explicitly invoke this principle; for him, it is just that things have gotten to the point where the defense of Islam demands what *paradoxical* Islam plainly forbids.

The overwhelming majority of Muslims (even many militants) are ambivalent about such actions. On the one hand, they find them deeply repugnant; on the other, they sometimes see no other way to deal with the situation they are in.[16] (For a rough parallel, quiz Americans of a certain age about the use of the bomb against Hiroshima and Nagasaki.) From the perspective of traditional Islamic jurisprudence, as we saw above, foreigners are in the country under the protection granted them by a Muslim government; so long as they observe the conditions of this protection, they are to be secure in their persons and property. As for government officials, they are liable to punishment only if they are apostates. The extremists would respond that these governments are precisely apostate regimes. As such, no Muslim can serve in them, and anyone who does is in effect an apostate. Likewise, they have no authority to extend their protection to any foreigner; such protection is simply null and void, and if a foreigner has accepted it in good faith, so much the worse for him. It is of course impossible to argue with someone who holds opinions of this kind, since he has made himself the sole judge of who is or is not a true Muslim.

The perspective of contemporary militants has deep roots in Islamic history. It is foreshadowed in the actions of the seventh- and eighth-century dissidents called Kharijites, and particularly in the extremist wing of that movement. The Kharijites were soon eradicated or driven to the desert and mountain margins of the Islamic world, but they have not been forgotten. Mainstream Muslims and even the more cautious activists point to them with alarm, as a frightening example of what happens when Muslims break away from the Community of Believers and arrogate to themselves alone the right to judge the conduct and beliefs of other Muslims. They label the contemporary extremists Kharijites, those who secede from the Community of Believers and thereby shred it into warring factions. The militants, in contrast, take the label "Kharijite" as a badge of honor that belongs to those who have taken personal responsibility to know, proclaim, and defend the faith, whatever the consequences.

The ancient Kharijites, for all their fanaticism and violence, paid little attention to the non-Muslim peoples surrounding the Islamic world; their struggle was directed against corruption and apostasy within the Community. And in spite of media headlines, much the same is true of their contemporary successors. These are bent, not on the expansion of Islam, but rather on saving it from its enemies. They do not see Islam triumphant, but Islam threatened from every side. In their view Islam certainly has enemies abroad—in particular, a malevolent and all-powerful United States in league with Zionism to humiliate and subjugate the Muslims—but its most dangerous enemies are the corrupt tyrants at home. Outbreaks of violence against tourists or spates of hostage taking are aimed not at foreigners and non-Muslims as such but at those who wittingly or not are collaborating with the internal forces of ruin. If they would go away and leave Islam alone, there would be no problem.

The neo-Kharijism of the Sunni militants finds a certain parallel in the most powerful and to date most successful of the Islamic movements, that which brought down the Shah of Iran and created an Islamic republic in that country. The Islamic Revolution was a remarkable combination of jihad and modern social revolution. It was carried out with the intention of building a modern, dynamic, progressive social order on the solid foundation of the eternal, unchanging truths of Islam. In a pattern that recalls the Islamic political movements of other countries, the dominant ideology of the revolutionary period had been shaped by a gifted layman, Ali Shariʿati, who died in 1977 (at the hands of the Shah's police, most people believed), but whose voluminous writings continued to inspire Iran's university students and modern professionals.[17] Like a number of

Iran's major twentieth-century intellectuals, Shariʿati was the son of a Shiʿite cleric. Unlike some of them, he did not reject his religious heritage, though he pursued a sharply different path in his formal education, for he earned a doctorate in sociology from the Sorbonne. He thereby combined traditional piety and the Western education of Iran's emerging technocratic-administrative elite. Shariʿati's intellectual aims were very ambitious, no less than a fully integrated synthesis of Islamic ethics and theology with modern (essentially Marxist) sociology. In common with many Asian and African intellectuals of this era, Shariʿati and his followers were seeking a third way, an ideology grounded in their own cultural traditions which would be neither "Western" (liberal/capitalist) nor "Eastern" (Marxist). His characteristic approach was to present the narratives of the Qurʾan as parables, whose true meaning could be unpacked through the tools of sociological analysis. For Iran's newly emerging university-educated class during the 1970s, Shariʿati's ideas were almost literally a godsend, for they showed how one could resolve the crisis of personal identity that afflicted so many. One could be modern and Iranian and Muslim, each quality simply a different dimension of one integrated personality. Shariʿati's thought also appealed because of its strong political element; as he presented the matter, Shiʿite Islam was in its essence a religion of revolution and social transformation, of struggle against tyranny and economic oppression.

It was in part Shariʿati's ideas that allowed Iran's Shiʿite clergy to take control of the Iranian revolution during the summer and autumn of 1978, for if Iran was to be rebuilt according to Islamic principles, who better than the clergy to guide this work? Ultimately leadership of the revolution (at first symbolic, then very real) fell to a classically trained scholar of law and theology who claimed lineal descent from the Prophet, the Ayatollah Ruhollah Khomeini. In his person Khomeini was the very embodiment of cultural authenticity and religious authority, and he used a very traditional rhetorical style. But he targeted the same frustrations and tensions as had Shariʿati—tyranny, imperialism, and Zionism on the political level, rootlessness and anomie on the personal. It is not surprising that many highly educated laymen, inspired by a vision of an Iran transformed through Islam, believed that Shariʿati and Khomeini were speaking with one voice. The Iranian revolution of 1978–1979 was a jihad in God's path, but it was one founded on a positive vision: not merely the overthrow and punishment of evildoers but the creation of a nation that would fully embody the equality and justice brought by Islam.

This complex vision was enshrined in the new constitution of 1979, a remarkable document that we have already examined in a different context. Here we need only note the role of jihad in the text. In spite of the Islamic Republic's perhaps overdrawn reputation for fomenting revolution and sponsoring international terrorism, there is very little about jihad in the body of the constitution, which generally reflects the principles of contemporary international law. Principle 143 states simply that "the Army of the Islamic Republic is responsible for safeguarding the independence and territorial integrity of the Islamic Republic and for maintaining public order therein"—unexceptionable marching orders by any standard. In Principle 152, we are told that the country's foreign policy is to be based on nonalignment and peaceful relations with nonbelligerent states, even while striving to protect the independence and rights of all Muslims. Principle 154 tries a balancing act that should be quite familiar to Americans: it eschews any interference in the internal affairs of other nations and simultaneously proclaims that Iran will "protect the struggles of the weak against the arrogant in any part of the world." Where the idea of jihad does come to the fore is in the long preface, which has no legal force but explains the constitution's historical roots and lofty goals; here the idea of jihad—both as the struggle against the forces of despotism and unbelief and as the intention to build a godly society—suffuses the whole text. Interestingly, the preface tends to portray the work of resistance as essentially completed (though obviously vigilance must be eternal) and stresses the work of rebuilding that lies ahead. It is admittedly jihad with a very contemporary flavor, and in fact the preface is very much a restatement of the concepts and ideals of ʿAli Shariʿati. The constitution of 1979 is as close as Shariʿati's ideas ever got to becoming a reality.

There are many reasons why the idealists of 1979—not only the laymen like Mahdi Bazargan (head of the provisional government until November 1979) and Abu'l-Hasan Bani Sadr (the first president elected under the new constitution), but perhaps even Khomeini himself—failed to achieve their goals. The war with Iraq swallowed up all the country's energies for eight years, not to mention the lives of several hundred thousand of its youth. In the end, Khomeini's personality and outlook—militant, vindictive, sure of Islam's enemies but not of what he hoped to build, unwilling to choose a socioeconomic policy but likewise unwilling to allow others to make the choice—did not enable him to lay the foundations for a new social and political system. But quite apart from historical accidents like the personalities of Saddam Hussein and Khomeini, Iran was by 1989 severely fragmented culturally and ideologically. No broad consensus could be found, and powerful political factions were bent on blocking one another's initiatives rather than trying to define coherent policy. But in the end, intriguingly, none of this has dampened the continuing effectiveness of the idea of jihad in Islamic culture; Iran's experience has not caused Islamic movements elsewhere to doubt in any way that Islam demands constant struggle against those forces of tyranny and corruption that defy God's will for mankind, and likewise constant struggle to build a community that truly embodies that will.

Where does all this leave us? Is the current militant, jihad-oriented trend within Islamic countries a quasi-permanent state of affairs, or should we expect it to abate, as it has so often done in the past? More important, in a world in which resistance and protest is primarily defined in terms of jihad, is there still a significant role for the quieter, more restrained virtue of "commanding the good"? Answers to questions like these can of course only be speculative, but they are worth asking simply because they help us grasp the often-hidden realities of a complex situation. Thus, to ask whatever happened to "commanding the good" is to recognize that it is still there, and still represents the outlook of the great majority of committed Muslims. A great deal of Islamic activism focuses, as it has throughout this century, on charitable and educational work, on trying to inculcate certain values and standards of behavior. But the presence of "commanding the good" has been masked by the sound and fury attached to calls for jihad. The militants have been extremely skillful in seizing the podium and focusing all attention on themselves, and both the media and fearful governments are naturally obsessed by their spectacular actions. But an excessive focus on the militants distracts us from asking what the Islamic movement means to the bulk of its adherents, and where they hope it will take their societies.

CHAPTER 9

WOMEN IN PUBLIC LIFE

Islamic Perspectives, Middle Eastern Realities

Westerners carry some very vivid pictures of Middle Eastern and Muslim women in their minds, and these pictures are neither flattering nor ennobling. They portray women draped head to toe in shapeless black cloaks, or shuffling along rural pathways almost doubled over under the weight of brushwood or sheaves of grain. There is another picture of a princess beheaded in a public square by a pitiless father outraged over some petty slight to his honor, and one of an American wife robbed of her children by a Muslim husband and pursued by religious fanatics. In a different vein, there are the pervasive sensual images of half-draped women languidly reclining on a chaise longue in the harem, awaiting the pleasure of their masters. Whatever the setting, we see pictures of women humiliated, subjugated, and terrorized by the men in their lives, not merely husbands but fathers and brothers as well. I will not argue that the Middle East is a feminist paradise, if we but knew the truth. In fact, women in the Middle East (and Muslim women in particular) do struggle against very severe challenges, but their situation is far more complex and nuanced than we usually imagine.[1]

To some degree women continue to have the same opportunities and to face the same constraints as they have throughout Islamic times. A good place to begin exploring this point is in the arena of high politics, if only because we have more stories about this aspect of life than any other. It is also an arena where women in most societies have had (until very recent decades) trouble carving out a visible and legitimate place for themselves. Our historical texts from the premodern Islamic world were all composed by men, who usually regarded it as unseemly if not immoral to publicize the doings of women. Even so, a reader quickly sees that women could at least on occasion play roles of extraordinary power and influence. Such behavior was sometimes an occasion for scandal, but just as often it elicits real respect from the narrator, and even a touch of awe.

The most famous or notorious case in early Islam was the very public political role taken by the Prophet's favorite wife, ʿAʾisha, after his death.[2] Since ʿAʾisha had married the Prophet very young and was only eighteen when she was left a widow, it is not surprising that we hear little of her for many years. But she became a prominent figure in the opposition to the caliph Uthman (reigned 644–656). Though she was not directly implicated in the murder of the aged caliph—she artfully left Medina before the final crisis broke—she did nothing to prevent it. The death of Uthman, however shocking or gratifying she may have found it, did not end her political career. For both personal and political reasons, she was extremely hostile to the new caliph proclaimed by the rebels, the Prophet's cousin Ali, and together with two male associates she launched an armed struggle to depose him. But this bold initiative quickly ended in catastrophe, with the death of her two allies and her own capture. Even in her later years under surveillance in Medina, however, she remained a lady of standing. Until her death some twenty years later, she played what would be arguably her most important and certainly least controversial role in Islamic history, as a uniquely privileged source for the religious teaching and personal life of the Prophet.

ʿAʾisha's misadventures poisoned the well for any legitimate public action by her sisters in later generations, but obviously that did not keep them out of politics. Their most common role was naturally that of trying to manipulate successions to the throne. In a world of plural marriage and concubinage, and one where the Shariʿa declared flatly that all sons were to have an equal share in their father's inheritance, it is obvious that there would be many rival candidates for the throne whenever the current ruler passed away. Down to the nineteenth century, almost every succession could turn into a major political crisis. Inevitably, every woman in the royal harem would try to ensure the throne for one of her own sons. This was not merely a matter of maternal affection, but also a matter of hardnosed political calculation, for the queen mother controlled the harem and its considerable financial resources, and she might often be one of her son's most trusted advisers. She certainly was one whom he could not easily ignore. (Some did try, of course, with unfortunate results. The caliph al-Hadi [785–786], exasperated by his mother Khayzuran's "meddling," tried to confine her to her quarters in the palace. She had him suffocated with a pillow and replaced by his more pliant younger brother, the famous Harun al-Rashid.)

The political roles of women in the royal household went beyond trying to manipulate succession crises to their own advantage, however. A number of them became the éminences grises, even the de facto rulers, of their states. This was normally resented by contemporary chroniclers, of course, and they have scathing things to say about the feeble, womanish "autocrats" who allowed themselves to be dominated by their mothers, wives, or sisters. But not always; a number of women were recognized (with some astonishment, to be sure) as prudent and far-sighted statesmen. A niece of Saladin named Dayfa Khatun became regent of the principality of Aleppo on behalf of her young grandson during the 1230s. She even issued royal decrees under her own name. Aleppo's independence was threatened on every side by powerful and ambitious neighbors, but contemporary writers universally attest her courage and skill in handling this very treacherous situation. They also admit that after her death in 1242, the principality's affairs never went quite as smoothly again.

A second case comes from the Ottoman Empire in the mid-seventeenth century. Later writers contemptuously referred to this period as "the sultanate of the women," but contemporary witnesses are far more admiring of the intelligence and firmness of character of the *valide sultans* (queen mothers), all of whom were concubines rather than legal wives. In spite of their seclusion in the imperial harem, they somehow managed to keep things going in a very troubled period.[3] One in particular, Kösem Sultan (the mother of three sultans, including the formidable Murad IV), became a cause célèbre when she was seized and executed in a palace coup in 1651; her death provoked a three-day general strike in the markets of Istanbul as well as riots that led to hundreds of deaths.[4]

One final case, by far the most famous but also the most aberrant, is provided by the colorful career of Shajar al-Durr. She had been the favorite concubine of Sultan al-Salih Ayyub of Egypt, though her son by him had not survived childhood. She was with the sultan in 1249 at his camp near the seaport of Damietta, where he had mustered his armies to try to fend off a massive new crusade led

by King Louis IX of France. But with the military situation in grave
doubt, al-Salih created a full-blown crisis by dying after a lingering
and extremely painful illness. Shajar al-Durr and the commander-
in-chief of the Egyptian army kept his death a secret and jointly
ran affairs of state for months while waiting for the dead sultan's
oldest son to reach the camp from his remote governorship in what
is now southeastern Turkey. On his arrival, they surrendered the
reins of power to him, but he proved a political disaster and was
soon assassinated by his own bodyguard. The assassins found no
appropriate successor to the murdered ruler and took the astonishing step of naming Shajar al-Durr sultan—that is, as head of state
in her own name—the first and only time before the twentieth century that any woman held supreme power de jure in an Islamic
country. She was tough and effective, but after a few months it was
clear that a government that was made up of a band of regicides
and headed by a woman monarch could have no political credibility
in the broader world. They therefore had Shajar al-Durr marry the
army commander-in-chief (*not* her old colleague) and named him
sultan in her place. The marriage lasted for seven years, but it was
not made in heaven. In 1257, for solid political reasons, Shajar al-
Durr had her husband murdered in his bath; his slaves in turn seized
her and beat her to death with her own clogs—a bloody if not unpredictable end to a fascinating career.[5]

As we move from the struggle for political power to the realms of
culture and religion, we find women in a more varied and (in the
eyes of their culture) more legitimate array of roles. This was so
even though women were far less likely than men to be literate, and
even though positions of religious leadership were reserved for men.
Shi'ite Islam recognized many women in the family of Ali as sacred
figures, and their tombs came to be thronged by pilgrims seeking
intercession and blessing. Shi'ite veneration naturally focused most
intensely on Fatima, daughter of the Prophet and wife of Ali. She
died only six months after her father, but not before bearing Hasan
and the martyred Husayn, thereby becoming the ancestress of all
the imams of every major Shi'ite sect. An enormous body of lore
has gathered around her, some of it reminiscent of the exaltation of
the Virgin Mary in Orthodox and Roman Christianity. But there were
many other deeply venerated figures as well—for example, Sayyida
Zaynab, the sister of Husayn, with her shrine in Damascus; and the

sister of the eighth imam (another Fatima), whose shrine in Qom was the foundation of that city's religious prestige.

The Sunni side of the ledger produced nothing quite like this, but women found a significant place there as well. Among the founders of the Sufi movement, none is more revered than Rabiʿa al-ʿAdawiyya (d. 800), whose poetry established the powerful and enormously influential image of the mystic as a lover longing for God the Beloved.[6] Sufism of course was (and remains) intuitive and experiential rather than rational. But even in the realm of the religious sciences, women could have a useful if limited role. The Arabic biographical literature reveals that many women were highly esteemed transmitters of the Prophet's sayings—an extremely important religious function, since the transmission of the Prophet's words from generation to generation was a key mechanism for establishing an unbroken continuity of doctrine and practice within the Community since its very beginnings. To give only one example (and there are others), the Damascene Ibn Asakir (d. 1176) prepared a separate volume on women in his enormous biographical dictionary of the scholars and religious leaders of Damascus. The whole compilation contains some nine thousand separate entries, and women account for about one-tenth of that number.

It is true that reporting Prophetic tradition was thought to be appropriate to a woman's intellect, since it required a reliable memory and a basic knowledge of Arabic but no serious understanding of jurisprudence or theology. However, there were some jurists who argued that women were perfectly capable of learning Shariʿa jurisprudence, and even of serving as judges. (So far as I know, no women held that office before the late twentieth century, and very few have held it since, but the point here is religious and intellectual capacity, not what actually happened.) And occasionally we do encounter a woman scholar widely recognized for her attainments. Amat al-Latif (d. 1243) belonged to a learned family and was the daughter of one of the leading scholars of Damascus. Her father saw to it that she received a thorough training in all the religious sciences, including jurisprudence. She ultimately became the close companion and mentor of a princess of the ruling family of Damascus, and somehow Amat al-Latif induced the princess to found a religious college specifically for her. She also managed at one point to

run afoul of one of the most powerful (and also suspicious and vindictive) rulers in Syria and spent some years in one of his jails. Amat
al-Latif was obviously a very exceptional figure, but it remains true
that her piety and learning were greatly respected and much praised
by her male peers.

Perhaps the largest role available to women in Islamic religious
life was that of patronage. A great many of the most important
mosques, colleges, and funerary complexes were built with their
money and at their behest. This we see from early times, and from
one end of the Islamic world to the other. The two central mosques
in Fez were founded by a pair of rival princesses who had taken
refuge in Morocco from the deadly political quarrels of Muslim
Spain. The caliph Harun al-Rashid's wife, his cousin Zubayda, was
famous for her lavish charities, including extensive wells, caravan-
serais, and facilities to ease the lot of pilgrims traveling between
Baghdad and Mecca. In thirteenth-century Damascus, some 15 percent of the roughly one hundred fifty mosques, colleges, and other
religious monuments were built or restored through the patronage
of women. Indeed, the women of the royal family funded fully half
of the work sponsored by the ruling dynasty.

Obviously all these women, like those who wielded political power,
belong to the most elite groups of their society—though since many
had begun their careers as slave concubines, they were not necessarily members of these groups by birth. But elite status, whether acquired by birth or talent or good luck, is precisely what we would
find for men as well. Serious political power was the affair of those
few people who had senior standing at a major court, and the patronage of religious architecture and institutions required both substantial wealth and considerable influence. The social background
characteristics of the women who could do these things were precisely
the same as those of men.

Court documents, which we have in abundance from the mid-
sixteenth century on, reveal the economic roles of a far broader cross-
section of women. In Shariʿa law, women have the full right to own
and dispose of property, whether they are married or single. Moreover, the property and incomes of a married woman may not be
used to support the household; that burden is borne entirely by her
husband. Hence the court registers reflect quite fully property and

contract transactions involving women. As to property transactions, some 25 to 40 percent of these involve women, usually in modest ways but sometimes on a very large scale.

In modern times the situation has become far more complex, but the old tradition persists in many ways. Women are still hewers of wood and carriers of water, as anyone can tell by going out to the villages, but the educated elites enjoy a significant role in the patronage of education and the arts. The latter would include such disparate figures as Shaykha Hussa of the Kuwaiti ruling house, who is the founder and principal donor of the Kuwait National Museum, and the wife of the late King Saud (reigned 1953–1964), who clandestinely began public education for girls in Saudi Arabia around 1960, at a time when to the country's religious traditionalists such a thing was unthinkable. As in medieval times, we encounter the gap between the narrow roles open to poor village women and the wide possibilities for action enjoyed by influential members of royal households.

But there are also women who have no real medieval counterparts. These are highly visible secular professionals, often with advanced degrees from major European and North American universities. Apart from their impressive educational and professional attainments, they have seized a public role in the political arena. They include Hanan Ashrawi (professor of English) and Bint al-Shati' ('A'isha 'Abd al-Rahman, professor of Arabic literature), Nawal Saadawi (physician, novelist, and gadfly), Mahnaz Afkhami (lawyer), Tansu Ciller (professor of economics and former prime minister of Turkey), and Fatima Mernissi (professor of sociology). Most women in this class would regard themselves as feminists (a word that covers many things, obviously), but not all; among them are those who speak very eloquently for Islamic tradition.

The role of universities in creating a female intelligentsia in the modern Islamic world is clear from the above list, and we obviously need to look at that role more closely. Women in the Muslim world, as in the United States, had a long struggle to be admitted to the modern-style secular universities that began to be founded around World War I and an even longer struggle to be accepted as equal members of the university community. No one could claim that the struggle has been won, but simply to walk onto the campus of Cairo University is to see how far they have come. Women constitute almost half of the undergraduate population, and they have a strong presence in every faculty except engineering. (Most American women will find this situation familiar if not altogether comforting.)

Saudi Arabia is a different case. Saudi ideology and policy demand a strict segregation between the sexes, and there is nothing merely pro forma about this demand; except within the sanctity of the family at home, adult men and women do not occupy the same space at the same time. So the Saudi universities have separate women's colleges, often on separate campuses. Male professors may lecture to women students, but only through the intermediary of closed-circuit television; the professor never sees his students. The women's colleges include faculties of arts, medicine, pharmacology, education, and so on, but also the traditional female faculties of nursing and home economics. They tend to receive secondhand equipment and less desirable facilities all around, but they are part of the public university system and they have a lot of students. At least one-third of the university students in this sternly conservative country are women. Obviously this fact will have a huge impact on Saudi social and political life in the long run, though it would be reckless to predict the exact nature of that impact. What is intriguing is the policy decision to admit women to the universities and to train them for at least limited professional roles. One suspects that a decision has been made, perhaps half-consciously, to prepare a way for a different future, without knowing what that future might be and while deferring it as long as possible.

Far more important in terms of numbers and everyday social impact are working women of the middle and lower-middle classes.[7] They have a high school education at least—many in fact are university graduates—and hold clerical and low-level professional jobs as nurses or schoolteachers. Their incomes by Western standards are very low but essential to whatever standard of living they and their husbands can command. They are the ones who have to contend daily for respect both as income-producing workers and as wives and mothers. Their husbands cannot do without their incomes, but their public roles, which bring them constantly into uncontrolled contact with strange men, somewhat compromise their respectability and moral standing. They must also define how they are going to imagine and present themselves as Muslim and Middle Eastern

212 Women in Public Life

women. A few years ago they tended to imitate Western dress as well as they could, and many were strikingly fashionable. Nowadays they are increasingly adopting some form of "Islamic dress," which can be anything from a loose dress, blouse, and jacket with an attractive headscarf to a bulky, fairly shapeless sack and a *jilbab*—a wimple pulled tightly around the head, leaving only the front of the face exposed. There is absolutely nothing "traditional" about the latter; it is a form of attire that looks nothing like what women were wearing in 1900. But it does meet the Islamic demand for modesty, for a form of dress that shelters women from the male gaze and in some sense segregates them from men. In this way, it also allows women to occupy the same public space as men without incurring censure for immodesty.

All this gives a fairly good idea of the social and cultural roles available to women in both premodern and contemporary Muslim societies. Obviously there have always been many severe constraints, but a perhaps surprising number of opportunities as well. Constraints and opportunities for women, or for any group, are not arbitrary; they are imbedded in and emerge from complex theological, legal, and cultural systems. Like most human institutions, these systems are both centuries old and constantly remaking themselves. But whether we see these systems from the perspective of tradition or innovation, it is important to know what they are and how they shape women's lives. Of course, this subject goes far beyond the scope of a single chapter. However, as with so many things in Islamic life, the Qur'an and the Shari'a provide the necessary starting point for any serious inquiry. Both have had enormous influence, because they are sacred—literally the word of God, either directly as in the Qur'an or indirectly as in the Shari'a. Accepting or rejecting their authority defines whether or not you are a real Muslim and what kind of Muslim you are. Finally, throughout this century the sections on women, the family, and personal morality have been the most vital and living elements of the Shari'a, and in the courts of most countries they are the only parts of it still enforced.

To put the matter baldly, the Qur'an is irredeemably patriarchal, in both tone and content.[8] It makes few explicit statements about family structure, or about appropriate relations between parents and children or between siblings. A striking exception to this assertion, but just about the only one, is the Qur'an's severe denunciation of female infanticide, which was a widespread practice not only in ancient Arabia but also in many premodern societies. The Qur'an's silence on these matters presumably implies that the kinship patterns and family structures of Arabian society were perfectly acceptable in God's sight. The Qur'an does provide a good deal of guidance on husbands and wives, and it is unmistakably clear that a wife must subordinate herself to the will and control of her husband.

The Qur'an (4:3) permits a man to marry several wives—apparently up to four, although the passage in question is notoriously muddy. But, as modern reformers correctly point out, the Qur'an seems to prefer monogamy in most cases, since it demands that a man treat each of his wives equally, and then adds that it is all but impossible to do equal justice to more than one (4:129). It is taken for granted that a man has the right to divorce his wife almost at will, though again he is called on to exercise this right with great restraint and humanity and to seek reconciliation where possible. A man is permitted to chastise his wife physically if she is flagrantly disobedient (4:34). Both men and women are called on to behave with modesty and decency, but the commandments regarding women are more detailed and explicit. Outside the realm of marriage, women continue to have a disadvantaged status. In matters of inheritance, they generally are awarded half as much as a similarly situated male; for example, a daughter gets one-half the portion of a son. In contractual disputes, the Qur'an requires the testimony of two women to equal that of one man (2:282).

All this having been said, the Qur'an recognizes the highly vulnerable position that women occupy and stresses over and over the need for equity, honorable treatment, and full recognition of their needs and rights. In the Qur'anic paradigm, the powers that men have over women are a burden, not a license for abuse and tyranny. The weight assigned a woman's honor is neatly indicated by the verses on slander (24:4–20). If a man accuses a woman of fornication, he must produce four reliable eyewitnesses to her misdeed; should he fail to meet this rather stiff evidentiary standard, he is to be punished by eighty lashes. On a more general plane, women and men enjoy what we would call spiritual equality. Women have the same hope of paradise and the same fear of hellfire as do men, and (with minor adjustments for matters like menstruation or childbirth, which create a state of ritual impurity) they bear the same ritual and moral obligations as men in their struggle to obtain salvation.

In broad lines, the Shariʿa follows the lines laid down in the Qurʾan, but it gives the Qurʾanic materials a rigid, legalistic twist.[9] Qurʾanic statements that would appear to favor women are treated as mere recommendations, while those that disfavor them are interpreted as strict commandments. For this there are many reasons— for example, that the Shariʿa draws on many sources besides the Qurʾan—but the main one no doubt is that the Shariʿa was developed by lawyers. What they sought was a set of clear-cut rules and procedures, not broad moral exhortation. Still, in spite of its restrictiveness, Shariʿa jurisprudence preserved an independent sphere for women. To repeat a point mentioned above, women retained full title to and disposal of their own property, whether they were married or single; a husband could not control his wife's property and could not use her wealth or income to support the household. In law this was his sole responsibility. The surviving Shariʿa court archives (which are quite rich for the centuries after 1500) make it clear that women's property rights were not mere words on a page; women did obtain and dispose of property of all kinds on a large scale.

In the arena of family life, although a woman could do nothing to block a divorce by her husband, she herself could go to court to seek a divorce in a few carefully defined situations such as abandonment or loathsome disease. The Shariʿa also permitted her to negotiate with her husband for a divorce, albeit at a considerable financial penalty. The area of law where a wife was most vulnerable probably lay in her husband's right to take a second wife without consulting her. In principle, this was not supposed to damage the first wife's financial interests, since her husband was obligated to maintain her and her children at the same level as before. In many cases, at least, the reality must have been quite different, though it is impossible to document this. In the final analysis, family law under the Shariʿa markedly advantages men, but women are not without recourse.

Legal changes in the twentieth century have on the whole preserved the rights and liberties that women had under a Shariʿa regime. It is hard to make any useful generalizations, since there are by now very wide differences in family law between one country and another, and these codes are subject to constant change. At one extreme lies Saudi Arabia, which adheres rigorously to traditional Shariᶜa principles and procedures. At the other there is Turkey, which simply tossed out its Shariᶜa-based legislation in 1927 and substituted the Swiss Civil Code for it. Everyone else has landed somewhere in between. Most commonly, men have retained their old prerogatives (unilateral divorce, plural marriage), but they must now register these acts with the court—or even obtain the court's permission—for them to be legally valid. In any event, however important the Qurʾan and the Shariᶜa may be, they state how things ought to be, not how they really are. For that we must look at popular custom, and this is both extremely varied and constantly changing. What you see in a High Atlas village in Morocco and a middle-class neighborhood in Cairo are not the same thing. They look different, and they are different.[10]

Custom overrides Qurʾanic teaching and formal Shariᶜa in many areas, but two examples will make the point. When a man becomes formally betrothed, he is required to pay a certain sum to his fiancée's male guardian (usually her father, but sometimes a paternal uncle or older brother). This sum is called *mahr*, usually translated in English—quite misleadingly—as "dowry" or "bride-price." The mahr is no nominal matter; the amount of money in question can be quite daunting. It is in any case determined by mutual agreement between the prospective groom and the woman's family, and the amount is stipulated in the marriage contract. Both the Qurʾan and the Shariᶜa state explicitly that the mahr belongs to the woman; it is her property to dispose of as she will, and she retains it on widowhood or divorce. It is in a sense her insurance policy. In spite of the plain words of scripture and law, however, it is common in smaller cities and villages for the bride's guardian to retain the bride-price. Few spend the money on themselves, to be sure; they use it to purchase a trousseau and household goods for their daughter. But if a girl has the misfortune to belong to a dysfunctional family, she has no effective way to compel her guardian to turn the money over to her. Going to court (where she would probably prevail) will only worsen her situation.

A second situation is also characteristic of village life. Both the Qurʾan and the Shariᶜa state that daughters must inherit a specified share of their father's land. Again, it is very common for fathers to "persuade" their daughters to turn over their shares to their brothers. The rationale for this practice is obvious: Qur³anic inheritance law will cause even a substantial piece of land to be subdivided into tiny garden plots in a few generations. Fathers are simply trying to guard their patrimony and to ensure that their sons have the wherewithal to live and count for something in the village. Daughters presumably will be provided for by their husbands. Even so, the practice skirts the plain intent of the Qur³an and the Shariʿa. If a daughter resists her father's demands, he can respond with some very credible threats—refusing to find a husband for her, for example.

The realm of custom, of what people actually do and think and feel, can be explored along two dimensions. The first is by looking at a familiar dichotomy, that men live and work in both the public and the private spheres, while women's lives, though complex and meaningful, are restricted to the arena of private life. How far this dichotomy works, and where it fails, will tell us much about the social structures of the Muslim world and what these mean for women. The second dimension is far more intensely personal. Sexuality has been almost from the beginning the focal point of Western imagination and fantasy about Muslim women. The blatant stereotypes and lurid images that Westerners have concocted make sexuality a very delicate topic, but the fact remains that it is the most intimate and revealing index of how women are situated, and situate themselves, within their culture.

The idea of separate public and private spheres is somewhat misleading from the outset, since women are out and about almost everywhere, even Saudi Arabia. (There are exceptions, admittedly. I remember spending whole days in certain small towns in eastern Turkey in 1973 without seeing a single woman on the streets. And Taliban rule in Afghanistan is notorious for having driven women out of professions like teaching and medicine.) As we have seen, women have important social roles outside the confines of the household. But there is a men's and a women's sphere; these overlap somewhat, but they are in fact far more separate and self-contained than in contemporary American society, or even the American society of Eisenhower's day.

As representatives of their families to the outside world, we can say that women represent their families chiefly before other women, and men before other men. But the sole fully acceptable arena of representation for women is the private or family quarters of the home, whereas for men there are many proper arenas: the public reception rooms of the home, the street, the marketplace, the mosque.

Within the economic realm, in conservative areas such as villages and small towns women's labor occurs largely in nonmarket sectors. This is not universally the case in Muslim lands: in solidly Muslim Java, the traditional retail markets are almost entirely run by women; if they went home, there would be precious little to buy. Even granting such exceptions, however, much of the most important work done by women is not officially counted as part of GDP. It thus tends to be devalued or at least taken for granted—that is, women are "supported" by their fathers or husbands or (where necessary) by brothers and sons. (American housewives will of course recognize this syndrome.) Men do a lot of nonmarket labor as well, especially in rural areas, but they very strongly dominate in the market-oriented or quantifiable sectors of the economy. They "invest" and "earn a living." In the major cities, however, things are quite different. Especially in clerical positions there are plenty of women, and the incomes they bring in, however modest, are essential to their families. But this fact creates tensions of its own: it is embarrassing to a man not to be able to support his family by his own (paid) labor, and working women gain little status or support for what they do.

Educationally, both boys and girls go to school nowadays. They do tend to go to separate schools from quite an early age, however, and certainly after completing the primary grades. Moreover, girls are far more likely to be pulled out of school when they finish elementary school, especially in rural areas and small cities—by no accident, since that is when they are approaching puberty, and their parents feel it necessary for the good reputation of their families as well as the girls' own moral protection to remove them from the public gaze.

Here an anecdote from a visit in 1990 to the High Atlas of Morocco may be useful. My interpreter, Ahmad, was yet another unemployed university graduate and was quite openly bitter about his situation, in particular the unending humiliation of pleading with foreign visitors to take him on as a guide. He regarded himself as very much a man of modern ideas and stated flatly that most young Berber intellectuals were, like him, strongly secularist in orientation. For whatever reason Ahmad wound up taking a liking to me, and he invited my wife and me to join him for supper at his home that evening. We were taken to a spacious but very spartan upstairs room, where we were joined by Ahmad, his brother (a prosperous and quite relaxed construction-materials dealer in a nearby city), and—most intriguingly—their niece, a very pretty fifteen-year-old.

Zaynab, to give her a name, sat quietly with us for about half an hour. She did not eat and spoke, very briefly, only when spoken to (in Berber) by Ahmad. Ahmad was very proud of his niece's achievements in school; she had always placed first in all her subjects. However, she had now completed her schooling (essentially eighth grade) and had already been engaged for a year or so to a young man in the village. She was in fact the cook of the excellent couscous we had been eating and, I believe, was the regular cook for the rather large household in which she lived. Ahmad was very critical of the extremely severe sexual ethic of his society—if a man saw a photograph of his wife, even a casual snapshot, in someone else's possession, it was instant divorce. But he bossed Zaynab around sharply in our presence and seemed to see nothing out-of-place in pulling this academically gifted young woman out of school in her early teens. He portrayed himself as a progressive, and of course he was: Zaynab had after all been allowed to sit in the company of a foreign man; she had completed several years of school, and was at least partially literate in French and Arabic. She enjoyed liberties well beyond those of most of her sisters in that village.

Politically, in most countries women have the right to vote, although this may not have any real impact on how things are run. Very rarely, women are elected to parliament, and a few have served as cabinet ministers or subministers. Whether there is a gender gap, in the sense of different political agendas as between men and women, and whether these women are able to assert specific interests of their own as women, is far less clear. Apart from Israel and Turkey, after all, researchers have had few opportunities to study Middle Eastern voting patterns in freely contested elections.

When we turn to sexuality, we obviously leave behind questions and ambiguities as to what is truly public or private.[11] As is the case almost throughout the world, sex is viewed with profound unease and ambivalence in Middle Eastern cultures. In contrast to the ancient values of Catholic Christianity, virginity is not valued in Islam for its own sake, as a symbol that one has transcended the body's carnal appetites or as a badge of spiritual purity. Virginity is valued, and indeed rigorously demanded, from those (both males and females, it should be stressed) who have not yet married. But the reason for this demand is to ensure the integrity of the patrilineal family—in effect, to ensure that everyone knows who the fathers are and that children can be situated within a secure line of descent. Virginity is a question of family honor, not of personal purity. From the very outset, Islamic teaching, like rabbinic Judaism, has assumed that adults should marry and produce children. The Qur'an very explicitly extols marriage as a source of sexual pleasure and procreation,[12] and a saying ascribed to the Prophet states, "There is no monasticism in Islam [*la rahbaniyyata fi al-Islam*]."

Once married, one is expected to stay within the fold—the demand for clear and unambiguous parentage is not relaxed. But before the twentieth century, men had a rather more relaxed mandate, though only a small percentage of them were in a position to take advantage of it. Men could (and legally still can in many Islamic countries) marry up to four wives simultaneously, so long as each wife can be supported adequately according to her station in life and so long as each receives equal financial support and accommodation. A husband is also required to share his nights equally among his wives; each has her turn (hence the same opportunity for sexual satisfaction, and more crucially, to conceive and bear children). Islamic polygamy is thus quite different from forms where there is a senior wife and the others are subordinate to her as well as to their (shared) husband. Plural marriage is obviously extremely expensive, and it is rare for co-wives to be terribly friendly. However, since they have separate apartments or quarters in the house, relations among them are normally correct. In any case, they need not see much of one another. Divorce is easy for men (albeit expensive as well), but some women will take the risk of trying to bully their husbands out of a second wife, and sometimes they get away with it.

There is one striking exception—perhaps we should call it a glaring loophole—to the requirement for equality between wives of a single husband. Before the twentieth century, when slavery was still legal and widespread in most Muslim countries, it was both lawful and appropriate for a man to purchase a serving girl to serve as his concubine. (In a few cases things went even further: for some centuries the Ottoman sultans did not marry at all; every sultan was the son of one of the royal concubines.) If she then bore his child, the child was "legitimate"—a full heir of the father's estate—and the mother, although still a slave, could not be sold even if her master grew tired of her. In an odd way, a concubine's position was more secure than that of a legal wife, though of course she had no family of her own to support her in conflicts with her master, as a wife normally would. Concubines also had the advantage of having been chosen because their purchasers found them attractive, and an astute woman could convert this attraction into a real bond of affection. Concubines often received a substantial bequest from their masters' estates, taken from the portion that a Muslim was permitted to dispose of as he wished. A concubine seldom enjoyed high status per se, but her situation was normal and accepted.

How did women feel about a system in which they were in effect bartered and traded, in which their own hopes and desires were secondary if not irrelevant to the political and economic needs of their families, or to the desires of a not necessarily appealing male who had literally taken them off the auction block in the market? On her wedding night, a girl who was still very young (14–16 years) would seldom know her husband; she would be deflowered literally by a stranger. Hardly less humiliating (though as much to her bridegroom as to her), first intercourse would take place on a white cloth. This cloth, stained by the blood of her lost virginity, was immediately passed to the women of her groom's family waiting outside the bridal chamber. Tenderness and courting, which might have eased the transition to a married state, were no part of the wedding night. To modern Westerners it may seem a kind of legalized rape. But in fact it is very hard for an outsider to "read" all this accurately, even if the outsider is a female anthropologist who is well known and trusted by her subjects. A bride's experience must be disorienting and alienating on a personal psychic level—or so we suppose—but it is one that is demanded, validated, and supported by her culture, including the female members of it. It is just how things are.

It is a difficult system for men as well, though they obviously have the better part of it. A man's bride is after all a stranger to him; he has to make love to a woman whom he has not seen before, who may not strike him as attractive in any way, toward whom he has had no opportunity to build up a fund of affection or focused desire. In that event he has some options, of course, whereas his bride does not; he can turn his back on her, divorce her, try to marry another wife. Even the institution of concubinage has serious emotional shortcomings. He may well have seen his new serving girl nude or nearly so, so he knows that she is physically appealing to him. But any emotional bonds, rooted in personality, character, and intelligence, will have to come later if at all. In spite of the difficult relations between the sexes in contemporary America, and in spite of the apparent tenuousness of the marriage bond, it remains very common for a man to say that his wife is his best friend. In the traditional Middle East that would have been an odd, almost incomprehensible statement.

Sad

Sexuality in Islamic societies is always connected in the Western mind with the institution of the harem, and so a word needs to be said about this. Anyone familiar with the paintings of Delacroix and Ingres (not to mention a host of lesser painters, most of them Frenchmen, as it happens) has an image of the "Oriental" harem—languid women, mostly or entirely nude, perched by the edge of tepid pools or lying outstretched on couches, in a luxuriant setting of rich brocades and filmy silks, where you can almost smell the perfumes and bath oils and the steamy air. I suppose that in the nature of things such places must have existed, though it is an absolute certainty that Delacroix and Ingres never laid eyes on one. But the overwhelming majority of harems were, I am sorry to say, sedate and even boring places.

Harem is the English form of the Arabic word *harim*, which means "forbidden" or "sacred."[13] It comes from the same root as *haram*, which refers to a sacred space, a sanctuary, such as the Dome of the Rock and the Aqsa Mosque in Jerusalem or the whole urban areas of Mecca and Medina. The harim is thus the sacred part of the home, the rooms that are reserved for the family and its private life, and are not to be visited by men who are not closely related to the women who reside there. Such visitors are accommodated in the public reception room toward the front of the house; the other chambers are none of their business. Typically the occupants of the family quarters consisted of a man's wife, their children, perhaps his mother if she was widowed, and a small number of female servants. If he was a wealthy man with more than one wife, each would have an apartment of her own, quite separate from that of her co-wives. A concubine would also have her own space, though she might share it with other slave women (but *not* any of the wives). The master of the household could enter the harem at will, of course, but for him it represented a retreat from the public world to spend time with his family. As to other men, the close blood relatives of a woman (essentially anyone she could not marry) could visit her, with appropriate permission, in her own chambers. And women were usually free to accept visits from other women. Except in the wealthiest households, the women of a harem had little time for the idle languor of our fantasies; they had to devote most of their waking hours to the hard work of running a home.

Among poorer families in all eras, and in the congestion of modern urban conditions even among families that are quite well off, it is difficult to maintain the traditional wall of separation between the public rooms and family quarters of a house. In slum or "popular" neighborhoods, several families will have small apartments overlooking a common courtyard, and the women of these households have to do a lot of their chores in this semipublic space. In modern high-rise apartment blocks, a man who is bringing a friend home may knock loudly before entering his own place to allow the women and children to retreat to the side rooms. And of course many people have adopted a more Western manner of life, one that permits a freer mingling of the sexes and assumes that women will be normal participants in public social gatherings—though even here it is easy for a foreigner to infringe unspoken but very real limits of propriety.

What the harem really represents and enforces is a strong cultural preference for a clear-cut segregation of the sexes, the assumption that most of the time men will spend their time with other men, and likewise women with other women. Obviously this preference is not a "separate but equal" arrangement, for it presupposes a high degree of control by men over the movements, indeed the whole lives, of the women in their households. It is extremely misleading, however, to assume that women are walled off from contact with the world. They simply interact with different (admittedly more limited) segments of it than do men.

Sometimes women must go out into public spaces, of course, and in this situation some form of veiling was traditionally used to maintain the desired barrier between the sexes. Veiling means many things, especially in the contemporary world; it ranges from rather stylishly worn headscarves to a full cloaking of the body, head, and face. But in any form it is meant to achieve two goals: (1) to minimize interaction between a woman and males not belonging to her household, by providing her with a degree of anonymity as she moves among strangers; and (2) to prevent her from becoming an object or cause of sexual temptation, by making it difficult to discern her features. Again, veiling assumes that women are to be supervised by men. But in a culture that values a high degree of gender segregation, veiling also allows women a far greater freedom of social interaction than they would otherwise have. It presents certain opportunities as well as obvious restraints.

In a society governed by such customs and constraints, it is hard to imagine a place for feminism—all the more because these practices were defined in terms of Islam. If ever there was an oxymoron in this world, it must surely be "Islamic feminism," or so one would conclude from the preceding discussion. And yet there are ongoing and serious efforts to build such a movement.[14] This will not be an easy task, but we would be foolish to dismiss it as foredoomed to failure. The difficulties, both historical and conceptual, are obvious and deep-rooted. Indeed, the whole notion of a specifically Islamic feminism might have seemed absurd twenty years ago, but that is no longer the case. The reason, ironically, lies in the struggle of the Islamic movements to recruit the broadest popular base possible, and one very strong element in current Islamic activism is its effort to mobilize women. Both literally and figuratively, the activists have invited women into the mosque, where they were in the past rather marginal figures if present at all. As this movement to mobilize women goes on, and as a highly educated and self-conscious generation of Muslim women tries to articulate its role within Islam, there will inevitably be very significant changes in the way Muslims conceptualize and act out their faith. (The parallels with feminism in contemporary Christianity are suggestive though admittedly very imprecise.) No doubt these changes will not be precisely those intended by the current generation of male activists, though it is far too early to say just what they will be.

It is hard to deny that Islam as it has been articulated over fourteen centuries, in almost every major variant, is a profoundly patriarchal religion. This begins, as we have seen, in the Qurʾan and becomes both more marked and far more rigid in the formulations of the lawyers. To review a few key points, the Qurʾan concedes "a degree" of superiority or preference to the male and places men in charge of the affairs of women (2:228; 4:34), but it insists on women's spiritual responsibility, property rights, and claims to fair and honorable treatment from their menfolk. The lawyers tend to minimize women's religious roles (though they never eliminate them), to narrow and formalize their property rights, and to permit (though they morally discourage) quite unethical treatment of wives by husbands. Thus a girl must be at least nine years old to marry and must give her consent to a marriage—but her male guardian (father, uncle, or brother) is the one who enters into a contract on her behalf, her silence implies consent, and she is given no substantial recourse against pressure from her guardian. In the realm of divorce, the Qurʾanic dicta could easily be interpreted to restrain the male prerogative and to permit women broad rights to initiate such proceedings, but the lawyers have never interpreted them in this way, at least until the later twentieth century. As we have seen, the culture at large is even more misogynistic than the law.

In light of these realities, it is perfectly natural that Middle Eastern feminism began in a rejection of traditional roles and symbols long sanctified by Islam—most theatrically, when Huda Shaʿrawi threw off her veil at Cairo's Ramses Station in 1921. From another, more positive perspective, it emerged as part of the larger movement to align Middle Eastern states and societies with specifically Western values and institutions—for example, representative government elected by universal suffrage, modern university education. None of this should seem surprising, for early Western feminism arose in the early and mid-nineteenth century in two countries (the United States and Great Britain) that had largely rejected religious belief and church membership as a basis for legal and civil rights. In so doing, they made it increasingly difficult to appeal to scripture or doctrine as a basis for excluding women from participation in pub-

lic life. One could of course base such an exclusion on the special
nature of women, on the different emotional and intellectual makeup
of the two sexes, but over time (a long time, admittedly) these arguments simply did not carry enough conviction to block women's
demands to be accepted as equal citizens. In short, in the West as in
the Middle East, the rise of feminism has been closely associated
with the progress of secularism.

Feminism in the Middle East has been pursued chiefly by a small
minority of highly educated, Western-oriented, upper-middle-class
women—in short, by those who had enough economic security to
violate widely held social taboos, and whose value orientation turned
them away from religiously-rooted norms toward secular liberalism or Marxism.[15] Even in relatively favorable climates, such as Republican Turkey (which supplanted Shariʿa with European civil and
criminal codes in the late 1920s), the Tunisia of Bourguiba, the Egypt
of Nasser and Sadat, and Iran during the Shah's last fifteen years in
power, progress toward a degree even of legal equality was slow
and fitful. In the last two cases, the personal influence of two well-
placed and strong-willed women, Mme Jihan Sadat and the empress
Farah Diba, was obviously a critical factor in such changes as were
made. But as things now stand, women's gains in Egypt are tenuous
and under constant Islamist pressure, while the Shah's new family
and personal-status code were swept away with his regime.

We should not exaggerate. The Islamic movements have focused
their antifeminism on the family and personal conduct in public. In
some arenas they have in fact confirmed the gains already made—
for example, the right to vote, or access to secondary and higher education. But even so, the tension between feminist and Islamist (not
to mention traditional Islamic) perspectives seems rooted in the very
self-identity of each movement.

Here we confront a paradox. If Islam, both as everyday culture
and as formal doctrine, insists on the strict control of women's roles
in society, and if feminism by any definition insists on the integrity
and autonomy of women and women's self-consciousness, how can
there be such a thing as Islamic feminism? The search for it is no
doubt rooted in the deeply felt need of educated Muslim women to
address two dimensions of their personal and social identities. On
the one hand, they want to assert their standing as women free and
able to act independently in the modern world. On the other hand,

they want to reaffirm their roots in the fourteen centuries of Islam, their continuing acceptance of the unique covenant that God offered to humanity through Muhammad. But mere psychic need does not make a quest intellectually valid or even pragmatically achievable.

A movement that wants to validate itself in terms of a historic tradition must be able to sink its roots in that tradition. And in fact Islamic history does offer contemporary women some interesting role models, though they must be interpreted quite boldly to serve effectively for modern purposes. Among the women whose lives we sketched at the beginning of the chapter, several might be made to serve an Islamic-feminist agenda: the Prophet's wife ʿAʾisha; the influential mystic Rabiʿa al-ʿAdawiyya; two queens, the famous Shajar al-Durr and the little-known but luckier and even more formidable Dayfa Khatun; the woman scholar Amat al-Latif. Apart from the rather problematical ʿAʾisha, however, not much has been done along these lines, though a small body of historical scholarship on women by women has begun to emerge in recent years.

A second angle, and one that is emerging in large part due to the Islamic activists themselves (no doubt to their horror, if they ever stop to think about it), is for contemporary Muslim women to claim an active part in defining what Islam is. The activists have struggled hard to bring women into the mosque, to make the mosque a kind of community center, and there are now an increasing number of women's Islamic study groups. Over an extended period, as literate and engaged women confront the sacred texts, especially the Qurʾan and Prophetic tradition, they will inevitably make something different of it than men have.[16] They may put aside the many misogynist statements (which are found in many sayings attributed to the Prophet but almost never in the Qurʾan, by the way) and retain those that confer some honor and status on women. They will certainly perceive the Qurʾan's humane and flexible tone as opposed to the rigidities of the jurists, and in light of this perception they will demand that Islamic legislation become more authentically Qurʾanic. Of course, none of this will come out in the way we now predict or imagine. But even in this most bitterly contested realm of life, we must never underestimate the capacity of Muslims to find original and effective solutions to the problems that beset them. Nor should we forget the infinite variety of resources that Islamic tradition will provide them for this search, if they will only allow themselves to use these freely.

CHAPTER 10

ISLAM AND HUMAN RIGHTS

Has Islamic thought produced any clear concept of human rights, or at least a body of values in which a doctrine of human rights can be firmly grounded?[1] The answer of course depends first of all on how we define human rights, a much-disputed issue. But if we stick to the definitions developed by the modern human rights movement, then "human rights" means those rights that belong to every individual as such—rights rooted in the very nature of what it is to be human. Even with this widely used definition, however, the answer to the above question is far from clear. This is especially so in connection with those rights that are particularly valued in American political culture: security of person and property against the arbitrary exercise of government power and a broad liberty of thought, speech, assembly, and peaceful action against one's government. These rights as Americans understand them also typically call for democracy, or at least for extensive rights to participate in government. This whole package of rights is firmly grounded in the notion of the autonomy and ultimate sovereignty of the individual. However, Islamic discourse, down to the nineteenth century at least, developed only an attenuated concept of individualism. It certainly never debated whether the individual, and his or her well-being and liberty, was the ultimate criterion of value. If this is in fact the case, we should not expect societies shaped by Islamic norms to have produced the same package of rights that seem so self-evident to Americans.

However, the individual is a final criterion of value only in a few highly exotic societies, like the modern United States. (I am not being ironic.) We therefore need to ask whether there are other grounds for human rights besides the untrammeled sovereignty of the individual. It is commonplace for representatives of authoritarian states to insist that freedom of thought and expression are specifically Western values, which Americans and Europeans have no right to impose on other societies and cultures. This imposition is not merely arrogant but a kind of cultural imperialism, which makes of the contemporary West the sole measure of value, the single arbiter of right or wrong. According to this argument, other rights (usually termed social and economic entitlements in Europe and North America) are primary and universal. These include the right to adequate health care, to decent nutrition and housing, to security from crime and violence. If a political system supplies food, drink, shelter, health, and personal security, and if that system seems generally acceptable to those who live under it, then outsiders have no business criticizing it.

We might counter that this is obviously a self-serving line of argument, and one that contains weaknesses both in logic and in fact. To start with, it takes for granted that authoritarian governments do in fact see to the material needs of their subjects—something that is true enough in Singapore or Saudi Arabia but is demonstrably not the case in many other places. Likewise, it does not address the problem of how citizens are to be protected from violence and injustice at the hands of their own governments, a regrettably common occurrence even in democratic countries. Finally, it is not clear why a right to the fulfillment of basic material needs should exclude rights of belief, expression, assembly, or due process. As any Swede or Dutchman will tell you, the two are not mutually contradictory. Why not have both?

Even so, we cannot just toss the anti-Westernist argument out of court. Cultures are in fact different and embody different values. It is natural, indeed inevitable, that they will come up with a different sense of their members' basic rights and obligations. The radical individualism of contemporary America has few parallels or antecedents in history, and we should not assume that everyone else in the world will find it appealing or constructive. Many are indeed appalled at what seems to them America's willful indifference to communal needs, its moral chaos, and its extraordinary level of random criminal violence.

In this light, if Muslim thinkers have over the centuries articulated a body of concepts that diverges from the Bill of Rights, their ideas still deserve our attention. At the same time, we need to keep in mind the fundamental axiom of the modern human rights movement stated above—namely, that all men and women, in all times and places, possess certain rights simply because they are human. "We hold these truths to be self-evident," said a well-known forebear of the movement, "that all men are . . . endowed by their Creator with certain unalienable rights."[2] Is this axiom indeed the case? And if such universal rights do exist, what precisely are they, and how (if at all) do they find expression within Islamic tradition?

To develop a yardstick for assessing how the ideas generated within Islamic tradition match up with our sense of how things ought to be, we can review very briefly the rights enshrined in two major documents: the U.S. Constitution and the UN's Universal Declaration of Human Rights. These latter are of course statements of ideals, not of realities, and they have been the subject of considerable skepticism and reserve even among those who framed them and formally subscribe to them. Still, they are the product of a long tradition of moral and political debate in the West, and they are what Americans are talking about when we "demand our rights."

These rights are wide-ranging, but they are all united by a common motive and purpose: they aim first and foremost to protect the individual citizen against the overwhelming power of the modern state. They include the following points:

1. Freedom of thought, of religious belief, and of expression so long as that expression does not wrongfully damage someone else.

2. Freedom of peaceable assembly, for almost any purpose.

3. The right to due process of law when one is charged with a crime.

4. The right to security against arbitrary arrest, against being compelled to testify against oneself, and against search and seizure without due cause.

5. Equal treatment under the law for every competent adult, regardless of race, gender, religion, and so on—a deeply imbedded but very hard-fought concept, whose implications are still being worked out.

6. The right to own and dispose of property, and to be compensated for it when it is taken over by a public entity.

7. The right to participate actively in the political life of one's country. This is the doctrine of popular sovereignty, holding that the

people are the sole source of political authority and that they have the right to designate those who will exercise this authority on their behalf.

8. Personal freedom; that is, no one's labor or body is to be subjected to the power of another, save through free and voluntary contract between legally equal parties.

These rights all presuppose a political context—they are only meaningful within an ordered social and political system, and only in such a system can they be either exercised or threatened—but they all focus on the individual. In effect, they define how the individual is to retain his or her innate, God-given autonomy in the face of social pressures to conform and the power of political authorities to coerce obedience.

Islamic tradition is extremely complex and many-sided. There is no single "Islamic" doctrine about anything except the oneness and uniqueness of God and the prophethood of Muhammad—and the meanings of even those concepts have been hotly argued over the centuries. Still, within the centuries-long debate about what Islam is and ought to be, we can identify two topics that throw a special light on the present inquiry: (1) the nature of law and (2) the obligations of the individual as a member of the Community of Believers. If we do not find a fully developed, self-conscious doctrine of human rights in the modern sense among pre-twentieth-century Islamic thinkers, we might still discover a body of practices and concepts that add up to something similar. Or if in the end we do not encounter that, we might at least discover some foundation on which a coherent philosophy of human rights could be erected.

In pursuing this problem, I will be referring constantly to the Shariʿa. Everyone knows, of course, that the Shariʿa is the Holy Law of Islam, laid down in the Qurʾan and in the authoritative teaching of Muhammad. Since the Shariʿa is God's Law, it is true now and forever, having existed without change from all eternity. If one wants to know what Islam teaches on any given issue, one goes to the Shariʿa to find out. In fact, such ideas are very misleading. The Shariʿa is indeed regarded by many contemporary Muslim activists, especially the militants with their terrifying shadeless clarity, as a closed and fixed corpus of commandments and prohibitions, a definitive and unchanging statement of what God has permitted and prohibited. But before the legal and political transformation of the nineteenth century, the Shariʿa was a field of debate, an arena of unceasing, vigorous, and occasionally vitriolic speculation and argumentation among the jurists. Although it is undeniable that this debate was increasingly limited by the burden of tradition, especially after the thirteenth century, the possibilities for originality and innovation were never blocked. Any reputable jurist could insist on reexamining supposedly settled questions. In what follows, then, when I talk about the Shariʿa, I am referring not to rigid commandments and statutes but to ideas on which a general (but never absolute) consensus had emerged over the centuries. More than that, I am talking about a set of concepts and a form of argumentation that shaped the debate—for if Muslim jurists did not always agree on conclusions, they did agree on what they were arguing about.

The logical place to begin a discussion of human rights in Islam is with the Arabic word *haqq* (pl., *huquq*), which means both "right" and "truth." Haqq at bottom does not refer to the abstract notion of "right" but to a concrete right—to a specific claim on or against someone. In this sense, haqq is a rightful demand that someone give you something that you are owed. In the broad arena of Islamic thought, stretching from the first revelations to Muhammad about 610 down to 1850, who was believed to possess rights in this specific sense, and from whom could these rights be demanded?

On these points, Muslim jurists were remarkably consistent. First and foremost, God possesses absolute rights against His creation, and in particular against mankind. There are scores of relevant verses in the Qurʾan, but they are all wonderfully subsumed in the following primordial oath of mankind before the Divine Majesty:

> Your Lord brought forth descendants from the loins of Adam's children and made them testify against themselves. He said, "Am I not your Lord?" They replied, "We bear witness that you are." This He did, lest you should say on the Day of Resurrection, "We had no knowledge of that," or, "Our forefathers were indeed polytheists. But will you destroy us, their progeny, on account of what the followers of falsehood did?" (Qurʾan 7:172–173)

God is the ultimate, and in the final analysis the only, absolute possessor of rights. In contrast, no man or woman has any rightful claims against God. They may have reasonable expectations, based

on God's sure promise of mercy to those who believe in Him alone
and endeavor to follow His commandments, but no rights. So far as
I am aware, the literatures of the Muslim world present us with no
figure like those tenacious biblical attorneys Abraham and Jacob.

Human beings do however have secondary or created rights—
rights that they can assert against one another. There is in fact a term
of jurisprudence, *huquq adamiyyin*, which might be literally translated as "human rights." However, *haqq adami* is not a general concept but a technical term; it refers to an individual's right to seek
redress from a malefactor or to receive compensation for a tort. In
God's order of things, there is an ideal set of relationships between
human beings, and these relationships are articulated in exhaustive
detail in His law, the Shariʿa. Here we have to make a distinction between God's law as He knows and defines it and God's law as human beings know and define it. The Shariʿa as it exists in the jurists'
treatises and debates is only an approximation of the real thing—it
is in effect our best guess about what God wants us to do. Still, it
is the closest we can come to the divine plan; as such, even in its
imperfect earthly form, the Shariʿa provides a divinely authorized
framework for the rightful claims of one person against another. Ultimately these claims will be vindicated by God Himself in the final
judgment, but here on earth we must settle for the efforts of all-too-
human rulers and judges.

Now, the Shariʿa recognizes only two "legal persons": on the one
hand, actual individuals, and on the other, the Community of Believers (*umma, jamaʿa*). There are no fictitious persons such as corporations or other legally constituted groups with the standing to act,
sue, and so on. The consequence is that the individual has rights and
obligations only vis-à-vis other individuals and the community as
a whole. But what is the nature of these mutual rights and obligations? If we can establish these, we might discern a basis for a coherent doctrine of human rights in Islamic thought.

In this effort to explore the rights of the Muslim vis-à-vis the community, one category of action provides an especially useful starting
point. This category is *al-amr biʾl-maʿruf waʾl-nahy ʿan al-munkar*, already discussed in chapter 8—the general obligation of every Muslim, within the limits of his or her power, to "command good and
denounce evil." We have seen earlier that the one strictly political
obligation of every Muslim toward the community is to reprimand

and correct conduct contrary to God's law. It is the obligation of every Muslim to help the Community to prosper, to save it from the divine wrath, and this can only be done insofar as he or she pushes the community to live in strict accord with the Shariʿa. Now, if a Muslim has the obligation to reprimand and correct, it necessarily follows that he must have the right to do so. That is, he can rightfully demand that the community (and most especially its rulers) afford him the scope and freedom of action necessary to carry out this religious obligation.

This right to reprimand and correct is a very specific and tightly focused one. It is not a First Amendment right to say whatever one likes, in whatever way one chooses. It is not a freedom to advocate a course of action based on one's own sense of right and wrong, or stemming from some personal desire to challenge the established order. Rather, it is the right to call other Muslims back to obedience to God, as obedience is defined and embodied in the Shariʿa. To put it simply, a Muslim has the right to speak the truth—that truth which the whole community recognizes and reveres, even if its members may have shamefully neglected or violated it. This truth may be extremely uncomfortable and unwelcome to the powers that be, but if it is genuinely grounded in the Shariʿa, in God's law, then a Muslim's right to proclaim it cannot be denied.

Since the Shariʿa is not a fixed code but a vast, amorphous, ever-changing record of debate—in effect, the literary residue of the endless search for truth among the learned—Muslims are also entitled to argue over some aspects of it. This debate cannot contest the idea of Shariʿa, of a divinely appointed path of righteous conduct, but it can ask what God wants one to do or not to do in particular cases. Again, one cannot conduct this debate to suit his own whims; he must show that his conclusions are in strict accord with the precepts of the Qurʾan and the teaching of the Prophet, and he must address the arguments developed by the great masters of the past. What about freedom to depart from the Shariʿa, to advocate the adoption of other systems of conduct, other values, other beliefs? Traditional doctrine held that no Muslim can do this, anymore than he can deny the unity of God; it is apostasy and is punishable by death.

Finally, what about non-Muslims living under a Muslim government? In the Middle East, at least, almost all such non-Muslims are

Christians, Jews, or (in Iran) Zoroastrians. (The situation in India, Southeast Asia, and Sub-Saharan Africa is obviously far more complex.) Again, the main traditions of Islamic thought have held that these peoples are adherents of scriptures that were valid when they were originally revealed, though they are now superseded by the definitive revelation vouchsafed to Muhammad. Peoples who follow the ancient revelations must be tolerated: they may practice their faiths quietly, and they are to enjoy security of person and property. They may not proselytize, however, and in any case they obviously have nothing to say about the Shariʿa or its application.

To sum up so far, the First Amendment finds only a few echoes in Islamic tradition. Muslims have the right to speak up and reprimand their fellows or the powers-that-be when they have departed from the straight path. They also have the right—which they would do well to exercise discreetly—to discuss the exact meaning of key theological truths (e.g, the unity of God, the nature of the next life), or to try to debate how God's law should be interpreted and applied to new or uncertain situations. But they have no right whatever to advocate falsehood and corruption. They cannot abandon Islam for another religion, or attack its fundamental doctrines, or allow others to do so. As to non-Muslims, if they accept a revelation recognized as previously valid by Islam, such as Christianity or Judaism, they are free within carefully defined limits to follow their traditional scriptures, but they are not free to seek converts, and they are of course subject to their own ecclesiastical authorities.

However, this line of analysis gives us too narrow a picture of how rights may be understood and applied within an Islamic framework. Although Americans are particularly exercised by issues of free speech and freedom of religion, a far more fundamental concern of the U.S. Constitution is to establish a government of law. And much the same is the case in Islamic traditions of political thought. The very nature of the Community of Believers implies a set of rights for Muslims. God is no arbitrary tyrant; He imposes commandments on His creatures, not whims, and these commandments have been part of the divine plan since all eternity. It follows that a community constituted for the purpose of realizing God's commandments must be a community of law, and Muslims can demand that they be treated according to that law.

The Shariʿa is not the Bill of Rights or even the U.S. Code of Civil

[margin note: tolerance is built in for dhimmis]

and Criminal Procedure, but it affords important and predictable rights to those governed by it. On the level of civil law, every free adult Muslim (both male and female, whether married or single) has the right to own and dispose of property, and all possess a broad freedom to make contracts and to have these contracts upheld in court according to well-defined rules of evidence and procedure. In matters of personal status, a freeborn Muslim cannot be enslaved for any reason whatever.

Criminal law is, not surprisingly, a bit more complex. This is so partly because certain actions (like assault and murder) are treated in Shariʿa jurisprudence as torts; they are wrongs committed against the victim and his or her kin, not against "the people," as American usage has it. Even so, such torts are supposed to be tried in court before a judge. Other matters that are not criminal acts in U.S. law— or are no longer so—are treated as such in the Shariʿa, and these have fixed penalties grounded in Qurʾanic commandments: consumption of alcohol (whether or not this leads to intoxication), adultery, false accusations of sexual misconduct against women. Theft and armed robbery are crimes in both systems. In criminal law generally, the Shariʿa envisages only two kinds of valid evidence: witnesses and sworn statements by the accused and accuser. In the absence of these, circumstantial evidence, however compelling, is not adequate to bring a conviction. If a man is accused of theft and there are no witnesses, he must be found innocent if he swears an oath that he did not commit the crime. However, he cannot remain silent; if he does not deny the deed on oath, he is presumed guilty. Many other acts— for example, fraud and extortion—are treated as crimes by Muslim jurists and likewise require confession or witnesses to establish guilt, but here the judge (or the government that has appointed him) has very broad discretion as to what kind of penalty to apply—typically some combination of flogging, imprisonment, and fines. There is then due process in Shariʿa. It goes without saying that such due process has not always been observed. Like everyplace else, the Muslim world has often been afflicted by brutal police officers and corrupt judges. But that is hardly the fault of the Shariʿa or of the lawyers who framed it.

This point brings us to another issue much debated among contemporary Muslims—that of social justice. The believer certainly has the right to demand justice from his or her fellow believers. But what is justice? In the framework of Islamic thought, justice is no abstract philosophic concept. On the contrary, justice is the whole body of obligatory and recommended behavior toward other persons described in the Shariʿa, and only that. Claims about "natural rights" that exist outside this framework are, in a strict sense, meaningless. Justice is what God says it is, not what we mortal creatures might desire or imagine it to be. In this light, the field on which contending ideas of social justice can struggle is perforce a narrow one. Likewise, the language within which one can frame this debate is tightly constrained.

What then does the Shariʿa demand in social relations? Here the answer is complex. First, not everyone is equal. Apart from children and mental incompetents, who are treated (much as in American law) as wards of their parents or legally recognized guardians, people are divided by three cleavages: Muslim versus non-Muslim, free versus slave, and (in many ways most crucially) male versus female. A person's rights and obligations under the Shariʿa are defined quite precisely according to the tripartite category into which he or she falls. The "default," or normative, category is of course the free adult male Muslim; the rights and duties of everyone else are defined in terms of his. The disparities between the different categories are quite marked, particularly as regards criminal liability, capacity to give witness or conclude independent contracts, and the right to bequeath and inherit. These disparities certainly affect a person's right to bear arms in a Muslim army or to take part in public office—that is, to represent or rule over Muslims.

Even so, things are not always what one might think. For example, women were undoubtedly subjected to a broad and highly arbitrary authority at the hands of their fathers and/or husbands; only in a few limited cases could they seek legal recourse against the males who were responsible for them. A woman normally inherits half as much as a man would in a similar blood relationship (e.g., the sisters of a decedent each receive one share of his or her estate, while their brothers each receive two shares). A married woman's body in effect belongs to her husband, except in cases of loathsome disease or great cruelty.

However—and in marked contrast to the common-law and Roman-law traditions followed in the West until the reforms of the last century—an adult woman retains full title and control over her own property, whether acquired before or during marriage. Nor can she be required to expend any of it toward the support of her husband or family. On another plane, anyone accusing a woman of adultery needs the support of four male eyewitnesses of good character to establish his complaint. If an accuser cannot meet this steep evidentiary standard, he is to be severely flogged for slander. In contrast, as far as the Shari'a is concerned, anyone can accuse a man of adultery with impunity.

In other arenas, non-Muslim subjects of a Muslim state remain subject to their own courts in all civil matters among themselves, including family and personal status cases, but they are free to appeal to the Muslim courts if these better suit their needs. Slaves have severely limited capacity to act on their own behalf, but they retain some legal personality: they may marry and have families, they may make contracts with their masters to purchase their freedom, and they may be chastised by their owners but not killed or severely injured. Islam grew up and flourished in a world where slavery was universal and had been practiced since the remotest antiquity; in that light, the Islamic code of slavery was almost certainly the most moderate and humane one ever produced in the ancient and medieval world.[3]

In regard to political rights, democracy, and popular participation in government, traditional Shari'a discourse has very little to say. Sovereignty belongs to God alone, as the Qur'an states in many places (e.g., 3:26). God of course can and does intervene directly in the affairs of this world, but He leaves the daily business of earthly government to His appointed representatives. These representatives are in the first instance the prophets whom He has sent, and they govern on God's behalf with plenipotentiary authority. But what happens when there are no prophets? From the outset, Islamic political thought, in every variant, accepted the idea that the community should invest its political powers in one man, who once named should be expected to rule for life. The ideas of regular elections, rotation of magistrates, and so on, never occurred to anyone, or at least were never regarded as remotely desirable. (To avoid misunderstanding, I must stress that the Qur'an does *not* demand one-man rule; in fact it has almost nothing to say about how communities should be governed in the absence of the prophets who founded them.) The criteria for rulership and the method by which the ruler should be selected were bitterly debated, and no universally accepted doctrine was ever reached. It can be said that even in the most "democratic," community-oriented theories, those who nominated the successor to the Prophet and God's vicegerent were a very small number, essentially the most prominent senior males living in or near the ruler's residence.

In chapters 5 and 7, I noted that as the caliphate ceased to be a functioning political institution in the course of the ninth and tenth centuries, it was replaced by warlords who seized power in various corners of the Islamic world through main force. For a long time such regimes had no color of legitimacy at all, and Muslims were counseled to obey them only because "sixty years of tyranny is better than one night of anarchy." But by the late eleventh century a new theory of Islamic government slowly began to emerge, and this theory was fully worked out among Sunni thinkers in the fourteenth century. It held that a regime was legitimate, however it had come to power, if it defended Islam and strove to govern in accordance with the Shariʿa. Legitimacy was conferred post facto; it represented a situation achieved by a ruler's actions once he had power, not by the process through which he gained power. Again, this revised theory focused on rule by one man; he should seek advice from wise and religious counselors, but in the end he made the decisions. Many modern Muslim reformers since the mid-nineteenth century have argued fervently and sincerely that Islam is "essentially" democratic. The argument may be true in itself—there is nothing in the Qurʾan to contradict it—but you will find no trace of this idea in traditional political theory. When the medieval theorists thought about democracy at all, they regarded it as little better than mob rule. In their eyes, just government was simply the good ruler ruling well.

What emerges from this long and rather tortuous discussion is something like this. On the one hand, we cannot really claim that traditional Islamic discourse, complex and variegated as it is, ever produced any body of human rights as comprehensive and absolute as those given in the U.S. Constitution (as amended over the last two centuries, of course) or in the UN Universal Declaration of Human Rights. It certainly does not provide for democracy or popular sovereignty. On the other hand, we do find in Islamic thought, and specifically in the Shariʿa, a limited but substantial body of doctrine that defines the claims that individuals can properly assert against the Community of Believers and its rulers, according to their religiolegal status within that community. These rights may be thought of as the right to participate in the life of the community, within the boundaries (and under the protection) of its recognized and God-given laws.

As far as the Shariʿa is concerned, in the framework of this life the individual does not exist in isolation, as an entity in his or her own right; rather, the individual derives social rights and obligations only from his or her membership (however qualified) in the community. In this context, the rights of the community are primary—or to put it differently, the claims of the community against its members take priority over those of individuals against the community. The rights of the individual are precisely those that are necessary if the community as a whole is to seek the divine blessing and secure the salvation of its members.

All this brings us to a crucial problem in Islamic history. For if Islamic legal discourse, as it crystallized in the Shariʿa, favors or even guarantees a certain concept of human rights, these rights have not always been observed by Islamic regimes—perhaps never less so than in the late twentieth century. (Obviously, Islamic countries are not alone in this; many of the states signatory to the Universal Declaration of Human Rights are not wholehearted devotees of it in practice.) This means that we must move our discussion on the nature and content of Shariʿa from the domain of the ideal and eternal, from academic discourse, to the domain of what has really happened. How has the Shariʿa actually been used, and how might it be used in the future?

The first question in this regard is whether the Shariʿa is law in the usual Western sense of the word. Is the Shariʿa a body of rules and sanctions that is actually enforced in the courts of Islamic countries, or is it just theory, the sophisticated but idle chatter of professors? Until the last few decades, it was an almost unquestioned dogma of Western scholarship that the Shariʿa was literally an academic enterprise—that is, a body of discourse produced by professors debating with one another—and that in the real world of rulers and judges it had little application. Only the chapters on family and personal status, so my teachers told me, were actually enforced in the courts. But recent research by Muslim and non-Muslim scholars has demonstrated that this is a gross misrepresentation. It is now clear that in almost every field of civil and even criminal law, the Shariʿa was for many centuries the real law applied in the courts. It had a considerable role even in the domain of public law (taxes, administration, etc.) where we would expect the immediate needs of the rulers to hold sway. Far from being abstract scholastic speculation, Shariʿa doctrines of contract, commerce, property, and so on, were intensely practical and readily applied to the real world. Shariʿa was often preferred by Jewish and Christian merchants and property holders even where they were free to follow other codes, if only because decisions made and documents registered in Islamic courts would be backed by the full authority of the state. The Shariʿa began to lose its central role only in the mid-nineteenth century, as increasing trade with Europe, the growing numbers of European merchants living in the Middle East, and—not least—the imperative demands of European governments compelled Middle Eastern regimes to substitute European-style commercial codes and court systems for those that had served them for so many centuries.

So far as the Shariʿa was actually followed, then, we can say that Muslims and non-Muslim subjects enjoyed the body of rights that it provides. These rights were, to repeat, not those expected by Americans, but they did provide a lawful framework for life, a set of regular rules and predictable consequences. But even though the Shariʿa was the law of the courts, its capacity to establish the rights of Muslims was severely limited. First of all, the Shariʿa was really only enforced in the towns, and down to the late nineteenth century these contained only 10 to 20 percent of the Middle East's population. Villagers and tribesmen were governed by highly variable local customs—customs more or less influenced by the Shariʿa, certainly, but independent of it. Second, in both the theory and the practice of autocracy in the Islamic world judges represented the autocrat; they were appointed by him, served at his pleasure, and could be replaced by him at any moment for any reason. Shariʿa law was formulated quite independently of the rulers, but the judges who had to interpret, apply, and enforce it were agents of the regime. In this light, the capacity of the Shariʿa to defend the rights of Muslims depended very heavily on who was in power at a given time and place, and the subjects seldom had any voice in choosing their rulers.

It should be stressed that Muslim thinkers of the premodern era recognized this problem very frankly, and in their advice to rulers they laid more stress on justice than any other dimension of rulership. Justice mirrored the divinely ordained order of things, they held; without justice the world would quickly fall into ruin. But they were never able to devise any institutional checks and balances that could assure even a rough approximation of justice; it would come about if and only if the ruler was himself a just man, unremittingly vigilant and energetic.

There was a more pervasive problem than tyranny. In theory the apparatus of government lay under the control of an all-powerful autocrat, but in reality Middle Eastern states before the mid-nineteenth century (like those everywhere else, really) were extremely weak. Even the most powerful and dynamic monarch had all he could do to rein in the senior ministers and army officers who resided in his capital. Provincial and local officials were effectively autonomous; only the very rare artisan or peasant who possessed enough time, money, and courage to wend his way to the supreme ruler's far-off court could hope for justice against these men. A king might appoint excellent judges to enforce the Shariʿa in his capital, but he could not guarantee the same level of justice for his remoter possessions.

In spite of these shortcomings, there were many rulers who worked hard to meet the demands laid on them by religion and philosophy, and their memories remained green for centuries. Even today Muslim activists appeal to them as models of what Islamic justice can and ought to be. There are differences of perspective, to be sure. For the Sunnis, for example, the second caliph, Umar ibn al-Khattab (634–644), is the finest exemplar of the just caliph, a man who united knowledge, piety, and action. Sunni sources portray him as dynamic and sleeplessly vigilant, possessing rigorous personal austerity and fierce integrity, unable to tolerate the merest whiff of corruption or favoritism. One of the Prophet's closest associates, he knew and understood his teaching like few others. In contrast, the Shiʿites find Umar heavy-handed and ignorant; many reject his title to the caliphate altogether, but even those who grudgingly recognize his legitimacy (on the grounds that Ali swore allegiance to him) find little to admire. Unquestionably sincere and devoted to Islam, he was nevertheless impulsive, often shortsighted, and negligent of the Prophet's rulings. In all, Shiʿites believe, Umar's legal judgments are gravely flawed and cannot serve as precedents for later generations. For

them, of course, the Prophet's cousin, son-in-law, and fourth successor, Ali ibn Abi Talib, is the man after God's own heart. He is not
only the perfect model of the just ruler but also an infallible imam
whose decisions constitute binding doctrine for all later rulers and
judges.[4]

On a more human scale, we could cite two of the great defenders
of Islam against the Crusaders, Nur al-Din (1146–1174) and Saladin
(1169–1193).[5] Nur al-Din portrayed his struggle not merely as a war
to expel the infidel from the lands of Islam and to recover the holy
city of Jerusalem, but as a systematic campaign to establish justice
and doctrinal unity within the lands he ruled. Toward this end, he
established literally scores of religious colleges in his domains to ensure the systematic dissemination of sound Islamic learning, and as
a way to ensure that his judges and high officials would have a solid
training in Islamic law. He took the business of judging very seriously, and in both his capitals, Damascus and Aleppo, he established
a new institution, the Palace of Justice, close to the central mosque
and the main marketplaces, where his subjects could have ready access to him and his judges. That Nur al-Din was absolutely sincere
in his protestations seems to be admitted by all his contemporaries;
even the great Crusader historian William of Tyre calls him "a monk
in warrior's clothing."

Saladin was a more colorful character, a man of great warmth
and charm in contrast to his dour predecessor. For most of his reign
he spent more time at war against his Muslim rivals than against
the Crusaders, and some contemporary observers regarded him
chiefly as an ambitious and successful empire builder. (Naturally he
pleaded that his war and diplomacy against other Muslim rulers
were essential for the successful prosecution of a decisive struggle
against the Crusaders. He may have been right, but it is hardly an
argument against interest.) In spite of criticism, Saladin was no less
concerned than Nur al-Din to project an image of justice, though he
was perhaps less scrupulous about seeing that his good intentions
were carried out. Saladin was no hypocrite, however; he appointed
good judges, men of high social standing and deep learning, and
when he himself sat in the judge's seat his decisions were recognized as sound and generous.

One last example of the just ruler from premodern times, and in
some ways the most remarkable, would be the Ottoman sultan Su-

leyman the Magnificent (1520–1566)—or as his own subjects called him, Kanuni Süleyman—Solomon the Lawgiver. He took his prophetic name very seriously; for some years he seems to have believed that he was the ruler appointed to usher in the Last Days. (Apocalyptic thought was in the air throughout Europe and the Middle East in the late fifteenth century and early sixteenth, as the names Savonarola, Martin Luther, and Shah Isma'il of Iran bear ample witness.) Even after the feverish atmosphere of his earlier years was calmed, he devoted himself to replicating the wisdom and justice of his biblical namesake. He codified the enormously complex administrative regulations of his vast empire and strove to harmonize these with the sometimes conflicting doctrines of the Shari'a. (Also like Israel's great king, Süleyman was much attracted to women, but that is another story.)

Finally, Süleyman had his imperial engineer Sinan, an architect worthy of the age of Bramante and Michelangelo and the Taj Mahal, erect a vast religious complex on one of the great hills overlooking the Golden Horn. The Süleymaniye includes a majestic mosque of extremely harmonious proportions, tombs for the sultan and his favorite wife, two colleges of law, a hospital, and a hospice for feeding and sheltering the poor. In this one complex all the central religious demands of Islam were addressed: worship and the confession of God's unity, the study of God's commandments, and charity for the needy. King Solomon had been a powerful symbolic presence in Constantinople from early times. When the Roman emperor Justinian, who had ruled in Constantinople precisely a millennium earlier (from 527 to 565) and who reminds one of Süleyman in many ways, completed the great Church of the Holy Wisdom (Hagia Sophia), he is said to have exclaimed, "This day, O Solomon, have I surpassed thee!" No doubt the great Ottoman sultan also had in mind the Temple of Jerusalem, and he could have repeated Justinian's exclamation with even greater pride.[6]

In short, among the best rulers of medieval Islam (and many lesser ones) justice was taken seriously, and they did what they could to imbed it within the political institutions that they bequeathed to their successors. The whole reason for being of these states was after all to defend and support Islam. Ensuring to their subjects the rights and immunities that the Shari'a bestowed on them was a vital element of this great task. For all sorts of reasons, such efforts were

Islam and Human Rights

bound to fall short of the mark, but we should not assume that the subjects of Muslim autocrats were worse off than their Christian counterparts in Western Europe, who lived under various combinations of Common Law, feudal custom, Roman law, and so on. Indeed, European observers of the Middle East as late as the seventeenth century tell us just the opposite.

In the nineteenth century, the old synthesis of autocracy and Shariʿa fell apart. The causes of this cataclysmic transformation (for so it was) are many and complex, but they can be boiled down to one great thing: European imperialism. The enormous advantage in economic dynamism and military power possessed by the great powers of Europe which became manifest by the 1830s made it impossible for the Muslim rulers of the Middle East and North Africa to carry on as before. The European states could no longer be ignored or treated as occasional foes and allies, as in generations past; they now dominated the economies of the Mediterranean Basin, and they dictated the rules of diplomacy and war. Any Middle Eastern regime that wanted to survive, let alone prosper, had to play Europe's game.

It was of course a contest of amateurs against professionals, and in the short term at least the outcome was foreordained. But the Middle Eastern states did not fall under European domination for lack of trying. The nineteenth and early twentieth centuries were marked by extensive administrative reforms and the adoption of codes and courts based on European models. In the legal and judicial arenas, "reforms" were often made reluctantly and under great foreign pressure, but they were made nonetheless. Since the regimes that adopted these reforms remained profoundly autocratic, the new institutions tended to enhance the regime's power over society. Where they did not do so, they often sowed corruption and demoralization. European-style bureaucracies and armies were extremely expensive to set up and maintain, and no Middle Eastern state had the fiscal resources to meet the challenge. Bureaucrats and judges had to be on the take just to make ends meet. Moreover, very few people in or out of government actually understood the new institutions or how to make them work effectively.

As part of the reform movement, the Shariʿa was bit by bit banished from the public realm and reduced to the crucial but narrow realm of family law. This was due in some degree also to changing values among the intellectual elite, who had lost confidence in the political-administrative tradition of their Islamic past and greatly admired (even while fearing) what French and British law and legal institutions seemed to offer. By World War I, almost all business in the Middle East was conducted according to some adaptation of the Code Napoléon and adjudicated before courts staffed by a mixed panel of European and local jurists. Much the same was true of criminal law. In this manner, the traditional protections and rights enshrined in the Shariʿa disappeared, to be replaced by unfamiliar laws and procedures, manipulated by a vastly more powerful state apparatus for its own benefit. In such a situation, the supposedly broader and more equal rights embodied in Roman law easily became a matter of pure theory for most litigants and defendants. This was true both in areas under direct colonial control (like French Algeria) and in those subject to a looser but still suffocating oversight (e.g., Egypt between the two world wars). The courts were no doubt more honest and efficient in areas of direct control, but law, procedure, and the cultural biases of the judges were heavily skewed in favor of Europeans and the Western-educated upper class. In the semi-independent countries, the judges were appointed by indigenous governments, but that did little to make them intelligible and accessible to the bulk of the population.

It must be said that during the high tide of European imperial domination (roughly three-quarters of a century, from 1870 to 1945) few Middle Eastern intellectuals were terribly worried about human rights as defined at the beginning of this chapter. (There were a few exceptions, however, most notably Ahmad Lutfi al-Sayyid of Egypt, whose active career as a journalist, political writer—rather in the Olympian manner of Walter Lippman—politician, and academic leader spanned the era from 1910 to 1940.)[7] For the great majority of them, the struggle for national independence enjoyed unquestioned priority. Once the imperialists are gone, they argued, once we are again in control of our political destiny, once we have regained control of our economic resources, then there will be time for democracy and human rights. These will indeed come about almost of their own accord. As earlier chapters have already shown, things did not turn out quite that way.

What needs to be stressed here is that the Middle East's sorry

Islam not responsible

record of police state tactics and tyrannical courts since 1945 cannot be attributed to Islam. The states most guilty of these things were often those most committed to *reducing* the role of Islamic tradition in official ideology, in public life, and even in society generally: Nasser's Egypt, Baathist Syria and Iraq, revolutionary Algeria, Tunisia in Bourguiba's later years, Iran under the Pahlavi shahs, Turkey during its periods of military rule (especially in the early 1980s). Indeed, the miserable human rights record of these states is one of the gravest and most effective charges brought against them by contemporary Islamic movements.

In response, it might well be argued that several (though not all) of these states worked to enhance the rights and status of women both within the family and in society generally. In this regard one could cite Iran's Family Protection Act of 1967, Sadat's presidential decree of 1979, and the Tunisian code of personal status of 1958. All these restricted male power by raising the minimum marriage age for girls, making polygamy much more difficult, requiring divorce proceedings to be heard and registered before a judge, and giving women broader grounds for seeking a divorce. Since women are a significantly disadvantaged class in traditional Islamic law, these points are obviously far from trivial. But in view of the enormous inertia of established cultural values and behavioral patterns, the human weaknesses of an almost all-male judiciary, and the inability of villagers and small-town folk to get to urban courts, such reforms could have only a limited impact. The new marriage laws were (and where still in force continue to be) of value mostly for educated middle-class women in the larger cities. In any case, they do little to protect the citizen against the state, which is the fundamental aim of human rights. And of course these efforts to enhance the legal status of women have proved extremely vulnerable to the region's political hurricanes, since they are precisely those that draw thunderbolts from Islamic activists concerned about the dissolution of the patriarchal family and the satanic influence of female liberation.

As things stand at the end of the twentieth century, the role that Islam has played and may play in the future in supporting and shielding human rights is far from clear. We have seen that traditional Islamic thought did address certain human rights issues, albeit in its own distinctive manner. But the capacity of Islam (or properly, of the Shari'a) to be effective in this role was attenuated by the nature of premodern autocratic government. In the nineteenth and early twentieth centuries, even this level of effectiveness was badly eroded by changes in the nature of the Middle Eastern state and by externally imposed administrative and legal reforms. The Middle Eastern states of the middle and late twentieth century—not all of them but many, including the largest and most important—have progressively abandoned or restricted Islamic legal principles and institutions for things that seemed more modern, dynamic, and progressive. Since the most important challenge to these secularist regimes now comes from the Islamic activists, we need to ask how these latter interpret human rights and how they would apply their interpretation once in power. Is there a distinctively *modern* Islamic doctrine of human rights that builds on traditional thought but is not bound by its premises and conclusions? If so, what legal and institutional form would such a doctrine take?

To some degree, the answers to these questions belong to the realm of prophecy rather than scholarly analysis. But not entirely, for there are now five self-described Islamic regimes in the Middle East (or six, if we include Pakistan): Morocco, the Sudan, Saudi Arabia, the Islamic Republic of Iran, and Afghanistan. These regimes differ greatly among themselves, and each has its own characteristic interpretation of Islam. Altogether, however, these states give us little grounds for confidence in an Islamist interpretation of human rights.

Of the five states, two are long-established and claim to be founded on traditional interpretations of Islam, although their respective interpretations are quite disparate: Morocco and Saudi Arabia. The modern Moroccan monarchy emerged in the early sixteenth century, and the current ruling dynasty, which claims lineal descent from the Prophet, rose to power in the 1660s. As a descendant of the Prophet, King Hasan II (1962–present) claims to be not only head of state but also the supreme and authoritative interpreter of Islam for his subjects.

Saudi Arabia is somewhat younger; its roots go back to a religio-political revivalist movement that emerged in the Arabian Peninsula's eastern steppe in the 1750s. After a period of eclipse in the late nineteenth century, the modern Saudi state took form under the aegis of the amir Abd al-Aziz, who seized control of the old Saudi heartland in eastern Arabia in the early 1900s and by 1924 was lord of most of Arabia. The Saudi monarchs have all been well educated in the Islamic sciences, but they do not claim religious leadership per se; rather, their job is to provide a political and administrative framework in which the Shariʿa, according to the severely conservative interpretation espoused by the Wahhabis, can be applied by authorized scholars. In the area of civil law, Saudi justice seems to be effective, and for criminal offenses, although the Saudis have a reputation for extreme swiftness and severity, they do not depart from the country's long-established social norms. The political arena is a different matter. As individuals, Saudi citizens have ready access to the monarch and the provincial governors and can apparently speak quite frankly to them about issues directly affecting themselves. But public criticism of the regime and its policies, even in the context of Islam (the traditional duty of "commanding the good"), is sharply discouraged, nor is there any institutional framework for broad public participation in government. Saudi Arabia is, quite literally, a family affair.

The rigid segregation of the sexes, and the extremely limited independence allowed women outside the home, is well known (not to say notorious) but seldom well understood. As we have already noted, this fact does have substantial human rights implications. While Saudi law may be rigid, it is not fossilized: women have been granted, or have discreetly seized, entree to important sectors in the economy, professions, and education. Although Saudi law forbids women to drive, and they are subject to all the controls of the traditional Islamic patriarchal household, about one-third of the students in the national universities are female, and women are well represented in such professions as medicine, nursing, and teaching. Moreover, women control a great deal of wealth in their own names, and a network of women's banks and investment firms has grown up to serve this considerable sector. Saudi institutions fit the framework of traditional Islamic thinking fairly well, though of course even the most moderate and pragmatic feminist will find them desperately wanting.

The other three regimes are the recent products of revolutionary action. It is perhaps unfair to judge Afghanistan, torn to pieces by civil war among the various factions who collectively expelled the Soviet occupation of their country, and now dominated by the Taliban—a militant movement recruited from among Afghan villagers driven from their homes by the struggle against the Soviets and jammed together in impoverished refugee camps in Pakistan, whose version of Islam seems extremist even to Saudi and Iranian commentators. The Sudan is also gripped by civil war, though here the military struggle is not between Muslim factions but between the predominantly Muslim north and the Christian and African-traditionalist regions of the south; for the civil war the policies of the Khartoum regime are largely though not entirely to blame. Even among Muslims, the Sudanese regime has a reputation for repressiveness and arbitrary rule. Whether this is connected with the inevitable characteristics of an embattled military regime or with the Islamic teachings of Hasan al-Turabi and his allies is open to debate.

The only firmly established revolutionary regime is that of Iran, and hence the Islamic Republic provides our only good model for asking how human rights are treated in a modern "Islamic state." Human rights receive much attention in the 1979 Constitution, both in the long, rhetorical preamble and in several Principles of the text proper (3, 8, 12–14, and most critically in chapter 3, "National Rights," Principles 19–42). The rights stated there are admittedly conditional in most cases; that is, they are to be interpreted in accordance with the principles of Islam, or are subject to regulation by law. Obviously such conditions or reservations can easily be abused. However, most Western governments possess (and use) the authority to regulate and limit the rights they grant their citizens, as one can quickly confirm by a glance at British, French, or German law. Moreover, the topics addressed in the Iranian Constitution—broad latitude in the practice of one's religion, freedom of assembly, freedom of speech and the press, equality before the law for all citizens and ethnic groups, due process of law in criminal and civil matters—are precisely those that preoccupy the human rights movement.

Ideals and realities are not the same thing, of course, and Iran's human rights record was, as one would expect, utterly miserable in the earliest years, between the Ayatollah Khomeini's return in February 1979 and the definitive seizure of power by the clergy in 1982. Since that time, as the revolution wound down and the new regime became firmly established in power, things have become more predictable, in spite of the long war with Iraq that ended in 1988. There are still occasional abuses and outrages—dragging unveiled women out of closed cars and beating them for "un-Islamic dress," or physically assaulting revered religious leaders who call for a restriction of the powers of the Faqih, for example—but in general the regime seems able to control its agents and "supporters" reasonably well. ("Failures" to control excess enthusiasm seem to reflect maneuverings between hostile factions within the government rather than governmental weakness or collusion per se.) As noted in previous chapters, there is an active parliamentary and political life, albeit within narrow bounds, as well as broad participation in the political process. The Islamic Republic is still in the process of inventing itself, of deciding what Islam is and what it means in the contemporary world, so perhaps here too we should defer final judgment on how it defines and strives to realize human rights.

Since existing regimes give us only limited insight into the meaning or role of human rights in modern Islam, we might well do better to look at the Islamic movements that are currently struggling, peaceably or violently, to control the future of the Middle East. One of the most effective charges they level against the status quo is the persistent abuse of human rights by these regimes—arbitrary arrest, lengthy detention without charges, torture, rigged trials, and so on. They also complain, with considerable justice, about the systematic suppression of democracy in the region. All this, they promise, will be rectified by true Islamic government. Islam, after all, is synonymous with the God-given dignity and autonomy of every person.

Since the Islamic movements are engaged in a long, bitter struggle to dislodge well-entrenched regimes, we should probably make some allowances for the inevitable moral ambiguities and shortcomings entailed by such a struggle. Most Americans, after all, supported the struggle against Nazi Germany wholeheartedly and felt (as they still do) that this evil had to be eradicated at whatever cost. However, anyone who has studied the war with any care knows how many ethically dubious decisions were made in pursuing it, from the internment of Japanese residents in the United States and Canada to the bombing of Dresden in March 1945. Even so, the tactics that a movement adopts in the struggle for power tell us something about its view of its opponents and how it may behave if it succeeds. In any struggle the means ought to be roughly commensurate with the ends.

By that criterion, the Islamic movements raise real qualms. The terror deliberately aimed against women, foreigners, and villagers in contemporary Algeria and (more sporadically) in Egypt reveals a frame of mind that is surely inimical to human rights by any meaningful definition. More disturbing are the assassinations of secularist spokesmen not affiliated with and often quite critical of existing regimes, such as Farag Foda in Egypt. Along the same lines we have the reprisals and death threats levied, sometimes with the support and collusion of self-styled Islamic governments, against "apostate" Muslims like Taslima Nasrin in Bangladesh, Suleiman Bashear in the West Bank, and most notoriously Salman Rushdie (a citizen of Great Britain) in Iran. Finally, there are disturbing incidents like the persecution of Tujan al-Faisal in Jordan and Nasr Hamid Abu Zayd in Egypt. The former was a television talk-show hostess and candidate for parliament, the latter an assistant professor of linguistics at Cairo University. In each case, and for quite different reasons, Islamic activists tried to get the courts to compel their spouses to divorce them, on the grounds that they had apostasized from Islam. In Jordan the courts ultimately rejected the suit, though only after much coming and going, and Tujan al-Faisal won her parliamentary seat. In Egypt, the initial trial court found for Professor Abu Zayd, but to the astonishment of most observers, that decision was reversed by the superior courts. Abu Zayd and his wife currently live in exile in Europe.[8]

In traditional Islamic doctrine, apostasy is a capital offense—one of the places where religious tolerance drew the line—but such cases still give one pause, since most of the targets of activist wrath (including Tujan al-Faisal and Abu Zayd) do not consider themselves apostates in any sense, but advocates of perfectly acceptable interpretations of Islam. Abu Zayd indeed grounds his arguments in the statements of highly regarded medieval authors. Islam, both would argue—and much of Islam's history would support them—is a "big tent" faith, with room for wide divergences in doctrine and practice. In other cases—the Islamic Republic of Iran and the brief phase of Islamist domination in Jordan in 1990–1993—women have been pressured out of public life, on the grounds that it is not appropriate for women to hold authority over men and the rightful place of women is in the home.

All in all, we perceive among many contemporary Islamic activists a fierceness and rigidity, an unwillingness to make any concessions to changing social mores and values, or even to ask if these changes might somehow be harmonized with traditional Islamic imperatives. Historically, Islam was highly adaptable to its social and cultural environment, even as Muslim thinkers worked to transform certain elements of that environment, but contemporary activists reject adaptation, at least in principle. Islam is for them eternal, unchanging, and absolute truth. Circumstances must be wrestled into compliance with this truth, not the other way around.

The activists' version of Islam is not the only one, although they have certainly been successful in seizing control of the podium and setting the public agenda for discussions of what Islam is or is not. There is also a strong modernist strain in twentieth-century Islam, and until twenty years ago or so the modernists were quite able to get a hearing for their perspectives. Indeed, they were regarded by most outside observers as the true representatives of Islam's future.

Modernists can be briefly defined as those Muslims who accept the Qur'an as authentic revelation and the authority of Muhammad's teaching and example but who strive to interpret and apply these sources within the framework of contemporary social structures, political institutions, and scientific knowledge. This strain of thought has a pedigree as old as fundamentalism, and perhaps older, for its key themes were enunciated as early as the 1860s and 1870s in the writings of the Ottoman bureaucrat and intellectual Namik Kemal (1840–1888) and the Indian Sir Sayyid Ahmad Khan (1817–1898). I have already mentioned the legacy of Muhammad Abduh (1849–1905), though it has sprouted two branches, one leading to modernism and the other to fundamentalist activism.

Even at their high tide, to be sure, the modernists had only limited success in getting their interpretations accepted among a broader public, but they had some important regime support (especially in Nasser's Egypt, Bourguiba's Tunisia, and Ayyub Khan's Pakistan). Most of all, they were confident that Islam possessed the intellectual resources to confront the modern world on its own terms and to shape that world in a dynamic, healthy direction. In the current

on the ebb of modernism

climate, however, they have been marginalized; their voices are diffident, their arguments defensive. Only in Indonesia (a very large exception, admittedly) do modernist writers still set the terms of debate, or at least participate on an equal footing. But even in Pakistan and the Middle East they are still present, and at some point that we do not now foresee the tide may well turn in their favor again. What then do the modernists have to say about Islam and human rights?

To begin with, they conduct their side of the debate outside, or at best on the margins of, traditional Shari'a discourse. Most Muslim modernists—like the great majority of fundamentalists, in fact—have been laypersons. They are highly educated men and women, but they are not formally accredited as interpreters of the Shari'a, because they have not completed the formal course of studies in an Islamic religious college which would qualify them to make authoritative pronouncements about the content and meaning of the Shari'a. One might well argue—and most modernists do—that this fact enables them to look at things with a fresh eye, to avoid getting mired down in the technical minutiae of traditional jurisprudence. But it also deprives them of a critical element of credibility in the struggle to influence public opinion, for how can the ordinary Muslim be sure that the new thought that modernists call for is truly rooted in the authentic teaching of the Qur'an and the Prophet? Here the fundamentalists have an advantage, because they invoke powerful symbols and cherished values—half-forgotten and often misinterpreted but still deeply embedded in Islamic culture and everyday patterns of life.

No one person can claim to speak for everyone in the modernist group, since their backgrounds and ideas diverge greatly. However, in recent decades one man was highly esteemed by all who knew him, and his personal integrity and intellectual sophistication establish a clear yardstick against which all modernist discourse can be measured. This was Fazlur Rahman, born in British India, educated at Oxford under the direction of the great orientalist H. A. R. Gibb after World War II, director of the Institute of Higher Islamic Studies in Pakistan during the late 1950s and early 1960s, and finally professor of Islamic Thought at the University of Chicago from 1968 to his death in 1986.[9] His Chicago years represented a compulsory exile from Pakistan, but they were also a period of productive and highly original thought. Although he was a native speaker of one major Islamic language (Urdu) and had a thorough command of Persian and Arabic, he wrote largely in English, and inevitably he found his audience largely among Muslim intellectuals who lived or had studied in Britain and the United States. Rahman was a deeply learned scholar, one of the world's leading students of the Avicennian tradition in Islamic philosophy. But in the realm of Shariʿa jurisprudence he was a layman, and that fact made his statements highly vulnerable to the attacks of self-appointed defenders of Islamic tradition. He also took Western scholarship on Islam seriously, though he often contested or rejected its conclusions, and for some critics this fact tarred him with the vice of "Westernism." Even so, his contributions to the rethinking of the Shariʿa's underlying premises and principles were penetrating and sophisticated. If and when a true modernist synthesis is achieved, his thought will be an important element in it.

During the 1950s and 1960s, Fazlur Rahman tended to focus on theological and historical questions, but during the 1970s he turned increasingly to issues of law and society. As his thought developed during these years, he focused on four major topics, which he regarded as the crucial elements in the renewal of Islam. Although the contemporary human rights movement was still in its infancy in this period, it will become clear as we proceed that Rahman's thought had direct implications for the subject.

In the realm of law, he stressed the concept of ijtihad, or independent judgment. In effect, *ijtihad* means to depart from existing and generally accepted rules of law, and instead to search for original solutions. Sometimes such innovative solutions are required because one is facing a new problem, one that none of the existing rules really covers. There is nothing very controversial about this in principle, although there are fierce disputes about the particular solutions put on the table through ijtihad. In contrast, proposing new solutions to old problems is far more controversial, simply because one is disrupting settled doctrine. A simple example may help make this clear. The traditional procedures used to draw up marriage contracts will not work for Muslims living in France, Great Britain, or the United States, because they are not valid within the civil codes of those countries. Hence new procedures are necessary, and these can only be framed through a process of ijtihad. However, if a scholar argues (as Rahman did) that the Qur'an virtually prohibits polygamy, and as a result the ancient doctrine permitting a man as many as four wives is simply wrong, he is proposing a new solution to an issue regarded as settled (indeed, set in concrete) for fourteen centuries. Such a use of ijtihad is bound to cause a firestorm.

By ijtihad, Rahman did not mean, as did many reformists and modernists, simply a limited revision of specific points in Shariʿa that now seemed outdated or embarrassing. On the contrary, he meant a wholesale rethinking and reconstruction of the Shariʿa from the ground up, based on a critical evaluation of the Qur'an's underlying themes as well as its specific commandments, the life of the Prophet, and the experience of the early Muslim community. He wanted a permanent, unceasing effort to shape law to the actual conditions of society, always of course in conformity with specifically Islamic criteria. The implications of this approach for a doctrine of human rights are obviously significant. At the very least, a commitment to systematic ijtihad would imply that Muslims have broad rights to debate the basic institutions of their society.

Closely linked to Rahman's concept of ijtihad, and no doubt also to his experience of the Anglo-Muhammadan courts of British India and independent Pakistan, was his concern for a reformed court system. Anglo-Muhammadan law suggested how this might be done, since it was a somewhat idiosyncratic but quite functional amalgam of Shariʿa-based statutes with English common-law reasoning and procedure. Apart from wigs and black robes for the judges, the most important common-law contributions to Anglo-Muhammadan law may well have been the concepts of precedent and judicial independence.

Precedent turns traditional Shariʿa practice inside out. In traditional practice, a judge's decision in court was binding on the litigants before him, but it did not bind any other court; it did not even bind him when he dealt with future cases. In contrast, in Anglo-American law, a judge's decision does establish (potentially) binding precedent. Precedent removes the power to develop, test, and alter law from the legal scholars—who had always held this power in Muslim countries before modern times—and turns it over to judges. It can thus be an instrument for assuring that the Shariʿa stays in close touch with changing social realities, with things as they are rather than things as they ought to be. But if judges are mere hand-maidens of the regimes that appoint them, then precedent can be an instrument of governmental tyranny.

For that reason, judicial independence is even more important as an instrument of reform than precedent, since it means that judges are no longer mere agents of the powers that be but authorities in their own right, bound only by their understanding of and commitment to the law. (In contemporary Pakistan, for example, it is illegal to criticize the judiciary, and this law is taken quite seriously.) The importance of judicial independence for human rights is obvious enough. From the standpoint of Islamic modernism, the point of a reformed judicial system is to expand the arena in which Muslims may freely and securely test the relationship of their society with the basic demands of Islam.

In common with almost all modernists and many fundamentalists, Fazlur Rahman was a strong advocate of popular sovereignty and constitutional government. (There is of course some irony in his having held the directorship of the Higher Institute for Islamic Studies under the first of Pakistan's military strongmen, Ayyub Khan, but I doubt that this should be regarded as anything more than the sort of hopeful accommodation with reality that most of us make in our lives.) This position, however self-evident it may seem to most Americans and Europeans, does seem to conflict with the Qur'anic dictum that sovereignty belongs to God alone. Moreover, that dictum had been and could continue to be a useful bulwark against governments that claimed totalitarian control over the lives of their subjects. But Rahman's response was simple: since God's sovereignty could only be implemented through human institutions and human agency, there was no reason in principle to prefer autocratic to democratic government. Moreover, a political-legal system based on continuous ijtihad required the whole community of Muslims to participate in the development of legislation and administration. Popularly elected legislatures might well be guilty of excesses and mistakes, but these could be adequately controlled through the courts and appropriate advisory councils of experts in Islamic law.

All these institutions—ijtihad, a reformed court system, and constitutional government—were essential to guarantee freedom of thought within Islam. Rahman was enough of a traditional Muslim to believe that the purpose of freedom of thought was to discover the truth, not to indulge one's ego, and he was always a bit uneasy with the First Amendment's blanket permission to say almost anything at all, no matter how hurtful or offensive. But as a victim of those who had demanded a rigid adherence to traditional dogma, he believed that a modern Islamic society needed to grant a very wide latitude to the search for truth in the realms of science, theology, law, and politics. As to such things as atheism or outright apostasy, I do not think he ever came to a clear conclusion.

To this point, we have been looking at Rahman's thought in the context of a homogenous society—that is, one made up entirely of adult male Muslims. But of course any society is by definition half female, and as a practical matter most Muslim countries have substantial non-Muslim majorities. Both of these classes were significantly disadvantaged under traditional interpretations of Islam. What was to be done about them? As regards non-Muslims, his position was quite straightforward: they should enjoy civil and political equality with Muslims, including the right to serve in the legislature and government. The one limitation might be that the head of state in a predominantly Muslim country should be a Muslim, but that was in any case almost a foregone conclusion. Women presented a more complex problem. Rahman believed that traditional jurists had often distorted or misunderstood the true teaching of the Qur'an, which (in his judgment) strongly encouraged monogamy and sought to restrict a husband's license to divorce his wife. Even the famous (or infamous) verse that seemed to demand male authority over women had been misconstrued: "Men have authority over the affairs of women in that God has preferred one to the other, and in that men expend their goods to maintain them" (Qur'an 4:34). The final clause, normally passed over, was in his view crucial: men had been given this authority only because in the society of Qur'anic times they were the sole source of financial support for the women in their household. In modern times, when women could earn a living on their own, the reason for this authority fell away—a very bold stroke of ijtihad! He used the same sort of reasoning in arguing that a woman's legal testimony in modern society should be equal to a man's—after all, women were now out and about in the world and had the same opportunity as men to know what was going on.[10] All of this led him to argue for a strong enhancement of women's place in the family (though the notion of complete parity between the sexes seemed unattainable and even meaningless) and their equality in the courts. As to political rights, he saw no reason why women should not vote or serve in parliaments.

In the final analysis, Fazlur Rahman's Islamic modernism yields a human rights agenda not greatly different from that found in the UN Universal Declaration, though there are a few ambiguities around the edges (as of course there are in U.S. constitutional law). No doubt that is by design. This fact leaves Rahman and other modernists open to the charge that they are really Westernizing secularists, and that their Islam is just a thin veneer applied to Western ideas to make them a bit more palatable to skeptical Muslims.

The modernists would respond that in the Prophet's time Islam addressed and challenged the world as it was, and Islam in the modern world must do the same or ultimately become an irrelevant fossil. Just as Muslims accept modern technologies without hesitation, so they must be open to the new values and aspirations that have taken root so widely in the world. Not every new idea is good, but each must be examined to see whether and how it fits with the primary purposes of God's revelation to Muhammad. Where these ideas can be linked to Islamic tradition and infused with Islamic meaning, their nature changes; they no longer represent mere human whim and desire. Rather, they become part of a vast ethical framework, grounded in divine revelation and guidance, that ensures prosperity in this world and leads to salvation in the next.

A final assessment of the relationship between Islam and human rights is very difficult to come to. Muslim thinkers, however great the differences among them, have always understood the distinction between the Community of Believers (or as they often say, "the Muslims") and the state. They have likewise seen the need to build some barriers between subjects and the power of the regime. In premodern times, they did this by insisting on the right of Muslims to live their lives in accordance with the Shariʿa. The Shariʿa, as we have seen, does accord some immunities and rights of due process to those who are subject to it, and thus ensures certain elements of human rights. However, a Shariʿa-based concept of human rights is very different from the concepts embodied in the U.S. Constitution and the Universal Declaration. Moreover, in traditional Islamic thought the barrier between the subject and the state was in some sense a theoretical one; insofar as a government could gain control of the mosques and the courts, it could use the Shariᶜa to impose its will on its subjects.

Contemporary Muslim activists, especially the more militant among them, have taken a rather paradoxical view of human rights. They vigorously oppose existing regimes on the grounds that they are not merely un-Islamic but tyrannical—that is, that they routinely violate the human rights of their people. Given the way things are, this is a highly credible line of attack. When Islamist movements do take power, however, their own human rights records are spotty at best. One sometimes suspects that the chief right that they advocate is the right to accept and live by their version of truth. They certainly believe that this version embodies a broad concept of human rights; not everyone will agree with them.

Finally, there is the modernist interpretation of Islam. For the most part, modernist concepts of human rights are quite close to those familiar in the West. There is, as we have seen, some ambivalence on certain points, but probably no more than many Westerners feel about these issues. The problem for modernists is that their agendas are really not part of the debate in much of the Muslim world. They talk, sometimes at considerable personal risk, but few people seem to be listening. The reasons for this are complex, but only a couple of points need to be made here. First, the Islamic-modernist discourse on human rights is very similar on the surface to secularist arguments. The result is that people who have strongly identified themselves with the "Islamic tendency" are put off by modernist statements, which seem foreign and Westernizing. But those who remain committed to secularist ideologies find the Islamic coloring of modernist thought only a distraction from the real issues. At best it provides a useful disguise when one is debating the Islamic movement; at worst it risks lending credibility to that movement. In response to rejection from both sides, the modernists can only say that Islam is, and inevitably will remain, an integral element of the human rights debate in Muslim countries. No human rights agenda can possibly be established among a Muslim people unless it is infused with Islamic values and framed in language that is meaningful and persuasive to them. If that argument is correct, Islamic modernists may well be able to reclaim a central place in the human rights debate. As to when that might come about, we must take refuge in the classic Muslim adage: God knows best.

TOWARD A CONCLUSION—
BETWEEN MEMORY AND DESIRE

It is tempting to dismiss Middle Eastern politics as a fascinating but incoherent tale of treachery, violence, and fanaticism, and to this temptation many commentators succumb. I myself can hardly claim to be superior to it, for these things are undeniably present in events that we witness almost every day. Even so, they are not the most important part of the story, often not even a major part of it. The genuinely crucial issues in the Middle East are sometimes difficult to make out through the cacophony, but I have tried to identify and examine a few of these in the preceding pages. First, there is the region's persistent economic stagnation and the intense social frustration that stems from it. Second, there is the struggle by the states of the region to assert some control over their own destiny within a vast and often hostile international political and economic system. One aspect of this struggle, and a particularly troubling one, is the need to resolve the ethnic and territorial conflicts created and left to fester by the World War I settlement eighty years ago. Third, we are witnessing an unending and as yet fruitless search for systems of government that can command the loyalty and support of the region's people. Fourth, both consequence and cause of everything else, there is the furious debate over the cultural and moral values that ought to drive political action and social policy.

Each of these problems has its own history, and to a considerable degree each can be analyzed separately. But it is perfectly clear that each is thoroughly implicated in all the others and that no one of them can be solved in isolation. For example, economic stagnation threatens the governments that try (and perpetually fail) to solve the economic crisis, even as the region's notorious inability to develop democratic and effective governments deprives it of the political tools essential for resolving the economic crisis. Likewise, the conflict over which ideas and values (liberal, Marxist, or Islamic, as the case may be) ought to be the foundation for political institutions means that any government in the region is open to attack from some group that believes that it is inherently wrong—that at bottom it has no right to exist. At the same time, these ideological conflicts are intensified and embittered by the repressive character of many governments, which permit little public debate or dissent even on practical policy issues.

These four basic issues—economic stagnation, weakness in the international arena, political instability, and ideological confusion—have endured throughout most of the twentieth century and show no signs of going away anytime soon. It is natural to wonder by now whether they can be solved at all, and if so, how. There is nothing in the preceding chapters to answer this question one way or the other, I am afraid. But a concise review of each issue will show us how things stand at the present hour, and in that process we may find some useful perspectives from which we can peer into a very murky future.

The book opened with the problem of economic stagnation and frustration, and that theme has recurred throughout in various guises. Is there any way to break a cycle that has characterized the Middle East throughout this century—momentary if uneven expansion, typically driven by favorable commodities markets (cotton, oil, etc.), followed almost inevitably by a collapse back to the previous level or even worse? On a solution to this problem almost everything else depends. In the real world, poor countries are weak countries, regarded with condescension by their neighbors and contempt by their own people. Likewise, governments that fail to provide a modicum of prosperity and economic security forfeit the loyalty of their citizens. Unable to rule through respect, they are constrained to rule through fear. Finally, perpetual stagnation and poverty simply reinforce the sense among a people that "nothing works"; in such an environment one can only expect ideological uncertainty—and in moments of crisis or sudden disruption, terrible outbursts of extremism. An effective economic policy is certainly not a sufficient condition for the resolution of every political impasse, but in the long run it is a necessary one.

The currency and banking crisis in East Asia that broke out in the summer of 1997 has demonstrated that even the most brilliantly successful strategy can come unglued in an instant. Indeed, the more brilliant the policy, the more skeptical we ought to be. In this light, both criticism and advice should only be offered with much humility. Even so, it does seem true that since World War II, centrally planned economies such as the Soviet Union or Maoist China have had only limited success. On the contrary, market-based and export-driven economies, based on the production of high-value-added goods, have seemed the surest path to rapid growth and prosperity. Japan, at least in the period 1955–1990, has surely been the model to emulate.

But quite apart from the current East Asian imbroglio, which is rooted in reckless speculation and corruption as much as in faulty policies, it is not clear that this model will be as effective in the future as it has been during the last half century. Some commentators have argued that the world faces a looming crisis of overproduction—that is, that there will be far more autos, televisions, and CD players than people with the means to buy them. If that is so (such prophets of gloom have been wrong more than once) it may be too late for the Middle East to imitate Japan and Singapore, even if they can figure out just how to do it.

Moreover, export-driven policies pose severe political problems for the regimes that adopt them. To finance the earlier stages of such policies, it is necessary to build savings as rapidly as possible and hence to keep wages low and consumption down. Occasionally this can be done through a people's self-imposed discipline, as was the case in West Germany and Japan. (The fact that both were staring into the abyss after the destruction of World War II may help account for the willingness of their citizens to accept short-term sacrifices.) But most often, as in Taiwan, South Korea, Indonesia, and China, such an approach involves considerable political repression for many years. It is undeniably true that Middle Eastern regimes have seldom hesitated to use very severe repression to fend off political opponents, but they do seem reluctant to use it simply to enforce an economic policy. They almost always back down quickly in the face of urban unrest when austerity measures are imposed and subsidies for staples like bread, sugar, and oil are cut. This tentativeness is due in part to the populism of these governments—one of the ways, we have seen, that they purchase a bit of legitimacy for themselves—and in part to their historical preference for state-controlled rather than market-oriented solutions, though that preference has eroded quite a bit over the last two decades.

In any case, it is a hard thing to tell Middle Easterners, who have endured so much political violence and economic deprivation, that they must be ready to endure yet more—and this in the name of policies that are far from a sure thing, that may well fail as abysmally as all the others that have been tried over the last century. Yet it is clear that any serious economic policy will require sacrifices from the population at large, and will put severe strains on any political system, whether authoritarian or democratic. The question is simply what kind of sacrifices will be imposed, and on whom, and how the resulting stresses will be restrained and channeled.

The international arena presents a scenario no less frustrating. Down through the seventeenth century, Muslim states in most of the world could at least hold their own against the rising ambitions of Europe, and sometimes (as with the Ottoman Empire) they could do better than hold their own. Since the early eighteenth century, however, the states of the Middle East and the Muslim world generally have been weak actors in the international arena. The Mughal Empire of India disintegrated and soon became a wholly owned subsidiary of the British East India Company. The Safavid Empire of Iran succumbed to civil war and invasion, emerging around 1800 not as a coherent state but as a vast tribal confederation with an autocratic superstructure. Only the Ottoman Empire managed to combine modest military resources, sporadically effective administrative reforms, and considerable diplomatic skill so as to preserve its independence (admittedly within steadily shrinking boundaries) and to enter World War I as a significant power. The era of direct colonial rule was, within the broad scheme of world history, very brief—roughly the seventy-five years between 1880 and 1955—but it left behind a congeries of new states that were for the most part weak and desperately poor. In the postcolonial period, the cold war gave some scope to bold and inventive leaders, most especially Nasser of Egypt, to find some room for maneuver. Moreover, Iran and Turkey benefited in many ways from their strategic position and close alliance with the United States, though nationalists in both countries found the price of such benefits excessive.

The decade of the 1970s opened new possibilities for the oil-rich states, due to the rapid run-up in prices after 1973. All raked in vast revenues, and many plunged into extremely ambitious development schemes. Even states like Egypt or Syria, which had very little oil of their own, benefited enormously from the flood of new money pouring into the region. Not everyone benefited, admittedly. Lebanon was shattered by civil war after 1975, and has hardly been patched back together even now. The Palestinian movement was quite generously funded, but for many reasons it could not convert money into an effective political and military strategy. Turkey's foreign reserves were sucked dry by foreign oil purchases, and it spun inexorably into financial chaos and political turbulence.

A few countries dreamed not only of wealth but also of power on the world stage. For a very few years Iran in particular could imagine itself a regional superpower. The Shah at last had the income to build a massive, well-equipped army—though in the end not the kind of army that was needed to keep him in power. He could also fill the vacuum left by the United States in the wake of the Vietnam debacle. He enjoyed all the advantages of solid American support for his regime combined with a great freedom of action to pursue his own interests. Iraq was a far smaller country in area and population, but under the Baathist regime of Hasan al-Bakr and Saddam Hussein it too exploited its special relationship with a superpower (in this case the Soviet Union) to amass a vast arsenal.

But all these glittering possibilities faded away as the 1980s unfolded. Oil prices collapsed suddenly after 1984, wiping out in a stroke all the economic gains of the previous ten years. Almost simultaneously the Soviet Union, already embroiled in an ugly war in Afghanistan that did much to sap its prestige in the Muslim world, slipped into political instability and then into dissolution. The tensions of the cold war were over, but so were the often-exploited opportunities to play the Soviets off against the Americans. Finally, there was the earthquake of the Islamic Revolution in Iran and the powerful shock waves this sent throughout the region. For a number of years, few governments could indulge themselves in dreams about their place in the international system; they had to focus on survival. In this political and economic turmoil, Iran and Iraq of course suffered most deeply and tragically, though their sufferings were to a great degree self-imposed.

The 1990s opened onto a strange new world, with no one knowing what the rules of the game were anymore, or even what game was being played. First of all, there was suddenly only one superpower in the world, though it was far from clear what adjustments the new situation might require. Within the region, Iran was in a period of uncertain readjustment after the death of the Ayatollah Khomeini in 1989, economically exhausted by eight years of savage warfare, no longer certain of its revolutionary mission, unclear where it should go now. Afghanistan was free of Soviet occupation but rapidly descending into long years of civil war and political chaos. Iraq did something absolutely without precedent when it invaded and occupied a sister Arab state. It then faced an equally unprecedented coalition of Western and Middle Eastern states determined to restore the status quo ante: the United States, Great Britain, and France (all erstwhile embodiments of Western imperialism), together with forces from Saudi Arabia, Egypt, and Syria. Finally, the PLO and Israel inched very painfully toward a modus vivendi in the Oslo Accords of 1993.

As I write, absolutely none of the uncertainties of 1990–1991 have been resolved. Afghanistan is still in turmoil, more or less under the control of the most exotic regime produced by the late twentieth century. Iran is still working out where it wants to go, though it is clear that for large numbers of Iranians the path of revolutionary Islam no longer seems desirable or appropriate. Saddam Hussein remains in power in Iraq and still looks to recoup the losses he suffered in 1991. Israel and the PLO cannot figure out how to take the next step. The United States remains by far the most important external force in the region, but without the sense of crisis provoked by Saddam Hussein's occupation of Kuwait, the American capacity to lead, to define goals and induce people to pursue them vigorously, has declined precipitously. Local forces can put their own agendas in the foreground and see how far they can push them. In short, the place of the Middle East in the international arena is as muddled as it has ever been.

Power at least can be measured on some scale; in this area governments know more or less where they stand. Legitimacy remains a far more elusive political commodity, harder to obtain and much harder to measure. Insofar as legitimacy is the right to make mistakes and still remain in power, regimes only know whether they have it when they are facing a crisis—when, in short, it is too late to do much about the situation if they do not. Insofar as legitimacy is the willingness of politically relevant individuals and groups to give power to someone else to act on their behalf, the makeup of such individuals and groups is constantly changing. The people whose consent was needed in 1950 in order to rule are not at all the same as those whose consent was needed even in 1960, let alone 1990. In many political systems, legitimacy is conferred through formal institutions (elections, parliaments, etc.) and legally defined procedures. But in much of the Middle East, such institutions and procedures are nonexistent or hollow. In such circumstances, regimes tend to gain legitimacy through sheer longevity. This quality exists in surprising abundance throughout the region, though we might want to avert our eyes from the means that many regimes have used to keep themselves in power. It remains a very serious question whether legitimacy of this kind can be transferred intact to the next generation.

In many ways the political systems of the Middle East still remain where they were back in 1975, and with many of the same actors. The hopes for a strengthened civil society awakened by the Gulf War, and for reforms favoring democratic rule, have been realized only in small part. Jordan has held contested and relatively honest parliamentary elections since 1989, but many observers believe that real democratic institutions there have developed only slightly. King Hussein knows how to use a parliament for his own purposes. Mubarak's Egypt, after a bit of loosening in the early nineties, has reverted to a far more authoritarian stance, though the country's very active political life continues to bubble, much as it has since Sadat came to power. Turkey remains as precariously balanced between electoral democracy and military intervention as she has been since 1960. Among countries in the Arabian Peninsula, Yemen seems to have the strongest commitment to democratic processes, but Yemen is too small and too far from the center to be an effective model for other states in the region. In spite of its place in American demonology, the Islamic Republic of Iran is almost surely the brightest beacon of hope for democratic aspirations, though only a madman would predict how things will evolve there over the next decade. In the final analysis, Middle Eastern governments do not trust their people, nor do their people trust them. The suspicions of both parties are well placed.

Finally, ideological confusion reigns supreme throughout the Middle East as in much of the Muslim world. The secularist ideologies that dominated the political stage in the 1960s are still embodied in such institutions as elections and parliaments, and God knows that secular interests and ambitions pervade politics and policy making from top to bottom. But a few countries aside (Syria, Turkey, Tunisia), secularism is no longer coin of the realm in public discourse. Even where secularism still holds sway, it does thanks largely to the overt repression of any alternatives. Nowadays, if some major policy has to be defined in terms of the basic values it serves, one must be ready to claim that it is essentially "Islamic."

Islam in some form dominates political discourse nowadays, but clearly "Islam" is a term with a thousand different meanings among those who invoke it. We have seen, I think, that Islamic religious thought *taken as a whole* provides a wealth of cultural and intellectual resources that can be used to address the challenges of the present day. The problem is that the militants have seized the podium and monopolized the agenda, and they do not like either complexity or open debate. In effect they read out of Islam anyone who departs from the very rigid and simplistic formulations (one might say slogans) they have adopted. (The parallel between this and attacks on "deviationism" in the days of Stalin and Mao is quite striking.) For Islam to produce meaningful answers to issues of women's roles in a modern economy, human rights, democratic government, development, and so on, Muslim thinkers must feel free to appeal to the full range of their intellectual tradition. But those who attempt this—Fazlur Rahman of Pakistan, Nasr Hamid Abu Zayd of Egypt—too often run the risk of exile, imprisonment, or even death at the hands of those who know that there is but a single truth.

In a milieu where the permissible terms of debate are narrowly defined and are all too often enforced by intimidation or terror, what seems most urgently needed is an authentic Islamic pluralism. Indeed, the frame of mind represented by pluralism—namely, both the willingness to include many contradictory voices in a debate and the commitment to take them seriously—is far more important than any specific program of Islamic reform or modernization, however appealing or imaginative it might be. In fact, pluralism is no stranger to Islam. On the contrary, pluralism has been an integral part of Islam throughout most of its history, though more as a matter of prac-

tice than of explicit principle. There was a widespread recognition
that Islam could include a wide range of theological doctrines and
devotional practices, that absolute unanimity on the content of the
Shari'a was neither obtainable nor even desirable, that due deference was owed to the differing customs of local communities. The
God-given limitations of human knowledge and reason, even when
guided by revelation, demanded a certain latitude. Obsessive demands for uniformity and purity could easily lead to unfortunate
excesses, and people who made such demands were often regarded
as dangerous agitators. It is no accident that Ibn Taymiyya (d. 1328),
the favorite medieval theologian of contemporary activists, was constantly in trouble with his colleagues and the authorities and that
he wound up spending a good many years in jail.

The late nineteenth century and the twentieth (let us say between
about 1875 and 1975) saw a real flourishing of new directions in Islamic thought. It is enough simply to recall the few names cited in
this book: the Ottoman Namik Kemal, the Egyptians Muhammad
Abduh and Ali Abd al-Raziq, the Iranian Ali Shari'ati, the Pakistani
Fazlur Rahman—as diverse a lot in background and intellectual style
as one could hope to find. In all this activity, conservative voices
like Rashid Rida and "fundamentalist" ones like Hasan al-Banna'
and Mawdudi were prominent and highly influential, but they did
not have a monopoly. They were part of a real debate on what Islam was and should become. It would be hard to argue that this
debate took place in an especially friendly external environment. It
occurred in political milieus that were repressive as well as sympathetic, in economic circumstances that were sometimes promising
but more often deeply frustrating. Some of the new thinkers enjoyed
a degree of official support, some faced studied indifference, some
had to spend their lives dodging the police.

This is not the place to explore in detail how a once-lively debate
came to be monopolized by a single tendency, nor how an atmosphere more conducive to pluralism might be restored—this time,
perhaps, a pluralism more consciously held and defended on the basis of well-defined principles. We can say that a revitalized Islamic
pluralism, if it is to be productive and able to hold its own in the
rough-and-tumble of contemporary politics, will have to achieve two
things simultaneously. Obviously it must be broadly inclusive, ready
to listen to many conflicting and contradictory voices, but it must

also decide how to set limits. Inclusiveness is not a principle that can stand on its own, since it would allow any and all ideas to claim that they were part of Islam. If pluralism is not to be an empty slogan, there must be some criteria for deciding which ideas are really part of an Islamic discourse. The defining and applying of boundaries must observe some limits of its own, however, for pluralism assumes that people have a right to be wrong, even outrageously wrong. It is all well and good to denounce an opponent as foolish and wrong-headed; demanding that he be outlawed is quite another matter. Pluralism cannot flourish in an atmosphere where *takfir* (proclaiming someone an infidel) is the first recourse of the offended.

Debate on the nature and proper role of Islam is of course steeped in a sense of the past, in memories of what Islam has been and how it has operated in society over a period of fourteen centuries. These memories are not mere shadows; they shape discussion and conflict in very direct ways. No group or tendency in contemporary Islam says that it aims to create something new. Rather, each claims—and surely believes—that it is trying to recapture the essence of the pure Islam that once existed. It is memory that identifies goals and purposes within the debate.

To a considerable degree, the same thing is true of the other issues reviewed here: economic stagnation, weakness in the international order, a lack of legitimate political institutions. There was an age—before colonialism, or before the Mongols, or in the time of the Prophet—when there was prosperity and abundance, when the Muslims were respected throughout the world, when justice reigned supreme, when the basic principles of a right social and political order were clear to all. These memories may be in various ways inaccurate or misplaced, but that does not lessen their vividness and force. They create a deep longing for the past, or at least for those things in the past that seem good and ennobling. But the impact of memory is not merely nostalgia, which is a delicious but unproductive emotion. Memory also provokes the hope of recapturing the past, and in so doing it identifies the goals that must be striven for in the future.

In the opening pages of this book I placed memory and desire in tension, almost in conflict, with each other. There seemed an unbridgeable gulf between images of the past, sometimes golden and sometimes bitter, and intense but always frustrated aspirations for the future. At this point, however, we may be able to see that memory and desire are simply reflections of each other. Memory creates the desire to regain the old and seize hold of the new, in the hope that they will be the same thing. But desire in its turn creates the memories that define past and future.

This process is not peculiar to the Middle East. It goes on in every society and culture, not least our own. Two things make the Middle East different (in degree, not in kind). First, memories there are intense and deeply felt yet poorly scrutinized and tested. Memory in the Middle East, we might say, tends to be embodied in myth rather than history. The preference for a mythic construction of the past is certainly understandable, for myth, with its grand confrontations between good and evil, inspires a people and moves them to action. Critical history, in contrast, douses everything in cold water; it induces skepticism, confusion, even cynicism. Yet only a historical approach to the past allows us to paint an honest picture of what was done and achieved, and hence what aspects of that past we want to recover and use to guide us toward the future.

Such an approach will be no easy thing to achieve, for historical analyses of a revered past violate deeply felt cultural taboos, not to mention the jealously guarded interests of suspicious governments. The Middle East does not lack for historians of skill and integrity, but they must work with great circumspection within a very treacherous environment. It will inevitably be a long time before memories of the past are shaped as much by history as by myth.

This brings us to the second point. Middle Eastern desires for the future, especially since 1960, have typically been transformative rather than ameliorative; they have aimed to create a new world, not to improve the one people actually live in. The reasons for this are clear enough; for many (perhaps most) Middle Easterners things are intolerable as they are, and it is far from clear what concrete steps really will make them better. At the same time, the twentieth century is full of evidence that complex societies are not readily transformed and that efforts at instantaneous transformation commonly end in disappointment if not catastrophe. Just as useful memories of the past can only be generated through a critical-historical approach to it, so productive aspirations for the future require a clear-headed sense of what is attainable. The art, a very delicate one, is to proclaim a bold and challenging vision that is just within one's grasp.

There is regrettably no set recipe for visions of this kind; the capacity to define them and set them in motion is the definition of political genius. The great majority of would-be political geniuses, of course, do not fulfill their early promise. But even granting all this, if such a vision could be found, it would take Middle Easterners a long way toward resolving the tension between memory and desire that has beset them throughout this century. These two impulses would no longer be a source of frustration and anger but would instead provide a surge of new energy for the difficult tasks before them.

NOTES

Preface

1. A convenient reference, though of course already out of date in important respects, is *The Cambridge Atlas of the Middle East and North Africa*, ed. Gerald Blake, John Dewdney, and Jonathan Mitchell (Cambridge: Cambridge University Press, 1987). It covers a wide variety of topics: physical environment, demography and economics, geopolitical issues, and so on.

2. T. S. Eliot, *The Wasteland and Other Poems* (San Diego and New York: Harcourt Brace & Co., 1934), 29.

3. A. J. M. Smith, ed., *Seven Centuries of Verse, English & American*. 2d rev. ed. (New York: Charles Scribner's Sons, 1957), 11.

Chapter 1. Hard Realities

1. The literature on the subjects touched on in this chapter is immense. A good recent synthesis is Alan Richards and John Waterbury, *A Political Economy of the Middle East: State, Class, and Economic Development* (Boulder, Colo.: Westview Press, 1990). Since I collected the data used in this chapter independently, there will be minor discrepancies between my numbers and those in Richards and Waterbury.

2. On Nasser's Cairo, see Janet L. Abu-Lughod, *Cairo: 1001 Years of the City Victorious* (Princeton: Princeton University Press, 1971), esp. Part III, "The Contemporary Metropolis," 169–239.

3. The nineteenth- and early-twentieth-century numbers are adapted from Charles Issawi, *An Economic History of the Middle East and North Africa* (New York: Columbia University Press, 1982), 93–103. For recent and current figures, I have used the World Bank, *Social Indicators of Development, 1994* (Baltimore: Johns Hopkins University Press, 1994), and idem, *World Tables, 1994* (Baltimore: Johns Hopkins University Press, 1994).

4. Peter Brown, *The Body and Society: Men, Women, and Sexual Renunciation in Early Christianity* (New York: Columbia University Press, 1988), 6.

5. An impression gathered on a personal visit in December 1993; I was accompanied by a few expert colleagues from my own university as well as by senior hospital staff.

6. I obtained these numbers by asking (through my interpreter) the child workers about their wages and hours during a visit to Fez in October 1990. I was told that the nine- or ten-year-old boys stitching shoes in one shop

would make about 10 dirhams (then equal to $1.25) per day. The small boys who were painting and sanding ceramic drums next door said that they got about 40 dirhams ($5) per week. They seemed to regard this as a fair enough wage.

7. The numbers in this and the following paragraph come from the tables in Andrew J. Pierre, *The International Politics of Arms Sales* (Princeton: Princeton University Press, 1979); and Yahya M. Sadowski, *Scuds or Butter: The Political Economy of Arms Control in the Middle East* (Washington, D.C.: Brookings Institute, 1993).

8. In 1995, Iran and Egypt spent only some $40 per capita on defense, as opposed to nearly $1,000 by the United States. As a percentage of gross domestic product (GDP), however, the numbers are almost equal: slightly under 4 percent for each country. In contrast, Iraq spent almost 15 percent of GDP on defense, Syria about 12 percent, and Saudi Arabia 10.6 percent. These numbers are from the International Institute for Strategic Studies, London. A good conspectus of the overall security situation is provided by Scott Peterson in the *Christian Science Monitor*, July 30, 1997, 7–14; Aug. 7, 1997, 7–14.

9. John Waterbury, *Hydropolitics of the Nile Valley* (Syracuse: Syracuse University Press, 1979). A more quantitative study is Dale Whittington and Giorgio Guariso, *Water Management Models in Practice: A Case Study of the Aswan High Dam* (New York: Elsevier Scientific, 1983).

10. I gathered this data on a personal visit to Jubail in December 1993. There is a recent book on the project, but I have had no opportunity to assess it: Andrea H. Pampanini, *Cities from the Arabian Desert: The Building of Jubail and Yanbu in Saudi Arabia* (Westport, Conn.: Praeger, 1997).

11. Roger Owen, *The Middle East in the World Economy, 1800–1914* (London: Methuen, 1981), provides a good analysis of the nineteenth century. There is no single summary of this caliber for the twentieth century, and a bibliography would be preposterously long: Charles Issawi, *An Economic History of the Middle East and North Africa* (1982), is concise but full of pertinent data and ideas; see esp. chaps. 8, 10. Obviously Issawi does not deal with the important changes of the last two decades.

12. The Khedive Isma'il was the grandson of Muhammad Ali, an Ottoman soldier of fortune who seized control of Egypt in the early nineteenth century. We cannot trace his remarkable career here. Though he was nominally the governor-general of Egypt on behalf of the Ottoman sultan, he governed the country as an effectively independent ruler. Feeling confined by the Nile Valley, he moved on to conquer much of the Sudan, and then Palestine and Syria. In 1838 he launched a war against his nominal overlord, the Ottoman sultan, and came within an ace of overthrowing him before being stopped by a British-engineered alliance in 1841. He retained the hereditary governorship of Egypt, however, and this passed to his grandson Isma'il in 1863. Isma'il had resided for some years in France and was an enthusiastic modernizer, though he never quite caught on to the wiles of French and Belgian bankers.

Chapter 2. From Imperialism to the New World Order

1. There is a thorough treatment of the British Empire in the postwar Middle East by William Roger Louis, *The British Empire in the Middle East, 1945–1951: Arab Nationalism, the United States, and Postwar Imperialism* (Oxford: Clarendon Press, 1984). A sequel covering the next six years is eagerly awaited. There is no similar study in English on the postwar French Empire; on the bloodiest and most tragic chapter of its decline, the Algerian Revolt, see Alistair Horne, *A Savage War of Peace: Algeria, 1954–1962* (London: Macmillan, 1977), and John E. Talbott, *The War without a Name: France in Algeria, 1954–1962* (New York: Knopf, 1980). Horne focuses on the struggle in Algeria, Talbott (a more analytic study) on the politics of the war in France itself.

2. The dates for the founding of Saudi Arabia are confusing. The amir Abd al-Aziz ibn Abd al-Rahman Al Saud began his campaigns to control central Arabia in 1902. Having consolidated his control of central and eastern Arabia by the end of World War I (with some financial assistance from Great Britain), he turned toward the Hijaz, where the holy cities of Mecca and Medina lay. These he conquered by 1925. In 1926 he proclaimed himself King of the Hijaz and Sultan of Najd. In 1932 the name of his realm was changed to the Kingdom of Saudi Arabia—i.e., it was named for the ruling dynasty, not the territories that it ruled—and this name it retains down to the present. The most recent history of the formation of the Saudi kingdom is Joseph Kostiner, *The Making of Saudi Arabia, 1916–1936: From Chieftaincy to Monarchical State* (New York: Oxford University Press, 1993).

3. There are a number of general histories of twentieth-century Iran. The deepest in its understanding of culture and intellectual life is the brilliant tour de force of Roy P. Mottahedeh, *The Mantle of the Prophet: Learning and Power in Modern Iran* (New York: Simon and Schuster, 1985). Political histories that pay serious attention to social, economic, and ideological developments are Nikki Keddie, *Roots of Revolution: An Interpretive History of Modern Iran* (New Haven: Yale University Press, 1981); and Ervand Abrahamian, *Iran between Two Revolutions* (Princeton: Princeton University Press, 1982). Since both were published just after the Islamic Revolution of 1979 they inevitably find it difficult to put this event in long-term perspective. On the vexed subject of U.S.-Iranian relations from World War II to Reagan, see the somewhat polemical but intelligent and well-researched study by James E. Bill, *The Eagle and the Lion: The Tragedy of American-Iranian Relations* (New Haven: Yale University Press, 1988).

4. Important recent books by Mangol Bayat are *Iran's First Revolution: Shi'ism and the Constitutional Revolution of 1905–1909* (New York: Oxford University Press, 1991); and Janet Afary, *The Iranian Constitutional Revolution, 1906–1911: Grassroots Democracy, Social Democracy, and the Origins of Feminism* (New York: Oxford University Press, 1996). The contemporary work by the great British Orientalist Edward G. Browne, *The Persian Revolution of 1905–1909* (Cambridge: Cambridge University Press, 1910), remains an irreplaceable classic, and captures much of the hope and idealism among Iranian constitutionalists during those years.

5. The voluminous literature on Mossadegh is intensely partisan and largely unreliable. Apart from the general histories mentioned at the beginning of this section, see the essays (by Iranian, British, and American authors) collected in William Roger Louis and James E. Bill, eds., *Musaddiq, Iranian Nationalism, and Oil* (Austin: University of Texas Press, 1988). Most recently, see Mostafa Elm, *Oil, Power, and Principle: Iran's Oil Nationalization and Its Aftermath* (Syracuse: Syracuse University Press, 1992).

6. Translations of the 1979 Constitution: "Constitution of the Islamic Republic of Iran," *Middle East Journal* 34 (1980): 181–204; Hamid Algar, *Constitution of the Islamic Republic of Iran* (Berkeley: Mizan Press, 1980). Algar's is the official translation; the version in *MEJ* comes from the U.S. State Department's Foreign Broadcast Information Service; it has some minor errors but appears to be quite usable. There were some minor amendments in 1989 (after Khomeini's death) which enhanced the authority of the president, but the jurist remains a powerful figure.

7. The literature on twentieth-century Egypt is immense, but no one book really brings it all together. Moreover, many of the most interesting studies are rather unapproachable for the nonspecialist. As a starting point, see Afaf Lutfi al-Sayyid Marsot, *A Short History of Modern Egypt* (Cambridge: Cambridge University Press, 1985). Since Gamal Abdel Nasser is the central figure in the following discussion, biographies of him should have pride of place. Again, we lack a really definitive one. Two older biographies by sympathetic Western contemporaries remain valuable: Jean Lacouture, *Nasser, a Biography* (New York: Knopf, 1973); and Anthony Nutting, *Nasser* (New York: E. P. Dutton, 1972). Nutting was the principal British negotiator of the 1954 Suez Canal Treaty and resigned from the government in protest over the Suez Canal imbroglio in 1956. A book by Nasser's confidant Mohamad Hassanein Heikal (Muhammad Hasanayn Haykal) is of course intensely partisan but gives a valuable Egyptian perspective: *The Cairo Documents: The Inside Story of Nasser and His Relationship with World Leaders, Rebels, and Statesmen* (Garden City, N.Y.: Doubleday, 1972).

8. A popular film released in 1993, *al-Mansi* (The Forgotten Man), is a funny but very pointed satire on this issue, and quite unmistakably links Mubarak's Egypt to that of King Farouk. A friend commented that he was surprised that the authorities had permitted it to be shown; it was certainly not complimentary to them.

9. On this subject the literature is incomprehensively vast; never in the history of human endeavor has so much ink been spilled on so small a piece of land. Charles D. Smith, *Palestine and the Arab-Israeli Conflict*, 3d ed. (New York: St. Martin's Press, 1996), is concise and reliable. Those desiring a full-length treatment will find it in the admirable synthesis by Mark Tessler, *A History of the Israeli-Palestinian Conflict* (Bloomington: Indiana University Press, 1994). On the Mandate period (1917–1948), Christopher Sykes, *Crossroads to Israel* (orig. pub. 1965; reprinted, Bloomington: Indiana University Press, 1978), was written before any of the official documents for the period were (legally) accessible, but it is vividly written and remains re-

markably astute in its assessment of British and Zionist policies, though markedly less insightful on the Arab side.

10. See now the comprehensive study by Yezid Sayigh, *Armed Struggle and the Search for State: The Palestinian National Movement, 1949–1993* (Oxford: Clarendon Press, 1997).

11. An excellent portrayal of the dead end into which Arafat and the PLO had worked themselves by the mid-eighties is given by Thomas Friedman, *From Beirut to Jerusalem* (New York: Farrar, Straus & Giroux, 1989), chap. 5, "The Teflon Guerilla," 106–125.

12. The Islamic Resistance in Palestine is a new movement and has only begun to receive serious attention; see Ziad Abu Amr, *Islamic Fundamentalism in the West Bank and Gaza: Muslim Brotherhood and Islamic Jihad* (Bloomington: Indiana University Press, 1994).

13. There is a great deal on the Intifada. Robert F. Hunter, *The Palestinian Uprising: A War by Other Means* (Berkeley and Los Angeles: University of California Press, 1991), provides a good narrative. A more analytical account (from a critical left-wing perspective) is Joost Hiltermann, *Behind the Intifada: Labor and Women's Movement in the Occupied Territories* (Princeton: Princeton University Press, 1991).

Chapter 3. The Strange Career of Pan-Arabism

1. Arab Nationalism has many synonyms in both Arabic and English; the most common are "Arabism" (Ar., *ʿuruba*) and "Pan-Arabism," and I will use both terms in this chapter. There have been many varieties of Arab Nationalism over the century of its existence; they differ both as to the region that they include within the Arab homeland and as to the characteristics (language, history, race, etc.) by which they define membership in the Arab nation. Pan-Arabism is that form of Arab Nationalism which seeks to unite all the Arabic-speaking peoples from Morocco to Iraq and Oman within a single country; in the Pan-Arabist perspective, all these peoples are fundamentally and eternally one in language, race, culture, and history, in spite of regional differences between them. The best presentation of the intellectual and political milieu in which Arab Nationalism developed remains Albert Hourani's classic *Arabic Thought in the Liberal Age, 1798–1939* (London: Oxford University Press, 1962), esp. chap. 11.

2. Malcolm Kerr, *The Arab Cold War: Gamal ʿAbd al-Nasir and His Rivals, 1958–1970* (orig. pub. 1965; rev. ed., New York: Oxford University Press, 1971).

3. Satiʿ al-Husri has been studied by William Cleveland, *The Making of an Arab Nationalist: Ottomanism and Arabism in the Life and Thought of Satiʿ al-Husri* (Princeton: Princeton University Press, 1971).

4. The literature on Syria is not large, but there are a few items of high quality. The French Mandate (1920–1946) is exhaustively treated in Philip Khoury, *Syria and the French Mandate: The Politics of Arab Nationalism, 1928–1945* (Princeton: Princeton University Press, 1987). Shorter, more readable,

278 Notes to Pages 74–79

and still valuable in spite of its age is A. H. Hourani, *Syria and Lebanon: A Political Essay* (London: Oxford University Press, 1946). The period between World War II and the formation of the United Arab Republic has been brilliantly recorded by Patrick Seale, *The Struggle for Syria: A Study of Post-War Arab Politics, 1945–1958* (London: Oxford University Press, 1965). The Baathist era (since 1961) is discussed in a concise but penetrating study by Nikolaos Van Dam, *The Struggle for Power in Syria: Politics and Society under Asad and the Baʿth Party* (London: I. B. Tauris, 1996). Patrick Seale, *Asad of Syria: The Struggle for the Middle East* (Berkeley and Los Angeles: University of California Press, 1988), is important because of the author's unrivaled access to Asad while writing it but is otherwise not on the same level as his earlier book.

5. See the vivid account in Friedman, *From Beirut to Jerusalem*, chap. 4, "Hama Rules," 76–105.

6. Among many general works on Lebanon, see Kamal Salibi, *A House of Many Mansions: The History of Lebanon Reconsidered* (Berkeley and Los Angeles: University of California Press, 1988), a series of essays on crucial problems in Lebanese history. A rather jaundiced but perceptive construction of the old order in its last years is Michael Gilsenan, *Lords of the Lebanese Marches: Violence and Narrative in an Arab Society* (Berkeley and Los Angeles: University of California Press, 1996). A well-balanced but passionless survey of the civil war is Itamar Rabinovich, *The War for Lebanon, 1970–1985*, rev. ed. (Ithaca, N.Y.: Cornell University Press, 1985). A substantial journalistic account of the early 1980s is given in Friedman, *From Beirut to Jerusalem* (1989).

7. The origins of Jordan are traced in Mary C. Wilson, *King Abdullah, Britain, and the Making of Jordan* (Cambridge: Cambridge University Press, 1987). For Jordan since independence, see Kamal Salibi, *The Modern History of Jordan* (London: I. B. Tauris, 1993).

8. Phebe Marr, *The Modern History of Iraq* (Boulder, Colo.: Westview Press, 1985), is a detailed and reliable survey of the country's twentieth-century history. Saddam Hussein's Iraq is not an easy place to study. The silence was broken by an Iraqi expatriate intellectual, Kanan Makiya (writing under the pseudonym Samir al-Khalil), *Republic of Fear: The Politics of Modern Iraq* (Berkeley and Los Angeles: University of California Press, 1989). His second book, *Cruelty and Silence* (New York: W. W. Norton, 1993), has a broader agenda than Iraq but is full of valuable information about the brutal anti-Kurdish campaigns in 1988 and the Shiʿite uprisings after the Gulf War.

9. It is not easy to carry out research in Saudi Arabia, and so serious books on the country are few. On its origins, see Joseph Kostiner, *The Making of Saudi Arabia, 1916–1936* (1993). The enormous changes undergone by the country since King Faysal took the throne in 1964 must be pieced together from a variety of sources; most recently, see the useful survey of David E. Long, *The Kingdom of Saudi Arabia* (Gainesville: University Press of Florida, 1997). Issued under official auspices, William Facey, gen. ed., *The Kingdom of Saudi Arabia* (London: Stacey International; many editions since

1977), has valuable information and contributions from a number of excellent scholars, though of course it must be used critically.

10. There is now a considerable body of good work on modern Yemen, though most of it is formidably academic. In any case, the old slur about "rushing headlong into the fourteenth century" is certainly no longer applicable, if it ever was. On the 1997 elections in unified Yemen, see William A. Rugh, "A (Successful) Test of Democracy in Yemen," *Christian Science Monitor*, May 28, 1997, 19.

11. Marvin Zonis and Daniel Brumberg, *Khomeini: the Islamic Republic of Iran, and the Arab World*, Middle East Papers, no. 5 (Cambridge: Center for Middle Eastern Studies, Harvard University, 1987).

Chapter 4. The Shaping of Foreign Policy

1. In 1996 this event was the subject of an extremely popular movie in Cairo, *Nasser '56*. Egyptians leaving the theater were heard exclaiming, "Those were the days!"

2. The most comprehensive study of the Suez Canal crisis in 1956 is Keith Kyle, *Suez* (New York: St. Martin's Press, 1991). For the history of the Suez Canal, see D. A. Farnie, *East and West of Suez: The Suez Canal in History, 1854–1956* (Oxford: Clarendon Press, 1969). A partisan but invaluable Egyptian perspective is provided by Mohamed Hassanein Heikal, *The Cairo Documents* (1973) and *Cutting the Lion's Tail: Suez through Egyptian Eyes* (London: R. Deutsch, 1986).

3. Kyle, *Suez*, 76.

4. The following scenario is adapted from Heikal's volumes.

5. The clearest presentation of the early years of the Islamic Republic is Shaul Bakhash, *The Reign of the Ayatollahs: Iran and the Islamic Revolution* (New York: Basic Books, 1984). A frank and detailed perspective on the fall of the Shah and the hostage crisis from an American policy maker's perspective is Gary Sick, *All Fall Down: America's Tragic Encounter with Iran* (New York: Random House, 1985). See also the relevant bibliography from the previous chapter. The best way to grasp Khomeini's political thought is of course to read his own writings and speeches; many of these are gathered in Hamid Algar, ed. and trans., *Islam and Revolution: Writings and Declarations of Imam Khomeini* (Berkeley: Mizan Press, 1981). The essay by Ervand Abrahamian, *Khomeinism: Essays on the Islamic Republic* (Berkeley and Los Angeles: University of California Press, 1993), is very readable and full of interesting insights but is perhaps a bit reductionist in its insistence that Khomeini represented little more than a variety of Third World populism.

6. There is rather little on how and why Saddam Hussein decided to occupy Kuwait. Hence all manner of theories (including a U.S. government conspiracy to entrap and destroy him) abound. An analysis of the crisis from an international-law perspective, and more sympathetic to Iraq than most, is the new book by Majid Khadduri and Edmund Ghareeb, *War in the Gulf, 1990–91: The Iraq-Kuwait Conflict and Its Implications* (New York: Oxford

University Press, 1997). Otherwise, this following account is based on a critical evaluation of news accounts of the crisis, along with a measure of controlled speculation.

Chapter 5. Military Dictatorship and Political Tradition in the Middle East

1. Since most of the references for this chapter would be the same as those for the preceding four, I will give references only for specific points. This chapter originated in a lecture delivered at the annual meeting of the Pacific Coast Branch of the American Historical Association, Kona, Hawaii, August 1991.

2. Leonard Binder, *In a Moment of Enthusiasm: Political Power and the Second Stratum in Egypt* (Chicago: University of Chicago Press, 1978).

3. A thorough exploration of this issue can be found in Augustus Richard Norton, ed., *Civil Society in the Middle East*, 2 vols. (Leiden: E. J. Brill, 1994–1995). One of the most articulate Arab advocates of this concept is the Egyptian sociologist Saad Eddin Ibrahim, several of whose works are available in English. A good place to start is *Egypt, Islam, and Democracy: Twelve Critical Essays* (Cairo: American University in Cairo Press, 1996).

Chapter 6. Profane and Sacred Politics

1. The topic of political Islam has produced an immense literature, of extremely uneven quality. Many of the major issues are laid out in the following three works, though each represents a very different approach to the subject: Emmanuel Sivan, *Radical Islam: Medieval Theology and Modern Politics* (New Haven: Yale University Press, 1985; rev. ed., 1990); John L. Esposito, *The Islamic Threat: Myth or Reality?* (New York: Oxford University Press, 1992); James Piscatori and Dale Eickelman, *Muslim Politics* (Princeton: Princeton University Press, 1996).

2. Ibn Khaldun, *The Muqaddima: An Introduction to History*, trans. Franz Rosenthal, 3 vols., 2d rev. ed. (Princeton: Princeton University Press, 1967), 1:385–388. His whole discussion on this issue is important: pp. 385–472.

3. The Ottoman codification of 1870 is called the *Mecelle* (with *c* pronounced like *j*). "Shariʿa" is commonly translated as "Islamic Law" or "Holy Law." This is extremely misleading. The Shariʿa is properly the whole body of duties incumbent on every Muslim, whether these duties pertain to religion (e.g., prayer and fasting), personal morality (e.g., proper dress and demeanor), civil law (e.g., correct procedure in drawing up contracts), or criminal violations (e.g., theft). Traditionally, the Shariʿa was not embodied in a fixed body of statutes. Rather, it was embedded in the whole body of debate and discussion among reputable legal scholars over the centuries. It is a little bit as if American federal judges reached their decisions not by consulting congressional statutes and Supreme Court decisions but by sifting through the law reviews published by the major law schools.

4. Michael Gilsenan, *Recognizing Islam: Religion and Society in the Modern Middle East* (London: I. B. Tauris, 1990; orig. pub. 1982), 9–11.

5. Mark Juergensmeyer, *The New Cold War: Religious Nationalism Confronts the Secular State* (Berkeley and Los Angeles: University of California Press, 1993). He calls this phenomenon "religious nationalism," a debatable but very suggestive turn of phrase. See also Bruce Lawrence, *Defenders of God: The Fundamentalist Revolt against the Modern Age* (San Francisco: Harper and Row, 1989).

6. A few years ago the hot show was "Dallas," but there is always some American TV series portraying the evils of power, greed, and lust among the wealthy. "The Bold and the Beautiful" was enormously popular during my visit to Cairo in 1993; it was also a favorite target of mosque preachers, who denounced it as the perfect symbol of the moral rot of contemporary America. Had it not existed, they would have had to invent it.

7. Hasan al-Turabi is a remarkable figure, as at home in English and Western political philosophy as in Arabic and Islamic thought. There is an interview with him in English: *Islam, Democracy, the State, and the West: A Roundtable with Dr. Hasan Turabi, May 10, 1992*, ed. Arthur Lowrie (Tampa, Fla.: World and Islam Studies Enterprises, 1993). However, one can legitimately suspect him of trimming his sails here to fit the values and outlook of an American audience. The interviews contained in a work by a Tunisian journalist may be more representative: Mohamed Elhachmi Hamdi, *The Making of an Islamic Political Leader: Conversations with Hasan al-Turabi* (Boulder, Colo.: Westview Press, 1998). His Arabic-language writings—which are of course the influential ones in the Middle East—have not been translated so far as I know. On the religious role of the monarch in Morocco, see the perceptive if idiosyncratic study of Elaine Combs-Schilling, *Sacred Performances: Islam, Sexuality, and Sacrifice* (New York: Columbia University Press, 1989). A more sober, and perhaps more persuasive interpretation is offered by a Moroccan scholar: Abdellah Hammoudi, *Master and Disciple: The Cultural Foundations of Moroccan Authoritarianism* (Chicago: University of Chicago Press, 1997).

8. There is no full-length study of this pivotal figure in English; a good short biography is that by the French scholar Henri Laoust in the *Encyclopaedia of Islam* (new edition): "Ibn ʿAbd al-Wahhab," 3:677–679.

9. It was once possible to regard the Sudan hopefully if not optimistically; see John and Sarah Voll, *The Sudan: Unity and Diversity in a Multicultural State* (Boulder, Colo.: Westview Press, 1985). By the early 1990s things looked far more somber; see John O. Voll, ed., *Sudan: State and Society in Crisis* (Bloomington: Indiana University Press, 1991). For the civil war and famine of the 1980s and 1990s, see J. Millard Burr and Robert O. Collins, *Requiem for the Sudan: War, Drought, and Disaster Relief on the Nile* (Boulder, Colo.: Westview Press, 1995).

10. Seyyed Vali Reza Nasr, *The Vanguard of the Islamic Revolution: The Jamaʿat-i Islami of Pakistan* (Berkeley and Los Angeles: University of California Press, 1994), discusses the history of the most influential and effective

Islamic group in Pakistan, from its founding in 1941 down to the present; it is clear enough that General Zia was trying to address and co-opt the energies generated by this and related movements in his own "Islamization" policies during the 1980s.

Chapter 7. Islam as a Political System

1. Translations of the Qur'an are discussed in the bibliographic note; the literature on it is of course beyond human reckoning. A particularly useful and accessible approach for those who want to follow up the topics discussed in this chapter is Fazlur Rahman, *Major Themes of the Qur'an* (Minneapolis: Bibliotheca Islamica, 1980). There is a terse but careful survey in Alford T. Welch, "Kur'an," *Encyclopaedia of Islam* (new edition), 5:esp. 421–427.

2. Biographies of Muhammad must number in the thousands. One of the most influential and widely read among Muslims is that by Muhammad Husayn Haykal (no relation to the noted journalist of Nasser's era), *The Life of Muhammad*, trans. Isma'il R. Faruqi (Philadelphia: American Trust Publications, 1976). A Western scholarly account is represented by W. Montgomery Watt, *Muhammad at Mecca* (Oxford: Clarendon Press, 1953), and *Muhammad at Medina* (Oxford: Clarendon Press, 1956). Watt's very sympathetic approach has given his work a certain audience even among Muslim readers. More recently, see F. E. Peters, *Muhammad and the Origins of Islam* (Albany: State University of New York Press, 1994). Peters follows the Arabic sources for Muhammad's career and quotes from them extensively, but he is more aware than either Haykal or Watt of the problems involved in evaluating and using these sources.

3. For the origins and development of the caliphate, see the general titles in the bibliography; among these, Marshall G. S. Hodgson, *The Venture of Islam: Conscience and History in World Civilization*, 3 vols. (Chicago: University of Chicago Press, 1974), 1:187–230, is particularly good. A very different view is given in the fascinating, though a bit over the top, study of Patricia Crone and Martin Hinds, *God's Caliph: Religious Authority in the First Centuries of Islam* (Cambridge: Cambridge University Press, 1986).

4. Edward Gibbon, *The Portable Gibbon: The Decline and Fall of the Roman Empire*, abridged ed., ed. Dero J. Saunders (New York: Viking Press, 1952), 105–106.

5. On the history of Shi'ism and its key political concepts, see Heinz Halm, *Shiism*, trans. Janet Watson (Edinburgh: Edinburgh University Press, 1991). An elementary but authoritative account from a Shi'ite perspective is Muhammad Husayn Tabataba'i, *Shi'ite Islam*, trans. Seyyed Hossein Nasr (Albany: State University of New York Press, 1975), esp. chaps. 1, 7.

6. The brief articles by H. A. R. Gibb in *Studies on the Civilization of Islam*, ed. S. J. Shaw and W. R. Polk (London: Routledge and Kegan Paul, 1962), on this issue are old but still perceptive: "Some Considerations of the Sunni Theory of the Caliphate," 141–150; "Al-Mawardi's Theory of the Caliphate," 151–165.

7. The definitive statement on "Perso-Islamic kingship" is the treatise by the eleventh-century vizier Nizam al-Mulk, *The Book of Government, or Rules for Kings*, trans. Hubert Darke (London: Routledge and Kegan Paul, 1960; rev. trans., 1978).

8. A. H. Hourani, *Arabic Thought in the Liberal Age* (1962); Şerif Mardin, *The Genesis of Young Ottoman Thought* (Princeton: Princeton University Press, 1962); Hamid Enayat, *Modern Islamic Political Thought: The Response of the Shīʾi and Sunni Muslims to the Twentieth Century* (London: Macmillan, 1982).

9. See chapter 2, notes 3 and 4.

10. See chapter 2, note 6.

11. See the selection of Khomeini's sermons and writings in Hamid Algar, *Islam and Revolution* (1981).

12. Translated by Algar as "Islamic Government" in *Islam and Revolution* (1981), 27–166.

Chapter 8. Jihad and the Politics of Salvation

1. In view of the countless books on jihad, perhaps the best place to start is with a collection of statements by Muslims: Rudoph Peters, ed., *Jihad in Classical and Modern Islam: A Reader* (Princeton: Markus Wiener, 1996), almost evenly divided between medieval and twentieth-century texts.

2. Qurʾanic injunctions to avoid force save when absolutely necessary: 2:190–193; 9:7–13; 48:24–25; among many others.

3. The standard account of the early Islamic conquests is now Fred M. Donner, *The Early Islamic Conquests* (Princeton: Princeton University Press, 1981). His analysis of this difficult subject is an impressive achievement, though I depart from it at a number of points.

4. The standard study remains Majid Khadduri, *War and Peace in the Law of Islam* (Baltimore: Johns Hopkins University Press, 1955). A terse but authoritative statement by a medieval Muslim jurist is given by the famous philosopher Averroës, in Peters, *Jihad in Classical and Modern Islam* (1996), chap. 4.

5. The best way of getting acquainted with these treaties is to read them. Fortunately we have an excellent cross-section of them in Jacob Hurewitz, *The Middle East and North Africa in World Politics: A Documentary Record*, 2 vols. (New Haven: Yale University Press, 1975). Vol. 1 covers the period 1535–1914 and is the relevant one here. Vol. 2 goes down to 1945; unfortunately vol. 3 has never appeared.

6. Rudolph Peters, *Islam and Colonialism: The Doctrine of Jihad in Modern History* (The Hague: Mouton, 1979).

7. Yet again, A. H. Hourani, *Arabic Thought in the Liberal Age* (1962), esp. chaps. 6, 7, 9.

8. Among many studies of Bannaʾ and the Muslim Brothers, the classic work remains Richard P. Mitchell, *The Society of Muslim Brothers* (London: Oxford University Press, 1969). The flavor of al-Bannaʾ's teaching comes across nicely in Charles Wendell, trans., *Five Tracts of Hasan al-Bannaʾ, 1906–1949* (Berkeley and Los Angeles: University of California Press, 1978).

9. Partial translation in Robert G. Landen, ed., *The Emergence of the Modern Middle East: Selected Readings* (New York: Van Nostrand Reinhold, 1970), 260–264.

10. Sayyid Qutb's first major treatise, *Social Justice in Islam,* denounced the corruption of Western culture and called for a thoroughgoing Islamic reform of society in the Muslim lands. The first edition of this treatise (1948) was translated in 1953 (reprinted New York: Octagon, 1970). The final version, far more radical in its attacks on the established order, has now been translated and analyzed by William Shepard, *Sayyid Qutb and Islamic Activism* (Leiden: E. J. Brill, 1996). His most influential tract has only recently become available in English: *Milestones* (Indianapolis: American Trust Publications, 1993).

11. On the group behind the Sadat assassination, see Johannes J. G. Jansen, *The Neglected Duty: The Creed of Sadat's Assassins and Islamic Resurgence in the Middle East* (New York: Macmillan, 1986).

12. On the Islamic movement in the Occupied Territories, see Ziad Abu Amr, *Islamic Fundamentalism in the West Bank and Gaza* (1994).

13. Robert Malley, *The Call from Algeria: Third Worldism, Revolution, and the Turn to Islam* (Berkeley and Los Angeles: University of California Press, 1996).

14. The Islamic movement in North Africa is treated in François Burgat and William Dowell, *The Islamic Movement in North Africa,* 2d ed. (Austin: Center for Middle Eastern Studies, University of Texas, 1997). As is often the case in current French writing, this is not an easy book, but it is important.

15. Jeffrey Goldberg, "From Peace Process to Police Process," *New York Times Magazine,* September 14, 1997, 62.

16. See a survey of Palestinian religious scholars: Ilene R. Prusher, "When Bombs Rip, Where Is Islam?" *Christian Science Monitor,* August 11, 1996, 1, 18.

17. Shariʿati's thought has been widely studied. A very interesting effort to situate Shariʿati within a broad intellectual-ideological movement is the recent study by Mehrzad Boroujerdi, *Iranian Intellectuals and the West: The Tormented Triumph of Nativism* (Syracuse: Syracuse University Press, 1996). Shariʿati was more an essayist than a systematic thinker, or at least he died before he could complete an overarching synthesis. A few of his essays are available in translations by Hamid Algar: *Lectures on the Sociology of Islam* (Berkeley: Mizan Press, 1979); *Marxism and Other Western Fallacies* (Berkeley: Mizan Press, 1980). Some critics have suggested that Algar's own ideological commitments may have caused him to misconstrue Shariʿati's meaning in certain passages.

Chapter 9. Women in Public Life

1. There is by now a huge literature, much of it by Muslim women. For readers wanting to plunge into this subject, a useful guide is Michelle R. Kimball and Barbara R. von Schlegell, *Muslim Women throughout the World: A Bibliography* (Boulder, Colo.: Lynne Rienner, 1997). One can begin with

the early classic by Fatima Mernissi, *Beyond the Veil: Male-Female Dynamics in Modern Muslim Society*, 2d ed., with new preface (Bloomington: Indiana University Press, 1987; orig. pub. 1975). A pioneer effort at a broad historical synthesis is Leila Ahmad, *Women and Gender in Islam: Historical Roots of a Modern Debate* (New Haven: Yale University Press, 1992).

2. A thought-provoking study of ʿAʾisha's place in Muslim cultural imagination is Denise Spellberg, *Politics, Gender, and the Islamic Past: The Legacy of ʿAʾisha bint Abi Bakr* (New York: Columbia University Press, 1994).

3. There is a superb study on this subject by Leslie Peirce, *The Imperial Harem: Women and Sovereignty in the Ottoman Empire* (New York: Oxford University Press, 1993).

4. Robert Dankoff, trans., *The Intimate Life of an Ottoman Statesman: Melek Ahmed Pasha as Portrayed in Evliya Çelebi's Book of Travels* (Albany: State University of New York Press, 1991), 89. Evliya gives us several portraits of the women of the Ottoman palace; particularly vivid is that of Melek Pasha's wife Kaya Sultan.

5. The only full-length study of Shajar al-Durr, I am sorry to say, is in German, but it is a very good one: Götz Schregle, *Die Sultanin von Ägypten* (Wiesbaden: Otto Harrassowitz, 1961). There is a short entry in the *Encyclopaedia of Islam* (new edition): L. Ammann, "Shadjar al-Durr," 9:176.

6. Margaret Smith, *Rabiʿa the Mystic and Her Fellow-Saints in Islam* (Cambridge: Cambridge University Press, 1928; reprinted 1984)—old but still very useful.

7. A fine study of this group in modern Cairo: Arlene Macleod, *Accommodating Protest: Working Women, the New Veiling, and Change in Cairo* (New York: Columbia University Press, 1991).

8. The most important passages in the Qurʾan on women are the following: 2:221–241; 4:1–35, 127–130; 19:1–36; 24:1–34; 58:1–4; 65:1–6. The layers of meaning given to these and other verses by Muslim culture can be explored in Barbara Freyer Stowasser, *Women in the Qurʾan, Traditions, and Interpretation* (New York: Oxford University Press, 1994).

9. The most important elements of Shariʿa in regard to women are covered in John Esposito, *Women in Muslim Family Law* (Syracuse: Syracuse University Press, 1982), which includes both classical and contemporary doctrines.

10. A controversial but important study on contemporary Muslim family law as applied in Iran and Morocco is Ziba Mir-Hosseini, *Marriage on Trial: A Study of Islamic Family Law, Iran and Morocco Compared* (London: I. B. Tauris, 1993). For the Shiʿite institution of temporary or fixed-term marriage, which has been revived in the Islamic Republic of Iran, see Shahla Haeri, *Law of Desire: Temporary Marriage in Shiʿi Iran* (Syracuse: Syracuse University Press, 1989).

11. Sexuality in the Islamic Middle East is much talked about but little studied. A wide variety of approaches can be found in Basim Musallam, *Sex and Society in Islam: Birth Control before the Nineteenth Century* (Cambridge: Cambridge University Press, 1983); Elaine Combs-Schilling, *Sacred Performances* (1989); Shahla Haeri, *Law of Desire* (1989); Carol Delaney, *The*

Seed and the Soil: Gender and Cosmology in Turkish Village Society (Berkeley and Los Angeles: University of California Press, 1991); and Erika Friedl, *Women of Deh Koh: Lives in an Iranian Village* (New York: Penguin Books, 1991). Friedl is a particularly useful place to start, because she tells stories—very good ones—about the lives of individual women in a village she knows well, constructed as far as possible from the perspective of those women.

12. Qurʾan 2:223.

13. Leslie Peirce, *The Imperial Harem* (1993), is the only scholarly study of the Ottoman harem. However, the letters of Lady Mary Wortley Montagu, wife of the British minister to Constantinople in the early eighteenth century, are very readable and perceptive: *The Complete Letters of Lady Mary Wortley Montagu*, ed. Robert Halsband, 3 vols. (Oxford: Clarendon Press, 1965–1967). From the royal harem of late-nineteenth-century Iran we have Taj al-Saltana, *Crowning Anguish: Memoirs of a Persian Princess from the Harem to Modernity, 1884–1914*, ed. Abbas Amanat, trans. Anna Vanzan and Amin Neshati (Washington, D.C.: Mage Publishers, 1993). A nearly contemporary account from Egypt is Huda Shaʿrawi, *Harem Years: The Memoirs of an Egyptian Feminist (1879–1924)* (London: Virago, 1986). Finally, mid-twentieth-century Morocco has given us the memoir of that notable sociologist and feminist Fatima Mernissi, *Dreams of Trespass: Tales of a Harem Girlhood* (Reading, Mass.: Addison-Wesley, 1994).

14. A starting point is Fatima Mernissi, *Women and Islam: An Historical and Theological Inquiry* (Oxford: Basil Blackwell, 1991).

15. We are just beginning to have some serious work on early Middle Eastern feminism. As is commonly the case, Egypt is the best-studied country: Margot Badran, *Feminists, Islam, and Nation: Gender and the Making of Modern Egypt* (Princeton: Princeton University Press, 1995); Beth Baron, *The Women's Awakening in Egypt: Culture, Society, and the Press* (New Haven: Yale University Press, 1994). Two of the most important contemporary Middle Eastern feminists, Nawal Saadawi (Egypt) and Mahnaz Afkhami (Iran), write from strongly secularist perspectives. Saadawi in particular passionately denounces many of the key traditional values of her society.

16. For example, Amina Wadud-Muhsin, *Qurʾan and Women* (Shah Alam, Malaysia: Penerbit Fajar Bakti Sdn. Bhd., 1992).

Chapter 10. Islam and Human Rights

1. Two general surveys of this issue are a good place to start: Ann Elizabeth Mayer, *Islam and Human Rights: Tradition and Politics* (Boulder, Colo.: Westview Press, 1991; rev. ed., 1995); Kevin Dwyer, *Arab Voices: The Human Rights Debate in the Middle East* (Berkeley and Los Angeles: University of California Press, 1991). Mayer's analysis is informed by a strong legal perspective. Dwyer's book is not as broad as the title implies; it really focuses on Morocco, Tunisia, and Egypt. However, it is based directly on extended conversations with human rights advocates in the region and thus reflects

Middle Eastern rather than Western perspectives. Among books in English by Middle Eastern authors, see Fatima Mernissi, *Islam and Democracy: Fear of the Modern World*, trans. Mary Jo Lakeland (New York: Addison-Wesley, 1992); Kanan Makiya, *Cruelty and Silence* (1993); Abdullahi An-Naʿim, *Toward an Islamic Reformation: Civil Liberties, Human Rights, and International Law* (Syracuse: Syracuse University Press, 1990) (An-Naʿim comes from a divergent theological perspective shared by few Muslims); and Saad al-Din Ibrahim, *Egypt, Islam, and Democracy* (1996). On North Africa (which is more widely studied than many regions because it is relatively open), see Susan E. Waltz, *Human Rights and Reform: Changing the Face of North African Politics* (Berkeley and Los Angeles: University of California Press, 1995).

2. The fullest statement of this and other principles ultimately embodied in the Bill of Rights is in fact the Virginia Bill of Rights of 1776; see esp. Article I: "That all men are by nature equally free and independent, and have certain inherent rights, of which, when they enter into a state of society, *they cannot by any compact deprive or divest their posterity* [my italics]." Quoted from Henry Steele Commager, ed., *Documents of American History*, 7th ed. (New York: Appleton-Century-Crofts, 1963), 103.

3. In view of the importance of slavery in premodern Islamic societies, the literature devoted to it is surprisingly thin. One can begin with Bernard Lewis, *Race and Slavery in the Middle East: An Historical Enquiry* (New York: Oxford University Press, 1990), though the book is too narrowly focused on African slavery and has a polemical undertone in places. See also the old but classic article by Robert Brunschvig, "ʿAbd," *Encyclopaedia of Islam* (new edition), 1:24–40.

4. There is, astonishingly, no serious political biography of ʿUmar in a Western language. Traditional Muslim views are available, however: (Sunni): al-Tabari, *The Conquest of Iran*, trans. G. Rex Smith, vol. 14 of *The History of al-Tabari*, gen. ed., Ehsan Yarshater (Albany: State University of New York Press, 1994), 103–128; a Shiʿite assessment of him is given by ʿAllamah Tabatabai, *Shiʿite Islam*, trans. Seyyed Hossein Nasr (Albany: State University of New York Press, 1976), 45–46.

5. There is a large literature on both men, but the best way to get at the Muslim views of their lives and work is via Francesco Gabrieli, *Arab Historians of the Crusades*, trans. E. J. Costello (Berkeley and Los Angeles: University of California Press, 1969), 68–72 (Nur al-Din), 87–113 (Saladin).

6. Again, there is no good political biography of Süleyman, though many aspects of his reign have been studied. A contemporary European perspective on him, both admiring and fearful, is provided by the letters of the ambassador of the Holy Roman Emperor Charles V: *The Turkish Letters of Ogier Ghiselin de Busbecq, Imperial Ambassador to Constantinople, 1554–1562*, trans. E. S. Forster (Oxford: Clarendon Press, 1927).

7. A concise and lucid introduction to his life and thought is in A. H. Hourani, *Arabic Thought in the Liberal Age* (1962), 170–181.

8. These incidents have inspired a considerable literature. Taslima Nasrin's case was widely covered in the American press. Suleiman Bashear was

an Israeli Druze convert to Islam, who adopted quite radical scholarly positions on the origins of his adopted religion; this came about in spite of the protections afforded by Israeli law. The most interesting reflections on Salman Rushdie are those by the noted Syrian philosopher Sadiq Jalal al-ʿAzm, "The Importance of Being Earnest about Salman Rushdie," *Die Welt des Islams* 31 (1991): 1–49. Ironically, and quite correctly, he excoriates the Western intellectual and literary establishment for its timidity, presumably in the name of multicultural sensitivity. My information on Tujan al-Faisal was supplied by my colleague Nancy Gallagher. On Abu Zayd, the fullest treatment is by Kilian Bälz, "Submitting Faith to Judicial Scrutiny through the Family Trial: The Abu Zayd Case," *Die Welt des Islams* 37 (1997): 135–155.

9. I will have to confess a personal interest here, since Fazlur Rahman was my (very senior) colleague during the years when I taught at the University of Chicago (1975–1980). I came to know him fairly well during that time, and developed an undying respect for his immense learning, his deep commitment to Islam, and his integrity. My feelings were widely shared among his colleagues and students.

He wrote many books—far too many to list here. For our purposes, see *Islam* (New York: Holt, Rinehart and Winston, 1966; reprinted with an additional chapter by the University of Chicago Press, 1979)—the book that made his reputation in the West and forced him to leave his native Pakistan; *Islam and Modernity: Transformation of an Intellectual Tradition* (Chicago: University of Chicago Press, 1982).

10. A recent article has demonstrated that a number of major medieval legal scholars held much the same opinion; Rahman would have been delighted, though I do not think he was aware of their arguments: Mohammad Fadel, "Two Women, One Man: Knowledge, Power, and Gender in Medieval Sunni Thought," *International Journal of Middle East Studies* 29, no. 2 (1997): 185–204.

A BIBLIOGRAPHIC NOTE

A list of all the books, articles, official documents, and other sources that I have used in writing this book would cover most of a lifetime's reading. And of course there is much else that I ought to have read but have not. A bibliography including all this would be at least as long as the book and would be of little value to anyone, least of all the "interested nonspecialist" whom I have tried to keep in mind as I wrote. As an alternative, I give a selection of books and articles in the notes to each chapter. These do not represent in any sense "a review of the literature"; they are chosen with the idea of helping readers take the next step on their own. For that reason I have favored good general surveys over detailed research monographs and new books over old ones—though a few favorite classics do sneak in here and there.

In this bibliographic note I focus on reference works and general studies, since these are indispensable for anyone who wants to understand the broader context of the subjects discussed in this book, or to clear up particular puzzlements. For the sake of utility, I normally include only titles in English (but including translations from Arabic, Persian, and Turkish), although occasionally it is impossible to overlook a crucial work in some other language. I also emphasize works by modern writers, both Muslim and non-Muslim, since these are written from points of view that are readily intelligible to us. At times, however, readers will be best served if they let the men and women of the medieval and early Islamic world speak for themselves. They were after all a voluble and very articulate people.

The Religion of Islam

Islam begins with the Qurʾan, and the Qurʾan is its very soul. Many readers will have noticed that I refer to it constantly, even in what seem to be unlikely places. There are a host of translations, though none is entirely satisfactory. None both conveys the eloquence and power of the Arabic text and presents its semantic content clearly and precisely. Most translations sound stiff, fussy, opaque, faux-antique—precisely the opposite of the Arabic original. The Qurʾan is admittedly a difficult text to crack, since it is in effect half of a telephone conversation, a loosely connected series of responses by God to a host of very concrete problems faced by Muhammad and his followers. But these questions and problems are seldom spelled out; they are only alluded to in terse, often cryptic ways. That was no problem for Muhammad and his contemporaries, of course; they knew what was going on and hence how the Qur'an's statements were to be understood and applied. But most often we do not know, and neither did later medieval interpreters, in spite of heroic efforts to recover the precise situations to which the Qur'an was addressed.

Fortunately, some translations overcome at least some of these difficulties. Among translations by non-Muslims, N. J. Dawood's *The Koran* (Harmondsworth: Penguin, 1956; often revised and reprinted since) reads like English, and he thereby removes the taint of exoticism and foreignness—but at the price of much of the Qur'an's unique eloquence. He also tends to paraphrase or to choose readily intelligible English words that may mask the precise meaning of the text. A. J. Arberry's quite literal translation, *The Koran Interpreted* (New York: Macmillan, 1955; often reprinted), gets close to the quality of the Arabic at times, but at other points seems mannered and Edwardian. He provides no notes at all, with the result that passages that are difficult in the original became wholly impenetrable in his translation.

There are many translations by Muslims, often by South Asians who are fully at home in English. These too present problems, however. They have the great advantage of coming to the text from within the tradition, to be sure, but they have to align themselves with one or another tendency within this tradition—that is, to give renderings that favor a particular modern doctrinal stance. Moreover, the mere fact of being a Muslim does not mean that one can solve correctly the manifold grammatical and lexical difficulties of this text. A translation widely used among English-speaking Muslims is that of Yusuf Ali, *The Holy Qur'an: Text, Translation, and Commentary* (New York: Hafner, 1946; often reprinted). This is an admirable effort, though Yusuf Ali translates in accordance with a rationalist theology that is rejected by many Muslims. Most recently, see Ahmed Ali, *Al-Qur'an: A Contemporary Translation* (Princeton: Princeton University Press, 1988), a widely praised version that attempts to follow current English usage.

For most Muslims, the teaching and example of the Prophet has been as important a source of religious and moral guidance as the Qur'an itself. The Prophet's unique place in Muslim religious life is eloquently described in Annemarie Schimmel, *And Muhammad Is His Prophet: The Veneration of the Prophet in Islamic Piety* (Chapel Hill: University of North Carolina Press, 1985). The Prophet's own teaching—or more precisely, what Muslims understand to be his teaching—is embodied in the form of thousands of sayings ascribed to him. Such a saying is called a Hadith (literally, a "report" or "story"). These Hadiths were sifted, assessed for authenticity, and collected in several classic compilations in the late ninth century. The question of their authenticity—that is, whether they really do represent the words and acts of Muhammad—has been seriously debated in Western scholarship since the late nineteenth century. However, that issue does not really concern us in this book, for the overwhelming majority of Muslims accept them at face value. There are many English translations of Hadiths, but most of them are published in Pakistan and so may not be easy to find. I am particularly fond of James Robson's meticulous translation of a comprehensive fourteenth-century collection by the Khatib al-Tibrizi, *Mishkat al-Masabih*, 4 vols. (Lahore: S. M. Ashraf, 1963–1965).

It is hard to find a really satisfactory introduction to Islamic belief and practice for non-Muslims. Most are written as undergraduate textbooks and hence have a certain odor of the classroom about them. Two are both sympathetic and reliable, though like all introductory texts they sometimes gloss over difficult or sensitive points: Frederick M. Denny, *An Introduction to Islam* (New York: Macmillan, 1985); and John L. Esposito, *Islam: The Straight Path*, rev. ed. (New York: Oxford University Press, 1991). A very different book, emphasizing Muslim spiritual experience and drawing on the rich artistic and literary expression of Islamic culture, is John Renard, *Seven Doors to Islam: Spirituality and the Religious Life of Muslims* (Berkeley: University of California Press, 1996).

Reference Works

Reference works are numerous, but only a few are of real use to most readers of this book. *The Encyclopaedia of Islam*, new ed., 9 vols., in progress (Leiden: E. J. Brill, 1954–) is the principal reference work for scholars. Due to its size and cost, it is likely to be found only in university or major public libraries. It is a pearl beyond price, but it assumes a good deal of knowledge on the part of its readers. For example, the articles are entered under Arabic, Persian, or Turkish headings—seldom a problem when one is looking up a person but sometimes a puzzle when one wants to look up "law" (*fikh*) or "history" (*ta'rikh*). Nevertheless, it is absolutely indispensable for anyone who wants to pursue any issue seriously. There is now a condensed version, which requires only space on one's desk rather than a whole shelf: *Islamic Desk Reference*, ed. E. J. van Donzel (Leiden: E. J. Brill, 1994).

The Oxford Dictionary of the Modern Islamic World, gen. ed., John L. Esposito, 4 vols. (New York: Oxford University Press, 1995), is also a scholarly reference tool, but it is aimed at a much broader audience and is printed in a more user-friendly format. It is particularly useful for readers of this book because it focuses on the twentieth century, though it has substantial historical depth. Broadly similar in size and scope is *The Encyclopedia of the Modern Middle East*, ed. Reeva S. Simon, Philip Mattar, and Richard W. Bulliet, 4 vols. (New York: Macmillan, 1996).

General Histories

Good general histories of the Islamic world are hard to find, though the situation is markedly better than it was ten years ago. Marshall G. S. Hodgson, *The Venture of Islam: Conscience and History in World Civilization*, 3 vols. (Chicago: University of Chicago Press, 1974), is really not a book for novices, since Hodgson's thought patterns are famously dense, sometimes opaque. It is also three decades old and hence seriously out of date on many subjects. But it was the first work that really embedded Islam in world history,

292 A Bibliographic Note

and it is intellectually and morally challenging beyond any other general survey of Islamic history.

I. M. Lapidus, *History of Islamic Societies* (Cambridge: Cambridge University Press, 1988), is up to date and very reliable. It deals in an extraordinarily balanced way with Islamic societies throughout the world, and is written with great clarity. It is not as probing as Hodgson, and some critics have felt that it achieves clarity at the cost of an overly schematic interpretation. But it remains an admirable achievement and can be recommended with confidence.

Life is short, so three shorter surveys should be mentioned. A. H. Hourani, *A History of the Arab Peoples* (Cambridge, Mass.: Harvard University Press, 1991), can be rather general and even bland·in its presentation of events and personalities. However, Hourani is extraordinarily good in his presentation of institutions and patterns of everyday life. In spite of the title, it is not strictly a history of the Arabs. The medieval portions (down to 1400 or so) deal with the whole Islamic world (at that time more or less coextensive with the modern Middle East and North Africa). The Ottoman chapters (ca. 1400–1800) describe the empire as a whole, including its Turkish and European provinces. Only when Hourani reaches the nineteenth and twentieth centuries does he really focus tightly on the Arabic-speaking lands.

Bernard Lewis, *The Middle East: A Brief History of the Last 2,000 Years* (New York: Scribner, 1995), is superbly written. Lewis is dauntingly learned and is really unequaled in his capacity to lay out complex problems with clarity, concision, and wit. I do wonder whether the very conciseness of this book may make it a bit difficult for newcomers to the subject. Moreover, some of Lewis's writing (not all by any means) has an unmistakable political edge, and in recent decades he has become a favorite target of attacks against "Orientalism." Whatever the value of these criticisms, the present work has most of his virtues and few of his weaknesses.

William Cleveland, *A History of the Modern Middle East* (Boulder, Colo.: Westview Press, 1994), is a reliable, judicious narrative focusing on the diplomatic-political dimensions of the Middle East (including Iran and Turkey) in the nineteenth and twentieth centuries. At the same time, it does not neglect social, economic, or cultural issues. The prose is not electric, but it is unfailingly clear. Written as an advanced undergraduate textbook, it is probably the most satisfactory general survey of the modern period now available.

John O. Voll, *Islam: Continuity and Change in the Modern World*, 2d ed. (Syracuse: Syracuse University Press, 1994), is a reliable and comprehensive overview of change and adaptation in Islamic thought and practice throughout the world from the eighteenth century down to the present. As such it is an invaluable complement to the political and social emphases of the other titles (except Hodgson) listed here.

INDEX

Ikhwan al-Muslimun. *See* Muslim
Brothers
Imam, 155, 160–61, 166. *See also* Caliph
India, 134, 135, 159, 163, 184, 185, 255,
264
Indonesia, 135, 136, 185, 217, 253
Infant mortality, 6–8
Intifada, 57–58. *See also* Arab-Israeli
conflict; Occupied Territories
Iran, 25, 26, 27–38, 75, 91, 92, 106, 107,
112, 162, 163–64, 225, 246, 264; ancient, 163–64, 180; Constitutional
Revolution, 31–32, 166; Constitution
of 1979, 36, 100, 202, 249, 276n6; economic development of, 17, 37, 265;
Islamic Republic of, 35–38, 129–30,
140, 144, 167–68, 247, 249–50, 251–52,
267; Islamic Revolution in, 34–35,
98–104, 200–203, 265; military expenditures of, 12, 13, 274n7; Qajar shahs
of, 30–32, 134; Shi'ite clergy in, 34–37,
99–101, 102, 135, 166, 201, 249. *See also*
Safavids
Iran-Iraq War, 12, 36, 37, 103–4, 105, 144,
202–3
Iraq, 25, 27, 50, 51, 62, 66, 67, 70, 74, 77,
78–79, 80, 82, 90–92, 94, 97, 113, 117,
119–22, 180, 265; and Arab Nationalism, 78–79, 91, 109, 110, 111; military
expenditures by, 12, 13, 274n8. *See also*
Gulf War
Islam: activists, xv; contemporary militants, xv, 194, 195–200; definition of,
xii–xiii, 148, 151–52, 154–55. *See also*
Fundamentalism, Islamic; Modernism, Islamic; Reform, Islamic
Isma'il, Khedive, 21, 274n12
Israel, 13, 26, 27–28, 77, 107, 109, 137,
181, 196, 199, 218, 266; religious
right in, 56–57. *See also* Arab-Israeli
conflict; Israelis; Jewish National
Home
Israeli-Egyptian Peace Treaty (1982), 12,
44
Israelis: sense of victimization, 47–48;
and European anti-Semitism, 48–49
Israel-Palestine. *See* Israel; Palestine
Istanbul, 3, 29, 67, 115, 120, 183–84, 243

Japan, 107
Java. *See* Indonesia
Jerusalem, 43, 180, 221, 242
Jewish National Home, 49, 71
Jihad, 172, 173–203; concept of, 174–78,
181–83, 194, 202; and European impe-
rialism, 184–87; in Islamic history,

178–81, 183–86; and Islamic Revolution in Iran, 200–203; and nationalism, 188–89; and term *Holy War*, 174,
175, 178
Jordan, 25, 26, 50, 51, 54, 62, 67, 71, 74,
75, 76–77, 90, 110, 193, 251, 267
Jubail (Saudi Arabia), 15, 16–17
June War (1967), 40, 52, 63, 69
Justice, concept of, in Shari'a, 235–37,
240–41
Justinian (Roman emperor), 243

Khalifat rasul Allah, 155. *See also* Caliph
Kharijites, 156, 199–200
Khatami, Muhammad, 36, 130
Khayzuran (mother of caliph al-Hadi),
206
Khomeini, Ayatollah Ruhollah, 35–36,
37, 81, 85, 86, 99–104, 112, 140, 144,
167–68, 201, 202–3, 249, 266
Kingship, medieval Islamic concepts of,
133, 163–64
Kösem Sultan, 206
Kurdistan, 91. *See also* Kurds
Kurds, 68, 78, 91, 120
Kuwait, 82, 85, 90, 97, 210; Iraqi occupa-
tion of, 104–11, 266

Labor force, 1–2, 3, 4, 10, 24, 273n6
Lebanon, 26, 27, 50, 51, 52, 62, 67, 71, 74,
75–76, 81, 193, 265; and Arab Nation-
alism, 75–76; Christians of, 75; civil
war in, 54; Israeli invasion of (1982),
12, 52, 54, 64, 106
Legitimacy (political concept), 124–26,
238, 266–67
Libya, 12, 25, 27, 76, 80, 113, 145
Likud, 56
Louis IX (king of France), 207
Lutfi al-Sayyid, Ahmad, 245

Macmillan, Harold, 94
Mahmud of Ghazna, 184
Mahmut Şevket Paşa, 120
Marriage and divorce, 213, 214–15, 219–
23, 224, 246
Mawdudi, Abu'l-'Ala', 269
Mecca, 79, 151–53, 154, 169, 209, 221
Medina, 29, 79, 143–44, 151, 153, 169,
175, 179, 205, 221
Mernissi, Fatima, 210
Middle East, definition of, xii–xiii
Military expenditures, 11–14, 274n8
Modernism, Islamic, 252–59. *See also*
Reform, Islamic
Mongols, 160, 162, 163, 184

* Great undergrad book
— also Rahman,

FR

* General impressions
* Reputation @ Chicago among faculty + students
* Major Themes
* Role of academic v. Islamic scholar
* Teaching style
* Relationship w/ Moslim v. non-Moslim

Nurcholish Madjid

* as student
* Afterwards

Ahmad Syafii Maarif

Binder

→ want to push beyond authenticity + authority
as explanations

→ Indonesia is different — more tolerant culture,
more Sufi-oriented, syncretic, implication
that its less Islamic

Acknowledgements:
→ Howard Federspiel, Phil Buckley, Leonard Binder, Stephen Humphreys,
Michael Feener, M. Ayoub, John A. Williams

Design: Nola Burger
Compositor: Prestige Typography
Text: 10/13 Palatino
Display: Gill Sans
Printer and binder: Maple-Vail Book Mfg.